# UNDERSTANDING THEOLOGY

## R. T. KENDALL

CHRISTIAN FOCUS

To the Deacons of Westminster Chapel

ISBN 1 85792 429 0
© R.T. Kendall
Published by Christian Focus Publications,
Geanies House, Fearn, Ross-shire, IV20 1TW, Great Britain

www.christianfocus.com

First paperback edition 1996,
reprinted in hardback 1998, 1999, 2000

Printed by WSOY, Finland

Cover design by Donna Macleod

# CONTENTS

# PREFACE

My heartfelt thanks to Mr Malcolm Maclean, my editor, and the people of Christian Focus for their confidence in publishing the edited notes that formed the basis for my lectures at our School of Theology. This book is about half of the lectures from 1992 to 1995.

I am particularly gratified by the warmth and support from people from all over Greater London who have attended and enrolled, also those who have subscribed to the notes by post or kept in touch by the unedited tapes of the talks.

But my special thanks go to my beloved Deacons who supported the idea from the beginning and have been truest of friends throughout. This volume is dedicated to them.

R T Kendall
Westminster Chapel
London 1996

# INTRODUCTION

I was not prepared for the response that came from our School of Theology on Friday evenings at Westminster Chapel. It has turned out to be the most successful venture we have come up with! But why? I can only assume that we have met a need that was far more present than had been thought. Ordinary people as well as church leaders have expressed a desire not only to know their Bibles better but theology as well. The response we have had has proved this.

'Theology put simply' has been our motto as well as governing principle as we have sought to come up with fresh lessons week after week. That phrase came to me as I thought about doing something different on Fridays. From 1972 to 1992 I had followed the pattern set out by Dr. Martyn Lloyd-Jones, choosing a book in the Bible and carefully 'inching' our way through it. We went through Galatians (in over three years), then the Epistle to the Hebrews (ten and a half years). I do not regret this for a minute, but I have to admit that these studies never took off as in the days of my great predecessor. I do not have his gift, neither was there apparently any great need to carry on on Fridays in much the same way as we were doing on Sundays.

Dr G. Campbell Morgan, who preceded Dr Lloyd-Jones, had conceived his own idea of a School of the Bible on Fridays earlier in this century. He actually filled the Chapel on Fridays. His idea somewhat gripped me, but I liked the idea of 'doing theology' rather than adopting his non-theological style. I'm not even sure he had a theology! And yet I feared that theology might be more off-putting than a Bible school. But I stayed with it.

One of the purposes of our School of Theology has been to show that theology is not a bad word. In fact it literally means 'word of God' (*theos*, God; *logos*, word). So it comes to the same thing – but it is still a bit different. One can become an expert in Bible knowledge and be utterly ignorant of theology. You can know the Bible without knowing theology, but it is unlikely that you can know theology (if it is sound) if you don't know the Bible. So by doing theology you get both – with a bit of church history, the 'laboratory of theology', thrown in.

I am hardly the world's greatest admirer of Karl Barth but I agree with at least one thing he said: 'Every Christian is called to be a theologian.' It is my view that the lack of theological-mindedness is a symptom of the superficiality of the modern church. Whereas there is the constant danger of being 'perfectly orthodox, perfectly useless', as Dr Lloyd-Jones put it, there is the obvious barrenness of Christians today who cannot tell you what or why they believe! I fear this may be true in some pulpits as well.

The main thing we have striven for, next to being simple, is balance: matching the practical with the cerebral, the Spirit with the Word. I do not say we have always succeeded, but that has been our goal.

What follows in this book is a selection of what we have done during our first four years. More may come down the road, but these chapters will give the reader a taste of what we have sought to do. The table of contents does not follow the original order. For example, the second chapter was a lecture that came in the third year but seems best put in the present volume as you will see.

Neither should one think for a minute that what you have in this book is all I think is needed! Hardly. I had no idea at all that my notes would find their way to print; otherwise, I might have done better in planning ahead! We just felt it would be good to give a sample of doing theology simply, that it might whet the reader's appetite to know God better. At the end of the day, that is all that matters. And if you found out you were a theologian after all, that too would be good!

# 1

# DISCOVERING THEOLOGY

## INTRODUCTION

### A. Why study theology?

1. Because theological-mindedness, assuming that it is centred on sound teaching and true spirituality, is the best remedy against being 'blown here and there by every wind of teaching and by the cunning and craftiness of men in their deceitful scheming' (Ephesians 4:14).

2. *Every Christian is called to be a theologian.*
   (a) You don't have to have a degree in theology to be a theologian.
   (b) You don't have to be a minister to be a theologian.
   (c) You don't have to be in full-time Christian service to be a theologian.

3. *The pastor's task is to prepare others for works of service 'so that the body of Christ may be built up... in the knowledge of the Son of God* (Ephesians 4:12-13).
   (a) 'Do your best to present yourself to God as one approved, a workman who does not need to be ashamed and who correctly handles the word of truth' (2 Timothy 2:15).
   (b) 'You, however, know all about my teaching' (2 Timothy 3:10).
   (c) 'For the time will come when men will not put up with sound doctrine' (2 Timothy 4:3).

4. *The present trend toward man-centredness and 'what's in it for me?' type of thinking has created a vacuum that has left the church in a powerless and superficial state.*
   (a) Too many Christians cannot tell you for sure what they believe or why they believe it.
   (b) Too many Christians know nothing of the history of the Christian church.
      (1) Church history is the laboratory of theology.
      (2) Knowledge of the past will help us to understand the present and face the future.

5. *All of us need motivation to be disciplined.*
   (a) This book may help motivate us to get on with learning that is long overdue.
   (b) It may help us discipline our minds that they will be filled with godly knowledge.

## B. Why theology and not just the Bible?

1. *One can learn facts about the Bible and miss the important principles that lie behind these facts.*
   (a) It is one thing to know the story of Adam and Eve, quite another, for example, to know:
      (1) The implications for marriage and the family.
      (2) The nature of sin, temptation and results of the Fall.
   (b) It is one thing to know that Jesus died on the cross, quite another to know:
      (1) What the blood of Jesus meant to God the Father.
      (2) What the blood of Jesus means to us.

2. *Theology is partly shaped by church history.*
   (a) None of us can live in isolation from the past.
      (1) We all have our biases.
      (2) They came largely from those who lived before us.
   (b) The Apostle Paul built his teaching on those who preceded him, e.g., Abraham and David (Romans 4:1-8).
      (1) Our minds have been shaped by great thinkers as well.
      (2) We often quote Luther and Calvin; they quoted Augustine and Athanasius.
   (c) Some say, 'But I will just read the Bible like Paul. I don't need Augustine or Athanasius or Calvin.'
      (1) Chances are, they will still have their prejudices.
      (2) We need to understand our prejudices, how we got them and how to correct them where necessary.

# 1 THEOLOGY: THE STUDY OF THE WORD OF GOD

## A. The word 'theology' comes from two Greek words:
1. *theos,* meaning 'God'.
2. *logos,* meaning 'word'.

## B. Theology is not a bad word!
1. *Theology was once regarded as the 'queen of the sciences'.*
   (a) Just two or three centuries ago the greatest minds aspired to be theologians or clerics.
   (b) Today the better minds aspire to be scientists or computer experts.

2. *On the Oxford University coat of arms are the words 'Dominus illuminatio mea' – 'the Lord is my light'* (Psalm 27:1).
   - (a) Since these words were written theology has passed behind a cloud.
   - (b) We want to help restore the honour of God's name by a return to theological-mindedness.

3. *Uninteresting preachers, dull theologians and less able men have moved in where spiritual giants once held sway.*
   - (a) Correcting this trend will not be easy.
   - (b) Learning theology may not come naturally.
     - (1) It will take effort.
     - (2) When Jesus said '*strive* to enter in' the Greek is 'agonize'.

## 2  SOUND THEOLOGY COMBINES BOTH THE MIND AND HEART

### A. One without the other will lead to a defect.
1. *Emphasis on the intellect alone is dangerous.*
   - (a) 'Knowledge puffs up, but love builds up' (1 Corinthians 8:1).
   - (b) The intellect is only one part of our personality.
   - (c) Intellectual stimulus alone breeds pride and leads to dulness and self-righteousness.

2. *Emphasis on the heart alone is dangerous.*
   - (a) 'The heart is deceitful above all things and beyond cure' (Jeremiah 17:9).
   - (b) The heart emphasis can lead to an over-emphasis on the emotions.
   - (c) Ignoring the intellectual side of personality can lead to false pride and self-righteousness.

### B. THE BEST THEOLOGY WILL BE SHAPED ON OUR KNEES.
1. Prayer is the antidote to dulness and intellectual pride.
2. Prayer is the vehicle by which our hearts remain sensitive to the Holy Spirit.
3. What the Holy Spirit does not reveal is not worth knowing.

## 3  GENERALLY SPEAKING, THEOLOGY HAS SEVEN BRANCHES

### A  Revelation.  The inspiration of the Bible.
1. *This is not a reference to the Book of Revelation, but to the doctrine of revelation.*
   - (a) Revelation comes from the Greek word meaning 'unveiling'.
   - (b) It means to unveil what is hidden.

2. *Revelation deals with the way God reveals Himself.*

3. *God has revealed himself in the Bible by the Holy Spirit.*
   (a) There is a sense in which revelation and Scripture are used interchangeably.
   (b) We know the Bible is the Word of God by the 'inner testimony of the Holy Spirit' (Calvin).

4. *The doctrine of the Trinity emerges under this heading, as well as providence.*

## B. Cosmology: the study of Creation.
1. From the Greek *kosmos* (world, or order of things) and *logos* (word).
2. Cosmology deals with the question: Did God create the universe and all in it or did it evolve or happen by chance?
3. Cosmology also deals with environmental issues.

## C. Anthropology: the study of Man.
1. *From the Greek* anthropos *(man) and* logos *(word).*
2. *Anthropology deals with the question: Was man created or did he evolve?*
3. *Anthropology also deals with issues such as:*
   (a) Is man fallen?
   (b) Is man a dichotomy (e.g. body and soul) or a trichotomy (e.g. body, soul and spirit)?
   (c) Human psychology.

## D. Soteriology: the study of Salvation.
1. From the Greek *soter* (saviour) and *logos* (word).
2. The words *salvation* and *redemption* are used interchangeably.
3. Soteriology is the widest area that will be covered most widely in future studies, dealing with such subjects as atonement, justification, predestination, the law, faith, sanctification and assurance.

## E. Pneumatology: the study of the Holy Spirit.
1. From the Greek *pneuma* (spirit) and *logos* (word).
2. This branch of theology overlaps with all of the above but is extended to subjects like the gifts, or anointings, of the Holy Spirit.

## F. Ecclesiology: the study of the church.
1. From the Greek *ecclesia* (the called out, or church) and *logos* (word).
2. Do not confuse *ecclesiological* (the study of the church and church government) with *ecclesiastical* (referring to work in a denomination, as in 'ecclesiastical appointment').
3. This branch of theology also includes baptism, the Lord's Supper and issues of church and state.

G. **Eschatology: the study of the last things.**
   1. From the Greek *eschatos* (last things) and *logos* (word).
   2. This branch of theology deals with subjects such as the Second Coming, unfulfilled prophecy, the final judgment, Heaven and Hell.

## 4 THEOLOGY AND ETHICS

A. **Closely parallel with the study of theology is the study of ethics.**
   1. Ethics means moral principles or values.
   2. Ethics deals partly with the relevance of theology.

B. **Theological ethics covers such subjects as**:
   Marriage and family issues, economics, politics, the environment, sociology, medicine and psychology.

## 5 THEOLOGY AND SPIRITUALITY

A. **Whereas the subject of spirituality overlaps with many of the above, for example, sanctification or the doctrine of the Holy Spirit, there is a need for particular emphasis on**:
   1. The place of prayer in the life of the church.
   2. The place of prayer in the life of the believer.
   3. Witnessing and soul-winning.
   4. How to read the Bible.
   5. The place of preaching.
   6. Worship.
   7. Revival.

B. **'Learning theology on your knees' is an aspect of our burden that will hopefully preserve us from an arid, sterile, irrelevant kind of emphasis that has not been helpful.**

## CONCLUSION

Studying theology in college is not an option open to all individuals. But through this book you have access to a range of teaching more usually available only in college. The benefits are twofold: we will be able to understand Scripture at a deeper level and our devotional times should be more productive.

The Holy Spirit will help in this task: he has promised to 'remind you of everything' you were taught (John 14:26). However, if we are empty-headed before we are Spirit-filled, we will be empty-headed afterwards. I believe Revival, another Great Awakening, is coming. Those who are equipped when it comes will be the most useful to God, the church and the world.

# 2

# HOW DOES GOD MAKE HIMSELF KNOWN?

## 1. INTRODUCTION

A. **The doctrine of revelation is vital to the Christian faith.**
   1. *This doctrine is basic to a proper understanding of:*
      (a) What we believe.
      (b) Why we believe.
      (c) Where we get our beliefs.
      (d) Why we believe these beliefs are true.

   2. *The importance of the doctrine of revelation is shown in that it is often the first subject dealt with in a theology text book.*
      (a) Revelation is to theology what epistemology is to philosophy, .
         (1) Philosophy: the search for wisdom which embraces epistemology (what is true?) and axiology (what has value?).
         (2) Epistemology: how do we know and how do we know it is true?
      (b) Epistemology is connected to *reason*, revelation to what is *given*.
         (1) Philosophers sometimes resent the idea that something is revealed, since it by-passes man's wisdom.
         (2) Revelation by-passes reason since it is assumed that what is true is knowable by God *giving* us the knowledge of himself.

B. **Revelation: the unveiling of absolute truth which had been previously hidden.**
   1. *Greek* apokalypsis: *'an uncovering, a laying bare, making naked'.*
   2. *It presupposes that something is hidden and that this something has been disclosed (revealed, or unveiled).*
      (a) A gossip columnist may say, 'I can now reveal that.....'
      (b) Many Christians seek a 'revelation' with regard to their lives, their future, etc.; this is why some are interested in a 'word of knowledge'.
         (1) This is a type of revelation, what is now laid bare that had been hidden.
         (2) It may also pertain to theological insight; one may say, 'I have a revelation on this verse.'

**C. Our study has to do with revelation of God himself and the truth about him.**

1. *There are therefore assumptions in our study:*
   (a) That God has revealed himself.
   (b) That God has revealed truth about himself.

2. *God is, therefore, knowable and we can know things about him.*

**D. Why is this study important?**

1. *It makes us face the most fundamental truth about our faith: how do we know the Bible is true and we are not being deceived?*

2. *It forces us to face some of the assumptions many of us have accepted uncritically – but which others have questions about.*

3. *It will help us to defend the faith when we are up against the secular, atheistic mind.*
   (a) 'Always be prepared to give an answer to everyone who asks you to give the reason for the hope that you have' (1 Peter 3:15).
   (b) Many of us have to rely on someone stronger or more able than ourselves to answer even the most fundamental question. This is not an impressive testimony.
   (c) True, not everyone is bothered with intellectual questions.
      (1) In such cases, our lives will be the greater witness.
      (2) But when we run into the more cerebral person, it will bring glory to God when he or she sees we have had to think through our faith.

4. *It will make us stronger and more confident in our own faith when we have wrestled with some of the questions we have swept under the carpet for too long.*

5. *It will make us thankful to see afresh that we really do have the absolute truth about God and his Son.*
   (a) Not that we understand everything!
   (b) But we may truly understand a lot more than we have known up to now.

6. *One of our greatest threats today is* pluralism. *Therefore, we need to be assured that Jesus Christ is the only way to God.*
   (a) Pluralism: the belief that there is more than one way to God, or to heaven.
   (b) With the growing numbers of Muslims, Hindus and other religions in Britain, along with so many churchmen sadly denying the necessity of knowing God through Christ alone, we must know where we are to stand.
   (c) How do we know it is the true God we are experiencing?

E. **By revelation we mean two things (in this order):**
   1. God unveiling himself.
   2. God showing things about himself (truths concerning him).

F. **This subject can be divided into two parts: non-redemptive revelation of God and redemptive revelation of God.**

## 1 NON-REDEMPTIVE REVELATION

A. **General revelation: to all people generally.**
   1. *All people have some knowledge, learning or awareness of God.*
      (a) That there is a God: 'since what may be known about God is plain to them' (Romans 1:19).
      (b) That there is a Creator: 'For since the creation of the world God's invisible qualities – his eternal power and divine nature – have been clearly seen, being understood from what has been made, so that men are without excuse' (Romans 1:20).
      (c) That this God is holy: this is implied by the words, 'divine nature'. Man's reaction is to 'suppress the truth by their wickedness' (Romans 1:18).

   2. *This knowledge of God is both* innate *(what we are born with) and* learned *(what we observe), and comes to us in three ways.*
      (a) The image of God in man, even though it is marred by the Fall
         (i) 'So God created man in his own image, in the image of God he created him; male and female he created them' (Genesis 1:27).
         (ii) The Fall: an event in history when our first parents, Adam and Eve, sinned in the Garden of Eden, leaving the human race helpless and sinful but with a non-redemptive knowledge of the Creator.

      (b) The conscience, the natural ability of man to reflect on himself in the light of what he knows is right or wrong.
         (i) 'Since they show that the requirements of the law are written on their hearts, their consciences also bearing witness, and their thoughts now accusing, now even defending them' (Romans 2:15).
         (ii) The conscience is what is left of the image of God in us, incapable of saving us and yet leaving us without excuse.

      (c) Reason, by which one can conclude that there is a Creator God were he honestly to follow through what his conscience tells him.
         (1) 'God did this so that men would seek him and perhaps reach out for him and find him, though he is not far from each one of us' (Acts 17:27).

(2) Medieval theologians, such as Thomas Aquinas (cosmological proof of God) and Anselm (ontological proof of God) demonstrated by reason why there must be a God.

(b) These three sources of awareness are further confirmed by the Creator Jesus Christ, 'the true light that gives light to every man coming into the world' (John 1:9). But note:
(1) This light does not save us.
(2) This light is essentially what is implied by all the above; the image of God, conscience and the ability to reason.

## B. Natural revelation: what people perceive of God through nature.

1. *This is a slightly different way of describing general revelation.*
   (a) It comes to all humans.
   (b) By focusing on nature it refers not merely to conscience, but to what we know must be true about God through nature.

2. *Natural revelation: that revelation of God given to all men either innately or in physical nature which brings everyone to an acknowledgement of God (Romans 1:18-25).*
   (a) This revelation does not save people.
   (b) This revelation brings all to an acknowledgement of God and yet it results in their refusal to acknowledge him!

## C. Biblical arguments for general revelation:

1. *Acts 17:24-28.*
   (a) God so ordered the affairs of men that they should seek God and find him.
   (b) Paul shows that men do not honestly search for him.
   (c) He shows that all men *ought* to recognise that God testifies to himself through nature and human affairs.

2. *Romans 1:18-25.*
   (a) Man recognises creation to be the handiwork of God.
   (b) Although God reveals himself in nature man does not make the appropriate response to God – in thanksgiving and worship – but becomes idolatrous.

3. The 'nature Psalms'.
   (a) Psalm 8:
   (1) The Lord is creator of nature.
   (2) This psalm displays God's goodness and majesty, testifying to these things.

- (b) Psalm 19:
  - (1) The heavens declare the glory of God.
  - (2) The regular succession of day and night speak of his glory.
- (c) Psalm 29:
  - (1) The voice of the Lord is over the waters, breaks the cedars and shakes the desert.
  - (2) The Lord thunders over the waters.
- (d) Note: these Psalms depict a natural revelation of God but are written by one who has been given a saving revelation – in order to respond in worshipful acknowledgement. It is not the response of natural man but of one who enjoys God's special revelation.

## D. General and natural revelation summed up:

1. *All men are given a limited knowledge of God.*
   - (a) It reveals God's creation and glory.
   - (b) It comes through nature and to the conscience.
2. *No-one is saved merely by this revelation; it is non-redemptive.*
3. *And yet it leaves men without excuse.*
   - (a) They choose not to acknowledge God.
   - (b) They suppress the truth by their sin.

## 2 REDEMPTIVE REVELATION

## A. Special revelation, as opposed to general revelation.

1. *Whereas general revelation comes to all via nature, and does not save, special revelation comes to some and is saving.*
   - (a) There are two inseparable instruments of special revelation:
     - (1) The gospel, which must be preached to all.
     - (2) The Holy Spirit, who applies the gospel to believers.
   - (b) We are required to give the gospel to all (Mark 16:15).
     - (1) God commands all people everywhere to repent (Acts 17:30).
     - (2) Only the Holy Spirit grants repentance and faith (Romans 2:4; Ephesians 2:8-9).
   - (c) The mere preaching of the gospel, the instrument of special revelation, does not in itself save (Acts 18:6).
     - (1) 'Many are invited, but few are chosen' (Matthew 22:14).
     - (2) The many are those who hear the gospel outwardly, the few are those who receive God's special revelation.

2. *The content of God's special revelation:*
   - (a) The gospel.
     - (1) The person of Jesus – the God-man.
     - (2) The work of Christ – his obedience, death and resurrection.

    (b)  The nature of God.
       (1)  His glory.
       (2)  His will.
    (c)  The sinfulness of man.
       (1)  Our inability.
       (2)  Our depravity (sinfulness).
    (d)  Judgement to come.
       (1)  The Second Coming of Christ.
       (2)  The final judgement.

  3.  *In Acts 17 Paul began with general revelation and ended with special revelation.*
    (a)  God 'made the world and everything in it ... so that men would seek him and perhaps reach out for him and find him' (Acts 17:24-27).
    (b)  'Now he commands all people everywhere to repent. For he has set a day when he will judge the world with justice by the man he has appointed' (Acts 17:30-31).

## B.  Supernatural revelation, as opposed to natural revelation.
Supernatural: above nature.
  1.  *The Bible, God's revealed will.*
    (a)  The Old Testament, consisting of 39 books.
    (b)  The New Testament, consisting or 27 books.

  2.  *The Holy Spirit, by which we know the Bible is God's Word.*
    (a)  There are two ways by which men may come to accept the Bible as true:
       (1)  External witness, such as archaeological discoveries, personal testimonies, etc..
       (2)  Internal witness, by the Holy Spirit.
    (b)  The Holy Spirit works effectually in believers by:
       (1)  Convicting of sin.
       (2)  Revealing the gospel.
       (3)  Creating faith and repentance.
       (4)  Convincing of the truth of the Bible.
       (5)  Showing God's will in how to live.

  3.  *The glory of Jesus Christ.*
    (a)  That he is God and man.
    (b)  That he is Creator.
    (c)  That he is the only Redeemer.
       (1)  That he is the unique Son of God.
       (2)  That he is the only way to God.

(3) That his death is saving for believers only.
(4) That he rose from the dead, ascended to God's right hand and reigns and intercedes for believers.
(5) That he is coming again to judge the world.

C. **The crucial difference between natural revelation (to all) and supernatural revelation (to believers) is the way the Holy Spirit works.**

1. *At the natural level the Holy Spirit blesses the unregenerate outwardly.*
   (a) 'He causes his sun to rise on the evil and the good, and sends rain on the righteous and the unrighteous' (Matthew 5:45b).
   (b) All good things in life come from God.
      (1) This is called 'common grace', God's goodness to all men.
      (2) Our intelligence, our health, our jobs, even government are by God's grace at the natural level.

2. *At the supernatural level the Holy Spirit works internally.*
   (a) It is the internal work of the Holy Spirit by which we know the Bible is God's Word.
   (b) It produces a faith so definite that:
      (1) 'You would stake your life on it a thousand times' (Luther).
      (2) 'You know you are not deceived' (Calvin).

## CONCLUSION

There is only one God – one Creator. He has revealed himself supremely in his one and only Son. All other religions have in common salvation by human effort and that salvation is initiated by human will. The Christian faith alone provides a Substitute – Jesus Christ – who saves by free grace. His resurrection from the dead proves he is the Son of God.

# 3

# INTERPRETING THE BIBLE

## INTRODUCTION

A. **This is an enormous venture.**
  1. *No-one would dare claim to be infallible with any subject in theology.*
     (a) No theologian or biblical scholar would claim to understand the Bible, except to a limited degree.
     (b) This study will not provide infallible guidelines, only suggestions that we believe will be helpful.

B. **We begin with an introduction to hermeneutics.**
  1. *Hermeneutics: the art or science of interpreting the Bible.*
     (a) Greek *hermeneuein*, to explain, interpret or translate.
     (b) Greek *hermeneia*, interpretation or translation.
     (c) It is used in the New Testament, e.g.:
         (1) 'And beginning with Moses and all the Prophets, he *explained* to them what was said in all the Scriptures concerning himself' (Luke 24:27).
         (2) 'The *interpretation* of tongues' (1 Corinthians 12:10).

  2. *We can only introduce this subject, giving a bit of history, a general look at selected sections of the Bible and some hints as to how certain books or themes can be understood.*
     (a) The Bible was written by approximately forty authors over a period of 1,500 years.
     (b) And yet we believe the Bible was written by the Holy Spirit; he is also the only infallible interpreter.
         (1) 'All Scripture is God-breathed and is useful for teaching, rebuking, correcting and training in righteousness' (2 Timothy 3:16).
         (2) 'Above all, you must understand that no prophecy of Scripture came about by the prophet's own interpretation. For prophecy never had its origin in the will of man, but men spoke from God as they were carried along by the Holy Spirit' (2 Peter 1:20-21).
     (c) It is helpful to remember the analogy between Jesus Christ and the Bible.

(1) Jesus was God as though he were not man and yet man as though he were not God.

(2) The Bible is the product of the Holy Spirit as though apart from men and yet it was written by men as though it was their own product.

## C. Here are some of the problems we face:

1. *The Bible is the Word of God, yet it has come to us in human form.*
   (a) The commands of God are absolute, yet the historical context of the writings appear to relativise certain elements.
      (1) Relativise: to put in relation or perspective to something else.
      (2) The command 'You shall not commit adultery' (Exodus 20:14) surely has greater weight than 'Do not cut the hair at the sides of your head or clip off the edges of your beard' (Leviticus 19:27). But why does the former have greater weight?
   (b) God who wrote through Moses also wrote through the apostle Paul; the style of each shows different purposes:
      (1) Moses said, 'Cursed is the man who does not uphold the words of this law by carrying them out' (Deuteronomy 27:26).
      (2) Paul said, 'But if you are led by the Spirit, you are not under the law' (Galatians 5:18).

2. *The divine message must be clear, yet some passages seem contradictory. Take, for example, the following passages that refer to the same event:*
   (a) 'Again the anger of the LORD burned against Israel, and he incited David against them, saying, "Go and count Israel and Judah" ' (2 Samuel 24:1).
   (b) 'Satan rose up against Israel and incited David to take a census of Israel' (1 Chronicles 21:1).

3. *We are dependent upon the Holy Spirit for instruction, yet knowledge of the cultural and historical contexts often enables us to grasp a passage more clearly.*
   (a) For women to have long hair was right in Corinth (1 Corinthians 11:15), but some women cannot grow long hair.
   (b) The ancient understanding of the oath and the covenant enables us to understand better its relevance to the law and the gospel.

4. *The Scriptures seem to assume a literal reading, yet we are also confronted by figurative passages.*
   (a) Jesus taught in parables (e.g. Matthew 13).
   (b) How are we to understand 'a woman clothed with the sun, with the moon under her feet and a crown of twelve stars on her head' (Revelation 12:1)?

5. *We all have our theological biases.*
   (a)  We naturally hope a passage means what we want it to mean.
   (b)  We don't give in to a contrary view quickly.
   (c)  The question is, Do we really want the *truth* or merely to be confirmed in our 'cherished' convictions?

6. *We all have our cultural biases.*
   (a)  Usually we tend to mix our theology with our culture, never realising that we are governed by the latter.
   (b)  Hermeneutics is designed to help us see how culture plays a far larger role than we perhaps want to admit.

## D. Why is this study important?
1.  All of us need help in understanding the Bible better.
2.  The Holy Spirit often works through the knowledge we have gone to the trouble to obtain.
3.  It can help us understand that we have biases that militate against a true understanding of a passage.
4.  To show how the Bible itself contains more than one kind of literature.
5.  To help the church leader to know how to interpret a passage when he is having to prepare a talk or sermon.
6.  To show that we need, above all, the anointing of the Holy Spirit; for he is the only infallible interpreter.

# 1  HISTORICAL APPROACHES TO INTERPRETING THE BIBLE

## A. Hermeneutics can be divided into two:
1. *Hermeneutics 'old-style': what the text meant.*
   (a)  One sought to get at the meaning of the text.
   (b)  One did this by close attention to grammar and the plain meaning within its context.
2. *Hermeneutics 'new style': what the text means.*
   (a)  How does one apply the text today?
   (b)  How do you bridge the gap between two cultures?
3. *The latter approach was born of theological liberalism that asked questions:*
   (a)  How can a person who has no connection with the first century read the Bible in the twentieth century? How can the two worlds come together?
   (b)  How can a world in which people believed in demons and resurrections be taken seriously by today's culture?
        (1)  How are we to understand foot washing today? The 'holy kiss'?
        (2)  What is the meaning of the Resurrection today?

(c)   People like Rudolf Bultmann saw the Bible as full of myths: fanciful, if not superstitious, beliefs.

(1)   In his view, Scripture must be 'de-mythologised', that is, you take away the myths and 're-mythologise', that is, you apply 'truth' without being literalistic.

(2)   Bultmann not only did this with the episode of the foot washing but with the whole of Scripture. For example, he would say that Peter did not literally walk on water but illustrates that we today can do extraordinary things.

(3)   Bultmann said that the primitive tendency to objectivise powers (e.g. demons, angels) that in reality do not exist must not be dismissed; he called for an existentialist interpretation (applying the word in the here and now) that did justice to primitive ideas without falling into literalism.

(4)   Jesus did not objectively rise from the dead but he can subjectively live in our hearts, said Bultmann. He could enjoy a hymn like 'You ask me how I know he lives, he lives within my heart.'

4.   *The one advantage of the 'new style' hermeneutics is that it stresses the importance of application.*

(a)   What it 'meant' *usually* is what it 'means'.

(b)   And yet things like foot washing and the holy kiss can be applied today without being literalistic.

(c)   But the truth of the Resurrection of Christ can only be upheld by holding to its being literal while also applying it.

(1)   You ask *me* how I know he lives?

(2)   Answer: Because he does! He is at God's right hand *and* in my heart by the Spirit.

## B.   Other methods of interpreting the Bible.

1.   *Allegory: by-passing the literal words for a deeper 'spiritual' meaning.*

(a)   This is one of the earliest methods of interpreting the Bible.

(b)   Augustine offered the following allegorical interpretation of the Parable of the Good Samaritan:

(1)   A certain man (Adam) went down from Jerusalem to Jericho.

(2)   Jerusalem (heavenly city of peace, from which Adam fell).

(3)   Jericho (the moon, signifying Adam's mortality).

(4)   Thieves (the devil and his angels).

(5)   Stripped him (of his immortality).

(6)   Beat him (persuading him to sin).

(7)   Left him half dead (he died spiritually, thus he is half dead).

(8) Priest and Levite (priesthood and ministry of the Old Testament).

(9) Samaritan (Christ).

(10) Bound his wounds (binding the restraint of sin).

(11) Oil (comfort of good hope).

(12) Wine (exhortation to work with a fervent spirit).

(13) Beast (the flesh of Christ's incarnation).

(14) Inn (the Church).

(15) The morrow (after the Resurrection).

(16) Two-pence (promise of this life and the life to come).

(17) Innkeeper (Paul).

(c) This style of interpretation plays around with coincidences of words and numbers.

2. *Typology: similar to allegory while taking seriously the literal meaning as well. For example:*
   (a) The Flood represents a type of the world under universal judgement.
      (1) God chose one man to be a saviour (Noah).
      (2) Noah provided a way of salvation: 'believe in order to enter the ark.'
   (b) Joseph is a type of Christ.
      (1) He was betrayed by his brothers.
      (2) Joseph totally forgave them; they had to bow down to him.

3. *Exegesis: bringing out the basic meaning of the text.*
   (a) This was the method used by the Protestant Reformers (e.g. Luther and Calvin), who rejected allegorizing.
   (b) The view here is that one should find the 'plain', if not literal, meaning of the text in its context.
   (c) The relevance of this was found in three-fold steps in preaching:
      (1) Exegesis: what it meant originally.
      (2) Exposition: bringing in the teaching or significance.
      (3) Application: how this teaching is applied to life.

## 2   HOW SHOULD WE INTERPRET SCRIPTURE?

### A. Consider the historical situation.

1. *When reading the Old Testament, keep in mind:*
   (a) Progressive revelation: the New Covenant had not been fully revealed, only promised.
      (1) We know what they didn't know. Do not charge them with knowledge or lack of knowledge that they could not help.

    (b)  The place of the Law.
       (1)  It came in with Moses, four hundred years after Abraham and thirteen hundred years before Christ.
       (2)  This is also helpful when reading difficult psalms.

  2.  *When reading the New Testament, keep in mind:*
    (a)  The Synoptic Gospels (Matthew, Mark, Luke) tell us what Jesus said and did.
    (b)  John's Gospel tells us what Jesus said, did and *meant*.
    (c)  Acts records the church's first church history.
    (d)  The Epistles were written mostly to answer questions or to deal with problems that arose in a church.
    (e)  The Book of Revelation contains mostly visions and symbols.

  3.  *Keep in mind ancient culture.*
    (a)  The people were people of their age, and cultures varied from location to location.
    (b)  Customs which were peculiar to them governed their thinking, for example: Women wearing gold; foot washing; the holy kiss.

  4.  *Keep in mind to whom a book was written and their particular situation, for example:*
    (a)  James is a Jewish epistle.
    (b)  Most of Paul's epistles answer questions.
    (c)  John's epistles deal with the effects of Gnosticism.
    (d)  Hebrews addresses discouraged Christians who were beginning to doubt essential truths.

**B.  Consider the type of literature, for example:**
  1.  Poetry (Song of Solomon, some Psalms).
  2.  Historical books (e.g., 1 and 2 Samuel, 1 and 2 Kings).
  3.  Apocalyptic (parts of Daniel, Zechariah, Revelation).
  4.  Parables (e.g., Matthew 13) which usually illustrate one basic truth and rarely stand 'on all four legs'.
  5.  Wisdom (Proverbs, Ecclesiastes).
  6.  Epistles.
  7.  Prophetic books, which contain history as well as prophetic utterances.

**C.  Practical helps:**
  1.  *Get a good translation.*
    (a)  The Authorised Version is often the most accurate and literal but its style and language are archaic.
    (b)  Read and compare several translations, if you are really wanting to understand.

2. *Aim for the most 'natural' meaning, considering the type of literature you happen to be reading.*
   (a) Ask, 'What is the plain meaning?'
   (b) Indications that you have found the meaning are:
       (1) Your mind is relieved.
       (2) Your heart is gripped. 'If a text gets a hold of you, chances are you've got a hold of it' (C. H. Spurgeon).
   (c) Martin Luther said that the best way to understand Romans 8 is to see its flow after reading Romans 1 to 7!
   (d) The first task of exegesis: careful study of a text within its context to discover its original, intended meaning.
       (1) 'A text outside its context is a pretext' (G. Campbell Morgan).
       (2) Beware of isogesis: putting in a meaning that was never intended.

3. *Having found what you believe to be the intended meaning, then ask: 'What does this mean to me?'*
   (a) This involves a lot of prayer.
   (b) This requires you to put yourself under, not above, the Word.

4. *Good tools:*
   (a) Bible dictionary; (b) Basic handbook; (c) Good commentaries.

5. *Learn to ask these questions:*
   (a) Is the teaching of scripture true because it's in the Bible?
   (b) Or is it in the Bible because it is true?
       (1) Some scriptures are hard to accept, but we accept them because they are a part of God's Word.
       (2) And yet one can develop a knowledge of truth so that you see a passage is true – even if it *wasn't* in the Bible.

6. *Remember that the Bible is often 'subtitled' GOD. e.g.:*
   (a) If any should lack wisdom he should turn to God/the Bible.
   (b) If you seek the Lord with all your heart you will look for him in his Word.

7. *Learn to think in an 'all round' manner.*
   (a) Remember that the people described were people like us. For example, Abraham, Jacob, Joseph (Genesis and Hebrews 11).
   (b) Some passages are explicitly doctrinal; you appreciate this when you read, for example, Romans or Galatians.
   (c) Some passages are pastoral, dealing with church problems or the ministry such as in the letters to Timothy and Titus.

8. *Be wary of quoting a verse out of its context unless you apply it as it was originally intended. Some examples are:*
   (a)  1 Timothy 5:23: 'Stop drinking only water, and use a little wine because of your stomach and your frequent illnesses.'
   (b)  Titus 1:12: 'Even one of their own prophets has said, "Cretans are always liars, evil brutes, lazy gluttons."'
   (c)  1 Corinthians 7:38: 'So then, he who marries the virgin does right, but he who does not marry her does even better.'

9. *Do not fall into the trap of expecting quick infallible guidance by opening the Bible at random.*

10. *Remember that the New Testament's manner of teaching the Old Testament is the ultimate, final and relevant meaning for us, even if its original use in the Old Testament meant something rather different, for example:*
   (a)  The quotation of Isaiah 7:14 by Matthew 1:23.
   (b)  The uses of the Law in Exodus, Leviticus, Numbers, Deuteronomy.

## D. The Holy Spirit: the forgotten Hermeneutic.
1. *The best way to understand the Bible is by being on good terms with the Holy Spirit – its infallible Author.*
2. *The Holy Spirit bridges history and experience.*
   (a)  Luke, who wrote Luke and Acts, was a historian; he anchors all he said in history.
   (b)  Thus he could say that behind the coming of the Holy Spirit described in Acts 2 was the literal person of Jesus.

3. *The Holy Spirit bridges the intellectual gap.*
   (a)  He makes the experience of the first century relevant today.
   (b)  We can have the same experiences they had because we have the same Holy Spirit.

## CONCLUSION
Remember that there is a purpose for all that is contained in the Bible. Learn to distinguish between the more important passages and those with less importance, and seek to master the former before you spend a lot of time with the latter. When giving a talk from a passage in the Bible, stick to those you are at home with rather than an obscure passage. The harder you work to understand God's Word the more the Holy Spirit will work in the end to clarify the meaning.

# 4

# THE TRINITY

## INTRODUCTION

A. **In this study we embark upon one of the most difficult subjects in Christian theology.**
1. *By the end of the day you may feel you are still all at sea.*
2. *At the least, you will learn something, at best perhaps you will have:*
   (a) A greater appreciation of the Trinity.
   (b) A greater ability to discuss, if not defend, the Trinity.

B. **The word 'Trinity' is not in the Bible.**
1. *It is a theological term not a biblical one.*
   (a) By 'theological' we mean that it is a term which best expresses what we believe the Bible teaches.
   (b) By 'not biblical' we mean that the word itself is never used in Scripture. However, it is of course pure biblical teaching!

2. *Some people feel that because it is not mentioned explicitly in the Bible – in and of itself – is sufficient reason to reject both the term and what it means.*
   (a) But should we reject the Book of Esther because the name of God is not found in that God-centred book?
   (b) The word 'only' or 'alone' is not used by Paul when he quotes Habakkuk 2:4, 'The just shall live by faith.'
      (1) Luther saw that faith alone is what was meant.
      (2) He was correct; but Paul did not add the word 'alone' or 'only'. It was implied!
      (3) Justification by faith alone is what gave Luther the theological breakthrough he needed for that wonderful teaching.

3. *We must not necessarily be suspicious of a word or of a phrase that is used to make a teaching clearer just because it is not found in the Bible.*

## C. Trinity: One God in three Persons: Father, Son, Spirit.

1. *God is one in his essential being but in this being there are three persons.*
   (a) Though there are three persons they do not compete with each other.
   (b) They are three modes or forms in which the divine being manifests himself to us.

2. *The three persons are self-distinctive in the one true God.*
   (a) The divine essence is wholly in each person.
   (b) This means the Father is wholly God, the Son is wholly God and the Spirit is wholly God.
      (1) Jesus is distinct from the Father but is truly God even as much as the Father is God.
      (2) The Holy Spirit is distinct from the Son and Father but is truly God as is either the Son or the Father.

## D. We may want to ask, 'Is the Trinity the teaching of the Bible or is it the teaching of the church?'

1. *In other words, is this a carefully expounded teaching in the Bible, or is it merely the church's way of explaining God?*

2. *The term* trinitas *(Latin) was first used by Tertullian (c. 200 AD), who also coined the term* persona *(Latin), to describe the manifestation of the Father, Son and Spirit.*
   (a) Those who say it is merely the teaching of the church point out that:
      (1) The term is not in the Bible.
      (2) The apostles were not bothered by the issue (as far as we can tell).
      (3) The term emerged over 150 years after Pentecost.

   (b) So is the teaching of the Trinity 'retroactive' truth?
      (1) Did the church use the term merely to explain what is obviously there in Scripture to be taught?
      (2) Was it therefore true from the beginning, truth however that had not been necessary to grasp at first? But nonetheless a truth that must be grasped now?

   (c) If the Trinity is merely the teaching of the church, do we have to believe it? It could be argued by some that the church did not always articulate it as we do. Why then must we believe it just because the term became orthodox in the eyes of the church?

3. *Church history is the laboratory of theology.*
    (a) Issues came up in due time that had not (apparently) bothered the apostles.
        (1) Some could say it did bother the apostles, this is why the teaching is there.
        (2) But clearly there are terms which are not in the Bible but which emerged later and explain best what the Bible meant.
    (b) Theology seeks to explain what the apostles wrote.
        (1) New terms are employed to make the apostles' meaning clear.
        (2) We cannot ignore the issues once they emerge.
    (c) For example, John 1:1 simply says, 'In the beginning was the Word and the Word was with God and the Word was God.'
        (1) John does not say the Word was 'co-equal' with God.
        (2) But surely he does say that!
        (3) The point is, a term was added to clarify the meaning.
        (4) Once a new term has been injected into the picture by church history we must either accept it or give a good reason for rejecting it.
    (d) So it is with the Trinity.
        (1) The term is with us, whether we like it or not.
        (2) If we believe that the Holy Spirit is a person – but one who is fully God – we are on our way to being Trinitarians in our theology.
        (3) If we say that Jesus Christ is a person – one who is fully God – we are on our way to being Trinitarians in our theology.
        (4) The term cannot be ignored; once we explain what we mean by it, it is either true or it is not.

4. *The development of thought on the Trinity. This is a brief outline of how the thinking of early church leaders developed from the second century*:
    (a) **The Apostolic Fathers**. This is the title given to those church leaders of the era immediately succeeding the New Testament period whose works in whole or in part have survived.
        (1) **Clement of Rome** (c. 96 ) co-ordinated the three in an oath: 'As God lives, and the Lord Jesus Christ lives, and the Holy Spirit.'
        (2) **Ignatius** (c. 107) used the triadic formula but described the Father, Son and Spirit in a way that gave rise to the idea of 'economic' Trinitarianism, i.e., regarding God as one in his essential being, the Son and Spirit being merely forms or modes of the Father's self-revelation, only distinguishable from him in the persons of revelation.

(3) **Hermas** (early second century) envisaged three distinct personages: the master, i.e., God the Father; his 'well-beloved son', i.e., the Holy Spirit; and the servant, i.e., the Son of God, Jesus Christ.

(b) **The Apologists.** This is the name given to early Christian writers (c. 120-220) who gave a reasoned defence of their faith to outsiders.

(1) **Justin Martyr** (c. 100-c. 165) co-ordinated the three persons (not calling them that however), sometimes quoting the baptismal formula and defending the veneration given to the Father, the Son and the 'prophetic Spirit'.

(2) **Irenaeus** (c. 180), the first great theologian after apostolic times, largely combated Gnosticism, but also made statements regarding the Godhead that anticipated orthodoxy, e.g., 'God the Father, not made, not material, invisible; one God, the creator of all things: this is the first point of our faith. The second point is: the Word, the Son of God, Christ Jesus our Lord ... was made man among men, visible and tangible. And the third point is: the Holy Spirit, through whom the prophets prophesied ... at the end of the age was poured out in a new way.'

(3) **Tertullian** (c. 200) gave the most advanced exposition of the Trinity, employing the terms 'person' (Lat. *persona*) and 'Trinity' (Lat. *trinitas*). He stated, 'We believe in only one God ... that the only one God has also a Son, his Word, who has issued out of himself ... which Son then sent, according to his promise, the Holy Spirit, the Paraclete, out of the Father.' He balanced the divine unity 'into Trinity, setting forth Father, Son and Spirit as three'.

(c) **The Apostles' Creed** (date and origin unknown) was one of the earliest creeds and shows the belief in the Father, Son and Spirit:

> 'I believe in God the Father almighty, and in Jesus Christ his only Son our Lord, who was born of the Holy Spirit and the Virgin Mary, who was crucified under Pontius Pilate and was buried. He descended into hell. The third day he rose from the dead. He ascended into heaven. And sits on the right hand of God the Father almighty. Whence he comes to judge the living and the dead. I believe in the Holy Spirit, the holy catholic church, the forgiveness of sins, the resurrection of the body, the life everlasting.'

- (d) **Council of Nicea** (325).
  - (1) The teaching of Arius (c. 250-c. 336) led to a major statement regarding Jesus Christ. Arius taught that the Word was God's creation, although God's greater creation.
  - (2) **Athanasius** (c. 296-373) refuted the rapidly growing Arianism. He asserted that the Word is co-substantial, co-equal and co-eternal with the Father. He also asserted equally the Deity of the Holy Spirit.
  - (3) **The Nicene Creed** (325) formally and officially condemned Arianism as heresy.

    'We believe in one God the Father All-sovereign, maker of all things visible and invisible; and in the Lord Jesus Christ, the Son of God, begotten of the Father, only begotten, that is, of the substance of the Father, God of God, begotten not made, of one substance with the Father, through whom all things were made... And in the Holy Spirit.'

- (e) **The Council of Constantinople** (381) made official what Athanasius taught also about the Holy Spirit, viz., that the Holy Spirit is equally co-substantial and eternal with the Father and the Son. Thus the Trinity was now explained in the simplest terms so far.

5. *We conclude that the Trinity is the teaching of the church; but, as we shall see, equally the teaching of the Bible.*

E. **A word of caution: do not let Muslims or Cultists accuse you of believing in three Gods.**
  1. *This is their simplistic (but clever) way of making Christians look stupid.*
  2. *Christian theology is never necessarily logical.*
    - (a) It is logical to claim that God is the author of sin and thus responsible for sin, that is,
      - (1) God is all-powerful.
      - (2) God is all-knowing.
      - (3) God had power to prevent man from sinning.
      - (4) God knew man would sin.
      - (5) Since God didn't stop man from sinning (when he could have done) this means God is the author of sin. That is logical. But nothing could be further from the truth!

(b) Theology must be understood analogically not logically.
    (1) Logic is like mathematics: two and two are four, four and four are eight, etc..
    (2) According to the Bible, however, two and two may not equal four.

(c) Analogical: to compare Scripture with Scripture.
    (1) We don't build a complete teaching on one verse.
    (2) We compare scripture with scripture: by analogy.
    (3) It is what Calvin called the 'analogy of faith', based upon Romans 12:6: 'If a man's gift is prophesying, let him use it in proportion (Greek: *analogia*) to his faith.'
    (4) What the Scriptures teach often defies logic.

(d) We therefore conclude:
    (1) God is not the author of sin (defies logic).
    (2) God is a Trinity (defies logic).

# 1 TO UNDERSTAND THE TRINITY WE BEGIN WITH JESUS (John 1:1).

## A. There are two questions:
1. *Was he a person? Yes.*
    (a) He was a man (1 Timothy 2:5).
    (b) He had personality:
        (1) He astonished with his teaching (Matthew 7:28).
        (2) His style had a definite impact (Matthew 22:16).
    (c) He had feelings (Matthew 14:14).
    (d) He had a will (Matthew 8:7).
    (e) He had a mind (Philippians 2:5).

2. *Was he God? Yes.*
    (a) He existed from the beginning (John 1:1).
    (b) He was creator (John 1:3; Colossians 1:16).
    (c) He was fully God (John 1:1; Colossians 2:9).
    (d) He was worshipped (Matthew 2:2; John 20:28).
    (e) He forgave sins (Matthew 9:2).

## B. Most people who object to the Trinity reject the deity of Jesus.
1. *If they accept the deity of Jesus they will usually accept the Trinity.*
2. *Some exceptions: those who call the Spirit an essence rather than a person claim to reject the Trinity.*
3. *For the most part, those who object to the Trinity have a hostility towards the belief that Jesus is God.*

   (a)   This is why we begin with Jesus to understand and to defend the Trinity.

   (b)   If Jesus is God, the Trinity will not be offensive, even if it is hard to grasp (and it is).

   (c)   Don't begin with the concept of a triune God when defending the Trinity. Ask: Do you believe that Jesus is God? It may be they will, sooner or later, accept Trinitarian theology.

## 2 THE HOLY SPIRIT IS THE THIRD PERSON OF THE GODHEAD

### A. The Holy Spirit is a person.

1. *Jesus described him as 'another' paraclete* (John 14:16).
   
   (a)   A paraclete (Greek, *parakletos*) is one who comes alongside.
   
   (b)   When Jesus called him 'another' paraclete this implied that the Holy Spirit is a person just as much as Jesus is a person.

2. *The Spirit is never an 'it' but a 'he'* (John 16:8,12-14; Romans 8:26).
3. *He has personality* (Acts 5:32). That is how he was recognised by the apostles.
4. *He has feelings* (Ephesians 4:30).
5. *He has a will* (Acts 16:6-7.)
6. *He has a mind* (John 3:8; Romans 8:27).

### B. The Holy Spirit is God.

1. He is creator (Genesis 1:2).
2. He is eternal (Hebrews 9:14).
3. He is called God (1 Corinthians 12:4-6; 2 Corinthians 3:17; Acts 5:3-4).
4. He gives life (John 6:63).
5. He convicts of sin (John 16:8).
6. He intercedes for us (Romans 8:26-27).

## 3 WHAT THE NEW TESTAMENT TEACHES EXPLICITLY ABOUT THE TRIUNE GOD EMERGES IMPLICITLY IN THE OLD TESTAMENT

### A. *The general term in the Old Testament for God is* Elohim.

1. The Hebrew word is plural.
2. This refers largely to the transcendence of God: his power and 'otherness'.
3. Elohim creates by means of the Word and Spirit (Genesis 1:1-3).

### B. *This teaching becomes clearer in Genesis 1:26*: 'Then God said, let us make man in our image, in our likeness.'

### C. *Both the creative activity of God and his government are at a later stage associated with the Word personified as Wisdom* (Job 28:23-27; Proverbs 8:22ff.).

D. *The Spirit is seen as the dispenser of all blessings and the source of strength, courage, culture and government* (Exodus 31:3; Numbers 11:25; Judges 3:10).

E. *The Spirit of God is given prominence in connection with redemption and revelation, and is assigned his office in the equipment of the Messiah for his work* (Isaiah 11:2; 42:1; 61:1).

F. *He would be the explanation for the response of faith and obedience* (Isaiah 32:15; Ezekiel 36:26,27; Joel 2:28).

G. *All prophets spoke as they did because the Holy Spirit was in them and behind their utterances* (2 Peter 1:21).

H. *See Psalm 51:11.*

## 4 ALL THE ABOVE MAKE CLEARER THE TRINITARIAN IMPLICATIONS IN THE NEW TESTAMENT

A. *The preaching of John the Baptist.*
   1. Repentance toward God (Matthew 3:2,7-8).
   2. Faith in a coming Messiah (Matthew 3:11).
   3. Baptism of the Holy Spirit (Matthew 3:11).

B. *The baptism of Jesus.*
   1. The presence of Jesus himself.
   2. The Father's voice from heaven (Matthew 3:17).
   3. The Spirit like a dove (Matthew 3:16).

C. *The announcement of Jesus' birth.*
   1. The agency of the Spirit in the incarnation (Luke 1:35).
   2. Jesus would be called the Son of God (Luke 1:35).
   3. The Lord God would give him the throne of his father David (Luke 1:32).

D. *The baptismal formula (Matthew 28:19).*
   1. Baptizing 'into the name' is a Hebrew form of expression.
   2. It carries with it a complete break with Judaism in including under a singular name not only the Father, but the Son and the Holy Spirit.

E. *The relationship between the Father and Son.*
   1. The Word was 'with' God shows a Trinitarian relationship.
   2. No one knew the Son except the Father, and vice versa (Matthew 11:27).
   3. The Father 'sent' the Son (John 6:44).
   4. The Father 'loves' the Son (John 5:20).
   5. The Father 'entrusts judgement' to the Son (John 5:22).

F. **Preaching of Peter** (Acts 2:32-33).
   1. Jesus was exalted to God's right hand.
   2. Jesus received of the Father the promise of the Spirit.

G. **Apostolic blessing** (2 Corinthians 13:14; Revelation 1:4-5).

H. **Note: unfortunately, 1 John 5:7, as found in the Authorised Version, is under a textual criticism cloud and is best not to be used with most people.**
   1. It may well have been in the original text.
   2. But doubt surrounding it suggests it is better not to use it.

## 5 RELATIONSHIP BETWEEN THE PERSONS OF THE GODHEAD

A. **They heap praise upon each other.**
   1. Father: glorifies the Son (Matthew 3:17; 17:5; John 5:20-23).
   2. Jesus: honours the Father (John 5:19, 30-31; 12:28).
   3. Spirit: honours the Son (John 15:26; 16:8-10,14).

B. **Secrecy is attributed to the Father.**
   1. *In the choice of a people* (John 6:37; Ephesians 1:4).
   2. *In the timing of events* (Mark 13:32; Galatians 4:4; Ephesians 1:9ff).
   3. *In the movements and ministry of Jesus* (John 5:16-17,19,30).
      (a) All that Jesus did, then, was what the Father told him to do and say.
      (b) Jesus was not 'his own man'. He had 'double vision' as it were; one eye on the Father, the other on those around him.

C. **Openness is attributed to the Son.**
   1. *He was clearly visible* (1 John 1:1,14; 20:27).
   2. *He made known what was invisible.*
      (a) The Father's will (John 14:20).
      (b) The Father's face (John 14:9).
      (c) The Father's plan (John 19:30).

D. **Clarification is attributed to the Spirit (John 16:13).**
   1. The purpose of the Son (Acts 2).
   2. The teaching of the Son (John 14:26; 1 Corinthians 2:10ff.).
   3. Assurance of salvation (Romans 5:5).
   4. The Spirit gives intimacy with the Father (Romans 8:15).

E. **Intercession is made for us by both the Son and the Spirit.**
   1. By the Spirit (Romans 8:26-27).
   2. By the Son (Romans 8:31ff.; Hebrews 7:25).

F. **There is no rivalry in the Trinity.**
   1. *You can pray to any person of the Godhead.*
      (a) Jesus said to pray to the Father (Matthew 6:9ff.).
      (b) But prayers were addressed to Jesus (Luke 23:42; Acts 7:59).

   2. *You can praise any person of the Trinity.*
      (a) Some take the Authorised Version translation of John 16:13 ('he shall not speak of himself') too far. The New International Version in fact translates like this: 'He will not speak on his own', which means that the Spirit is like Jesus as he describes himself in John 5:19 and 30.

G. **The relationship of the persons of the Trinity regarding the salvation of sinners can be summarised as:**
   1. The Father thought it (Ephesians 1:9).
   2. The Son bought it (1 Corinthians 6:20).
   3. The Spirit wrought it (John 6:63).

## CONCLUSION

The doctrine of the Trinity is central to the Christian Faith. Any teaching that does not affirm the Trinity is heresy. Heresy is a strong word; it means false doctrine – heterodoxy – and is the opposite of orthodoxy. Orthodoxy refers to the historic Christian faith as affirmed by the ancient creeds and councils. But beware of a head knowledge that is not matched by a warm heart.

# 5

# INTRODUCING THE GOD OF THE BIBLE

## INTRODUCTION

### A. 'Your God versus the God of the Bible'.
1. *The German philosopher, Ludwig Fuerbach (1804-1872), is known for at least three things:*
    - (a) His thinking anticipated Marxism.
    - (b) He coined the phrase, 'Man is what he eats.' He was not talking about good health; he was denying man is a spiritual being, with a soul.
    - (c) He claimed that 'God is nothing but man's projection upon the backdrop of the universe'.

2. *We must ask: Would man have come up with the God of the Bible?*
    - (a) Man may project (i.e., fancy or imagine) a God he believes is there – or hopes is there.
    - (b) But would man *ever* have dreamed up the God that is:
        - (1) Revealed in Scripture?
        - (2) The very God who revealed himself to man?

### B. Romans 1 shows that man by nature believes there is a God.
1. *This is a reference to the conscience* (Romans 1:19-20).
2. *John 1:9 shows that the entry point into every man's heart is Jesus Christ.*
    - (a) A so-called 'God framework' or Christian background is not necessary for belief.
    - (b) The way we believe in God is by Jesus Christ (1 Peter 1:21).
        - (1) There was no God-framework in Corinth (1 Corinthians 2:2).
        - (2) There was no God-framework in Ephesus (Ephesians 4:20-21).

### C. In short: belief in God comes by revelation.
1. *The first level of revelation is by the conscien*ce (Romans 1:20).
    - (1) Insufficient to save (Romans 2:12).
    - (2) Sufficient to condemn (Romans 2:15).
2. *The second level is by the Holy Spirit* (John 16:8).
    - (1) Through preachers (Romans 10:14).
    - (2) Through preaching (1 Corinthians 1:21).

## 1 THE GOD OF THE BIBLE

### A. There is no attempt to prove God's existence in the Bible.
1. *The Bible* assumes *God* (Genesis 1:1; John 1:1).
2. *The challenge in Malachi 3:10 is possibly the closest any of the Bible writers come to proving God.*

### B. The only safe route to belief in God is by faith.
1. *This is how we believe in creation* (Hebrews 11:3).
   - (a) Science may generally affirm creation one day.
   - (b) But science will never by-pass faith as the safe route.

2. *Mere belief in God in a sense proves nothing.*
   - (a) The devil believes in God (James 2:19).
     - (1) He knows his final doom (Matthew 8:29).
     - (2) He knows his time is short (Revelation 12:12).
   - (b) There are no atheists in hell (Luke 16:27).

3. *Two things precipitate faith:*
   - (a) Preaching (Romans 10:14; 1 Corinthians 1:21).
   - (b) The Holy Spirit (John 16:8).
     - (1) Faith comes by God's will (James 1:18).
     - (2) Faith is God's gift (John 6:44, 65; Ephesians 2:8).

### C. Medieval scholastics (as they are called) devised 'proofs' of God.
1. *They popularised what we now call apologetics (the science of defending the faith).*
   - (a) The first Christian apologists defended the faith against rising Gnosticism.
     - (1) Justin Martyr (c.100-c.165).
     - (2) Irenaeus (c.130-c.200)
   - (b) The two best known apologists of the Middle Ages were:
     - (1) Thomas Aquinas (c.1225-1274)
     - (2) Anselm of Canterbury (c.1033-1109).

2. *Aquinas devised what we call:*
   - (a) Cosmological proof of God (Greek *kosmos*: 'world').
     - (1) Every event has a cause.
     - (2) God must be an 'unmoved mover'.
   - (b) Teleological proof of God (Greek *telos*: 'end'), from the idea that the world has design and thus purpose (an end). It is also called 'argument from design'.

3. *Anselm devised the ontological proof of God.*
   - (a) Ontology: being.
   - (b) There is an idea in my mind 'than which no greater can be conceived'; such exists independently of the mind.

D. **Note: all attempts to prove God are valid only for those who already believe.**
   1. *They seldom if ever* convince *an unbeliever.*
      - (a) They may leave him without a good answer.
      - (b) But 'a man convinced against his will is of the same opinion still'.

   2. *The only way in the end to a living faith in God is by a revelation of the Holy Spirit.*

## 2  KNOWING ABOUT THE GOD OF THE BIBLE

A  **Who he is.**
   1. *He is a personal God.*
      - (a) This not only means he is knowable personally but that he is a person.
        - (1) All the members of the Trinity are persons.
        - (2) God therefore is never 'it' but 'he'.

      - (b) When we are discerning the God of the Bible we are referring to him essentially in two ways:
        - (1) As *Elohim*, which refers to his power and transcendence, i.e., that he is 'way out there', beyond our reach (1 Kings 8:27).
        - (2) As *Yahweh*, which refers to his personal being ('I am that I am') and immanence, i.e., close at hand (Exodus 3:14). This aspect of God became clearer when he was revealed by Jesus as the Father (Matthew 6:9; 11:27).

      - (c) The God of the Bible is seen as essentially masculine.
        - (1) All persons of the Trinity are referred to as 'he'.
        - (2) When God made Adam the latter was in God's own 'image' (Genesis 1:26), hence Adam was masculine not feminine.
        - (3) Woman was made *for* man and *from* man (Genesis 2:22-23).
        - (4) Any attempt to make God feminine is contrary to the plain revelation of him in the Bible.

2. *He is a holy God* (Exodus 3:5; Leviticus 11:44).
   (a)  A good synonym for holiness is 'otherness', which means:
       (1)  God is wholly 'other' (Exodus 9:14).
       (2)  There is nothing beside God that is quite like him (Exodus 15:11).
   (b)  God is without any sin, fault or defect (Deuteronomy 32:4).
       (1)  He hates sin (Exodus 20:1-17; Psalm 7:11).
       (2)  He is incapable of error (2 Samuel 22:31; Psalm 18:30).
   (c)  This is why man needs a substitute (Habakkuk 1:13).
       (1)  The sacrificial system was introduced to show not only God's mercy but also the seriousness of sin (Hebrews 10:1ff.).
       (2)  The substitute must be without spot or blemish (Exodus 12:5; Hebrews 4:15; 1 Peter 2:22).
   (d)  This is why his people are to be holy (1 Peter 1:16).
       (1)  Conversion leads to holiness (Ephesians 4:22).
       (2)  Sanctification (the process of being made holy) is required of each of us (1 Thessalonians 4:3).

3. *He is a merciful God* (Exodus 34:7).
   (a)  This means he chose not to punish us (Exodus 33:19; 2 Peter 3:9).
       (1)  Jesus Christ is the lamb slain from the foundation of the world (1 Peter 1:19-20).
       (2)  The plan of redemption was revealed in Genesis 3:15.
   (b)  God's mercy was extended to his people, called the 'chosen' or 'elect' (Psalm 33:12; Romans 8:33).
       (1)  They were known from the foundation of the world (Acts 13:48; Ephesians 1:4).
       (2)  They were chosen by sheer grace not works (Romans 9:11-15; 2 Timothy 1:9).
   (c)  This mercy is revealed in the gospel (John 3:16).
       (1)  It is called a righteousness revealed (Romans 1:17).
       (2)  It is assured to us by faith alone (Romans 4:5).

4. *He is a just God* (Exodus 34:7).
   (a)  This means justice or fairness (Psalm 89:14).
       (1)  This is not man's view of fairness (Isaiah 55:8-9).
       (2)  But what God calls righteousness (Psalm 9:8).
   (b)  This means he must punish sin (Exodus 34:7).
       (1)  He will not clear the guilty (Numbers 14:18).
       (2)  All the world is guilty before God (Romans 3:19).
   (c)  God punishes sin in a number of ways, e.g.,
       (1)  By letting man continue in sin (Romans 1:26ff.).
       (2)  By sending calamity (Deuteronomy 32:35).

    (d)  God's immediate promise to punish sin is by death (Genesis 2:17; Romans 6:23).

    (e)  God's ultimate punishment for sin is done in one of two ways:
        (1)  By the sacrifice of blood (Exodus 12:13).
        (2)  By everlasting hell (Matthew 25:41).

    (f)  God's temporal punishment is called chastening, or disciplining (Hebrews 12:6).
        (1)  It does not come to the non-Christian (1 Corinthians 11:32).
        (2)  It is for true Christians only (Hebrews 12:7-11).

5. *He is a jealous God* (Exodus 20:5; Isaiah 42:8).
    (a)  He will tolerate no rival (Exodus 34:14).
    (b)  He hates any form of idolatry (Deuteronomy 4:23-24; 6:14ff.).
    (c)  He is jealous for his people (Zechariah 1:14; James 4:5).

6. *He is a faithful God* (Lamentations 3:23; 1 Corinthians 1:9).
    (a)  He will never leave us or forsake us (Matthew 28:20; Hebrews 13:5).
    (b)  He will supply all our need (Philippians 4:19).
    (c)  He will make a way of escape in trial or temptation (1 Corinthians 10:13; 2 Peter 2:9).

7. *He is a truthful God* (Titus 1:2; Hebrews 6:18).
    (a)  He requires truth in our dealings with him (Psalm 51:6).
    (b)  His Son is truth (John 14:6).
    (c)  His Spirit is truth (John 14:16-17).
    (d)  His Word is truth (John 17:17).

## B. The attributes of the God of the Bible.

*Note*: There is obviously some overlapping of meaning between God's character and his attributes. The character of God, speaking generally, relates to his honour; the attributes refer to his infinitude (having no limit).

1. *He is eternal* (Genesis 21:33).
    (a)  He has no beginning (Genesis 1:1).
    (b)  He has no end (Deuteronomy 32:40).

2. *He is unchangeable* (Malachi 3:6; Hebrews 13:8).
    (a)  His plans and purposes are the same forever (Psalm 33:11).
    (b)  He is not 'moody' (James 1:17).

3. *He is omniscient or all-knowing* (Psalm 139:1-4; Romans 11:33).
    (a)  He knows everything that is going on (Proverbs 15:3).
    (b)  He knows everything that will happen (Isaiah 44:7; 46:10).

4. *He is omnipresent or everywhere* (Psalm 139:7-10).
   (a) His glory surpasses the heavens (Psalm 8:1).
   (b) His glory fills the whole earth (Numbers 14:21; Isaiah 6:3).

5. *He is omnipotent or all-powerful* (Exodus 15:6).
   (a) Nothing is too hard for God (Jeremiah 32:27).
   (b) With God nothing is impossible (Luke 1:37).

6. *He is invisible* (Exodus 33:20; Colossians 1:15).
   (a) No-one has seen God (John 1:18).
   (b) God is Spirit (John 4:24).

7. *He is incomprehensible; he cannot be fully understood or figured out!* (Isaiah 40:12; Romans 11:33).
   (a) We cannot understand how he does things (Job 5:9; Psalm 40:5).
   (b) He keeps us from knowing him perfectly – at least here on earth (Isaiah 45:15; Micah 4:12).

## C. Other descriptions of the God of the Bible.

1. Creator (Ecclesiastes 12:1).
2. Redeemer (Psalm 19:14).
3. Spirit (John 4:24).
4. Saviour (Isaiah 45:15).
5. Holy One (Isaiah 10:17).
6. King of kings (1 Timothy 6:15).
7. The Father (Matthew 11:25).

## D. When all of the above is summed up in one word we may safely affirm that the God of the Bible is a God of *glory* (Acts 7:2).

1. The glory of God is the sum total of his character.
2. The glory of God is the sum total of his attributes.

# 3  KNOWING THE GOD OF THE BIBLE

## A. There is a difference between knowing *about* God and knowing God.

1. *Illustration: I had long been fascinated with the land of Israel.*
   (a) For years I looked at pictures of Israel and studied the maps. But one day I had the privilege of visiting Israel itself – it made a vast difference. Since 1969 I have visited Israel at least ten times; I'm still learning about the land and the people.

   (b) It is the same with God. There is a difference between knowing about him from what we read in the Bible and actually knowing him.

2. *All of the information, given in the previous section,* about *the God of the Bible is accessible to anybody.*
   (a) It is not required that one actually know God to grasp most of what we looked at above.
   (b) The rest of this lesson has to do with just *knowing* God.

B. **The God of the Bible is knowable – at the most intimate level.**
   1. *One old Puritan as he lay dying gave this charge to a younger man at his bedside: 'Please tell people that God deals familiarly with men.'*
   2. *Jesus said to his disciples, 'I no longer call you servants... Instead, I have called you friends'* (John 15:15).
      (a) Abraham was called God's friend (Isaiah 41:8).
      (b) The Lord spoke to Moses 'as a man speaks with his friend' (Exodus 33:11).
   3. *The witness of the Spirit wells up in us so that we may cry, 'Abba, Father'* (Galatians 4:6).
   4. *The Lord* confides *in those who fear him* (Psalm 25:14).

C. **Knowing God is achieved in two main stages:**
   1. *Conversion. This must be experienced before anybody can know the God of the Bible. This too is in two stages:*
      (a) Hearing the gospel.
         (1) The general call: preaching – 'many are invited'.
         (2) The particular call: the Holy Spirit – 'but few are chosen' (Matthew 22:14).
      (b) Affirming the gospel.
         (1) Confession with the mouth.
         (2) Believing in the heart (Romans 10:9-10).
      (c) If you have been through these two stages it means that you believe that:
         (1) Jesus of Nazareth is God in the flesh – that is, that Jesus Christ is the God of the Bible in the flesh (John 1:14).
         (2) Jesus fulfilled the Law by his life and death (Romans 5:1-21).
         (3) Jesus Christ was personally and bodily raised from the dead (Romans 4:25).

   2. *Growth in grace* (2 Peter 1:5-8; 3:18).
      (a) At this stage there is more than one way to proceed but here is the order I would lay down:
         (1) Bible reading (at least one chapter a day).
         (2) Private prayer time (aim for thirty minutes daily, the more the better).
         (3) Teaching/preaching (don't expect to grow much apart from these).

       (4) Church involvement (for fellowship and finding your niche in a Bible-believing church).

       (5) The Lord's Supper (see it as a special time for which there is no adequate substitute).

  (b) Walking in the light (1 John 1:7).

       (1) Openness to the Holy Spirit.

       (2) Eagerness with regard to anything God will show you.

       (3) Sensitivity to what grieves the Spirit.

       (4) Confession of sin you had not been previously aware of.

       (5) Instant obedience regarding anything God shows you.

  (c) Speaking personally, here is what I have had to come to terms with over the years:

       (1) Dignifying the trial God allows me to have.

       (2) Totally forgiving those who have hurt me.

       (3) Personal witnessing.

       (4) Care for the poor.

       (5) Contempt for my own reputation.

## 4  SEEING GOD ACT

### A. Knowing the God of the Bible is to know his ways.

  1. *'They have not known my ways,' God lamented with reference to the children of Israel* (Hebrews 3:10).

  2. *In order to know his ways it follows:*

    (a) We are eager to know whatever pleases or displeases him.

    (b) We spend time with him.

    (c) We listen to him when he speaks.

### B. There are certain things we will invariably discern:

  1. *The God of the Bible wants to be worshipped.*

    (a) He is a God of glory. He wants this recognised.

    (b) He is a jealous God. He will tolerate no rivals.

    (c) He loves praise.

    (d) He tells us *how* he wants to be worshipped.

  2. *The God of the Bible wants to be talked to.*

    (a) He gives us access to him – it is called prayer.

    (b) He wants us to share our hearts.

    (c) He wants us to be totally honest before him.

    (d) He wants to know our needs.

    (e) He wants us to acknowledge him in everything.

3. *The God of the Bible answers prayer.*
   (a)  He doesn't always say 'Yes' to each request.
   (b)  When he says 'No' it is for our good.
   (c)  He wants to say 'Yes' whenever he can.
   (d)  Until he says 'No' we should keep on asking.
   (e)  When he says 'Yes' we know we have pleased him.

4. *The God of the Bible reveals himself.*
   (a)  He will begin to show his heart.
   (b)  He will show you what pleases him/displeases him.
   (c)  He will help you to develop a sensitivity to his voice.
   (d)  You will get to the place where you can hear him.
   (e)  You will know you are on good terms with him.

## CONCLUSION

The character and attributes of the God of the Bible may be learned. What God desires, however, is that we move beyond head knowledge to know him personally.

Sometimes God chooses to reveal himself in spectacular ways both to individuals (the baptism of the Holy Spirit) and to the church (in revival).

In the meantime the best thing we can do is to learn to hear his voice.

# 6

# THE SOVEREIGNTY OF GOD

**INTRODUCTION**

A. **For some this will be the most important study we have had.**
   1. *It will be a breakthrough for some; old hat (perhaps) to others.*
   2. *It may for others be a very hard pill to swallow; indeed, you may not swallow it at all!*

B. **Sovereignty of God: God's right and power to do whatever he pleases with everyone at any time (Psalm 115:3).**
   1. *In medieval times people believed in the 'divine right of kings'.*
      (a) This meant that the king could do anything, including breaking the rules that would apply to anyone else. King Henry VIII is an example of this.
      (b) This 'right' however is not biblical and was eventually discredited, although the idea that those born to 'privilege' are a law to themselves sadly exists with some to this day.

   2. *In recent years 'human rights' has been an issue of considerable discussion.*
      (a) This issue extends to international politics; diplomats appeal to 'human rights' as a reasonable point of view when dealing with dictators.
      (b) This issue has also been extended to individuals at the level of racial tension, poverty, housing, education, health, etc..

   3. *Parallel with human rights has been 'animal rights'.*
      (a) This extends from the protection of whales to birds and dogs.
      (b) Those defending these rights are often highly motivated. Ironically, they are sometimes hostile to the rights of unborn children.

   4. *God's rights are almost totally neglected today.*
      (a) God has a right to be God.
      (b) The question is, Will we 'let God be God'?

## C. Why is this study important?

1. *It lets us view theology from God's perspective.*
   - (a) There are two basic ways of 'doing theology':
     - (1) From man's point of view – the common approach nowadays.
     - (2) From God's point of view – the biblical approach.
   - (b) The Bible is God's 'in house' publication.
     - (1) Not only is it his Word but also it is expressed in a God-centred context.
     - (2) It therefore calls for theology from God's point of view.

2. *Most theology today errs towards anthropology (the study of man); the sovereignty of God is the purest theology.*
   - (a) The word 'theology' came from two Greek words:
     - (1) *theos*, God.
     - (2) *logos*, word.
   - (b) Thus to do pure theology is truly to handle God's own Word.
     - (1) This means a divine perspective, not man's perspective.
     - (2) The glimpse of the sovereignty of God gives us a taste of *theology* in its purest form.

3. *Today's generation has lost real respect for God.*
   - (a) There is no real fear of God in the land, or among God's people.
   - (b) This is the 'me generation', the 'what's in it for me?' era, when the 'health and wealth', or prosperity gospel, has great appeal.
   - (c) The irony is the more theology is presented from man's perspective the less people fear God and the less they care about him.
   - (d) A robust view of the sovereignty of God, which puts him back on the throne, will be what brings people to their senses.
   - (e) The biblical teaching of the sovereignty of God will help correct this perspective.

4. *This subject enables us to get better acquainted with the God of the Bible.*
   - (a) The God of the Bible is the only true God.
   - (b) A short route to grasp the glory of God is via the sovereignty of God (Exodus 33:18-19).

## 1  GOD'S RIGHT

### A. Two meanings are implied in God's right to do whatever he pleases.

1. *First, his privilege, or prerogative.*
   - (a) Aristocrats are said to be 'born to privilege'.
     - (1) Whether these are just rights to them is another matter.
     - (2) Indeed, so much seems to be unfair and quite wrong.

    (b)  But God was not 'born'; he always was, is and shall ever be.

        (1)  What are the privileges, then, of being God?

        (2)  Does he have a 'right' to do this or that because he is God?

2.  *Secondly, his rightness – indeed, righteousness – in what he does.*

    (a)  God makes the rules; what he does is right.

        (1)  But does this mean he can break his own rules?

        (2)  Does he teach us one thing but live another way himself? The answer is a definite 'No'.

    (b)  God's right or privilege cannot be divorced from his unchanging characteristics:

        (1)  He is holy; (2) He cannot lie.

**B.  However, although God doesn't break the rules, neither does he have to explain himself along the way.**

1.  *Why? Because God is God.*

    (a)  He is answerable to no-one (Hebrews 6:13).

    (b)  He is at peace with himself (Psalm 16:11).

    (c)  He is perfectly free (Isaiah 57:15). The greatest freedom is having nothing to prove.

2.  *Having to explain ourselves all the time, or prove something, is a sign of insecurity.*

    (a)  God is secure within himself.

    (b)  This security is mirrored in the person of Jesus.  e.g.:

        (1) To the chief priests (Matthew 21:27); (2) To Herod (Luke 23:9).

## 2  GOD'S POWER

**A.  When the phrase 'sovereignty of God' emerges it is difficult to know which, if either, has priority: God's will or his power.**

1.  *Probably, his will.*

    (a)  Ephesians 1:11: 'In him we were also chosen, having been predestined according to the plan of him who works out everything in conformity with the purpose of his will.'

        (1)  This is a clear declaration of God's sovereignty.

        (2)  What surfaces at once: God's will.

    (b)  Psalm 115:3: 'Our God is in heaven; he does whatsoever pleases him.'

        (1)  This too arises out of the assumption that whatever God does is acceptable.

        (2)  Thus the idea of his will, or prerogative, is what we think of most.

2. *But behind the assumption that God can exercise any right which he is pleased to do lies the equal assumption that he* can *do anything; that is, he has the power to do what he chooses to do.*
   (a) Some who sit on a throne may exercise their will, but do they have the power to pull it off?
   (b) It is said of the Queen: She does not rule; she reigns. But God, however, not only reigns but rules; he controls and carries out what he is pleased to do.

## B. The word 'power' has two basic meanings: force and authority.
   1. *Indeed two Greek words are often translated* power *in English.*
      (a) *dunamis* – 'power', from which we get the word 'dynamite'. It refers to force or energy. It is used in Luke 24:49; Acts 1:8.
      (b) *exousia* – 'authority' which means 'having the right', or 'privilege'. It is used in Matthew 28:18; John 1:12; John 17:2.

   2. *The sovereignty of God encompasses both words.*
      (a) God has the power to do anything because he can make it happen!
         (1) He has power over creation (Psalm 19:1-6).
         (2) He has power over nature (Psalm 75:6-7).
         (3) He has power over Satan (Job 1).
      (b) And yet equally God alone has the right, or privilege, to do these things.
         (1) He controls our destinies (Romans 9:18).
         (2) It is by his mercy that we are not consumed (Lamentations 3:22).

   3. *In short: God can do anything and whatever he does is right.*

## 3  GOD'S SOVEREIGNTY WITH REGARD TO CREATION

## A. The realm of nature
   1. *God made the heavens and the earth according to his own will* (Genesis 1).

   2. *He thus gave shape, substance, space and time to all that is* (Acts 17:24-28).
      (a) All that is was not always there; matter is not eternal (Hebrews 11:3).
      (b) What is there was put there by God (Colossians 1:15ff.).
         (1) The earth's surface – land and sea.
         (2) The earth's inhabitants – plants, animals, human beings.

## B. The nations
1. *Language* (Genesis 11)
   - (a) God is the architect of language differences.
   - (b) God equally has the power to bestow the gift of language, or its interpretation (1 Corinthians 12:10).

2. *Peoples* (Genesis 11)
   - (a) God made nations, determining their origins and destinies.
   - (b) God thus has power to topple a nation and to put the leader he chooses there (Psalm 75).
   - (c) God will one day judge the nations (Matthew 25:31ff.).

## C. Common grace
1. *Common grace: God's goodness to all men.*
   - (a) Calvin: 'Special grace within nature'.
   - (b) This kind of grace does not refer to conversion, regeneration or sanctification

2. *Our natural abilities are by common grace.*
   - (1) Gifts, talents, intelligence.
   - (2) Our job, our income.

3. *The existence of law is by common grace* (Romans 13:1-5).
   - (a) Where would we be without the fear of punishment?
   - (b) God graciously establishes governments for our sakes – even those which have no connection whatever with the church.

4. *The weather is controlled by common grace* (Matthew 5:45).
   - (a) God controls nature from rain to earthquakes.
   - (b) Why he allows things that are not good in our eyes belongs to the mystery of his sovereignty (Psalm 115:3).

## D. Our individual creation and existence.
1. *God chose to give each of us birth* (James 1:18).
   - (a) None of us is an 'accident'.
   - (b) You may say 'My parents didn't want me.' I answer: God did.

2. *From this we rightly conclude:*
   - (a) God chose our parents (Psalm 139:16).
   - (b) God therefore chose the time and place of our birth!

# 4 GOD'S SOVEREIGNTY WITH REGARD TO REDEMPTION

## A. The words redemption and salvation may, generally speaking, be used interchangeably.

1.  Redemption means God 'bought us back' by the blood of his Son (1 Peter 1:18-19).
2.  Salvation means God spared us from the wrath to come by the blood of his Son (Romans 5:9).

B.  **God chose to save us before the Fall and yet in the light of the Fall.**
    1.  *The Fall (man's sin in the Garden of Eden; Genesis 3) did not take God by surprise.*
        (a)  Christ is the lamb chosen before the creation of the world (1 Peter 1:20).
        (b)  God did not panic when Adam and Eve sinned but began the process of redemption in the Garden of Eden itself (Genesis 3:21).

    2.  *God chose to have a people.*
        (a)  This choice was made before the world began (Ephesians 1:4).
        (b)  The people God chose were given to the Son (John 6:37).
        (c)  Those people are predestined to be saved (Romans 8:30).
        (d)  The choice was not based upon their works (2 Timothy 1:9).
        (e)  Those God chose believe in time (Acts 13:48).

    3.  *Why did God choose some but not all? The nearest we come to an answer is in the words of Jesus:* 'Yes, Father, for this was your good pleasure' (Matthew 11:26).
        (a)  Some things remain a mystery, like earthquakes.
        (b)  Adopt Abraham's answer: 'Will not the Judge of all the earth do right?' (Genesis 18:25).

## 5  GOD'S SOVEREIGNTY WITH REGARD TO HIS VARIOUS DEALINGS WITH US

A.  **The explanation for our status, calling, profile or position lies solely and wholly within the mystery of God's sovereignty.**
    1.  *Some can say with David:* 'The boundary lines have fallen for me in pleasant places; surely I have a delightful inheritance' (Psalm 16:6).
        (a)  David was highly favoured, like Mary (Luke 1:28).
            (1)  David was a man after God's own heart (1 Samuel 13:14).
            (2)  David was Israel's greatest king!
        (b)  Perhaps many of you humbly and gratefully acknowledge: 'I will sing to the LORD, for he has been good to me' (Psalm 13:6).
            (1)  It may be God's goodness not only at the level of saving mercy but also at the level of common grace.
            (2)  It may be God's role for you in his kingdom.
            (3)  It could be he has spared you of hurt – or embarrassment (Psalm 103:10).

2. *Some are more like Mephibosheth* (2 Samuel 9).
  (a) Mephibosheth was crippled.
    (1) Some are lame from birth, or have some handicap from birth.
    (2) Others develop a problem – either through an illness or through an accident.
  (b) Some Christians seem destined to continual suffering and can hardly recall when there were not problems – financial, emotional, physical or social.
  (c) Why? It lies within the mystery of God's sovereignty – and certainly for his glory (John 11:4).

B. **The explanation of God's strategy for his kingdom lies within the sphere of God's sovereignty.**
  1. *Our calling, or anointing* (1 Corinthians 12)
    (a) Some have greater gifts.
    (b) Some are the eye, or head; others the intestines! (1 Corinthians 12:12ff.).

  2. *Our faithfulness and hard work vis-a-vis those who are equally rewarded without any effort!* (Matthew 20:1-16).
    (a) Some work for years to get to where others are in a day.
    (b) God may pass over the gifted person at the last minute.

C. **The explanation for God's chastening.**
  1. *God may chasten (discipline) one for a sin or fault which another gets away with!* (Hebrews 12:5-11).
    (a) Some have to wait for years to 'discover' their errors (Lamentations 4:22).
    (b) Others are dealt with immediately (Jonah 1).

  2. *God may use chastening, or suffering, to refine one's character.*
    (a) Another may get this refinement by a sudden filling of the Spirit.
    (b) Either belongs to God's secret will (John 21:21-22).

D. **The explanation for success.**
  1. *God uses Billy Graham, to the dismay of many hyper-Calvinists!*
  2. *God may withhold success, or vindication, from those who may seem so worthy.*
    (a) Some get a promotion; others do not.
    (b) Some get married; others do not.

## 4   ALL THAT HAS BEEN SAID ABOUT THE SOVEREIGNTY OF GOD MAY BE ASCRIBED EQUALLY TO JESUS CHRIST

**A. To do justice to the sovereignty of Christ we need a separate study.**

**B. And yet all that pertains to the will and power of God the Father can be ascribed to the Son.**
1. At the level of creation (Hebrews 1:1-2).
2. At the level of redemption (John 5:21).
3. At the level of individual dealings (John 21:21).

### CONCLUSION

God is sovereign: he has the right and the power to do whatever he pleases. He is in control of all that happens and has happened, both for nations and individuals.

We can trust the Holy God to order things aright, even though they remain a mystery to us. Remember Isaiah 55:8-9: 'For my thoughts are not your thoughts, neither are your ways my ways,' declares the LORD. 'As the heavens are higher than the earth, so are my ways higher than your ways and my thoughts than your thoughts.'

Can you affirm the above as Jesus did in Matthew 11:26?

# 7

# HUMAN RESPONSIBILITY

## INTRODUCTION

**A. This study follows the one on the Sovereignty of God, and with good reason!**

1. The initial reaction to the teaching of God's sovereignty is sometimes: 'What does it matter? Why bother? If God is sovereign, there is no need for us to do anything.' Such a reaction, however, is wrong.

**B. God's sovereignty and human responsibility are an antinomy: two parallel principles that are irreconcilable but both equally true.**

1. *When applied to theology, an antinomy, as J I Packer puts it, is two parallel principles that are 'apparently' irreconcilable.*
   - (a) In other words, they are not really irreconcilable; they only appear to be so.
   - (b) C. H. Spurgeon said that truths like these are parallel here on earth but meet in eternity!

2. *The point is, we believe both equally, even though they appear to contradict each other.*
   - (a) If God is powerful and sovereign and at work, it would seem to suggest that we sit back and do nothing!
   - (b) No. Human responsibility always comes into the picture; we must act and work as though everything depends on our efforts.

3. *There are other theological antinomies:*
   - (a) Jesus is God as though he were not man and man as though he were not God.
   - (b) The believer is 'simultaneous saint and sinner' (Martin Luther); holy and yet with a heart 'prone to wander' (Jeremiah 17:9).

**C. In the light of the teaching of the sovereignty of God we must guard against certain attitudes which the devil may use.**

1. *Bitterness.*
   - (a) Many react in a hostile way to this teaching.
     - (1) They may say that this hostility is not towards God himself, but towards the teaching.
     - (2) This assumes that the teaching is false, that God is not absolutely sovereign.

(b) But if the teaching is true (and it is), the hostile feeling is not directed at the teaching but at God himself.

    (1) There is that in all of us that wants to blame God.

    (2) Although this feeling may seem justified at first, it is absolutely wrong, and must be confessed and cleansed.

(c) The reasons we feel this bitterness and hostility toward the teaching of God's sovereignty are these:

    (1) We feel betrayed that such a God turns out to be different from the one we had been worshipping!

    (2) We feel betrayed that we were not we taught this teaching before.

    (3) We like to feel that we are in control; the teaching of God's sovereignty takes away our control.

    (4) This teaching is alien to our natural feelings; if we aren't careful we will confuse the natural with the spiritual and will think we are being led by the Spirit when it is the flesh that is governing our thinking.

2. *Becoming passive*

(a) The man who hid his talent may be thought as having had a high view of God's sovereignty (Matthew 25:24-25).

(b) It is sad but true that there are Christians who accept the teaching of God's sovereignty but who are irresponsibly passive.

    (1) I'd prefer an Arminian to remain an evangelistically-minded and godly Christian than to become an inconsistent Calvinist.

(c) We can become passive in two areas if we are not careful:

    (1) In *evangelism*. If God is sovereign, why be evangelistic? A good book on this subject is J I Packer's *Evangelism and the Sovereignty of God*.

    (2) In *holy living*. If God is sovereign, why live a holy life?

(d) It is theologically sound to believe in the teaching of the absolute sovereignty of God and yet be as zealous as any Christian that ever lived!

    (1) The same Bible which gives us the teaching of God's sovereignty also gives us commands!

    (2) We can worship the awesome sovereign God by taking seriously those passages that tell *us* what *we* are to do!

    (3) We are fools if we take on the teaching of the sovereignty of God and neglect those passages that urge human responsibility!

## D. Why is this teaching important?

1. *It gives us theological, as well as practical, balance.*
   (a) It is my aim that the theology I teach will never (knowingly) be one-sided or out of balance.
   (b) I believe in the deity of Jesus Christ; I equally believe in his humanity.
   (c) I believe in the sovereignty of God; I equally believe in evangelism.
   (d) I believe that once saved, always saved; I equally believe in holy living.

2. *It will enable us to see a wonderful biblical teaching in a more complete perspective.*
   (a) The teaching of the sovereignty of God is only one side of the coin.
   (b) The teaching of human responsibility is the other.

3. *It will help bring us into a tradition of Christians and church leaders of former days who did not let their robust teaching on the sovereignty of God slow them down. For example:*
   (a) The Reformers: Luther and Calvin.
   (b) Men used in great revival:George Whitefield and Jonathan Edwards.

4. *It will provide a corrective, if not alternative, to the widespread superficiality of the present time.*
   (a) Many have not been exposed to this kind of teaching at all.
   (b) It is my conviction that this perspective can make a difference in Christian lives; and if enough of us truly believe these truths we can make a difference in Britain itself!

# 1 GOD'S PROMISES USUALLY ASSUME OUR OBEDIENCE

## A. The 'fleeces' in the Bible.

1. *Gideon's fleece* (Judges 6:36-40).
   (a) God made it doubly clear he was with Gideon to defeat the Midianites.
   (b) But Gideon still had to act – both in obedience and with shrewdness (Judges 7:1-25).

2. *Jonathan's proposition* (1 Samuel 14:9-10).
   (a) Jonathan concluded from God's answer that he and his armour-bearer should attack the Philistines (1 Samuel 14:12).
   (b) But they still had to get on with it and act courageously (1 Samuel 14:13ff.).

### B. Promises where the honour of God's Name is at stake.

1. *God's promise to Abraham.*
   - (a) God made a stunning promise to Abraham concerning his seed when he was already elderly and without any heir (Genesis 15:4-5).
   - (b) But Abraham believed it; the result was that Abraham's faith counted for righteousness (verse 6).

2. *God's promise to Moses.*
   - (a) God gave extraordinary words to Moses when the children of Israel were under Pharaoh's cruel bondage (Exodus 3:7-22).
   - (b) But the people had to follow Moses during a time of disillusionment for all of them, and keep on trusting, before these promises were fulfilled.

3. *God's promise to Joshua.*
   - (a) God made it clear that the Israelites would be given the land of Canaan – 'every place where you set your feet' (Joshua 1:3).
   - (b) But the first major battle – overcoming the walled city of Jericho – was not won until they followed God's instructions, which may have seemed ridiculous! (Joshua 6:3-16).

4. *God's promise to David and Jerusalem.*
   - (a) The Bible clearly says God had chosen Zion, or Jerusalem (Zechariah 3:2; cf. Zechariah 1:14).
   - (b) But what David and Joab had to do to conquer Jerusalem originally was a most extraordinary feat (2 Samuel 5:6-10).

5. *God's promise via prophets.*
   - (a) Elijah promised rain (after a famine of three years) to Ahab, but a major battle had to be fought first (1 Kings 18).
   - (b) Elisha told Naaman he would be cleansed of leprosy – but only after he washed himself in the Jordan seven times! (2 Kings 5:10).

### C. Other general promises.

1. *Wisdom and knowledge* (Proverbs 1:7; 9:10).
   - (a) The fear of the Lord is but the 'beginning' of knowledge, or wisdom.
   - (b) That we fear the Lord does not mean we will be endowed with wisdom or knowledge automatically.
   - (c) Indeed, the proof that we truly fear the Lord is that we press on and learn all we can from the Lord. This means effort.

2. *Guidance* (Proverbs 3:5-6).
   - (a) We have the promise of God's guidance but on the condition that we 'acknowledge him in all our ways'.

(b) God can let us get off the rails to warn us, lest we take his guidance for granted.

(c) The more details we put before him in our prayer life, the better!

3. *Material or spiritual blessing* (Proverbs 3:9; Malachi 3:8-10).

   (a) When we honour God with the tithe, there is promise of blessing; both material and spiritual blessings are implied.

   (b) God *is able to* bless us, whether or not we tithe – and has done so many times.

   (c) But to presume on God's mercy is not honouring to him; he may rebuke us for lack of care for what is his.

4. *Protection* (Psalm 91)

   (a) The devil quoted Psalm 91:11-12 to Jesus when trying to get him to throw himself down from the highest point of the temple (Matthew 4:5-6).

   (b) But Jesus replied: 'Do not put the Lord your God to the test' (Matthew 4:7).

   (c) Therefore it is irresponsible to claim a promise and not act responsibly (see Ezra 8:22-23).

5. *Closeness to God* (Psalm 27; James 4:8).

   (a) If we want a close walk with God we will make an effort.

   (b) A close walk with God comes not merely from saying 'Yes, Lord' in church.

   (c) It comes from a commitment that is carried out in detail.

6. *Getting the desires of our hearts* (Psalm 37:4).

   (a) God promises to give us the desires of our hearts – on condition that we delight ourselves in him.

   (b) When we truly delight ourselves in him, the desires will increase or diminish, depending on what delights the Lord!

## 2   THE LIFE OF JESUS

### A. When it comes to human responsibility and the sovereignty of God, let Jesus be our supreme model.

1. Nobody had a more robust view of the sovereignty of God than Jesus (Matthew 11:25ff.).

2. Nobody acted more lovingly and responsibly than Jesus.

### B. Christ was the lamb slain from the foundation of the world.

1. *This would imply, in one sense, that it was all 'cut and dried'; that God could not lose.*

2. *But Jesus had to fulfil everything to the last detail.*

(a)  To become a baby in the fulness of time (Galatians 4:4).

(b)  To humble himself to death on a cross (Philippians 2:5-8).

C.  **In daily life his faith and actions were done with common sense and responsibility.**

1.  *In resisting the devil* (Matthew 4).

(a)  Temptation to unbelief.

(b)  Temptation to pride.

(c)  Temptation to act irresponsibly.

2.  *In resisting all temptation generally*

(a)  Sexual sin (Hebrews 4:15).

(b)  Self-vindication (1 Peter 2:22-23).

3.  *In his prayer life*

(a)  Jesus prayed like no person before or since.

(1)  In the morning (Mark 1:35).

(2)  In the evening (Matthew 14:23).

(3)  All night long (Luke 6:12).

(b)  He prayed all night prior to calling the Twelve (Luke 6:12-13).

(1)  From this we conclude he prayed for guidance.

(2)  Though he was the God-man, Jesus prayed as though needing strength and guidance from outside himself!

## 3  THE LIFE OF THE APOSTLE PAUL

A.  **Paul regarded himself as an 'example' for those who would believe on Jesus (1 Timothy 1:16).**

1.  Paul had a robust view of God's sovereignty (Romans 9:11-18).

2.  But Paul was anything but a passive man!

B.  **Paul knew his conversion was wholly and absolutely by sheer sovereign grace (Acts 9:1-6).**

1.  He had done nothing whatever to deserve it.

2.  He also could say: 'I was not disobedient to the vision from heaven' (Acts 26:19).

C.  **He himself knew hardship and rough times when, surely, God must have seemed to be far away.**

1.  *His ordeal at sea* (Acts 27).

2.  *His being put in prison* (Acts 16:24ff.; 23:10, 35).

3.  *See also 1 Corinthians 4:11ff; 2 Corinthians 11:23-29.*

(a)  He was pleased that Onesiphorus worked so hard looking for him (2 Timothy 1:17).

(b)  He told Timothy to act responsibly regarding his health (1 Timothy 5:23).

D. **As an evangelist Paul was consistently wanting to be a soul-winner.**
1. When he was 'in between times' he took the opportunity to witness in the market place (Acts 17:16-17).
2. He wanted to preach where no-one had been! (Romans 15:20).


## CONCLUSION

God is sovereign in all that he does – from salvation to healing. But we are commanded to do all in our power: we are told to go into all the world with the gospel (Matthew 28:19); we are told to pray for the sick (James 5:14ff.).

God is powerful, sovereign and at work; yet we have a responsibility to work and act as if everything depended on our efforts in winning souls, in prayer, in walking in the light.

If we are negligent in these areas, no matter how 'high' our view of the sovereignty of God is, we are fools.

# 8

# THE GLORY OF GOD

## INTRODUCTION

**A. The glory of God is my favourite theme.**
1. It is truly the heart of God.
2. Our love for his glory is an indication of whether our own hearts have been touched by him.

**B. Most theology today has lost its God-emphasis and is really anthropology (the study of man).**
(1) Most theology today is done on the assumption that:
   (a) Man is the centre of the universe.
   (b) God owes man an explanation of things.
(2) Theology today is largely existential.
   (a) Existentialism: emphasis on our 'existence' in the here and now.
   (b) 'What's in it for me?' versus the God who is *there* and the one before whom I will stand *then*.

**C. Why study the glory of God?**
1. *It is an introduction to the true and only God: the God of the Bible. He is called the 'God of glory'* (Acts 7:2).
2. *It teaches us what matters most – God's own glory* (Isaiah 42:8).
3. *It shows us what we fall short of; why we know we are sinners* (Romans 3:23).
4. *We are on holy ground; we are entering the most sacred area I know of* (Exodus 3:1-6).
5. *If we grasp and affirm from our hearts the glory of God, it will be life-changing.*
   (a) It will transform our sense of worship (Isaiah 6:1-4).
   (b) It will humble us (Isaiah 6:5a).
   (c) It will lead to obedience (Isaiah 6:6-8).

6. *It will help us understand the aim of our lives as believers: to see God's glory in all things* (1 Corinthians 10:31).
7. *Sooner or later, in our quest to know God, we will come up against this theme. Love it or hate it, we will never be the same again.*

(a)  If we come to love the glory of God, it will be because we have got to know the true God – and still love him!

(b)  We will realise with awe that we are treading where the greatest of men and women, the spiritual greats both in the Bible and Church History, have trod.

## E.  The glory of God is the dignity of his person.

1.  *This succinct definition obviously needs to be unpacked; the whole of this study will seek to do just that.*
    (a)  Dignity: worthiness, honour or respect.
    (b)  Person: God's essential being; that he is a personal God.
    (c)  The Trinity is God in three persons.

2.  *There are two words in the ancient languages that must be observed: each is translated 'glory'.*
    (a)  Old Testament: *kabodh* is a Hebrew word meaning 'heaviness' or 'weight'. It refers to one's weight, or stature.
        (1)  We sometimes refer to someone 'throwing his weight around'.
        (2)  God's 'weightiness' is the basic idea of his glory in the Old Testament where the word is used no fewer than 222 times.
    (b)  New Testament: *doxa* is the Greek word from which we get 'doxology'; it means 'praise' or 'honour'.
        (1)  It comes from a root word that means 'opinion'.
        (2)  The New Testament thus brings out a meaning inherent in the Old Testament, that connects to God's opinion, or will. It is used no fewer than 168 times in the New Testament.

3.  *The two words combined lead us to a number of subsidiary definitions, all of which are correct.*

4.  *John used* doxa *to describe Jesus:* 'The Word became flesh and lived for a while among us. We have seen his glory, the glory of the One and Only Son, who came from the Father, full of grace and truth' (John 1:14). Yet its use in John 1:14 mirrors the Hebrew meaning.
    (a)  The ancient Hebrews referred to the Shekinah glory.
    (b)  The Greek word that is translated 'lived for a while' means 'tented' or 'tabernacled', from a word that is almost certainly taken from the idea of Shekinah.

5.  *Paul used* doxa *to describe the gospel:* 'The god of this age has blinded the minds of unbelievers, so that they cannot see the light of the gospel of the glory of Christ, who is the image of God' (2 Corinthians 4:4). The result of the gospel, then, was 'to give us the light of the knowledge of the *glory of God* in the face of Christ' (2 Corinthians 4:6).

## 1   GLORY IS THE SUM TOTAL OF GOD'S ATTRIBUTES

### A. Attributes are the characteristics of a person.

1. God is a personal God, a 'he' not an 'it' (Exodus 3:13).
2. God is holy (Leviticus 11:44). He hates sin.
3. God is merciful (Exodus 34:7). He does not want to punish.
4. God is just (Psalm 89:14). He is absolutely fair.
5. God is jealous (Exodus 20:5). He tolerates no rivals.
6. God is faithful (Lamentations 3:23). He will never desert us.
7. God is truthful (Hebrews 6:18). He cannot lie.
8. God is eternal (Genesis 21:33). He has no beginning or end.
9. God is unchangeable (Malachi 3:6). His character stays the same.
10. God is omniscient (Psalm 139:1-4). He knows everything.
11. God is omnipotent (Exodus 15:6). He is all-powerful.
12. God is omnipresent (Psalm 139:7-10). He is everywhere.
13. God is invisible (Exodus 33:20). No-one can see him.
14. God is incomprehensible (Romans 11:33). No-one can fully understand him or figure him out!
15. God is Creator (Ecclesiastes 12:1). He made all that is out of nothing.
16. God is Redeemer (Psalm 19:14). He bought us back with the blood of his Son.
17. God is Spirit (John 4:24). He cannot be seen or touched.
18. God is Saviour (Isaiah 45:15). He saves us from our sins and from his wrath.
19. God is King of kings (1 Timothy 6:15). All the kings of the earth must bow to him.
20. God is Father (Matthew 11:25). This is what he becomes to us through Jesus Christ.

### B. 'Glory' is the one word which sums up all the above.

1. *'Glory' is the nearest we come to describing God in one word.*
    (a) Stephen called him 'the God of glory' (Acts 7:2).
    (b) Later Stephen saw 'the glory of God' (Acts 7:55).

2. *'Glory' is God's 'essence'.*
    (a) Essence: all that makes something what it is; its nature.
    (b) The nature, or essence of God, in one word, is glory.

3. *God is the 'weightiest' being there is.*
    (a) We may ask: 'Who carries the most weight?'
        Royalty; politicians; wealthy persons; those with power.
    (b) God is the most powerful, awesome being that is – which is his *glory.*

## 2   WHERE CREDIT IS DUE 'ASCRIBE TO THE LORD THE GLORY DUE HIS NAME' (1 Chronicles 16:29).

### A.  Glory means credit. Who gets the credit?

1. *For creation* (Psalm 19:1).
   - (a)  Who gets the credit for our being created? God.
     - 1)  'I will praise you because I am fearfully and wonderfully made' (Psalm 139:14).
     - (2)  How contemptible to speak of creation by chance or evolution.
   - (b)  Who gets the credit for the beauty of creation? God.

2. *For redemption* (Ephesians 1:14).
   - (a)  Who gets the credit for our being predestined? God.
     - (1)  'And those he predestined, he also called; those he called, he also justified; those he justified, he also glorified' (Romans 8:30).
     - (2)  How silly to speak of salvation in terms of what we have done for God!
   - (b)  Who gets the credit for purchasing our salvation? God.
     - (1)  'In him we have redemption through his blood, the forgiveness of sins, in accordance with the riches of God's grace' (Ephesians 1:7).
     - (2)  How absurd for one to speak of salvation in terms of our good works!
   - (c)  Who gets the credit for drawing us? God.
     - (1)  'No-one can come to me unless the Father who sent me draws him, and I will raise him up at the last day' (John 6:44).
     - (2)  How ridiculous that we should say we made the first move toward God!
   - (d)  Who gets the credit for our being kept? God.
     - (1)  'For I am convinced that neither death nor life, neither angels nor demons, neither the present nor the future, nor any powers, neither height nor depth, nor anything else in all creation, will be able to separate us from the love of God that is in Christ Jesus our Lord' (Romans 8:38-39).
     - (2)  How ludicrous to suppose we keep ourselves saved!

3. *For all the benefits that are ours in Christ* (Psalm 103:2).
   - (a)  *Our gifts*: 'For who makes you different from anyone else? What do you have that you did not receive? And if you did receive it, why do you boast as though you did not?' (1 Corinthians 4:7). How arrogant for us to take credit for what we have!

(b) *Our position*: 'No-one from the east or the west or from the desert can exalt a man. But it is God who judges: He brings one down, he exalts another' (Psalm 75:6-7). How thoughtless of us if we say we got to where we are by our own cleverness!

(c) *Our guidance*: 'Surely goodness and love will follow me all the days of my life, and I will dwell in the house of the LORD for ever' (Psalm 23:6). How ungrateful we are should fancy that we cope in our strength.

**B. All that we are and have and hope to be can be summed up in this: to God be the glory!**

## 3   THE DIGNITY OF HIS PLEASURE (Exodus 33:19).

### A. The dignity of God's pleasure comes to two things:
1. *The dignity of his presence: what his presence does and means.*
2. *The dignity of his will: how his opinion should be regarded.*
   (a) Moses made a stupendous, if not impertinent, request to see God's glory! (Exodus 33:18).
       (1) And yet Jesus would later say, 'Did I not tell you that if you believed, you would see the glory of God?' (John 11:40).
       (2) Stephen saw the glory of God (Acts 7:55).
   (b) God replied to Moses: 'I will cause all my goodness to pass in front of you, and I will proclaim my name, the LORD, in your presence. I will have mercy on whom I will have mercy, and I will have compassion on whom I will have compassion' (Exodus 33:19).
       (1) This referred to God's presence (cf. Exodus 33:14).
       (2) This referred to God's will, what he would be pleased to do.

### B. We should pray that God will be *pleased* to show himself.
1. *His presence is to be valued above anything.*
   (a) The first time God's presence is referred to is in Genesis 3:8.
   (b) God's presence was promised to Moses. 'The LORD replied, "My Presence will go with you, and I will give you rest"' (Exodus 33:14).

2. *God's presence graced Solomon's temple (1 Kings 8:10-11).*
   (a) The presence of God was visible – it is described as a cloud.
   (b) We are immediately told that this was the glory.
       (1) This came to be known as the Shekinah.
       (2) There is no way of knowing exactly what this was like, although some contemporary testimonies give some hints.

(3) Any sense of God's presence is owing to his will. He may be pleased to show or withhold his glory (Romans 9:15).

## C. There are various manifestations of God's presence.
1. A healing presence (Luke 5:17).
2. A presence of judgment (Acts 5:1-11).
3. A praise presence (Acts 2:46-47).
4. An intercessory prayer presence (Acts 4:24ff.).
5. A presence of wisdom (Acts 6:5, 10).
6. A special presence at the Lord's Supper (1 Corinthians 11:29).
7. A presence that issues in conversions (Acts 2:41).

## D. The presence of the glory of God is to be coveted above all else – if the church is to have any respect.
1. *It is properly called the church's 'genius'.*
   (a) It is what will make a church – or break it, should it be absent.
   (b) The worst thing that can be said of the church: 'The glory has departed.'
      (1) The Ark was a symbol of God's glory. When it was taken it was said that the glory departed (1 Samuel 4:21-22).

2. *The church's genius is not:*
   (a) Its wealth.
   (b) Its gifted clergymen or ministers.
   (c) Its numbers.
   (d) Its buildings or architecture.
   (e) Its music.

3. *The church's genius is the presence of the glory of God.*

## CONCLUSION
Jonathan Edwards taught us: The one thing which Satan cannot successfully counterfeit is a love for the glory of God. It is the grace that distinguishes us as true believers, for no unconverted person can love God's glory. If you do love it, you are without doubt a true child of God.

Sometimes the presence of God in the soul is so overwhelming that one simply wants to exclaim 'Glory!' (Psalm 29:9).

# 9

# THE NAME OF GOD

## INTRODUCTION

**A. This study is quite close to the subject of the glory of God.**
   1. We saw that the glory of God is the main key to understanding the heart of the God of the Bible.
   2. Not far removed from this is another key, that of God's Name.

**B. When Moses learned that God had chosen him to be the deliverer of the children of Israel from Pharaoh's bondage he said, 'Suppose I go to the Israelites and say to them, "The God of your fathers has sent me to you," and they ask me, "What is his name?" then what shall I tell them?' (Exodus 3:13).**
   1. *Perhaps Moses asked this because he feared that the people of Israel already knew that he didn't know God's name – and it would be their way of testing him.*
      (a) Moses felt like an outsider.
      (b) He assumed (perhaps) that the people would know God's name backwards and forwards.
      (c) He needed to prove to them that he already knew something of this God so that they would trust him.

   2. *It is also possible that Moses himself was curious.*
      (a) He was eager to know more about God.
      (b) He also needed authority to approach the children of Israel.

**C. Name: a word or words by which one is known.**
   1. *It primarily refers to one's identity.*
      (a) We identify a person by his or her name.
      (b) It is what distinguishes him or her from another individual.
   2. *It also refers to one's reputation.*
      (a) We will say, 'He has a good name.'
      (b) Proverbs 22:1: 'A good name is more desirable than great riches; to be esteemed is better than silver or gold.'
   3. *It can refer to one's influence.*
      (a) A person's name as a reference can be powerful.
      (b) Having a person with a good name behind you will help give you a good name.

4. *It also may refer to being a substitute for someone: 'I come in so-and-so's name'; 'I am representing so-and-so'.*
   (a) One is therefore authorised to speak on behalf of another.
   (b) For example, an ambassador speaks for his country.
   (c) A policeman may arrest in the name of the law.

5. *God's name will incorporate all the above meanings.*

## D. Why is this study important?
1. It will teach us to have a deeper respect for God. The third commandment is, 'You shall not misuse the name of the LORD your God, for the LORD will not hold anyone guiltless who misuses his name' (Exodus 20:7).
2. It is a good way to know a lot more about the God of the Bible.
3. It has tremendous relevance for prayer.

# 1  GOD'S IDENTITY

## A. The term 'God' does not itself give identity.
1. *'God' is a generic term and does not necessarily mean the Christian view of God.*
   (a) This is why we refer to 'the God of the Bible'.
   (b) This is why we refer to 'the God and Father of our Lord Jesus Christ' (2 Corinthians 1:3).

2. Elohim *(Hebrew) refers to God as a powerful being.*
   (a) It is the first term used in the Bible for the Creator God (Genesis 1:1).
   (b) It is also a plural noun in Hebrew, suggesting the Trinity; hence, 'God said, "Let us make man in our image, in our likeness" ' (Genesis 1:26).

## B. *Yahweh* is the Old Testament word that clearly identifies the name of the true God.
1. *It is translated LORD and most versions have all four letters in upper case to let you know it means Yahweh.*
   (a) The Authorised Version wrongly translated *Yahweh* as 'Jehovah':
      (1) The original Hebrew word was not vocalised; the 'tetragrammaton' YHWH was considered too sacred to pronounce.
      (2) When vowels were combined with the consonants YHWH it was assumed the spelling should be 'Jehovah'. This form was first attested at the beginning of the twelfth century AD.

    (b)  Scholarly studies since have shown that the pronunciation should be 'Yahweh' and such is indicated by transliterations of the name into Greek in early Christian literature.

        (1)  There is no hint that ancient Jews did not pronounce the name.

        (2)  Not pronouncing 'Yahweh' but substituting *Adonai* was probably a medieval superstition that gave Jews a righteous feeling.

  2.  *Strictly speaking, Yahweh is the only 'name' of God.*

    (a)  *Yahweh*, in contrast to *Elohim*, is the name of a person, though this person is divine.

    (b)  'Yahweh' brings God near to man so that he speaks to us as a friend.

    (c)  Yahweh means, literally, 'one who is' or 'one who causes to be', or 'I will be what I will be'.

        (1)  Moses asked, 'What is his name?'

        (2)  God said, 'I am who I am .... I AM has sent me to you'.

        (3)  'This is my name for ever, the name by which I am to be remembered from generation to generation' (Exodus 3:15-17).

    (d)  God said to Moses, 'I am the LORD (*Yahweh*). I appeared to Abraham, to Isaac and to Jacob as God Almighty, but by my name the LORD (*Yahweh*) I did not make myself known to them' (Exodus 6:3).

    (e)  When you transliterate the Greek for Jesus back into Hebrew it comes out as 'Joshua' -- 'The LORD is salvation'.

C.  **Other words are used to describe God; sometimes we may refer to them as names although, technically, they are descriptions:**

  1.  El. *This merely means god in the widest sense; even an image is treated as a god* (Genesis 35:2).

    (a)  'I, the LORD your God, am a jealous God (*El*)' (Deuteronomy 5:9).

    (b)  'The God (*El*) of Bethel' (Genesis 31:13).

  2.  El Elyon, *'the most high God' as worshipped by Melchizedek* (Genesis 14:19; cf. Numbers 24:16; Psalm 7:17; Daniel 7:22).

  3.  El Olam, *the eternal God* (Genesis 21:33).

  4.  El Elohe-Israel, *the God of Israel* (Genesis 33:20).

  5.  Jahweh-jireh, *the Lord provides* (Genesis 22:8,14).

  6.  Jahweh-nissi, *the Lord is my banner* (Exodus 17:15).

  7.  Yahweh-shalom, *the Lord is peace* (Judges 6:24).

  8.  Yahweh-tsidkenu, *the Lord our righteousness* (Jeremiah 23:6).

  9.  Yahweh-shammah, *the Lord is there* (Ezekiel 48:35).

  10. Yahweh-shebot, *the Lord of hosts.*

    (a)  This is translated the Lord Almighty in the New Iinternational Version (1 Samuel 1:3; 1 Samuel 17:45).

      (b)  It is used to show Yahweh as Protector of his people, the 'hosts' being all the heavenly powers ready to carry out the Lord's command. It is used 88 times in Jeremiah.

  11. Quedos Israel, *the Holy One of Israel – a favourite with Isaiah (used 29 times). Similarly:*

      (a)  The mighty One of Israel (Isaiah 1:24).

      (b)  The Glory of Israel (1 Samuel 15:29).

  12. *Ancient of Days* (Daniel 7:9, 13, 22). *It alternates with Most High* (Daniel 7:18, 22, 25, 27).

## 2  GOD'S REPUTATION

**A.  The God of glory cares greatly about the honour of his name (Joshua 7:9).**

  1.  'Moses said to the LORD, "Then the Egyptians will hear about it! By your power you brought these people up from among them. And they will tell the inhabitants of this land about it .... If you put these people to death all at one time, the nations who have heard this report about you will say, 'The LORD was not able to bring these people into the land he promised them on oath; so he slaughtered them in the desert' " ' (Numbers 14:13-16).

      (a)  God was prepared to destroy Israel and start all over again with a different people.

      (b)  Moses interceded and reminded God of his reputation – and what the enemies of Israel would say!

  2.  *All that God's people do should reflect his honour.*

      (a)  Rahab told the Israelite spies how the courage of the people of Canaan failed them because of all they had heard, 'for the LORD your God is God in heaven above and on the earth below ....' (Joshua 2:10-12).

      (b)  Israel's reputation was the Lord's reputation.

      (c)  What God does in the lives of his people reflects on his name.

  3.  *All that we are, who are called by his name, can bring him dishonour.*

      (a)  David's sin (adultery and murder) 'made the enemies of the LORD show utter contempt' (2 Samuel 12:14).

      (b)  The incestuous sin in Corinth brought great dishonour. It was 'of a kind that does not occur even among pagans' (1 Corinthians 5:1).

**B.  The first thing the disciples were to learn about the Father in the Lord's Prayer was, 'Hallowed be your name' (Matthew 6:9).**

  1.  *'Holy and awesome is his name'* (Psalm 111:9; Isaiah 57:15).

2. *This would refer to Yahweh.* 'I am the LORD; that is my name! I will not give my glory to another or my praise to idols' (Isaiah 42:8).
   (a) God's reputation was implied when David wanted to build the Temple (2 Chronicles 6:7-8).
   (b) God's reputation was implied when he told the nation of Israel the way back, should they wander. 'If my people, who are called by my name, will humble themselves and pray and seek my face and turn from their wicked ways, then will I hear from heaven and will forgive their sin and will heal their land' (2 Chronicles 7:14).

C. **The third commandment was to protect the name of the Lord from abuse: 'You shall not misuse the name of the LORD your God, for the LORD will not hold anyone guiltless who misuses his name' (Exodus 20:7).**
   1. *This was not merely a warning against swearing, that is, cursing.*
   2. *The fundamental meaning of the third commandment is to 'let God be God' and not bring his name into it.*
      (a) This is the way Jesus interpreted it in the Sermon on the Mount (Matthew 5:33-37).
         (1) When one swears an oath he must appeal to the greater, as Hebrews 6:16 puts it.
         (2) To appeal to the name of God when swearing is to lower him.
      (b) James warned mistreated Christians against claiming God as being with them over against other Christians (James 5:12).
         (1) To claim 'God is with me rather than you' is to abuse his name.
         (2) We should 'keep God out of it' when we are personally involved.

D. **When we pray 'Glorify your name' we are praying that God's reputation will be enhanced.**
   1. *We need to ask ourselves: What will bring glory to God's name?*
      (a) Increased numbers?
      (b) Holy living?
      (c) Miracles?
      (d) That which shames wicked men?
      (e) A government that recognises God and righteousness?
   2. *As Christians, who are called by God's name, we should be conscious of that which truly brings glory to him.*

E. **God gave new meaning to his name by giving his name to Jesus (Philippians 2:9).**
  1. *The name that is above every name is none other than Yahweh.*
     (a) A father will sometimes give his name to his son.
     (b) God the Father has given his name to Jesus.
         (1) This was not the name Jesus, which was God's name for his Son at his birth (Matthew 1:21).
         (2) This naming was after Jesus ascended to heaven.

  2. *This meant that Jesus had the total approval of his Father.*
     (a) Not just at his baptism (Matthew 3:17) or when he was transfigured (Matthew 17:5).
     (b) Now that he had finished his mission the Father bestowed on Jesus his own name.
     (c) 'The Son is the radiance of God's glory and the exact representation of his being, sustaining all things by his powerful word. After he had provided purification for sins, he sat down at the right hand of the Majesty in heaven. So he became as much superior to the angels as the name he has inherited is superior to theirs' (Hebrews 1:3-4).

  3. *This is one more proof (if needed) of the deity of Jesus.*
     (a) Compare Isaiah 42:8 with Philippians 2:9.
         (1) God will not give his glory to another (to man).
         (2) But he gave it to Jesus!
     (b) God put the whole of his own reputation in the name of his Son!

## 3  THE NAME OF GOD AND INFLUENCE

A. **We have already seen how the dread of God's name fell on the land of Canaan even before the people of Israel entered it (Joshua 2).**
  1. *This is because God's name had influence.*
  2. *Influence is the power to produce an effect.*
     (a) This is taking the reputation of God's name a step further.
     (b) It is when the very mention of the name of the Lord produces an effect.
         (1) With God's enemies: fear (Judges 7:14-15).
         (2) With God's people: praise (Psalm 115:1).

B. **Influence with God (John 14:14).**
  1. *The Father is influenced by his Son.*
     (a) The Father, as we have seen, was pleased with his Son.
     (b) Whatever Jesus asked for he got.

      (1)  Jesus never knew unanswered prayer.

      (2)  When he did not do many miracles in a certain place it was not his lack of faith but the people's (Matthew 13:58).

      (3)  Jesus only did what the Father wanted him to do (John 5:19).

  (c)  Whenever Jesus asked for anything it was because he was simultaneously prompted by the Father to do so.

      (1)  Jesus never went against the Father's will.

      (2)  He always prayed in the Father's will.

2.  *This authority has been promised to us now that Jesus is in heaven.*

  (a)  However, asking in Jesus' name means more than repeating the words 'We ask this in Jesus' name. Amen.'

      (1)  We can repeat the words 'In Jesus' name' and not really mean what Jesus intended.

      (2)  We could also repeat these words in unbelief.

  (b)  To pray in Jesus' name means to embrace the authority to speak to the Father as Jesus himself did.

      (1)  When we come in the name of Jesus we know that we are really speaking for him – that is, we would pray in the Father's will as he did (1 John 5:14-15).

## CONCLUSION

God's name is bound up with his identity, who he is. He is Yahweh, the 'one who is', the great I AM. This God of glory is jealous for the honour of his name and all that we, his people, say and do should reflect his honour and reputation. All the authority that is in the name of God has been transferred to the name of Jesus.

# 10

# THE LAW OF GOD

## INTRODUCTION

A. **The Law of God has to be one of the most difficult subjects that can be raised in the study of theology.**
 (1) One Scottish divine long ago observed: 'He who can bring together the real connection between the law and the gospel, will be a good theologian.' Indeed; to show the mutual relevance of the law and the gospel has been perhaps the hardest task a theologian has faced since the Great Reformation of the sixteenth century.

B. **Martin Luther had two 'successors', that is, men who claimed to know what he believed and who claimed to speak for him.**
 1. *Andreas Osiander (1498-1552), who stressed the righteousness of the law as being the inevitable outcome of being justified by faith.*
   (a) This is often referred to as imparted righteousness.
   (b) This stresses not Christ's righteousness put to our credit but the transference of his righteousness to the believer.

 2. *John Agricola (1494-1566), who argued that the righteousness of the law had no relevance for the believer.*
   (a) He stressed imputed righteousness.
   (b) This refers to Christ's righteousness put to our credit to the extent that the law has no place in the life of the Christian.

 3. *The term* Antinomianism *emerged as a result of Agricola's views.*
   (a) Antinomianism comes from two Greek words:
     (1) *Anti:* 'against'; (2) *Nomos:* 'law'.
   (b) Antinomianism is the heresy (false doctrine) that has no place for the law in the believer's life.

 4. *Who best interpreted Luther? The answer: neither.*
   (a) Osiander said things Luther did not dream of.
   (b) Agricola said things Luther was afraid of.

C. **The law: the law of Moses. We sometimes refer to it as the Mosaic Law, given by God through angels (Galatians 3:19; Acts 7:38) at Sinai (Exodus 19-20). It is understood in three ways:**

1.  *The Moral Law or the Ten Commandments* (Exodus 20:1-17).
    (a)  This refers to moral righteousness, or personal righteousness –
         the way the people of God were to live their lives.
    (b)  No higher outward standard has ever emerged in human history,
         in so far as a code of conduct is concerned.

2.  *The Civil Law* (Exodus 21-23 and other places in Leviticus, Numbers
    and Deuteronomy).
    (a)  This dictated how the nation of Israel should govern itself.
    (b)  It had largely to do with relationships between the people of Israel.

3.  *The Ceremonial Law* (mostly the Book of Leviticus).
    (a)  This shows how the people of Israel should worship God.
    (b)  This covered the details of the sacrifices, holy days and the
         tabernacle.

## 1  THE RIGHTEOUSNESS OF THE MORAL LAW

## A.  A brief exposition of the Ten Commandments is as follows:

1.  *'You shall have no other gods before me'* (Exodus 20:3).
    (a)  Idolatry: giving priority to anything that is displeasing to God.
         (1)  This may refer to an idol of wood or stone.
         (2)  It refers equally to *anything* that comes between us and God.
    (b)  It also shows God's jealousy, which comes out more clearly in
         the second commandment.

2.  *'You shall not make for yourself an idol in the form of anything in
    heaven above or on the earth beneath or in the waters below. You
    shall not bow down to them or worship them; for I, the LORD your
    God, am a jealous God, punishing the children for the sin of the
    fathers to the third and fourth generation of those who hate me,
    but showing love to thousands who love me and keep my
    commandments'* (Exodus 20:4-6).
    (a)  This shows more clearly what God meant by the first
         commandment.
         (1)  God is opposed to visible forms to which one gives adoration.
         (2)  Such forms go against true faith (Hebrews 11:1).
    (b)  This anticipates not only faith but the nature of faith that comes
         not by seeing but by hearing.

3.  *'You shall not misuse the name of the LORD your God, for the LORD
    will not hold anyone guiltless who misuses his name'* (Exodus 20:7).
    (a)  This reveals God's jealousy for his name; its power and reputation.
         (1)  It refers of course to swearing, that is, cursing by using
              God's name.

(2) But it mainly refers to abusing God's name by claiming he is on your side (even if he is!).
   (b) This means we should not use God's name in an argument in order to support our point of view.

4. *'Remember the Sabbath day by keeping it holy. Six days you shall labour and do all your work, but the seventh day is a Sabbath to the LORD your God. On it you shall not do any work, neither you, nor your son or daughter, nor your manservant or maidservant, nor your animals, nor the alien within your gates. For in six days the LORD made the heavens and the earth, the sea, and all that is in them, but he rested on the seventh day. Therefore the LORD blessed the Sabbath day and made it holy'* (Exodus 20:8-11).
   (a) This refers to the seventh day, that is, from sunset on Friday to sunset on Saturday.
      (1) It was to be a day of complete rest, even for animals.
      (2) This was given for the sake of our bodies, that need a break!
   (b) This became one of the most controversial items of Jesus' ministry (his healing on the Sabbath).
   (c) It has been assumed that Sunday became the Sabbath.

5. *'Honour your father and your mother, so that you may live long in the land the LORD your God is giving you'* (Exodus 20:12).
   (a) This stresses God's concern for the family and the respect that is due the parents. It indicates the authority given to all parents.
   (b) Children are to obey parents, not the other way around. The apostle Paul points out that this is 'the first commandment with promise' (Ephesians 6:2).

6. *'You shall not murder'* (Exodus 20:13).
   (a) This reveals God's opinion on the sanctity (sacredness or holiness) of human life.
   (b) It may or may not refer to going to war (that is a complicated issue), but it surely refers to abortion.

7. *'You shall not commit adultery'* (Exodus 20:14).
   (a) This shows God's jealousy for the sanctity of the family.
      (1) The only sexual intercourse God approves of is between husband and wife.
      (2) This demonstrates God's care for the security of the marital relationship.
   (b) This further shows God's care for the security of the children, often those most hurt when infidelity occurs.

8. *'You shall not steal'* (Exodus 20:15).
    (a) This reveals God's respect for private possessions.
        (1) It assumes some things will be ours.
        (2) This law protects a person having his possessions taken by someone to whom they do not belong.
    (b) This further shows God's care for our personal security and well-being.

9. *'You shall not give false testimony against your neighbour'* (Exodus 20:16).
    (a) This of course refers to lying.
        (1) It shows God wants us to tell the truth.
        (2) It mainly shows how God wants no slander when we talk about others.
    (b) This reveals God's care for our integrity as well as our reputation.

10. *'You shall not covet your neighbour's house. You shall not covet your neighbour's wife, or his manservant or maidservant, his ox or donkey, or anything that belongs to your neighbour'* (Exodus 20:17).
    (a) Covet: 'to desire eagerly'.
        (1) This is the first command that refers to the inner person.
        (2) All the above refer to outward conduct.
    (b) This commandment slays all of us, even showing how much we have broken all of the above in our hearts (Matthew 5:21-22; 27-28; Romans 7:7).

## B. The Moral Law, then, refers to personal righteousness.

1. *This study is an introduction only, and so cannot deal with the whole of the law.*
    (a) The Civil Law was more relevant to Israel than to us.
        (1) Some would bring in the Civil Law upon nations today.
        (2) They would impose a theocracy on a nation (that God would actually govern by Israel's ancient laws).
    (b) The Ceremonial Law was totally fulfilled in Christ.
        (1) His parents kept the law for him until he became of age – e.g., his circumcision, etc..
        (2) Holy days and the sacrificial system were absolutely fulfilled in Christ – they have no contemporary application.
2. *The rest of this study includes the whole of the law but mainly the place of the Moral Law.*
    (a) Matthew 5:17 is of special relevance: 'Do not think that I have come to abolish the Law or the Prophets; I have not come to abolish them but to fulfil them.'

        (1)  In a sense this was Jesus' most daring statement.

        (2)  But that is exactly what he did; he fulfilled the law.

   (b)  In other words he kept it for us, the whole of it.

        (1)  He did it as our substitute.

        (2)  All he did for us is ours by faith; it is as though we kept it ourselves.

3.  *The Big Question then is this: Since Christ kept the law for us, to what extent are we obliged to keep it?*

   (a)  We are saved by faith (Galatians 2:16; Ephesians 2:8-9).

   (b)  Why then should we be bothered with the law which was perfectly fulfilled by Christ?

## 2  THE PURPOSE OF THE LAW

### A.  The precipitating cause (Galatians 3:19).

1.  *Israel's transgressions led God to bring in the Law.*

   (a)  The people of Israel turned to sin in the wilderness (1 Corinthians 10:1-11): idolatry (Exodus 32:1-6); sexual sin (Numbers 25:1-9); murmuring (Exodus 16:3).

   (b)  God stepped in with a Moral Code of Righteousness.

2.  *The implication of Galatians 3:19 is that, had the people not murmured and had God not seen their unbelief, there would have been no cause to bring in the law.*

   (a)  Both sin and righteousness had been in existence before the law was given (Romans 5:13). What the law did was to give a conscious understanding of both.

        (1)  Murder was regarded as sin before the law came in (Genesis 4:1-12).

        (2)  Adultery was regarded as sin (Genesis 39:9).

   (b)  Gross disobedience was the reason God superimposed the law.

### B.  The effectual purpose (1 Timothy 1:9-10).

1.  *To restrain (hold back) sin.*

   (a)  The children of Israel were getting carried away. When Moses was not around, they gave in to the flesh.

   (b)  Something had to be done. So God intervened by giving the law.

2.  *The restraint came through fear of punishment.*

   (a)  God instituted punishment for various offences.

        (1)  The punishment for murder was death (Numbers 35:30).

        (2)  The punishment for adultery was death (Leviticus 20:10).

   (b)  The whole of the civil law was enforced through fear of punishment (Exodus 21-23).

3. *By the way, it works!*
    (a)  This is why we have law today.
    (b)  People keep the law because they don't want to get caught, and fined or sent to prison!

## C. The spiritual purpose (Psalm 19:7-14; Romans 7:12).

1. *To reveal the character of God* (Leviticus 11:44; 1 Peter 1:16).
    (a)  God is holy.
    (b)  The holiness of God is revealed in the law.

2. *To show the standard of righteousness God requires of his people.*
    (a)  This is revealed clearly in the Ten Commandments.
    (b)  This standard has not changed (Malachi 3:6).

3. *Without the law there is no objective standard by which we can gauge what true righteousness is.*
    (a)  It is imprinted on the conscience (Romans 2:15).
    (b)  But at the end of the day one does not appeal to conscience, but to the external written code.

## D. The convicting purpose (Romans 7:7).

1. *To show the seriousness of sin* (Exodus 20:18-19).
    (a)  Had the law not been given, the people may have not been bothered by their sin.
    (b)  The law demonstrated:
        (1)  How much God hates sin.
        (2)  How serious it is to commit sin.

2. *The sacrificial system (a part of the ceremonial law) also showed the seriousness of sin.*
    (a)  That man could not atone for his own sin; he must go outside himself.
    (b)  He needed:
        (1)  A sacrifice of blood (Leviticus 17:11).
        (2)  A substitute (Hebrews 9:22).

## 3   THE PARENTHESIS OF LAW

## A. The law came 'in between' Abraham and Christ (Galatians 3:19).

1. *The word translated* added *in Romans 5:20 and Galatians 3:19 means* came in aside.
    (a)  This coheres with Section 2 above: had not gross sin come about, the law would not have come in at all.
    (b)  For sin was already known to be sin.

    2. *The law was 'added'; it was superimposed because of the trans-*
      *gressions.*
      (a)  The gospel had been revealed to Abraham (Galatians 3:8).
          (1)  Abraham is our example of justification by faith.
          (2)  All who believe are children of Abraham (Romans 4:12).
      (b)  Jesus said, 'Abraham saw my day and was glad' (John 8:56).
          (1)  We therefore do not go back to Moses.
          (2)  We go back to Abraham.

## B. The law came in 430 years after Abraham (Galatians 3:17).
    1. *It therefore came late!*
    2. *The parenthesis therefore meant:*
      (a)  The law was added.
      (b)  The law was not permanent.
      (c)  The law would eventually be fulfilled.
          (1)  It was fulfilled in Christ (Galatians 3:19).
          (2)  What Christ promised to do he did! (Matthew 5:17).

## C. In the meantime (during this parenthesis) the law was a tutor (Galatians 3:24).
    1. *Through the law it was learned:*
      (a)  The righteousness God requires.
      (b)  The seriousness of sin.
      (c)  The need for a sacrificial substitute.
    2. *But once Christ came 'we are no longer under the supervision of the law'* (Galatians 3:25).
      (a)  The law was fulfilled in Christ.
      (b)  When we are in Christ the law's requirements are complete (Galatians 2:17).
    3. *In short: those in Christ are no longer under the law* (Galatians 3:19, 25; cf. 5:18).

## 4  THE RELEVANCE OF THE LAW (1 Timothy 1:8-11).

## A. To show what Jesus was required to do (Matthew 3:15; 5:17).
    1. *The law having come in had to be fulfilled* (Galatians 3:19).
    2. *Jesus did what no human being had ever done* (Acts 15:10).
      (a)  The law could not impart life (Galatians 3:21).
      (b)  The one who fulfilled it can (John 5:21).

## B. To show what we have in Christ (1 Corinthians 1:30).
    1. *When he came he fulfilled it:*
      (a)  By perfect obedience (Romans 5:10).
      (b)  By his death (Romans 5:9).

2. *All that he did becomes ours by faith* (Romans 4:5).
   (a) He was without sin (Hebrews 4:15).
   (b) He was even baptised for us! (Matthew 3:15).

## C. To show what the law cannot do (Romans 8:3).
1. *It is unable to save us* (Galatians 3:10).
   (a) If a person prefers to be saved by the law, he must keep the *whole* of the law (James 2:10).
2. *It is unable to sanctify us* (Romans 7:14-24).
   (a) If one wishes to be sanctified by the law he must remember the spiritual requirements as well (Matthew 5:21-22,27-28).
   (b) The tenth commandment shows the impossibility of any of us being sanctified by the law (Romans 7:7ff.).

## D. To show that faith in Christ fulfils the law (Romans 10:4).
1. *That is the purpose of justification by faith.*
   (a) Faith achieves the righteousness required by the law (Galatians 2:16ff.).
   (b) Faith means that God puts to our credit a righteousness that makes it as though we kept the law.
2. *The law was put in charge that we might be justified by faith* (Galatians 3:24).
   (a) The law shows what we cannot do.
   (b) It follows that faith alone achieves this righteousness.

## E. To show the minimum standard of righteousness required for the believer (Romans 8:4).
1. *We were not justified by faith to remain in sin* (Romans 6:1ff.).
   (a) The faith that was given by the Spirit leads to a life of holiness (Romans 6:22).
   (b) The holiness we are led to is the righteousness of the law (the Ten Commandments).
2. *It is a test of righteousness whether or not we are walking in the Spirit* (Galatians 5:16).
   (a) Anyone who claims to be walking in the Spirit must be tested by his life.
   (b) If his life matches the righteousness of the law it is a good sign that he is truly walking in the Spirit.
3. *Note: the righteousness of the law is not a pre-condition of being justified by faith.*
   (a) This was the error of some of the Puritans.
      (1) They claimed you enter into a covenant to keep the law.
      (2) It was a condition you met before you could claim to be justified by faith.

(3) This led to works and legalism.

(4) Nobody ever knew for sure if he/she was justified.

(b) The righteousness of the law is not a condition of salvation but a debt of gratitude; sanctification is gratitude.

(c) Is it binding upon the Christian? Yes.

(1) Not as a condition to be saved.

(2) Rather as a minimum standard of life-style that shows you are saved – and grateful.

## CONCLUSION

Significantly, the Day of Pentecost, which occurred fifty days after the Passover, is the commemoration of the giving of the law. It was also the occasion when the Spirit came as a consequence of the glorification of Jesus who had fulfilled the law perfectly. It was then that the Spirit replaced the law which had never produced holiness. This inability was not in the law itself, but in sinful human nature (Romans 8:3-4). What is done through fear of punishment is not true holiness. Holiness, rather, is the response of gratitude!

The Spirit who convicts unbelievers of sin (John 16:8) also leads believers to live holy lives (Romans 8:4). He causes them to practise the ethic of Jesus, which was the law of love (John 13:34). As believers, we are under the law of Christ (1 Corinthians 9:21; Galatians 6:2). If we attempt to live our lives by the law, the result is bondage and self-righteousness. But if we live by love we will fulfil the law (Romans 13:8-10).

# 11

# THE COVENANT OF GOD

**INTRODUCTION**

A. **The focus of this study is upon God's relationship with people.**
   1. It gets to the heart of the gospel and the way God relates to us.
   2. God has chosen to relate to us by what is called 'covenant'.

B. **Covenant: a promise made binding by an oath. It is often defined as 'an agreement between two parties', but this is only one kind of covenant.**
   1. *Until the oath is taken the promise may be said to be:*
      (a) Conditional, that is, a promise will be kept if certain conditions are met.
      (b) Temporary, that is, a promise may be withdrawn after a certain period of time elapses.
      (c) On offer but awaiting the oath.

   2. *Oath: a solemn declaration – by swearing – that one will or will not do a certain thing.*
      (a) Generally speaking there are two levels through which God communicates to us:
         (1) By promise; his declaration to do or not do a certain thing; this is usually given with conditions.
         (2) By oath; when God swears his declaration; this is always permanent and without any conditions.
      (b) What is the purpose of God's oath?
         (1) To make the promise more believable so that one is sure it is really true.
         (2) To 'put an end to argument' so that there is no doubt about it (Hebrews 6:16).
         (3) To reward our faith; the swearing of an oath by God usually follows a period of time during which we proved we could stand the test he put us through.
         (4) To prepare us for the future – sometimes for the long haul ahead.

   3. *Since a covenant is a promise made binding by an oath, the terms 'oath' and 'covenant' can sometimes be used interchangeably.*

       (a)  But there are some differences between the two: for example, a covenant may be initiated and await a lapse of time before it is consummated by the oath.

       (b)  Sometimes a covenant is not what we accept from God but what we offer to him, which he may or may not accept.

## C.  Why this study?  Is it important?

  1.  *Have you ever made a promise to God?*

       (a)  If so, what good did it do?

       (b)  Was it an oath or a vow that you made?  See Ecclesiastes 5:4.

  2.  *It gets to the heart of the way God deals with people.*

  3.  *It points to the very contents of the Bible.*

       (a)  The Old Testament (covenant) contains 39 books.

       (b)  The New Testament (covenant) contains 27 books.

  4.  *The promise of a 'new covenant' (Jeremiah 31:31) is precisely what we otherwise call 'the gospel'.*

  5.  *Understanding the nature of covenant will lead us to see how so many theological subjects come together, e.g.:*

       (a)  The connection between covenant and justification by faith.

       (b)  The connection between covenant and assurance.

       (c)  The connection between covenant and rewards at the Judgement Seat of Christ.

       (d)  The connection between the law and the gospel.

  6.  *Any word that is used so often in the Bible (286 times in the Old Testament, 33 times in the New Testament) should get our attention.*

  7.  *Understanding this topic may be the nearest 'short cut' to good theology that there is.*

## 1   THE KINDS OF COVENANT

## A.  There are generally two kinds of covenant:

  1.  Unconditional covenant, when one pledges to another no matter what that other party does.

       (a)  One may swear to another without any conditions attached.

       (b)  This means that he who swears must come through with what is promised no matter what!

  2.  Conditional covenant, when an agreement is mutually accepted.

       (a)  It is, however, based upon certain conditions.

       (2)  These conditions must be met by both parties.

2. *In the ancient Near East there were three types of covenant; I am
   indebted to Dr Michael Eaton for these insights:*
   (a) Parity (equality) covenants between two equal parties.
      (1) An example is given in Genesis 26:28: 'They answered, "We
          saw clearly that the LORD was with you; so we said, 'There
          ought to be a sworn agreement between us' – between us
          and you. Let us make a treaty with you"' (cf. Genesis 21:27,
          31; 31:44, 53).
      (2) One of the best known parity covenants was that between
          Jonathan and David: '"But if my father is inclined to harm
          you, may the LORD deal with me, be it ever so severely, if I
          do not let you know and send you away safely. May the LORD
          be with you as he has been with my father." ... So Jonathan
          made a covenant with the house of David, saying, "May the
          LORD call David's enemies to account." And Jonathan made
          David reaffirm his oath out of love for him, because he loved
          him as he loved himself' (1 Samuel 20:13,16-17).
      (3) The other notable parity covenant is the marriage relationship
          (Malachi 2:14-15).

   (b) Covenants of grant (what is generously given), whereby the
       emphasis falls on the one who is being generous – the senior
       partner being generous to the junior partner.
      (1) The senior partner promises on oath to do something for the
          junior partner.
      (2) This falls into the category of unconditional covenant (above).
      (3) The party in a superior position binds himself to some
          obligation for the benefit of an inferior.
      (4) This was the basis for God's covenants with Noah and Abraham.

   (c) Covenants of law, whereby the emphasis falls on the obligation
       of the junior, or inferior, partner and in which the junior partner
       takes the oath.
      (1) This was the basis of the Mosaic or Sinai-covenant (which
          God gave to Moses at Sinai).
      (2) It was the people who took the oath, not God. 'Everything
          the LORD has said we will do' (Exodus 24:3).
      (3) God is the senior and for this reason (to restrain sin) imposed
          his will on the people and demanded their obedience.
      (4) On God's side the Mosaic covenant is without an oath – a
          point that Hebrews 7:20-22 makes use of.

B. **Note: all ancient covenants were ratified by a sacrifice or the
   shedding of blood.**

## 2  OLD TESTAMENT COVENANTS

### A.  God's covenant with Noah.

1. *The first time the word 'covenant' is used in scripture is in Genesis 6:18, before the flood.*

   (a)  The Hebrew word is *berith*. However, it is used in various ways.

   (b)  Taken as it is first revealed, the covenant of God:

       (1)  Is a covenant of grant.

       (2)  Is universal in its scope; it embraces not only Noah but his seed after him and every living creature.

       (3)  Shows that the grace bestowed is not dependent upon intelligent understanding or favourable response.

       (4)  Is unconditional; there is no obligation for Noah and his seed, hence the thought of breaking the covenant is irrelevant.

       (5)  Is what God himself will do; there is no contribution to the agency by which the promises are fulfilled.

       (6)  Is everlasting.

2. *After the flood the covenant was established* (Genesis 9:17).

   (a)  All that was true of the above covenant (before the flood) is established.

   (b)  The sign of the covenant is the rainbow: 'Whenever I bring clouds over the earth and the rainbow appears in the clouds, I will remember my covenant between me and you and all living creatures of every kind. Never again will the waters become a flood to destroy all life' (Genesis 9:14-15).

   (c)  The covenant with Noah is a sovereign administration of grace: (1) universal; (2) unconditional; (3) unending; (4) undeserved.

### B.  God's covenant with Abraham (Genesis 15).

1. *Promises were given.* 'Then the word of the LORD came to him: "This man will not be your heir, but a son coming from your own body will be your heir." He took him outside and said, "Look up at the heavens and count the stars – if indeed you can count them." Then he said to him, "So shall your offspring be"' (verses 4-5).

2. *Responded to by faith alone.* 'Abram believed the LORD, and he credited it to him as righteousness' (Genesis 15:6).

3. *Preceded in fact by sovereign grace.* 'He also said to him, "I am the LORD, who brought you out of Ur of the Chaldeans to give you this land to take possession of it" ' (Genesis 15:7).

4. *Related to assurance.* 'But Abram said, "O Sovereign LORD, how can I know that I shall gain possession of it?"' (Genesis 15:8).

5. *Some observations of God's covenant with Abraham:*
    (a) It is not related to either request for obedience or statement of obedience.
        (1) Obedience is not mentioned as the ground of the covenant.
        (2) Abraham's lapses (Genesis 16, 20) do not hinder the covenant.
        (3) It comes in before obedience is invited. 'When Abram was ninety-nine years old, the Lord appeared to him and said, "I am God Almighty, walk before me and be blameless"' (Genesis 17:1).
    (b) The covenant came in where Abraham had faith but was not free of doubt; he needed more assurance.
    (c) The covenant came in before Abraham had been tested (Genesis 22:1) and before it was confirmed (Genesis 22:12).
    (d) While Abraham showed obedience of faith, the covenant was none the less not built on Abraham's obedience.
    (e) God took the oath – by himself: 'The angel of the LORD called to Abraham from heaven a second time and said, "I swear by myself, declares the LORD, that because you have done this and have not withheld your son, your only son, I will surely bless you .... Your descendants will take possession of the cities of their enemies, and through your offspring all nations on earth will be blessed, because you have obeyed me"' (Genesis 22:15-18).
        (1) Abraham did not enter into an obligation.
        (2) The oath meant unconditional grace to Abraham.
    (f) The assurance Abraham wanted he got: '"Do not lay a hand on the boy," he said, "Do not do anything to him. Now I know that you fear God, because you have not withheld from me your son, your only son"' (Genesis 22:12).
    (g) This assurance followed Abraham's obedience: 'because you have obeyed me' (Genesis 22:18).
    (h) The sign of the covenant is circumcision (Genesis 17:10-11).
    (i) The covenant is extended to Isaac's seed not Ishmael's (Genesis 17:19).

6. *The oath and covenant in the life of Abraham are spread over many years:*
    (a) The promise (Genesis 12:1-3).
    (b) The covenant ceremony (Genesis 15).
    (c) The oath (Genesis 22).
        (1) In Genesis 15 the covenant is 'on offer', as Dr Michael Eaton puts it.

(2) The oath in Genesis 22 is 'the consummation of the covenant-on-offer'.

## C. The Mosaic Covenant (Exodus 20-24; cf. Galatians 3).

1. *It came 430 years after the covenant with Abraham and his seed* (Galatians 3:17).
2. *It was brought in because of the people's sins* (Galatians 3:19).
3. *It motivated people to holiness out of fear of punishment. Exodus 20:20; Deuteronomy 11:28.*
4. *God took no oath; only the people swore an oath* (Exodus 24:7; cf. 2 Kings 23:3; 2 Chronicles 15:12-15).
5. *It is a covenant of law: moral, civil, ceremonial (Exodus 20-24; Leviticus,* passim).
   (a) The covenants of God to Noah and Abraham were covenants of generosity; God took the oath.
   (b) In the Mosaic covenant it is the 'junior' or 'inferior' partner who takes the oath.
6. *The fruition of blessing depended upon obedience to the law (Deuteronomy 11:26-27).*
7. *Not to obey the law was to be under a curse (Deuteronomy 11:28; 27:26; Galatians 3:10).*
8. *Note: the covenant was renewed under Josiah (2 Kings 23).*

## D. God's covenant with David.

1. *That Messiah would come through his seed.*
   (a) 'You said, "I have made a covenant with my chosen one, I have sworn to David my servant, I will establish your line for ever and make your throne firm through all generations"' (Psalm 89:3-4).
   (b) This is what lay behind Nathan's words in 2 Samuel 7:12-16.

2. *The oath concerning Melchizedek* (Psalm 110:4).
   (a) This foretold the abolition of the Levitical priesthood (Hebrews 7:11-14).
   (b) It anticipated Christ's priesthood (Hebrews 7:20-22).

## E. There were four major positive oaths from God in the Old Testament:

1. To Noah (Genesis 6-9).
2. To Abraham (Genesis 17-22).
3. To David regarding his seed (Psalm 89).
4. To David regarding Melchizedek (Psalm 110).

## 3    THE COVENANT IN THE NEW TESTAMENT

### A.   It was anticipated by the covenant with Abraham and explicitly prophesied by Jeremiah 31:31-34.

1. *Abraham received the gospel.*
   (a)   God's covenant with Abraham is called 'the gospel in advance' (Galatians 3:8). This is partly why Jesus could say that Abraham saw the day of Christ and was glad (John 8:56).
   (b)   The essential ingredients of the gospel are found in the Abrahamic covenant: (1) election; (2) promise; (3) faith; (4) the shedding of blood; (5) inheritance; (6) assurance.

2. *Paul was at pains to show that the Mosaic covenant:*
   (a)   Came in 'aside'; it was 'added' (Romans 5:20; Galatians 3:19).
   (b)   That our gospel is analogous to the covenant of Abraham, not that of Moses (Galatians 3:7ff.).
   (c)   That the law's coming in did not 'do away with the promise' (Galatians 3:17).
   (d)   The law's coming in was a temporary thing: 'Now that faith has come, we are no longer under the supervision of the law' (Galatians 3:25).

### B.   Jesus announced the new covenant at the Last Supper.

1. *'In the same way, after the supper he took the cup, saying, "This cup is the new covenant in my blood, which is poured out for you'* (Luke 22:20; cf. Matthew 26:28; Mark 14:24).
2. *This then was the fulfilment of Jeremiah's prophecy and the completion of what God announced to Abraham. It meant that:*
   (a)   Jesus would shed his blood.
   (b)   This shedding of blood was not an accident, but was expressly for the new covenant.
   (c)   The new covenant promised forgiveness of sins.

### C.   In Hebrews 9:16-17 covenant means 'testament'.

1. *The Greek word* diatheke *is carried over from the Hebrew word* berith.
   (a)   Both words mean 'covenant'.
   (b)   But in Hebrews 9:16-17 *diatheke* takes on the idea of testament.

2. *Testament: what one leaves by will after death.*
   (a)   We refer to a person's 'last will and testament'.
   (b)   This is what is meant in Hebrews 9:16-17: 'In the case of a will, it is necessary to prove the death of the one who made it, because a will is in force only when somebody has died; it never takes effect while the one who made it is living.'

3. *Here is a summary of the relevant teaching of Hebrews 9:*
   (a) The blood of Jesus gives us eternal redemption (verses 11-12).
   (b) The blood of Jesus give us daily cleansing (verses 13-14).
   (c) Then comes a third thing: the blood of Jesus can get us our inheritance (reward).
       (1) Salvation is one thing.
       (2) Reward, or inheritance, is another.

D. **The new covenant also points to a last will and testament (and illustrates the ancient meaning of 'covenant of generosity', when the senior swears to the junior).**
   1. *A testament involved a benefactor (the generous senior person):* God in Christ (Matthew 26:28).
   2. *A testament involved a bequest, a legacy (what is willed by a person before he dies):* 'Father, I want those you have given me to be with me where I am, and to see my glory, the glory you have given me because you loved me before the creation of the world' (John 17:24).
   3. *A testament involved a people who are designated for the bequest:* 'My prayer is not for them alone. I pray also for those who will believe in me through their message' (John 17:20).
   4. *A testament might involve a condition in the receiving person. In this case:*
       (a) Faith was the condition for receiving Christ's legacy (John 3:16; Romans 3:26).
       (b) Further conditions were attached to receiving the inheritance – which was not 'automatic' but offered 'that those who are called *may* receive the promised eternal inheritance' (Hebrews 9:15). The conditions were: (1) staying open to the Spirit; (2) hearing God's voice; (3) daily cleansing.
   5. *A testament is dependent on the death of the benefactor. Christ has died!*

## CONCLUSION
The covenant and oath to Abraham contain the essential ingredients of the new covenant. In this covenant, faith alone unconditionally assures believers of their eternal salvation, but their entering into their inheritance (reward) is conditional on their obedience to God. Therefore, under the new covenant Christians are to walk in the light (1 John 1:7) – this is the condition for experiencing fellowship with God.

# 12

## PROPHECY AND THE BIRTH OF CHRIST

### INTRODUCTION

**A. Old Testament prophecy**
1. Prophecies concerning Christ, the coming Messiah, are given in grea number in the Old Testament. These prophecies are often detailed and precise

**B. Prophecies that he would be male, not female.**
1. *Although Genesis 3:15 refers to his death rather than his birth, the assumption is that the person referred to is male*: 'And I will pu enmity between you and the woman, and between your offspring and hers; he will crush your head, and you will strike his heel.'
   (a) This is relevant today in the light of an extremist feminist poin of view. Some feminists resent the facts that God is Father (no mother) and that Messiah is man (not woman). The Bible, however is unequivocal: the Messiah is God.

2. *Isaiah 7:14: 'Therefore the LORD himself will give you a sign: The virgin will be with child and will give birth to a son, and will cal him Immanuel.'*
   (a) The clear reference is to a 'son'.
   (b) He is to be called 'Immanuel'.

3. *Isaiah 9:6: 'For to us a child is born, to us a son is given, and the government will be on his shoulders. And he will be called Won derful Counsellor, Mighty God, Everlasting Father, Prince of Peace.*

4. *Isaiah 53:2: 'He grew up before him like a tender shoot, and like a root out of dry ground. He had no beauty or majesty to attract us to him, nothing in his appearance that we should desire him.'*

**C. Prophecies that he would be a human being, not an angel.**
1. *The virgin would be giving 'birth to a son'* (Isaiah 7:14).
2. *For 'to us a child is born'* (Isaiah 9:6).
   (a) The writer to the Hebrews stresses that the Old Testamen prophets did not have an angelic being in mind (Hebrews 1:5).
   (b) The prophecies remove any doubt that though the Messiah would be a supernatural figure, he would be natural, as we are.

### D. Prophecy that he would have no earthly father.

1. *'Therefore the LORD himself will give you a sign: The virgin will be with child and will give birth to a son, and will call him Immanuel'* (Isaiah 7:14).

   (a) The Hebrew *almah* may mean virgin, or young woman.

      (1) Some liberal scholars have seized upon the latter interpretation and wanted to say that the mother of Jesus needed not have been a virgin (cf. Isaiah 7:14, RSV).

      (2) *Almah* however always was understood to be a virgin; in those days a young woman was a virgin.

   (b) When the LXX (Septuagint, the Greek translation of the Old Testament) translated *almah* in Isaiah 7:14 they used the Greek word that could only be translated 'virgin' (*parthenos*).

      (1) This shows how the ancient rabbis understood *almah*. It did not cross their minds to use any other word.

      (2) Note: the LXX was in existence many years before Jesus was born.

   (c) Thus when Matthew 1:23 was written under the inspiration of the Holy Spirit the LXX translation was used.

2. *What is more, both Matthew and Luke make the explicit point that Mary was a virgin.*

   (a) 'This is how the birth of Jesus Christ came about. His mother Mary was pledged to be married to Joseph, but before they came together, she was found to be with child through the Holy Spirit' (Matthew 1:18).

   (b) 'How will this be,' Mary asked the angel, 'since I am a virgin?' (Luke 1:34).

### E. This son would be God.

1. This is why he would be called Immanuel, which means 'God with us' (Matthew 1:23).

2. Isaiah 9:6 elaborates: 'He will be called ... Mighty God, Everlasting Father. As a 'son' he was natural; as the Son of God he was supernatural. He was God as though he were not man; he was man as though he were not God.

3. Jesus himself interpreted Psalm 110:1 as declaring the deity of the Son and stopped the mouths of his critics: 'The LORD says to my Lord: "Sit at my right hand until I make your enemies a footstool for your feet."' The Pharisees said that the Christ was the son of David (Matthew 22:42). Jesus asked then, 'If then David calls him "Lord," how can he be his son?' (Matthew 22:45). The only conclusion: Christ was the Son of God.

4. The New Testament is therefore full of affirmation of Christ's deity: John 1:1; Romans 9:5; Philippians 2:5-6; Colossians 1: 15-16; 1 Timothy 3:16; Hebrews 1:1-3; 1 John 5:20.

## F. The son would come from Israel; from Judah; from David.

1. *Israel.* 'For to us *a child is born...*' (Isaiah 9:6).
    (a) This means the people of Israel could gladly boast that God's Messiah was coming to them and from them.
        (1) 'He came to that which was his own, but his own did not receive him' (John 1:11).
        (2) The gospel was 'first for the Jew' (Romans 1:16).
    (b) 'For I could wish that I myself were cursed and cut off from Christ for the sake of my brothers, those of my own race, the people of Israel. Theirs is the adoption as sons; theirs the divine glory, the covenants, the receiving of the law, the temple worship and the promises. Theirs are the patriarchs, and from them is traced the human ancestry of Christ, who is God over all, for ever praised! Amen' (Romans 9:3-5).

2. *Judah.* 'The sceptre will not depart from Judah, nor the ruler's staff from between his feet, until he comes to whom it belongs and the obedience of the nations is his' (Genesis 49:10).
    (a) David was of the tribe of Judah (1 Chronicles 2:15).
    (b) Jesus was born of the tribe of Judah (Matthew 1:3, 6; Hebrews 7:14).

3. *David.* 'Your house and your kingdom shall endure for ever before me; your throne shall be established for ever' (2 Samuel 7:16; cf. 1 Chronicles 17:13).
    (a) This prophecy was made by the non-canonical prophet, Nathan.
    (b) It was understood by the writer of Hebrews (1:5) as referring to the son of David, that is, his seed, being from David's loins.
    (c) 'So Joseph also went up from the town of Nazareth in Galilee to Judea, to Bethlehem the town of David, because he belonged to the house and line of David' (Luke 2:4).

## G. The prophet Micah foretold that the Messiah would be born in Bethlehem. 'But you, Bethlehem Ephrathah, though you are small among the clans of Judah, out of you will come for me one who will be ruler over Israel, whose origins are from of old, from ancient times (Micah 5:2).

1. The ancient authorities understood this to mean that Messiah would be born in Bethlehem (Matthew 2:5-6). And so he was (Luke 2:4-6).

## H. That this Son would be a King.

1. *The prophet Nathan was given to see this* (2 Samuel 7:4-17).
   (a) This was a prophecy to David which had immediate reference to Solomon.
   (b) But its *ultimate* relevance was to Christ. 'He is the one who will build a house for my Name, and I will establish the throne of his kingdom for ever' (2 Samuel 7:13).

2. *Isaiah saw this as well.* 'Of the increase of his government and peace there will be no end. He will reign on David's throne and over his kingdom, establishing and upholding it with justice and righteousness from that time on and for ever' (Isaiah 9:7).
   (a) The Son would establish a government, an everlasting government.
       (1) The Jews saw this as proof that Jesus could not be Messiah; his death on a cross vindicated their rejection of him (Isaiah 53:4).
       (2) The early church however saw that his reign began at his ascension and will continue after his second coming.

3. *Gabriel's announcement to Mary brings this home:* 'He will be great and will be called the Son of the Most High. The Lord God will give him the throne of his father David, and he will reign over the house of Jacob for ever; his kingdom will never end' (Luke 1:32-33).

## 2 HOW PROPHECIES OF CHRIST'S BIRTH CAME TO BE FULFILLED

## A. The cryptic nature of Old Testament prophecy.

1. *Many of the Old Testament prophecies concerning the birth of Christ were uttered cryptically?*
   (a) Cryptic: concealing the message in a puzzling way.
   (b) For example, few of the prophecies were uttered with literal clarity:
       (1) We are not told the names of Mary or Joseph in advance; we are only told of a virgin who would give birth to a son.
       (2) A 'root out of dry ground' (Isaiah 53:2) could never be figured out in advance; only looking back after its fulfilment could it be understood.
   (c) Bethlehem is given as the place of birth; but no-one could see in advance how it would happen.

2. *Why were the Old Testament prophecies given cryptically:*
   (a) God wants to keep some surprises for his people to the very end.
       (1) This keeps all interpreters of prophecy humble.

(2) God would not allow any 'expert' to have the final word on how, when, who, where and why things would happen.

(3) This should help some of us to lower our voices lest we try to be the 'first' to understand all the events concerning Christ's second coming!

(b) God wanted to keep things hidden from Satan..

(1) Perhaps this is why no explicit prophecy mentions that the parents of Jesus would be from Nazareth.

(2) It was assumed they would be natives of Bethlehem (Matthew 2:5ff.).

(3) Therefore Satan could have no way of knowing that the parents of the Lord would be from Nazareth.

## B. There were three prophecies to be fulfilled that no-one could have put together in advance.

1. *The birthplace of Jesus* – Bethlehem (Micah 5:2).

2. *The prominence of Galilee.* Isaiah 9:1, which Matthew applies with regard to Jesus' ministry but which could equally refer to his being from Nazareth (Matthew 4:12-16).

3. *The fulfilment of Hosea 11:1*: 'When Israel was a child, I loved him, and out of Egypt I called my son' (Matthew 2:15).

## C. God alone knew that it would in fact be this way:

1. Joseph and Mary were from Nazareth.

2. Caesar Augustus would call for a world-wide census (Luke 2:1).

3. This edict required Joseph and Mary to register in Bethlehem.

4. This came while Mary was ready to give birth to her child – which she did, in Bethlehem.

5. Herod would seek to have all male children under two years of age killed (Matthew 2:16).

6. God would warn Joseph through an angel to escape to Egypt (Matthew 2:13).

7. When it was safe for them to return to Nazareth, they did; then the prophecy of Hosea 11:1 was fulfilled!

8. In the meantime it became clear that Jeremiah's prophecy of 'A voice is heard in Ramah, mourning and great weeping ... because her children are no more ' had a dual fulfilment. It probably was regarded as pointing to events in the days of the Babylonian captivity. Yet its ultimate fulfilment came as a result of Herod's wickedness (Matthew 2:17-18).

## 3 IMMEDIATE PROPHECIES CONCERNING JESUS AFTER HIS BIRTH

A. The angelic prophecy to the shepherds: 'Today in the town of David a Saviour has been born to you; he is Christ the Lord. This will be a sign to you: You will find a baby wrapped in cloths and lying in a manger' (Luke 2:11-12). This was fulfilled (Luke 2:16).
B. The warning in the dream of the Magi (Matthew 2:12).
C. The angelic warning to Joseph (Matthew 2:13).
D. The angelic word to Joseph (Matthew 2:19-20).
E. The promise of Simeon and his prophecy (Luke 2:25-32). This was an encouragement to Joseph and Mary (Luke 2:33). Simeon then prophesied to Mary (Luke 2:34-35).
F. The account concerning the prophetess Anna (Luke 2:36-38).

**CONCLUSION**
There are more prophecies concerning Christ's coming than we have referred to above. These however are sufficient to show how God raised up prophets to predict details of the Messiah and his work. As I have shown, in advance of the event prophesied they are sometimes cryptic. But when the prophecies are fulfilled they prove to have been clear enough!

# 13

# THE CROSS OF CHRIST

## INTRODUCTION

A. **This study focusses on the heart of the gospel.**
   1. *The cross is the reason God sent his one and only Son into the world.*
   2. *The death and resurrection of Christ are the most important events in the history of the world.*
      (a) One may ask: Which was more important, Passover or the crossing of the Red Sea?
      (b) Answer: Either would be incomplete without the other.
      (c) So too with the death and resurrection of Jesus Christ.

B. **Why deal with this subject?**
   1. *The cross is the heart of soteriology (doctrine of salvation).*
      (a) We must never let any branch of theology become more important than soteriology.
         (1) In decision making one must learn to tell the difference between what is important and what is essential – and always be sure to do the latter.
         (2) Soteriology is essential.

   2. *We need constantly to be brought back to the Main Thing – lest we lose our focus on what is essential.*
      (a) Spiritual warfare, signs and wonders, and so on are interesting subjects. But to become advanced theologians (which is what I want all of us truly to be) means constantly returning to the Main Thing.

   3. *Often the Main Thing in theology turns out to be what we understand the least!*
      (a) So I will presume nothing and be very simple.
      (b) This way the most mature Christian will be reminded of what he or she knows – and the newest Christian can learn.

C. **Definitions**
   1. *The Cross of Christ:*
      (a) Literally, the cross on which Jesus died.
      (b) Symbolically, the event that combines:

      (1) The way we are saved.
      (2) The shedding of blood.
      (3) The shame or stigma that surrounds Jesus' death.

2. *Crucifixion: the ancient Roman method of capital punishment.*
3. *Atonement: the theological description that is applied to Jesus'
   crucifixion – Christ dying for our sins.*
   (a) At the natural level, what happened on Good Friday was only a
       crucifixion.
   (b) At the level of the Spirit Christ died for our sins.
   (c) In a sense, any crucifixion was atonement: one paid his debt to
       society by dying for his *own* sins. 'To atone for' a wrong is to
       take some action which cancels out the ill effects that wrong has
       had.
   (d) Jesus was sentenced to die for his own sins, so it was claimed.
   (e) But by the Spirit we know that Jesus never sinned; even Pontius
       Pilate testified to this (John 19:4; cf. 2 Corinthians 5:21; Hebrews
       4:15). He died not for his own sins but for ours (1 Corinthians
       15:3; 1 Peter 2:24).

# 1  CRUCIFIXION IN GENERAL

## A. The public shame
1. Partly as a warning to other potential offenders, the condemned man
   was made to carry his cross along the public roads and to the execution ground, which itself was nearly always in a public place.
2. There he was stripped of all his clothing.
3. Affixed to the cross, he could not care for his bodily needs, and was
   the object of taunts and indignities from passers-by.
4. On the way to execution a tablet was hung around the offender stating
   the crime, and this was affixed to the cross after execution so that all
   could see.

## B. The torture
1. Crucifiction was notorious for being the worst form of punishment.
   Cicero called it the supreme penalty; the most painful, dreadful, and ugly.
2. The cruelty of this form of capital punishment lay not only in the public shame but also in its slow physical torture.
3. It damaged no vital part of the body.
4. The victim was fastened to the cross by nails through the hands or
   wrists, and through the feet or above the heels.
5. On the ground he was bound with outstretched arms, with the body
   fastened to the upright post. There was no footrest.

6.  Ropes bound the shoulders or torso to the wooden frame.
   (a)  The victim was then held immovable, unable to cope with heat or cold or insects.
   (b)  Death came slowly – often after many days – as the result of fatigue, cramped muscles, hunger and thirst.
   (c)  Sometimes the victim was offered a drug to deaden the pain.
7.  Rome reserved this form of punishment for slaves and foreigners.
   (a)  Hence Jesus could be crucified.
   (b)  Paul, who had Roman citizenship, could not have been.
8.  In Palestine, crucifixion was used to punish robbery, tumult, and sedition (rebellion against the State).
   (a)  This served as a public reminder of the Jews' servitude to the foreign power.
   (b)  Crosses were a familiar sight in Galilee and provided a metaphor for Christian discipleship (Matthew 16:24).
9.  Scourging often preceded the crucifixion.
10. Usually the body was left to rot on the cross.

## C.  The cross

1.  Literally, it was an upright stake, pale or pole.
2.  As an instrument of execution it was sunk vertically into the ground.
3.  Usually a horizontal piece was attached to the vertical post, sometimes at the top to give the shape of a T, sometimes just below the top.
4.  The height of the cross varied.
   (a)  It was usually rather more than a man's height.
   (b)  It might be even higher when the offender was to be held up for public display at a distance.

## 2   THE CROSS OF JESUS

### A.  Jesus' cross is mentioned in all four Gospels (Matthew 27:32ff.; Mark 15:21ff.; Luke 23:26ff.; John 19:17ff.).

1.  Pilate ordered that Jesus be scourged (whipped) with thongs (Matthew 27:26).
2.  Simon of Cyrene was compelled to carry Jesus' cross for him (Matthew 27:32).
3.  Matthew says Jesus knew his death would be by crucifixion (Matthew 20:19; 26:2).
4.  The exact spot of the crucifixion of Jesus is not known. It was somewhere outside the city (Hebrews 13:12), probably beside one of the main roads leading into Jerusalem (Matthew 27:39).
5.  Jesus refused the drink offered to deaden his pain (Matthew 27:34).
6.  Two other men were put to death at the same time (John 19:18).

(a) One of them joined in the derision (Matthew 27:44; Luke 23:39), perhaps hoping to gain favour at last by siding in with the rulers.

(b) One appealed to Jesus: 'Jesus, remember me when you come into your kingdom' (Luke 23:42).

7. A sign, indicating the crime for which he was condemned, was placed on the cross ( Luke 23:38).

## B. The shame

1. Jesus hated the shame: 'Let us fix our eyes on Jesus, the author and perfecter of our faith, who for the joy set before him endured the cross, scorning its shame, and sat down at the right hand of the throne of God' (Hebrews 12:2).

2. Jesus' cross evidently stood rather higher than usual (Mark 15:32, 36).

3. He was insulted: 'Those who passed by hurled insults at him, shaking their heads and saying, "You who are going to destroy the temple and build it in three days, save yourself! Come down from the cross, if you are the Son of God!"' (Matthew 27:39-40).

4. Chief priests, teachers of the law and the elders mocked him: '"He saved others," they said, "but he can't save himself! He's the King of Israel! Let him come down now from the cross, and we will believe in him"' (Matthew 27:42).

5. He was naked (John 19:23-24).

6. All this was before his mother, his mother's sister, Mary the wife of Clopas, and Mary of Magdala (John 19:25).

## C. The torture

1. Nothing is said directly about how much pain Jesus must have experienced. This is left to us to contemplate.

2. Roman scourging was so severe that victims often died under it; for one charged with sedition, as Jesus was, it would have been merciless.

3. The nearest we get to experiencing his physical suffering was Jesus' comment to those who 'wailed' for him: 'Daughters of Jerusalem, do not weep for me; weep for yourselves and your children' (Luke 23:28).

## D. The spiritual suffering

1. This is apparently what Jesus dreaded most (Luke 22:42ff.; cf. Hebrews 5:7).

2. For a time he was not allowed to communicate comforting words to those at the cross, so as to allay their fears and bewilderment.

3. The worst moment was when he felt deserted, even by his Father: 'My God, my God, why have you forsaken me?' (Matthew 27:46).

4. This was the only hint at the time, although nobody understood it, that atonement was taking place (2 Corinthians 5:21).

E. **What Jesus said while hanging on the cross.**
   1. 'Father, forgive them, for they do not know what they are doing' (Luke 23:34).
   2. 'When Jesus saw his mother there, and the disciple whom he loved standing near by, he said to his mother, "Dear woman, here is your son," and to the disciple, "Here is your mother"' (John 19:26-27).
   3. 'I tell you the truth, today you will be with me in paradise' (Luke 23:43).
   4. 'I am thirsty' (John 19:28).
   5. 'My God, my God, why have you forsaken me?' (Matthew 27:46).
   6. 'It is finished' (John 19:30).
   7. 'Father, into your hands I commit my spirit' (Luke 23:46).

### 3   WHAT REALLY HAPPENED ON GOOD FRIDAY?

A. **In limiting our study to the Cross of Christ we must pass over many relevant and interesting matters, for example:**
   1. The 'trial' of Jesus (which was no legal trial at all).
   2. The cowardly roles of Herod and Pilate.
   3. The shouts and demands of the people.
   4. The role of the Roman soldiers.
   5. The burial of Jesus.

B. **Good Friday must be understood by the Holy Spirit, not merely from the external act of the crucifixion.**
   1. *An old spiritual asks: 'Were you there when they crucified my Lord?'*
      (a) The truth is, had you been there you would have seen nothing but a spine-chilling crucifixion: 'When all the people who had gathered to witness this sight saw what took place, they beat their breasts and went away' (Luke 23:48).
      (b) There was nothing that you could have seen at the time that would have told you that this was the atonement for the sins of the world, that it was when God in Christ was reconciling the world to himself.
      (c) More likely one would concur with Isaiah's prophecy that foretold how the Jews felt safe in their self-justification: 'We considered him stricken by God, smitten by him, and afflicted' (53:4). It looked as though God was against Jesus and that Jesus was getting what he deserved.

   2. *The only way the events of Good Friday can be accurately interpreted is by the Holy Spirit.*
      (a) Even after the resurrection itself the disciples did not know why Jesus was crucified – or why he was raised from the dead.

(b) It was not until the Spirit fell on the disciples at Pentecost that the whole event came together. Then Peter and the disciples understood it all for the first time.
   (1) They then saw that it was for our sins that Jesus died.
   (2) They saw that it was all a part of God's pre-determined plan: 'This man was handed over to you by God's set purpose and foreknowledge; and you, with the help of wicked men, put him to death by nailing him to the cross' (Acts 2:23).

3. *Therefore, to examine the four Gospels apart from the Holy Spirit and to look for the meaning of the crucifixion is almost like looking for a needle in a haystack!*
   (a) Of course, with the Holy Spirit and the Bible we can understand it all very well.
   (b) But to put yourself back at the scene of the Cross without the aid of the Holy Spirit is to find little evidence that God was at work.

## C. **There is proof, however, that God was at work at the time.**

1. *The tearing of the curtain of the Temple from top to bottom* (Matthew 27:51). This was no coincidence for it came 'from top to bottom', proving God did it. And it came at the precise moment that Jesus cried out in a loud voice, 'It is finished.'
   (a) This tearing of the curtain showed divine affirmation of the Cross. This showed that God put his own seal of approval on what Jesus did. It officially ended the sacrificial system as far as God was concerned.

2. *The bodies of many saints arose from the dead.*
   (a) This showed God's approval (Matthew 27:52-53).
   (b) It was an immense encouragement to those who had been believers.

3. *The confession of the Roman centurion.* 'When the centurion and those with him who were guarding Jesus saw the earthquake and all that had happened, they were terrified, and exclaimed, "Surely he was the Son of God!" ' (Matthew 27:54).

4. *One might be inclined to add the words of Jesus,* 'It is finished' (John 19:30).
   (a) But this too is only grasped by the Spirit.
   (b) 'It is finished' is the English translation of *tetelestai*, a colloquial expression in the ancient marketplace that meant 'paid in full'.
      (1) But those who heard the Aramaic may have assumed Jesus only meant 'It's over' – or that he had paid for his own sin.
      (2) Only the Spirit will make *tetelestai* precious to us.

### D. **What *ought* those present to have seen?**
1. *The fulfilment of Passover.*
   (a) It was the very time of Passover.
   (b) All that happened when Jesus was hanging on the Cross mirrored the shedding of blood.
       (1) 'When I see the blood, I will pass over you' (Exodus 12:13).
       (2) 'Take a bunch of hyssop, dip it into the blood in the basin and put some of the blood on the top and on both sides of the door-frame.  Not one of you shall go out of the door of his house until morning' (Exodus 12:22).

2. *The fulfilment of Isaiah 53.*
   (a) A part of this chapter shows how the Jews would regard their Messiah (Isaiah 53:2-4).
   (b) But the truth was: 'The LORD has laid on him the iniquity of us all' (Isaiah 53:6).

### E. **What is it that we grasp by the Spirit?**
1. *Jesus bore the punishment of our sins.*
   (a) He did not die for his own sin; he was sinless.
   (b) He died for our sins.

2. *Jesus was our substitute.*
   (a) He got what we deserve – the punishment of God's wrath.
   (b) He literally took our place.

3. *That Jesus' blood satisfied the justice of God.*
   (a) 'When I see the blood, I will pass over you.'
   (b) God looked at that blood and passed over our sins.

### CONCLUSION
The relevance of all this for us is that what happened on Good Friday is the way – and the only way – we are saved. We should honour what Jesus did by recalling these words from Paul: 'For I resolved to know nothing while I was with you except Jesus Christ and him crucified' (1 Corinthians 2:2). The Cross, the greatest possible stigma, was to Paul the greatest thing one could uphold. Instead of presenting Christianity in the 'best' possible light to a godless generation, Paul put forward the 'worst' possible offence! 'May I never boast except in the cross of our Lord Jesus Christ, through which the world has been crucified to me, and I to the world' (Galatians 6:14).

This is the heart of the gospel. It is God's way of saving us. It is the only way we can be saved, assuming that the Holy Spirit has worked faith in our hearts.

# 14

## THE RESURRECTION OF JESUS

**INTRODUCTION**

A. **The person of Jesus was literally raised from the dead on Easter Sunday, having died on a cross on Good Friday. This is what is known as the resurrection.**
   1. *He was crucified on a Roman cross, the means of capital punishment at the time.*
      (a) 'When they came to the place called the Skull, there they crucified him, along with the criminals – one on his right, the other on his left' (Luke 23:33).
      (b) 'This man was handed over to you by God's set purpose and foreknowledge; and you, with the help of wicked men, put him to death by nailing him to the cross' (Acts 2:23).

   2. *He was buried.*
      (a) 'Joseph, a member of the Council, a good and upright man, who had not consented to their decision and action. He came from the Judean town of Arimathea and he was waiting for the kingdom of God. Going to Pilate, he asked for Jesus' body. Then he took it down, wrapped it in linen cloth and placed it in a tomb cut in the rock, one in which no-one had yet been laid' (Luke 23:50-53).
      (b) 'At the place where Jesus was crucified, there was a garden, and in the garden a new tomb, in which no-one had ever been laid. Because it was the Jewish day of Preparation and since the tomb was near by, they laid Jesus there' (John 19:41-42).

   3. *He was resurrected.*
      (a) 'The angel said to the women, "Do not be afraid, for I know that you are looking for Jesus, who was crucified. He is not here; he has risen, just as he said. Come and see the place where he lay"' (Matthew 28:5-6).
      (b) 'But God raised him from the dead, freeing him from the agony of death, because it was impossible for death to keep its hold on him' (Acts 2:24).
      (c) 'Therefore let all Israel be assured of this: God has made this Jesus, whom you crucified, both Lord and Christ' (Acts 2:36).

### B. Why is this study important?

1. *It is essential to the Christian faith.*
   - (a) If there had been no resurrection of Jesus, there would be no such thing as Christianity.
   - (b) What kept the message of Jesus alive was his resurrection; otherwise he would have been forgotten beyond his own generation.

2. *It is essential to our salvation.*
   - (a) There would be no reason to value his death if he had not also been raised from the dead.
   - (b) 'And if Christ has not been raised, your faith is futile; you are still in your sins' (1 Corinthians 15:17).

3. *It is essential to our future hope.*
   - (a) If Christ was not raised there is no hope that we too will be raised one day.
   - (b) 'And if Christ has not been raised, our preaching is useless and so is your faith. More than that, we are then found to be false witnesses about God, for we have testified about God that he raised Christ from the dead. But he did not raise him if in fact the dead are not raised. For if the dead are not raised, then Christ has not been raised either' (1 Corinthians 15:14-16).

4. *If we do not come to terms with the essential details of Christ's resurrection we are not going to be able to answer these questions:*
   - (a) Was it the soul of Jesus only that was raised – or the body?
   - (b) What kind of resurrection do we expect for ourselves?
   - (c) What kind of body did he have after he was raised?

## 1  THE RESURRECTION HAPPENED TO JESUS, NOT TO THE CHURCH

### A. Some claim that the resurrection of Jesus is something that happened to the church – not Jesus.

1. *That something happened to the church is not doubted.*
2. *They really did believe that Jesus was resurrected, or else they would not have been so excited.*
3. *Some maintain, however, that the resurrection was the church's subjective experience not what was objectively true of Jesus.*
   - (a) The premiss here is sheer atheism, or humanism.
   - (b) At heart is the denial of the supernatural; it is not possible that a dead man really and truly was raised from having been dead.

B. **Luke stresses that Jesus was objectively raised from the dead**: 'After his suffering, he showed himself to these men and gave many convincing proofs that he was alive. He appeared to them over a period of forty days and spoke about the kingdom of God' (Acts 1:3).

1. *The empty tomb makes this point.*
   - (a) 'On the first day of the week, very early in the morning, the women took the spices they had prepared and went to the tomb. They found the stone rolled away from the tomb, but when they entered, they did not find the body of the Lord Jesus' (Luke 24:1-3).
   - (b) 'In addition, some of our women amazed us. They went to the tomb early this morning but didn't find his body. They came and told us that they had seen a vision of angels, who said he was alive' (Luke 24:22-23).
   - (c) 'So she came running to Simon Peter and the other disciple, the one Jesus loved, and said, "They have taken the Lord out of the tomb, and we don't know where they have put him!" ... Then Simon Peter, who was behind him, arrived and went into the tomb. He saw the strips of linen lying there, as well as the burial cloth that had been around Jesus' head. The cloth was folded up by itself, separate from the linen' (John 20:2, 6-7).
   - (d) Cf. Matthew 28:1-6 and Mark 16:1-8.

2. *This was the testimony of the angels.*
   - (a) The angel said to the women, 'Do not be afraid, for I know that you are looking for Jesus who was crucified. He is not here; he has risen, just as he said (Matthew 28:6).
   - (b) As they entered the tomb, they saw a young man dressed in a white robe .... and they were alarmed ... 'Don't be alarmed, ' he said. 'You are looking for Jesus the Nazarene, who was crucified. He has risen! He is not here' (Mark 16:5-6).

3. *This is why the witnesses of the empty tomb were afraid.*
   - (a) 'So the women hurried away from the tomb, afraid yet filled with joy, and ran to tell his disciples' (Matthew 28:8).
   - (b) 'Trembling and bewildered, the women went out and fled from the tomb. They said nothing to anyone, because they were afraid' (Mark 16:8).

4. *Those who went to the tomb were not expecting it to be empty; they went to anoint Jesus' body* (see Mark 16:1; Luke 24:1)

**C. Jesus himself testified to the reality of the resurrection.**

1. As they were coming down the mountain, Jesus instructed them, 'Don't tell anyone what you have seen, until the Son of Man has been raised from the dead' (Matthew 17:9; cf. Matthew 16:21; Mark 8:31; Luke 9:22).

2. 'Look at my hands and my feet. It is I myself! Touch me and see; a ghost does not have flesh and bones, as you see I have' (Luke 24:39).

3. Then he said to Thomas, 'Put your finger here; see my hands. Reach out your hand and put it into my side. Stop doubting and believe' (John 20:27).

## 2  JESUS' RESURRECTION BODY WAS A TRANSFORMED, PHYSICAL AND SPIRITUAL, BODY

**A. The gospel writers emphasise that it was Jesus' physical body that was raised.**

1. *Suddenly Jesus met them. 'Greetings,' he said. They came to him, clasped his feet and worshipped him'* (Matthew 28:9).

2. *It was only his body that they could think of when they saw the empty tomb.*
   (a) 'But [they] didn't find his body... him they did not see' (Luke 24:23-24).
   (b) 'Sir, if you have carried him away, tell me where you have put him, and I will get him' (John 20:15).

3. *Jesus stressed that it was his physical body that had been raised (Luke 24:39) and to prove it:*
   (a) 'They gave him a piece of broiled fish, and he took it and ate it in their presence' (Luke 24:42-43).
   (b) 'He was not seen by all the people, but by witnesses whom God had already chosen – by us who ate and drank with him after he rose from the dead' (Acts 10:41).

4. *A physical resurrection is the only thing that made sense to them.*
   (a) This was Thomas's only concern, having missed seeing Jesus the first time he appeared to the disciples. 'When the other disciples told him that they had seen the Lord, he declared, "Unless I see the nail marks in his hands and put my finger where the nails were, and put my hand into his side, I will not believe it" ' (John 20:25).
   (b) This is why Peter stressed, 'God has made *this Jesus*, whom you crucified, both Lord and Christ' (Acts 2:36; AV: 'that same Jesus').

**B. And yet Paul also calls Jesus' body a spiritual body.**

1. *This does not mean that Paul didn't believe Jesus' resurrection body was a physical body.*
   - (a) 'That he was buried, that he was raised on the third day according to the Scriptures, and that he appeared to Peter, and then to the Twelve. After that, he appeared to more than five hundred of the brothers at the same time, most of whom are still living, but some have fallen asleep. Then he appeared to James, then to all the apostles, and last of all he appeared to me also, as to one abnormally born' (1 Corinthians 15:4-8).
   - (b) 'For he has set a day when he will judge the world with justice by the man he has appointed. He has given proof of this to all men by raising him from the dead' (Acts 17:31).

2. *Paul is saying that Jesus' resurrection body, though the same body, is none the less different; it is a transformed body.*
   - (a) Called the 'last Adam', he was 'a life-giving spirit' (1 Corinthians 15:45).
   - (b) Showing that our bodies will be raised 'spiritual', Paul infers that this is what Jesus' resurrected body was (1 Corinthians 15:44-49).
   - (c) It was a transformed body, both physical and spiritual.

3. *This would explain Jesus' sudden appearances and disappearances during the forty days between his resurrection and ascension.*
   - (a) Though the disciples met behind locked doors, Jesus turned up in the room 'and stood among them' (John 20:19).
   - (b) He broke bread with the two people who met him on the way to Emmaus and then 'disappeared from their sight' (Luke 24:31).

**C. Jesus' resurrection is the 'firstfruits' of the dead; therefore showing the kind of body we will have in heaven (1 Corinthians 15:20).**

1. *Firstfruits: the first of a season's agricultural products.*
   - (a) It may refer to the first results of one's work.
   - (b) It may refer to the first profits or first effects of anything.

2. *It comes to this: the first of a kind.*
   - (a) Jesus was not the first to be raised to life (1 Kings 17:17-24; Luke 7:11-15; John 11). These others would eventually die again.

3. *Jesus is the first to be raised from the dead who would never die.*
   - (a) 'But Christ has indeed been raised from the dead, the firstfruits of those who have fallen asleep' (1 Corinthians 15:20).
   - (b) 'I am the Living One; I was dead, and behold I am alive for ever and ever! And I hold the keys of death and Hades' (Revelation 1:18).

4. *Jesus' resurrection shows the permanence of bodily life in heaven.*
   (a) Unlike angels, which are spirits (Hebrews 1:14), bodies are visible and recognisable.
   (b) Bodily life will continue in heaven (1 Corinthians 15:35-44).
       (1) The spiritual existence of souls at death is a temporary thing.
       (2) When Jesus comes the souls will be reunited to resurrected bodies (1 Thessalonians 4:14-17).

5. *The resurrection of Jesus and of our bodies shows the continuity between the present and the future.*
   (a) We will be the same persons.
       (1) Jesus was recognisable (Matthew 28:9; John 20:19ff.).
       (2) So we will be transformed yet with some likeness (1 John 3:2).
   (b) From this we may conclude:
       (1) We will have our memories in heaven.
       (2) We will know one another in heaven.

## 3  THE RESURRECTION OF JESUS IS BELIEVED AND UNDERSTOOD ONLY THROUGH THE HOLY SPIRIT

A. **This may well be the most forgotten and underestimated aspect of Jesus' resurrection.**
   1. *Seeing the empty tomb convinced no-one at the time that Jesus was alive.*
   2. *Those who actually saw him alive after his death were not without some unbelief:* 'When they saw him, they worshipped him; but some doubted' (Matthew 28:17).
      (a) If TV cameras had been stationed at the tomb and caught the entire event for us to see on video: many would remain unconvinced and many would find something to justify their fears and unbelief.
      (b) If people saw Jesus alive face-to-face but still doubted, why should we expect people to believe today?
          (1) 'A man convinced against his will is of the same opinion still.'
          (2) No apologetic (that is, defence of the faith) is strong enough to create faith where unbelief is present.

   3. *Those who actually saw him still did not have full assurance of the answer to these questions:*
      (a) Who was he?
      (b) Why did he come to earth?
      (c) Why did he die?
      (d) Why was he raised?

4. *The disciples were still filled with questions that reflected their own self-interest.* 'So when they met together, they asked him, "Lord, are you at this time going to restore the kingdom to Israel?"' (Acts 1:6).

   (a)  Jesus' reply was, 'It is not for you to know the times or dates the Father has set by his own authority. But you will receive power when the Holy Spirit comes on you; and you will be my witnesses in Jerusalem, and in all Judea and Samaria, and to the ends of the earth' (Acts 1:7-8).

   (b)  His last words were these: 'I am going to send you what my Father has promised; but stay in the city until you have been clothed with power from on high' (Luke 24:49).

## B. After the Spirit fell on the Day of Pentecost these questions were answered.

1. *This is why Jesus said, 'But I tell you the truth: It is for your good that I am going away. Unless I go away, the Counsellor will not come to you; but if I go, I will send him to you'* (John 16:7).

   (a)  The disciples did not understand these words (John 16:17-18).

   (b)  They were not happy about Jesus' introduction of the Holy Spirit (John 16:6).

2. *But when the Spirit came down the reasons for Jesus' coming, death and resurrection (and ascension) came together for them.*

   (a)  Jesus was as real to them at the level of the Spirit as he had been at the natural level.

      (1)  John 16:19-24 made sense to them.

      (2)  So real was Jesus that Peter quoted Psalm 16:8 (Acts 2:25).

   (b)  What is more, the resurrection was now as clear to them as it can be to us!

      (1)  We may feel deprived that we have not had their privilege of seeing Jesus alive in the flesh.

      (2)  But we have the same Holy Spirit that they had!

   (c)  The renewal of the Spirit did it for them again (Acts 4:33).

## C. We are at no disadvantage for not having been present with those who saw Jesus alive with their own eyes.

1. *The resurrection of Jesus is to be believed – by faith not sight* (John 20:29).

2. *It is therefore by the Spirit that we know:*

   (a)  Who he was – the God-man.

   (b)  Why he came – to die.

   (c)  Why he died – to save us from our sins.

   (d)  Why he was raised – to vindicate the cross.

## D. Easter: the vindication of the cross (Romans 4:25).

1. *The cross is the heart of Easter.*
    (a) Good Friday cannot be separated from Easter.
        (1) Jesus' death would have been of no value had he not been raised.
        (2) His resurrection would have been of no value had he not shed his blood for our sins.
    (b) It is like trying to separate Passover from the crossing of the Red Sea. The Israelites would have been unable to cross the Red Sea without Passover. To separate these two is out of the question.

2. *Good Friday and Easter mutually excel the other in importance and glory.*
    (a) One is no less important or glorious than the other.
    (b) They cannot be separated.

## CONCLUSION

Jesus' death and resurrection are two aspects of the greatest event in human history. To represent Easter without the cross smacks of being ashamed of the cross. To represent the cross without the resurrection smacks of sentimentalism and defeat. But Jesus is alive because God vindicated who he was (Romans 1:4) and what he did (Romans 4:25).

# 15

# THE ATONEMENT

**INTRODUCTION**

A. **As always, especially when dealing with the 'heavier' subjects, we tend to stress how important the subject in hand is.**
   1. *This would be particularly true when it came to subjects like the Trinity, the Holy Spirit and the Law of God.*
   2. *But what could possibly be more important than the Atonement?*
      (a) Atonement: the making of amends; making up for error or deficiency.
      (b) Atonement of Christ: the making up for the sins of the world by his death on the cross.
         (1) Atonement is the theological way of describing what a secular historian would merely call a crucifixion.
         (2) There were many crucifixions in the ancient Roman world; but only one of them was atonement – when Jesus by his death made up for the sins of the whole world.

B. **Why is this subject so important?**
   1. *It focuses on the reason Jesus came into the world in the first place.*
      (a) He came to die (Matthew 1:21).
      (b) The crucifixion was no accident; nothing 'went wrong'; the crucifixion of Jesus was the reason God sent his Son into the world (John 3:16).
   2. *It tells us how we are saved.*
      (a) It is what makes the gospel 'good news'.
      (b) We are not saved by our works but by his death on the cross.
   3. *It tells us why we are saved.*
      (a) Not because we earned it or were good enough.
      (b) But because God affirmed what his Son did on the cross.
   4. *It is what separates Christianity from every other religion.*
      (a) The difference between Christianity and natural religion is who initiates what you do.
      (b) All other religions (without exception) have in common the idea of personal merit not sovereign grace.
   5. *It is what divides true belief from superficial liberalism.*
      (a) Many churches will in measure dignify Jesus' death on the cross.
      (b) But how many affirm that we are saved by his death alone?

6. *It is the heart of the gospel.*
    (a) Rolfe Barnard used to say, 'Be wrong on anything else but be right on this!'
    (b) If we truly understand the atonement:
        (1) Our Christology will be sound.
        (2) Our soteriology will be sound.

7. *It is what will give us certainty of our own salvation.*
    (a) Nothing assures us of being saved like a clear understanding of the atonement.
    (b) This is because it is not great faith that saves but only faith in a great Saviour!

C. **When we examine the doctrine of Atonement in church history, we should be thankful for the perspective we now have.**
    1. *Like justification by faith alone, which most Protestants now take for granted, the understanding of the atonement was not always clear in church history.*
    2. *We know (or should know) a lot more theology than those who preceded us.*
    3. *A historical perspective gives us a decided advantage.*
        (a) 'From everyone who has been given much, much will be demanded' (Luke 12:48).

# 1 HISTORICAL THEORIES OF THE ATONEMENT

A. **Generally speaking there are three major views that have been taken seriously in church history.**
    1. *The 'ransom' theory, dating back to Origen (c.185 - c.254), the Greek church father.*
        (a) The death of Christ was the ransom paid to Satan.
            (1) Satan crucified Jesus, but it was really nothing more than God 'tricking' the devil to do this.
            (2) Satan had acquired rights over man by the Fall; sinners thus belong to Satan because of their sin.
            (3) In the death of Christ God paid the price of the sinners' redemption.
            (4) Satan accepted Jesus in place of sinners but Satan could not hold him.
            (5) On Easter Day Jesus rose triumphant, leaving Satan without both his original captives and their ransom.
        (b) This theory upholds an objective transactional view, but the 'business' that took place was between God and the devil rather than between God and Christ.

2. *The 'moral influence' theory, dating back to Abelard (1079-1142), the medieval scholastic theologian.*
    (a) The death of Christ had a profound 'effect' on man.
        (1) We contemplate the love of God and are overwhelmed.
        (2) We are moved to repent and love him in return.
        (3) We are thus transformed by the death of Christ.
    (b) Note: this theory is especially attractive to those who object to an objective transaction between the Father and the Son, or the Father and the devil. It is only a subjective view of the atonement and often appeals to liberal theologians.

3. *The 'penal satisfaction' view, dating back to Anselm (c.1033-1109), whose classic book* Cur Deus Homo? *(Why the God-man?) became the essential view of most evangelicals.*
    (a) Sin, being an infinite offence against God, required a satisfaction equally infinite.
        (1) No finite being, man or angel, could offer such satisfaction.
        (2) It was necessary that the infinite being, namely God himself, should take the place of man.
        (3) This was done by the death of the God-man on the cross.
        (4) Thus by Christ's death complete satisfaction was made to the divine justice.
        (5) Hence the death of Christ was not a ransom paid to the devil but a debt paid to the Father.
    (b) This theory upholds the objective transaction between the Father and the Son. The Reformers taught along these lines.
        (1) Martin Luther taught that Christ, in becoming by voluntary substitution the punishment due to man, was reckoned by God a sinner in his place.
        (2) John Calvin taught the Christ bore in his soul the tortures of a condemned man.

## C. There is something attractive in all three of the above views.
1. We need not accept any single one to the exclusion of the others.
2. Only the second view (moral influence theory) is inadequate by itself and has merit only when one sees it as secondary.
3. If one had to choose but one, the penal satisfaction theory is the most biblical. My own view is predominantly penal satisfaction, but with a fond appreciation for the truth contained in the ransom theory, which we will explore further.

## 2  SYNONYMS, OR INTERCHANGEABLE WORDS,  FOR ATONE-MENT.

### A.  General terms.
1. *Redemption.*
    (a) One Greek word is *apolutrosis*: setting free for a ransom (Romans 3:24; 1 Corinthians 1:30; Ephesians 1:7; Colossians 1:14).
        (1) Ransom: the release of a captive in return for money or other payment demanded by his captors.
        (2) In ancient literature a ransom referred to prisoners of war, slaves and criminals condemned to death.

    (b) Another Greek word is *lutroo*:  to buy back by a ransom, to redeem (Luke 24:21; Titus 2:14; 1 Peter 1:18).
        (1) Root word *luo*: 'to loose' (Matthew 16:19; John 11:44).
        (2) Noun is *lutron*: 'ransom' (Matthew 20:28; Mark 10:45).

    (c) The picture is this: we have been redeemed (bought back) by God, the price paid for our release being the blood of Christ.
        (1) We fell to Satan in the Garden of Eden and have been held captive ever since.
        (2) But Jesus Christ by his blood bought us back; we are now owned by God – bought with a price (1 Corinthians 6:20).
        (3) The life of Christ was apparently an agreed price paid to secure our freedom from bondage to Satan, but it is not absolutely clear to whom the ransom was paid. Note: so much of the Atonement still remains a mystery.

2. *Reconciliation.*
    (a) Greek word is *katallage* from *katallassoo* which, in Hellenistic literature, referred to the reconciliation between husband and wife.
        (1) Reconcile: to restore friendship between people after an estrangement or quarrel.
        (2) This term is used only by Paul (Romans 5:10-11; 11:15; 2 Corinthians 5:18-19).

    (b) God has taken the initiative to restore friendship with man who by sin has been alienated from God.
        (1) God has done this through his Son by both his death and life.
        (2) It was done for the world  (2 Corinthians 5:19).

3. *Salvation*
   (a) Greek word is *soteria* (salvation) from *sozo* (to make safe, sound).
       (1) To deliver from a direct threat.
       (2) To bring safe and sound out of a difficult situation.
   (b) The two meanings above are to be seen in the New Testament.
       (1) We are saved from the wrath of God (Romans 5:9).
       (2) We are delivered from our sins (Matthew 1:21).
   (c) This salvation comes by God's initiative and provision.
       (1) By Christ's blood (Romans 5:9);
       (2) by Christ's life (Romans 5:10);
       (3) by God's purpose (2 Timothy 1:9);
       (4) by God's grace (Ephesians 2:8-9).

## B. Specific terms

1. *Sacrifice*
   (a) Greek word is *thusia* (Hebrews 5:1; 7:27; 8:3; 9:9, 23, 26; 10:12).
   (b) Sacrifice: the slaughter of a victim or presenting of a gift or doing of an act in order to win divine favour (Matthew 9:13; Romans 12:1; 1 Peter 2:5).
   (c) All of the above terms (redemption, reconciliation, salvation) are inseparably connected to the idea of sacrifice.
       (1) In the Old Testament it was of animals (Hebrews 5:1; 10:1).
       (2) In the New Testament it was the body of Christ (Hebrews 10:5).

2. *Substitution*
   (a) Although this is not a biblical word it is clearly implied by two Greek words:
       (1) *anti* 'for', 'in place of' (Matthew 5:38; 20:28; Mark 10:45).
       (2) *huper* 'for', 'in behalf of' (John 10:15; Romans 5:8; Galatians 1:4; Hebrews 2:9; 1 Peter 3:18).
   (b) When one combines the idea of sacrifice with the ideas of redemption, reconciliation and salvation, one comes to an obvious conclusion:
       (1) Christ was our sacrifice – in our place.
       (2) He was therefore our substitute.

3. *Propitiation*
   (a) Greek word is *hilasterion* (Romans 3:25; Hebrews 9:5).
       (1) Propitiation: to win the favour of; to appease; to placate.
       (2) It is carried out with reference to another party, or person – not a thing.
   (b) In Luke 18:13 the verb *hilaskomai* means 'be merciful to' and is used of God's attitude toward the sinner.

    (c)  We propitiate (win the favour of) a person rather than a sin (1 John 2:2).
        (1)  Expiation refers to removal of sin, and forgiveness.
        (2)  Propitiation refers to God, to whom satisfaction is made: the removal of wrath by the offering of a gift.
    (d)  C H Spurgeon said: 'There is no gospel apart from these two words: substitution and satisfaction.'
        (1)  Jesus Christ was our substitute – both by his death and also by his life.
        (2)  Jesus Christ was our satisfaction, since his precious blood satisfied the justice and wrath of God.

## 3  ASSUMPTIONS UNDERLYING THE DOCTRINE OF THE ATONEMENT

### A.  God is holy (Leviticus 11:44).
  1.  *The holiness of God refers to his purity, sinlessness and 'otherness'.*
    (a)  God is pure (1 John 1:5-6).
        (1)  Brilliant brightness (1 Timothy 6:16; see Acts 9:3; 22:6; 26:13).
    (b)  There is no frame of reference by which we can fully understand God.
        (1)  Some theologians call him 'wholly other'.
        (2)  That means he is unlike anything or anyone we know.

  2.  *God is just* (Psalm 89:14).
    (a)  This means God is fair and righteous (Psalm 25:8).
        (1)  The Civil Law was based on fairness (Exodus 21-23).
        (2)  God withholds nothing from those who walk uprightly (Psalm 84:11).
    (b)  But this equally means he is a God of justice.
        (1)  One day he will clear his Name.
        (2)  In the meantime, sin must be punished (Exodus 34:7).

### B.  We are sinners (Romans 3:23).
  1.  *All the world is guilty before God* (Romans 3:19).
    (a)  There are no exceptions (Romans 2:1).
    (b)  Sin is anything that comes short of the glory of God.

  2.  *The purpose of the sacrificial system: it was designed to show:*
    (a)  The seriousness of sin (Psalm 7:11).
        (1)  That no-one can atone for sin within himself (Revelation 5:2ff.).
        (2)  He must go outside of himself – a sacrifice of an animal.

(b) The need for a substitute.
- (1) Sin was transferred to the animal once the priest put his hands on the animal.
- (2) The expiation (passing over of sin) was not due to the quality of the person's life (who is the sinner) but the quality of the sacrifice (which must be perfect).

## C. God is merciful (Ephesians 2:4).

1. *Mercy is not getting what we deserve – punishment* (Exodus 33:19).
   - (a) When we ask for mercy we ask for what we don't deserve.
   - (b) We have no bargaining power within ourselves.

2. *God has shown mercy by unveiling his desire to be reconciled to man.*
   - (a) He provided man with a substitute in the Garden of Eden (Genesis 3:21).
   - (b) This is the reason for the sacrificial system in the Old Testament.

## D. The Atonement explains how God can be just and merciful at the same time.

1. *His justice had to be satisfied; it was* (John 19:30).
   - (a) Jesus fulfilled the Law:
     - (1) The Law was fulfilled by his death, according to the ceremonial demands.
     - (2) The Law was fulfilled by his life, according to the moral demands.
   - (c) Jesus never sinned (Hebrews 4:15).
     - (1) He was the God-man (1 John 1:1, 14).
     - (2) The God-man offered the complete satisfaction to the Father (2 Corinthians 5:21).

2. *His mercy was just because justice had been carried out* (Romans 3:25-26).
   - (a) It may not seem fair that our confession of sin results in cleansing, but it does (1 John 1:9).
   - (b) This is why it is called 'such a great salvation' (Hebrews 2:3).

## 4   ANALOGY BETWEEN THE ALTAR OF THE TABERNACLE AND THE CROSS OF CHRIST

## A. The Day of Atonement (*yom kippur*).

1. *Once a year the High Priest went into the Most Holy Place* (see Hebrews 9 and Leviticus 16).
   - (a) He first offered a sacrifice for his own sin.
   - (b) He then offered a sacrifice for the sins of the people.

2. *The sacrificed animal was slaughtered openly on the altar.*
   (a)  The high priest then collected blood that came from the animal.
   (b)  He took this blood and offered it on the Mercy Seat (place of atonement) inside the Most Holy Place.
      (1)  The animal was an offering when it was on the altar; a pledge before all.
      (2)  Atonement did not take effect until the very blood was sprinkled on the Mercy Seat behind the veil.

B.  **Christ fulfilled the ancient sacrificial system (1 Corinthians 5:7).**
   1. *What he did was done once and for all* (Hebrews 10:10).
      (a)  He did not need to offer sacrifices for his own sin (Hebrews 4:15).
      (b)  All he did was for *our* sins (1 Peter 2:24).

   2. *Jesus shed his blood openly on the cross.*
      (a)  That is our pledge that we will be saved (Hebrews 2:9).
      (b)  But atonement took effect when Christ entered the heaven of heavens by his own blood (Hebrews 9:24).
         (1)  He died for all (2 Corinthians 5:14-15; 1 Timothy 2:6).
         (2)  He intercedes only for those who come to God through him (Hebrews 7:25).
         (3)  In short: the atonement takes effect for believers only (Romans 3:22-26).

C.  **The Lord's Supper mirrors both the ancient Tabernacle and Christ's death on the cross.**
   1. *We do the Lord's Supper in two parts:*
      (a)  The Bread, symbolising Christ's broken body.
      (b)  The Cup, symbolising Christ's shed blood.

   2. *This mirrors the ancient pattern:*
      (a)  The offering of a sacrifice.
      (b)  The application of the blood.

## CONCLUSION

This has been a complicated study, although it is a very basic introduction to the Atonement. The most important thing to remember from it is this: we know that our sins are dealt with because Jesus died for us.

# 16

## THE ASCENSION OF JESUS

**INTRODUCTION**

A. **His ascension is one of the great events in the life of Jesus and the life of the church. It is described in a number of places:**
   1. 'When he had led them out to the vicinity of Bethany, he lifted up his hands and blessed them. While he was blessing them, he left them and was taken up into heaven. Then they worshipped him and returned to Jerusalem with great joy' (Luke 24:50-52).
   2. 'After he said this, he was taken up before their very eyes, and a cloud hid him from their sight. They were looking intently up into the sky as he was going, when suddenly two men dressed in white stood beside them. "Men of Galilee," they said, "Why do you stand here looking into the sky? This same Jesus, who has been taken from you into heaven, will come back in the same way you have seen him go into heaven"' (Acts 1:9-11).
   3. 'After the Lord Jesus had spoken to them, he was taken up into heaven and he sat at the right hand of God' (Mark 16:19).
   4. 'Therefore, since we have a great high priest who has gone through the heavens, Jesus the Son of God, let us hold firmly to the faith we profess' (Hebrews 4:14; cf. Ephesians 4:8).
   5. Jesus hinted at his ascension in John 6:62: 'What if you see the Son of Man ascend to where he was before!'
   6. It is implied in Ephesians 1:20; Philippians 2:9; Colossians 3:1; 1 Thessalonians 1:10; 1 Timothy 3:16; Hebrews 1:3; 1 Peter 3:22.
   7. It is prophesied in Psalm 16:8-11, Psalm 110:1 and Luke 22:69.

B. **After Jesus was raised from the dead he appeared several times over a period of forty days, but these appearances were temporary (Acts 1:3).**
   1. At the empty tomb (John 20:10-17).
   2. On the road to Emmaus (Luke 24:13-35).
   3. To ten of the disciples in Jerusalem (Luke 24:36-49; John 20:19-23).
   4. To the disciples with Thomas present (John 20:24-29).
   5. In Galilee (John 21).

C. **Without answering their question Jesus left them for the last time.**
   1. *Their question shows what was really on their mind: 'Lord, are you*

*at this time going to restore the kingdom to Israel?'* (Acts 1:6).
  (a)  This reveals partly why they had been following Jesus; they were not without a 'What's in it for me?' mentality.
  (b)  It certainly shows that:
    (1)  They did not know why he was crucified.
    (2)  They did not know why he was raised from the dead.
    (3)  They did not know why Jesus came at all!

2.  *Instead of answering the question Jesus directed them to the Holy Spirit.*
  (a)  He told them, 'Don't leave Jerusalem' (Luke 24:49; Acts 1:4).
  (b)  He gave a prophecy: 'But you will receive power when the Holy Spirit comes on you; and you will be my witnesses in Jerusalem, and in all Judea and Samaria, and to the ends of the earth' (Acts 1:8).

3.  *It was then that Jesus ascended to heaven, and the disciples no longer saw him in the flesh* (Acts 1:9).

## E.  Why should we study the Ascension?
1.  It is an essential link between the resurrection of Jesus and the coming of the Holy Spirit at Pentecost.
2.  It tells us where Jesus went after he ascended..
3.  It tells us what happened after he arrived.
4.  It tells us where he is now and what he is doing there.
5.  It tells us why he will come again!
6.  It explains a number of verses in the Old Testament which were of immense comfort to the early church who searched the scriptures to understand what was happening.

## 1  PERTINENT FACTS REGARDING THE ASCENSION

## A.  Jesus went up: 'He ascended on high' (Ephesians 4:8).
1.  *Greek* anabaino: *to arise from the depths to the heights.*
2.  *The word is actually used 81 times but most of these do not refer to Jesus' ascension but merely to 'going up', for example:*
  (a)  'He went up out of the water' (Matthew 3:16).
  (b)  'He went up on a mountainside' (Matthew 5:1).
  (c)  'As Jesus was going up to Jerusalem' (Matthew 20:17).

## B.  He disappeared: 'He was taken up before their very eyes, and a cloud hid him from their sight' (Acts 1:9).
1.  *This means one moment they saw him and the next they didn't!*
2.  *This shows how literal the event was.*

    (a)   Bible-denying liberals love to deride the idea of Jesus' Ascension.

    (b)   The Ascension is not a myth nor a symbol; it was a literal, distinct event.

## C. He disappeared behind a cloud: 'A cloud hid him from their sight' (Acts 1:9).

1. It is not certain whether this was a literal cloud in the sky – which I am inclined to believe.

2. It may have been a spiritual phenomenon, like the pillar of cloud (Exodus 13:22), which enveloped Jesus after he was a few feet off the ground.

## D. His Ascension was unexpected.

1. When the disciples asked their question (Acts 1:6), they had no idea it would be their last or that these appearances would come to an end.

2. They therefore were not prepared for his final departure from the earth, even though he had said, 'I am going there' – to the Father's right hand – 'to prepare a place for you' (John 14:2).

## E. His Ascension was visible: 'He was taken up before their very eyes' (Acts 1:9).

1. This further demonstrates that no faith was needed for this to be believed.

2. Unlike the resurrection, for which there were no eye-witnesses, the Ascension was visible to the naked eye.

## F. It was a bodily Ascension.

1. *Like the resurrection, Jesus arose bodily.*

    (a)   It was a transformed body, yes.

    (b)   But it was the same Jesus: 'Touch me and see; a ghost does not have flesh and bones, as you see I have' (Luke 24:39).

2. *The same Jesus went to heaven: 'This same Jesus, who has been taken from you into heaven'* (Acts 1:11).

    (a)   Jesus' body remained his after he entered heaven.

    (b)   At this moment there is a man in glory, visible as ever to those in heaven: 'There is one God and one mediator between God and men, *the man* Christ Jesus' (1 Timothy 2:5; cf. Acts 7:55ff.).

## G. Jesus ascended from the Mount of Olives (Acts 1:12).

1. Luke 24:50-52 says that he ascended from the 'vicinity of Bethany'.

2. But Bethany is 'at the Mount of Olives' (Mark 11:1).

H. **This event was approximately forty days after the resurrection (Acts 1:3).**

    1. If this was literally forty days after the resurrection, it meant that the disciples only had eight days or so to wait in Jerusalem before the Spirit fell on them.

    2. Pentecost is fifty days after Passover, but apparently the Ascension came forty days after the resurrection not the Passover, which roughly coincided with the time of Jesus' death.

    3. Whether there is any significance in the number 40 is not certain.

        (a) The Flood was the result of rain for 'forty days and forty nights' (Genesis 7:4).

        (b) Jesus fasted for 'forty days and forty nights' (Matthew 4:2).

## 2  THE SIGNIFICANCE OF THE ASCENSION OF JESUS

A. **The Ascension was his return to heaven.**

    1. *He came from heaven in the first place.*

        (a) Until the Incarnation he was the *Logos*.

        (b) He was God but he was also 'with God' (John 1:1).

    2. *He prayed: 'And now, Father, glorify me in your presence with the glory I had with you before the world began'* (John 17:5).

        (a) The Ascension was the answer to Jesus' own prayer.

        (b) He was now restored to the glory he had with the Father before the world began.

    3. *But there was one important difference: he was now there in a body.*

        (a) Before he entered the womb of the Virgin Mary he was fully God but without a body.

        (b) Once he was in the womb of Mary he 'became flesh' (John 1:14).

            (1) 'A body you prepared for me' (Hebrews 10:5).

            (2) The eternal Son returned to heaven with a body he will have throughout the endless eons of eternity.

    4. *He would have been welcomed home by the Father and the angels and possibly the sainted dead such as Abraham, Isaac and Jacob* (cf. Matthew 22:32).

        (a) His return home may have been the fulfilment of Psalm 24:7-10:

        (b) What an historical, significant and indescribably thrilling moment it must have been!

            (1) This moment was what kept Jesus going (humanly speaking) when he endured the cross.

            (2) He was to experience 'the joy set before him' (Hebrews 12:2).

**B. At the Ascension he took his seat at the Father's right hand (Ephesians 1:20).**
1. *This is what the Psalmist saw prophetically: 'The LORD says to my Lord: "Sit at my right hand until I make your enemies a footstool for your feet"'* (Psalm 110:1).
   (a) The LORD (Yahweh) says to my Lord (Jesus).
   (b) The Father welcomed his Son home and invited him to take his seat at the right hand of God the Father.

2. *The term 'right hand' was a symbol of power and authority.*
   (a) It was to show that Jesus was God and equal with God – as the Word had been from the beginning (John 1:2).
   (b) It was not only symbolic but literal: Jesus is not only strategically at the right hand of God but also at the right side of the Father.

**C. The Ascension was his personal vindication (Acts 4:11).**
1. *His vindication had been subjective until then.*
   (a) Subjective: what he himself felt and knew. It was by the Spirit alone (1 Timothy 3:16).
      (1) He got his sense of purpose and identity by the witness of the Spirit who he had without limit (John 3:34).
      (2) This gave him all the fulfilment he needed, despite his being rejected.
   (b) Objectively, he had been rejected by the authorities of Rome and Israel.

2. *Now in heaven it was an open and objective vindication.*
   (a) The Father vindicated Jesus by giving him his seat at the right hand of God.
   (b) The angels and saints witnessed this – so it was objective.
   (c) But he is still being vindicated here below by the Spirit that is in us (Romans 12:3).
      (1) We know that his vindication is objective.
      (2) But no-one can know this unless they have the Holy Spirit!

**D. The Ascension was his exaltation (Acts 2:33; Philippians 2:9).**
1. *In heaven Jesus was given the honour that had been due him all along.*
   (a) Here below 'he was despised and rejected by men' (Isaiah 53:3).
   (b) Here below he was the stone 'set at nought' (Acts 4:11, AV).

2. *Even after Jesus was raised from the dead he showed himself only to those who had been believers.*

     (a)  On one occasion he appeared to more than five hundred (1 Corinthians 15:6).

     (b)  But never once did he appear before his accusers!

3.  *Jesus is exalted in heaven not on earth (except by believers).*
     (a)  He 'sits' at the right hand of God, which shows his sovereign authority (Hebrews 1:3).
     (b)  This position not only shows his dignity, but is proof that his atonement is complete and final (Hebrews 10:12).

E.  **At the Ascension he was given 'the Name that is above every name' (Philippians 2:9).**
  1.  This was the ultimate seal of approval by the Father.
  2.  The Father – known as Yahweh by the Jews of ancient Israel – gave to Jesus his very own name. (See chapter 9, The Name of God.)

F.  **The Ascension was the beginning of his reign as King Jesus.**
  1.  *He admitted to being the King of the Jews* (John 18:37).
     (a)  He was rejected partly for this reason.
     (b)  'Pilate had a notice prepared and fastened to the cross. It read: JESUS OF NAZARETH, THE KING OF THE JEWS' (John 19:19).
  2.  *But his reign began in heaven at God's right hand.*
  3.  *This reign will last until he has put all his enemies under his feet (1 Corinthians 15:25). This will happen after the last person to be saved is saved!*
  4.  *One day he will be openly and objectively vindicated by* all – *in heaven and earth – as 'King of kings and Lord of lords'* (Revelation 19:16).

G.  **It was at the Ascension that Jesus began his role as our great high priest (Hebrews 4:14).**
  1.  *It is here that the blood he shed on the cross is applied.*
     (a)  His blood was shed for the sins of the world (Hebrews 2:9).
     (b)  It is applied and made effectual by the intercession of Christ (John 17:9).
  2.  *Peter said, 'Exalted to the right hand of God, he has received from the Father the promised Holy Spirit and has poured out what you now see and hear'* (Acts 2:33).
  3.  *It was at the right hand of God that he began interceding for us.*
     (a)  'Who is he that condemns? Christ Jesus, who died – more than that, who was raised to life – is at the right hand of God and is also interceding for us' (Romans 8:34).

(b) 'Therefore he is able to save completely those who come to God through him, because he always lives to intercede for them' (Hebrews 7:25).

4. *He is there as the only mediator between God and men* (1 Timothy 2:5).

5. *This will continue until he returns to earth a second time.*

## 3  THE SIGNIFICANCE OF THE ASCENSION FOR US

A. **After Jesus disappeared in the cloud, here is what happened with the disciples:**
1. They waited; they walked to Jerusalem from the Mount of Olives (Acts 1:12).
2. They stayed in Jerusalem.
3. They went 'upstairs to the room where they were staying' (Acts 1:13).
4. They worshipped and praised God continually (Luke 24:52-53).
5. They prayed (Acts 1:14).

B. **On the day of Pentecost the Holy Spirit came down on the disciples (Acts 2:1-4).**
1. *All this was the consequence of two things:*
   (a) Jesus' advice to tarry – not to leave Jerusalem.
   (b) Jesus' intercession at the right hand of God.

2. *When Peter preached, which came as a result of having to refute the charge that they were drunk on new wine (Acts 2:13ff.), his sermon was preoccupied with Jesus' death, resurrection and ascension.*
   (a) Psalm 16 was applied to Jesus' death, resurrection and ascension (Acts 2:25ff.).
   (b) Psalm 110 was explicitly quoted to show that its fulfilment was in Christ's ascension (Acts 2:33ff.).

C. **The significance for us now.**
1. *That we never forget where Jesus is now.*
   (a) It was one thing for the earliest disciples to claim that Jesus was raised from the dead.
   (b) They then had to explain why, if he was raised from the dead, he did not turn up and prove to all that he is alive.
   (c) Their reply: he has been exalted to God's right hand.
      (1) 'Therefore let all Israel be assured of this: God has made this Jesus, whom you crucified, both Lord and Christ' (Acts 2:36).
      (2) 'He must remain in heaven until the time comes for God to

restore everything, as he promised long ago through his holy prophets' ( Acts 3:21).

  (3)  'God exalted him to his own right hand as Prince and Saviour that he might give repentance and forgiveness of sins to Israel' (Acts 5:31).

  (d)  We too must realise that Jesus is alive and well – in heaven – and looks the same as he did when last seen by the naked eye (Hebrews 13:8).

2.  *We pray to the Father through the Mediator, the man in glory* (1 Timothy 2:5).
  (a)  The ascension of Christ is our basis for prayer (John 14:14).
  (b)  The reason we have access to God is because Jesus is there, interceding for us  (Hebrews 7:25).
  (c)  In Calvin's words: the Son beckons the attention of the Father to himself to 'keep his gaze away from our sins'.

3.  *Our affection should be directed to 'things above, where Christ is seated at the right hand of God'* (Colossians 3:1).
  (a)  This is what Paul meant when he said, 'And God raised us up with Christ and seated us with him in the heavenly realms in Christ Jesus' (Ephesians 2:6).

D. **There is a close connection between Christ's ascension and his Second Coming. Although the parallel should not be drawn too far, it has been noted that the similarities between the Ascension and the Second Coming are found in Acts 1:9-11.**
  1.  The ascension was unexpected; so too Christ will come as a thief (Matthew 24:44; 2 Peter 3:10).
  2.  He passed behind a cloud; he will come with clouds (Matthew 24:30).
  3.  His ascension was visible; so too 'every eye will see him' (Revelation 1:7).
  4.  He ascended bodily; he will return bodily: 'this same Jesus' (Acts 1:10-11).
  5.  Some go so far as to contend he will even return to the very place from which he ascended! (Zechariah 14:4).

**CONCLUSION**
Christ is alive and well. He has been totally vindicated in heaven. One day 'every knee' will bow and everybody confess who he is (Romans 14:11; Philippians 2:9-11).

# 17

# THE PRIESTHOOD OF CHRIST

## INTRODUCTION

A. **Immediately after his Ascension Jesus began his role as our great high priest (Hebrews 4:14).**
   1. The only book in the New Testament where we find Jesus referred to as our high priest is the Epistle to the Hebrews.
   2. John Calvin was the first theologian to make the three-fold distinction in the office of Christ – as prophet, king and priest.

B. **Priesthood of Christ: Christ's intercessory work at the Father's right hand.**
   1. *Priest: a mediator, that is, one who acts as a go-between or peacemaker between opposing sides.*
   2. *Christ is the one mediator between God and men* (1 Timothy 2:5).
      (a) All Christians are called priests in the New Testament (1 Peter 2:5,9). (See Chapter on the 'The Priesthood of All Believers'.)
      (b) The office of priest in terms of official ministry is essentially an Old Testament concept.

C. **Why is this study important?**
   1. *It lets us see what Jesus is doing now at the right hand of God.*
   2. *It provides us with the right foundation for prayer.*
   3. *It sheds further light on what is meant by praying in Jesus' name.*
   4. *It lets us see further why our salvation is secure – that is, why 'once saved, always saved' is true.*
   5. *It forces us to go back to the Old Testament and work out our theology – just as those in the early church had to do.*
      (a) It shows the relevance of the Tabernacle in the wilderness.
      (b) It shows the relevance of the Day of Atonement.
      (c) It shows the relevance of Psalm 110.

## 1 OLD TESTAMENT ROOTS

A. **The emergence of the priesthood.**
   1. *Moses and Aaron were of the tribe of Levi* (Exodus 2:1; 4:14).
      (a) Aaron led the people into apostasy (falling away) with the golden calf (Exodus 32:25ff.).

129

(b) But the sons of Levi avenged the Lord's honour by punishing many offenders (Exodus 32:28).
  (1) The Lord rewarded the tribe of Levi for this (Exodus 32:29).
  (2) The result: the tribe of Levi were given the responsibility for ceremonial worship.

2. *The Levites became the most prestigious tribe in ancient Israel.*
  (a) They were responsible for the worship of God.
  (b) Although they had no geographical inheritance, they had the responsibility for the ceremonial worship:
    (1) The Tabernacle and all that pertained to it.
    (2) The sacrificial system.

## B. The Tabernacle (a movable tent).

1. *This was the provisional meeting place of God and his people* (Exodus 33:7-11).
2. *The Tabernacle and all that pertained to it was erected by Moses but 'according to the pattern' shown to him by God* (Exodus 25:40).
  (a) Just outside the Tabernacle was the altar on which sacrifices were slain.
  (b) The Tabernacle itself was in two parts:
    (1) The Holy Place, in which were the lampstand, the table and the consecrated bread.
    (2) A curtain separated the Holy Place from the Most Holy Place in which was the Ark of the Covenant.
  (c) The Ark of the Covenant was a rectangular box made of acacia wood and covered with gold.
    (1) It measured about 4 feet by 2½ feet and was 2½ feet high.
    (2) The lid was called the Mercy Seat.

## C. Day of Atonement (Leviticus 16).

1. *The High Priest alone entered into the Most Holy Place.*
2. *This was done once a year – on the Day of Atonement – and never without blood* (Hebrews 9:7).
  (a) The sacrifice was slaughtered on the altar just outside the Tabernacle.
  (b) The High Priest went behind the veil and sprinkled blood on the Mercy Seat.

## D. Priest after the order of Melchizedek (Genesis 14 and Psalm 110).

1. Abraham paid tithes to Melchizedek, King of Salem, after a stunning victory (Genesis 14:20).
2. David prophesied of a priesthood that would come 'after the order of Melchizedek' (Psalm 110:4).

## 2 NEW TESTAMENT FULFILMENT

A. **Jesus is pictured in the Epistle to the Hebrews in a two-fold manner.**
   1. *The sacrifice for sin* (Hebrews 9:28).
      (a) He died on a cross, shedding his precious blood.
      (b) He thus was 'the Lamb of God, who takes away the sin of the world' (John 1:29).

   2. *High Priest* (Hebrews 9:11).
      (a) He entered 'the greater and more perfect tabernacle that is not man-made ... by his own blood, having obtained eternal redemption' (Hebrews 9:11-12).
      (b) This was not repeated year after year but done 'once for all' (Hebrews 9:26).

B. **But there remained a problem for the writer of Hebrews to solve.**
   1. *Jesus was not of the tribe of Levi but of Judah* (Hebrews 7:14).
   2. *Jesus came to fulfil Psalm 110:4, 'in the order of Melchizedek'* (Hebrews 7:15-22).
      (a) This proves that the Levitical priesthood was temporary (Hebrews 7:18).
      (b) The priesthood of Melchizedek was the one that would permanently replace the old order (Hebrews 9:21).

C. **When Jesus died on the cross the veil of the Temple was 'torn in two from top to bottom' (Matthew 27:51).**
   1. This shows what God thought of what Jesus did.
   2. This shows that the old order had passed away.

D. **After Jesus rose from the dead he took his seat at God's right hand.**
   1. This is when Psalm 110 was fulfilled.
   2. Jesus has been at God's right hand to this day – as our Great High Priest (Hebrews 4:14).

## 3 THE NATURE OF CHRIST'S INTERCESSION

A. **Intercession: to intervene on behalf of another.**
   1. *To intervene: to step in by words or deeds.*
      (a) The timing is therefore crucial.
      (b) The nature of what is done is crucial:
         (1) Who it is and the influence he has.
         (2) What he says can make a difference.

 2. *'Intercession' and 'mediating' can be used here interchangeably.*
  (a) Either word assumes that two parties need reconciling.
  (b) The assumption moreover is that the one interceding has influence with both parties.
   (1) Influence with the offended party.
   (2) Influence with the one who did the offending.

## B. Christ's intercession is unique.
 1. *He alone has influence with both parties* (1 Timothy 2:5).
  (a) With the one who is offended – God.
  (b) With the offenders – us.

 2. *He is the only person who could ever qualify.*
  (a) No man on earth could come up to the standard God requires.
   (1) Jesus alone is worthy (Revelation 5:3-5).
   (2) Jesus is the only way to God (John 14:6; Acts 4:12).
  (b) No other person could identify with our problem.
   (1) He bore our sins in his body (1 Peter 2:24).
   (2) He understands our feelings and nature (Hebrews 2:18; 4:15).
  (c) Jesus has access to the Father.
   (1) He has entered the Most Holy Place, 'heaven itself' (Hebrews 9:24).
   (2) He has remained there since he ascended (Hebrews 10:12-13).

## C. What exactly does Jesus do now?
 1. *He carries out the secret will of God.*
  (a) The ancient high priest followed an inflexible plan.
   (1) He could not do what he personally wanted to do.
   (2) He had to do what had been prescribed.
  (b) Even when Jesus was on earth he was not 'his own man', as it were.
   (1) 'Jesus gave them this answer: "I tell you the truth, the Son can do nothing by himself; he can do only what he sees his Father doing, because whatever the Father does the Son also does" ' (John 5:19).
   (2) 'By myself I can do nothing; I judge only as I hear, and my judgment is just, for I seek not to please myself but him who sent me' (John 5:30).
  (c) This obedience continues at the right hand of God.
   (1) Jesus doesn't 'think up' what to do or who to pray for.
   (2) He carries out God's secret will.

2. *He prays for those given to him by the Father.*

  (a) 'All that the Father gives me will come to me, and whoever comes to me I will never drive away' (John 6:37).

  (b) Those given to the Son – God's elect – are the object of Christ's intercessory prayer.

    (1) 'I pray for them. I am not praying for the world, but for those you have given me, for they are yours' (John 17:9).

    (2) They alone are interceded for.

  (c) The reason that anybody believes has its sole explanation in Christ's intercession.

    (1) No-one would ever believe in and of himself or herself.

    (2) We are born 'dead' in 'transgressions and sins' (Ephesians 2:1).

  (d) The Son sends the Spirit to give life to God's elect people.

    (1) The Son obeys the Father (John 5:19, 30).

    (2) The Spirit obeys the Son (John 14:16).

3. *Jesus* applies *what he did on the cross* (Hebrews 9:11-12,24ff.).

  (a) He shed his blood openly.

    (1) His crucifixion was visible (Matthew 27:36).

    (2) The slaying of the sacrifice was visible on the altar (Leviticus 16:3-7).

  (b) His intercession is secret – out of view.

    (1) He went behind the veil (curtain) (Hebrews 6:19).

    (2) What the ancient high priest did was to apply the blood 'behind the curtain' (Leviticus 16:15).

  (c) Atonement takes effect not when the sacrifice sheds blood but when that blood is *applied.*

    (1) Jesus died for all – but not all are saved.

    (2) What Jesus did on the cross must be applied (John 3:16).

  (d) The application of Jesus' work on the cross is carried out, then, in this order:

    (1) Jesus prays for those who have been chosen.

    (2) The Holy Spirit creates faith in God's elect.

    (3) Those in whom the Spirit has worked, believe.

  (e) Once a person has believed we may know that Christ's blood has been *applied.*

    (1) The death of Jesus is one thing; it *provides* salvation.

    (2) His intercession is another; it *applies* salvation.

    (3) All that Jesus did for the salvation of the human race is of no value for us until we believe.

    (4) No-one is saved 'automatically' by Jesus' death; this is why he needed to be our Great High Priest.

4. *Jesus* upholds *his people by his continuous intercession.*
    (a) His prayer is that none will be lost (John 17:11-12).
    (b) His prayers are answered!
        (1) He prays with a perfect faith (John 3:34).
        (2) Paul could say, 'I live by the faith *of* the Son of God' (Galatians 2:20, AV).
    (c) Our eternal security is guaranteed by Christ's intercession.
        (1) 'Who is he that condemns? Christ Jesus, who died – more than that, who was raised to life – is at the right hand of God and is also interceding for us' (Romans 8:34).
        (2) 'Therefore he is able to save completely those who come to God through him, because he always lives to intercede for them' (Hebrews 7:25).
    (d) As long as Jesus prays for us we may know we cannot be lost.
        (1) His intercession never stops!
        (2) We therefore can never be lost!
    (e) Question: How do we know for sure that Jesus is praying for us as individuals? Answer:
        (1) We begin by looking to the cross; for it was there he provided salvation for *all.*
        (2) We could not have been directed to the cross but by the Spirit who was at work in us.
        (3) C. H. Spurgeon said: 'Don't ask, "Am I elected?" Ask, "Do I believe?"'
        (4) All this is summarised in Hebrews 7:25.
        (5) Those who come to God by Jesus are saved; those who come to Jesus are never refused (John 6:37).

## 4   THE RELEVANCE OF CHRIST'S INTERCESSION AND PRAYER

A. **We have direct access into God's presence by the blood of Jesus (Hebrews 10:19-21).**
    1. *What the ancient high priest could do only once a year we now can do all the time.*
        (a) But this is with one condition: by blood.
            (1) The high priest never entered the Most Holy Place without blood (Hebrews 9:7). This aspect has never changed.
        (b) We therefore may enter the Most Holy Place – heaven itself – but never without blood.
            (1) We, therefore, must be continually conscious that we enter God's presence by the blood of Jesus.
            (2) The continuous intercession of Christ is done on the basis of his own blood.

2. *We therefore must be mindful of three things when we pray:*
   (a) That we never outgrow the need of a mediator (1 Timothy 2:5).
   (b) That we come to God by Jesus (John 14:6).
   (c) That our access is by the blood he shed on the cross and which he has sprinkled on the heavenly Mercy Seat.

B. **When we pray we must pray in Jesus' name – or at least plead the merit of his name.**
   1. *In a previous lesson we learned:*
      (a) Praying in Jesus' name is speaking to God on behalf of Jesus, as if speaking *for* Jesus.
      (b) This assumes we are praying in the Spirit and consciously reflect the will of God.

   2. *However, we do not always know what the will of God is* (Romans 8:26-27).
      (a) If we *do* know the will of God, we will know that we get what we ask for (1 John 5:14-15).
      (b) But if we don't know the will of God we can always plead the *merit* of Jesus' name even if we don't know we are speaking Jesus' will.

C. **Behind all this is the consistent truth that Christ's intercession will be according to the Father's will.**
   1. *Jesus never intercedes outside the Father's will.*
   2. *Jesus always prays in the will of God.*
   3. *We too must pray in the will of God if we are to receive anything.*
      (a) We may not *know* we are praying in the will of God.
         (1) That is why John said 'if' in 1 John 5:14-15.
         (2) This is a big 'if' and yet we should hope it will be the case with each of us!
      (b) But even if we don't *know* we are praying in God's will - that prayer *will* be answered if it is in God's will.
         (1) Any prayer prayed in the will of God will be answered.
         (2) The only prayer that is answered is that which is in God's will.
   4. *We are not going to twist the Father's arm to go against his own will for us. He knows what is right and good for us.*

## CONCLUSION
The old order of priesthood has gone. Jesus is our high priest and sacrifice for ever. He is a sympathetic mediator; a high priest who knows our needs and our weaknesses and will 'filter' our requests, passing to the Father only those requests that are acceptable to him. The one prayer we know for sure is answered is that we will never be lost (Hebrews 7:25).

# 18

## MAN, SIN, SALVATION

### INTRODUCTION

A. **This study can aptly be described as 'purest theology'.**
1. *From time to time we must touch on the essentials.*
    (a) The subject is probably the most important of them all.
        (1) It has been suggested that Christology (the doctrine of Christ) is more important.
        (2) But this lesson in fact includes Christology; it moreover assumes that our doctrine of Christ is already correct!
    (b) It deals with *the* reason God sent his Son into the world.
    (c) It deals with our own souls – where we will spend eternity.
        (1) If there is a heaven and a hell, and we go irrevocably and irretrievably to one or the other when we die, nothing is more important than going to heaven.
        (2) We must know that we are saved.

B. **Soteriology: doctrine of salvation.**
1. *It comes from two Greek words: (a)* Soter: *saviour; (b)* Logos: *word.*
2. *Soteriology deals with two questions:*
    (a) Does man need to be redeemed? (b) If so, how?
3. *'Saved' is thought to be an old-fashioned word.*
    (a) Some refer to being 'converted' or 'committed'.
    (b) The Bible's word is unashamedly 'saved'.
        (1) 'She will give birth to a son, and you are to give him the name Jesus, because he will save his people from their sins' (Matthew 1:21).
        (2) 'Not that I accept human testimony; but I mention it that you may be saved' (John 5:34).
        (3) 'Salvation is found in no-one else, for there is no other name under heaven given to men by which we must be saved' (Acts 4:12).
        (4) 'He then brought them out and asked, "Sirs, what must I do to be saved?"' (Acts 16:30).
        (5) 'That if you confess with your mouth, "Jesus is Lord," and believe in your heart that God raised him from the dead, you will be saved' (Romans 10:9).

C. **This study will give a panoramic view of the biblical history of redemption.**
  1. *The terms 'salvation' and 'redemption' can be used interchangeably, but each has its own meaning.*
     (a) Salvation: saved from the wrath of God (Romans 5:9). This will necessarily includes being saved from the penalty and power of sin.
     (b) Redemption: being brought back. This refers to Christ's blood buying us back from the lost condition into which we were born.

  2. *To understand the need for salvation and redemption we need to look at the doctrine of man:*
     (a) Man as he was created – before the Fall.
     (b) Man as he became after sin came in – after the Fall.
         (1) The Fall: the moment of Adam's sin in the Garden of Eden.
         (2) The Garden of Eden was a place on the map; the Fall was a date in history.

D. **The first major theologian to articulate the theology of sin and salvation after the apostle Paul was St Augustine (354-430).**
  1. *When asked why no-one since Paul had dealt with this matter he replied, 'No-one had to counter the error of Pelagius' (c.400).*
     (a) Pelagius, a British monk, was angry when he read Augustine's famous prayer, 'Give what Thou commandest, and command what Thou wilt.' He wrote a treatise attacking the predestinarian implications of Augustine's thinking.
     (b) Augustine replied to Pelagius; the result was the first major treatment of the subject of sin and salvation.
     (c) The doctrine of salvation in church history was never the same again. From then on, a person was either Augustinian or semi-Pelagian (a view that anticipated what many today would call Arminianism).

  2. *Augustine's soteriology can be summarised generally by his famous 'four stages' of man in the history of redemption.*
     (a) *Posse peccare* – 'able to sin'.
         (1) This is man as he was created – before the Fall.
         (2) He was thus created sinless but with the possibility of sinning.
     (b) *Non posse non peccare* – 'not able not to sin'.
         (1) This is man after the Fall.
         (2) Man was thus unable to do other than sin after sin emerged; a condition into which all men were born.

(3) Note: Pelagius regarded all people as being born as Adam
was before the Fall.
(c) *Posse non peccare* – 'able not to sin'.
(1) This is man after being saved.
(2) Man was thus able, by the power of the Holy Spirit, not to
sin.
(d) *Non posse peccare* – 'not able to sin'.
(1) This is man after he is glorified (Romans 8:30.
(2) In heaven man will not be able to sin.

## E.  Why is this study important?
1. *It is absolutely essential that we have a right understanding of this
aspect of theology.*
2. *Our soteriology assumes a correct Christology.*
   (a) We may have a correct Christology and a faulty soteriology.
   (b) But a correct soteriology almost certainly presupposes a correct
   Christology.
3. *When it comes to witnessing to others, the doctrine of salvation is
what we'd better be sure about!*

## 1   MAN BEFORE THE FALL

## A.  Man was created in the image of God (Genesis 1:26-27).
1. *A spiritual being. We sometimes refer to this as conscience.*
   (a) This means man was made with *more* than the physical senses (to
   see, smell, touch, hear, taste).
   (b) He was given a yearning to worship the Creator.
   (1) He had pure fellowship with God, and conversed with God.

2. *Free will.* 'And the LORD God commanded the man, "You are free to
eat from any tree in the garden; but you must not eat from the tree of
the knowledge of good and evil, for when you eat of it you will surely
die"' (Genesis 2:16-17).
   (a) In his unfallen state man had the power to choose.
   (b) He was 'able to sin'.

3. *Immortality*
   (a) God alone is immortal (1 Timothy 6:16).
   (b) And yet God gave immortality to man when he was created; an
   essential part of his being made in God's own image (Genesis 2:17).

4. *Intelligence*
   (a) Man was superior to all other created beings (Genesis 1:28).
   (b) God let man name the creatures (Genesis 2:19-20).

5. *Work and responsibility*
   (a) Essential to unfallen man was the capacity to do work (Genesis 2:15).
   (b) Unfallen man however did not find work hard or tiring.

## B. Man was created innocent and sinless (Genesis 2:25).
   1. Innocence: without any guilt or shame.
   2. Man was not created sinful but without any sin whatever.

## C. Note: there is a lot more to be studied with reference to man before the Fall. For example:
   1. The need for earthly fellowship (Genesis 2:18).
   2. The implications of the role of man and woman (Genesis 2:23-24).

## 2 MAN AFTER THE FALL: THE EMERGENCE OF SIN

## A. The unhappy event that led to man's sin is recorded in Genesis 3:1-7.
   1. The devil came to Eve in the form of a serpent (verse 1).
   2. The devil twisted God's word to man (verses 1-5).
   3. Eve gave in to temptation (verse 6).
   4. Adam followed her (verse 6).

## B. The consequence of their sin.
   1. *Death* (Genesis 2:17; Romans 6:23).
      (a) The moment they ate, death set in.
         (1) They continued to live on for a good while.
         (2) But it was only a matter of time before they would die.
      (b) Spiritual death entered in (Ephesians 2:1-3).
   2. *Shame* (Genesis 3:8).
      (a) Before they sinned they were not self-conscious about their nakedness.
      (b) Immediately after they sinned they felt a need to cover their bodies (Genesis 3:7).
   3. *Refusal to accept responsibility because of self-righteousness* (Genesis 3:12-13).
      (a) Adam blamed Eve; (b) Eve blamed the serpent.
   4. *Fear* (Genesis 3:10).
   5. *Note: there are other consequences of the Fall, for example:*
      (a) Punishment for the woman (Genesis 3:16).
      (b) Punishment for the man (Genesis 3:19)
      (c) Punishment for the rest of creation (Genesis 3:17ff.).
         (1) The ground is cursed.
         (2) There is every reason to believe that the whole of earthly creation was adversely affected (Romans 8:20ff.).

### C. Further consequences of the Fall.

1. *The whole human race fell as a result of our first parents*: 'Therefore, just as sin entered the world through one man, and death through sin, and in this way death came to all men, because all sinned – for before the law was given, sin was in the world' (Romans 5:12-13a.).

   (a) This means that all born after Adam and Eve inherited the condition of Adam and Eve as they were *after* the Fall (not before).

      (1) Man has never been born as Adam was – in his unfallen state.

      (2) He inherits Adam's death, shame, self-righteousness and fear.

   (b) In a word: we are not sinners because we sin; we sin because we are born sinners.

      (1) 'Surely I have been a sinner from birth, sinful from the time my mother conceived me' (Psalm 51:5).

      (2) 'Even from birth the wicked go astray; from the womb they are wayward and speak lies' (Psalm 58:3).

2. *The image of God is defaced, or marred.*

   (a) It has not been totally obliterated, just seriously damaged.

   (b) This means there is a vestige (a trace) of what the image of God in man was, but not as it was before the Fall.

      (1) Man still has a conscience; there is a 'God-shaped blank' in every man (Pascal).

      (2) Man is still illuminated to some extent by Christ (John 1:9).

      (3) But man's conscience is unable to save.

3. *Free will, as Adam once had, is forfeited. Is man a free moral agent?*

   (a) Man is in subjection to sin; he is hardly free (Ephesians 2:1).

   (b) Man is not moral; he is 'full of cursing and bitterness' (Romans 3:14).

   (c) Man is not the agent in his salvation; the Holy Spirit – God's drawing power – is the agent (John 6:44).

   (d) Note: as if to drive this point home, God 'drove the man out, he placed on the east side of the Garden of Eden cherubim and a flaming sword flashing back and forth to guard the way to the tree of life' (Genesis 3:24).

   (e) In short, man was 'not able not to sin'.

## 3  SALVATION

**A. The first promise of salvation is found in Genesis 3:15: 'And I will put enmity between you and the woman, and between your offspring and hers; he will crush his head, and you will strike his heel.'**

1. *This word was addressed to the serpent.*
    2. *It was the promise that Jesus would die on a cross.*
        (a) God could have chosen to let man perish or utterly destroy the devil then and there.
        (b) Instead he chose to send a redeemer and to deal with evil in stages.

    3. *The first hint of God's love and the way he would save us was when he 'made garments of skin for Adam and his wife and clothed them'* (Genesis 3:21).
        (a) The garments of skin meant:
            (1) The sacrifice of a substitute.
            (2) The shedding of blood.
        (b) The clothing pointed to the covering of righteousness that would be needed.

B. **The history of redemption in the Old Testament.**
    1. *Abel* (Hebrews 11:4).
    2. *Abraham.*
        (a) The gospel was preached to Abraham (Galatians 3:8).
        (b) Abraham saw Jesus' day and was glad (John 8:56).
    3. *The Law* (Romans 5:20).
        (a) The sacrificial system was explicitly introduced (Hebrews 10:1).
        (b) This pointed to its fulfilment in Christ (Galatians 3:24).

C. **The coming of the redeemer (Galatians 4:4ff.).**
    1. *Jesus was born of a virgin.*
        (a) He was man as though he were not God (Hebrews 5:8).
        (b) He was God as though he were not man (John 1:1).
    2. *Jesus promised to fulfil the Law* (Matthew 5:17).
        (a) This meant he would be the first person who never sinned.
            (1) For no-one had kept the Law (Acts 15:10; Romans 3:23).
            (2) Jesus never sinned ( 2 Corinthians 5:21; Hebrews 4:15).
        (b) He said on the cross, 'It is finished' (John 19:30).
            (1) This meant he succeeded in what he come to do.
            (2) It meant our debt was paid by him.
    3. *Three things were needed to save mankind.*
        (a) Sacrifice: the shedding of blood.
            (1) This meant that salvation lay outside of man's hands.
            (2) This meant the 'types' of sacrifice under the Law must have their ultimate fulfilment.
            (3) The Lord Jesus Christ accomplished all the above.
        (b) Substitution: to take man's place.
            (1) This required a perfect, sinless life.

        (2)  This required a perfect sacrifice in death.

        (3)  The Lord Jesus Christ fulfilled all the above.

   (c)  Satisfaction: to appease God.

        (1)  This required that a holy God be satisfied in terms of his justice.

        (2)  This required that a holy God be no longer angry.

        (3)  The Lord Jesus Christ fulfilled all the above.

## D. The need for faith (Romans 3:22).

1. *We might well wish that Romans 1:17 had said that the righteousness of God is revealed by faith – full stop.*
    (a) Had this been the case, then the very person and work of Jesus Christ would have guaranteed salvation for all.
        (1) Jesus died for all ( 2 Corinthians 5:15; Hebrews 2:9).
        (2) But we know that not all are saved.
    (b) This is because the righteousness (justice) is revealed 'from faith to faith' (Romans 1:17 AV – which is what the Greek says).
        (1) This means that what Jesus Christ did was not sufficient to save in and by itself – by God's own decree.
        (2) Our faith must be joined to what he did – or we will not be saved.

2. *But the righteousness of God comes only 'to all who believe'* (John 3:16; Romans 3:22)..
    (a) If we believe, we are saved (John 5:24).
    (b) If we do not believe, we are condemned (John 3:36).

## E. The need for preaching (1 Corinthians 1:21).

1. *No-one believes without being witnessed to* (Romans 10:14).
2. *We are commanded to witness to all* (Matthew 28:19; 2 Corinthians 5:20).
    (a) If our view of salvation does not lead us to witness to the lost, we are disobedient to Christ.
    (b) If we are balanced theologians it will be impossible to tell which we emphasise more:
        (1) Being sound in our theology.
        (2) Being obedient in our witnessing.

## F. The need for faith to be imparted (Ephesians 2:8).

1. *Man cannot, in and of himself, believe.*
    (a) He is born 'dead' (Ephesians 2:1-5).
    (b) Jesus said, 'No-one can come to me unless the Father who sent me draws him' (John 6:44).

2. *What is required: regeneration (being born again).*
   (a) We were powerless and passive in our natural birth.
   (b) We are likewise powerless and passive in our spiritual birth (John 1:13).
   (c) Regeneration is the work of the Holy Spirit.
      (1) It is what God must 'begin' (Philippians 1:6).
      (2) It is effectual by the Spirit alone (1 Thessalonians 2:13; 2 Thessalonians 2:13).
   (d) In a word: faith is the gift of God.

3. *Who believes?*
   (a) Those given to Jesus by the Father (John 6:37).
   (b) Those who were appointed to eternal life (Acts 13:48).
   (c) Those who were predestined and called (Romans 8:30).

4. *What happens to believers?*
   (a) They are given an 'imputed' righteousness (Romans 4:1-12).
   (b) They are kept (John 6:37,44; 10:28).
   (c) They are given power not to sin (Romans 6:1-22). 'Able not to sin'.

## G. The need for glorification (Romans 8:30).
1. *God might have decreed that all who are saved are not only sanctified but also simultaneously glorified.*
2. *But he designed that redemption be completed in two stages.*
   (a) Satan's defeat is in two stages:
      (1) At the cross (Genesis 3:15).
      (2) Final doom (Revelation 20:10).
   (b) Our redemption is in two stages:
      (1) By faith (Romans 5:1).
      (2) By glorification – when Jesus comes (1 John 3:2). 'Not able to sin'.

## CONCLUSION
All born after Adam inherit Adam's fallen condition. God could have chosen to let man perish or to destroy the devil totally there and then. Instead, however, he had a plan for our salvation, to save humanity from God's wrath, from the power and penalty of sin. He sent a Redeemer, Jesus Christ, the perfect sacrifice.

# 19

# THE BELIEVER'S POSITION 'IN CHRIST'

**INTRODUCTION**

A. **This study focuses on how we get to heaven: by being 'in Christ'.**
   1. *Largely a Pauline phrase, 'in Christ' (or its equivalent) appears in his epistles no fewer than 146 times.*
      (1) 18 times in Romans; (2) 22 times in 1 Corinthians; (3) 11 times in 2 Corinthians; (4) 9 times in Galatians; (5) 31 times in Ephesians; (6) 19 times in Philippians; (7) 16 times in Colossians.
   2. *In Ephesians 1:4-13 it appears no less than 11 times!*
      (a) Sometimes it is 'in Christ', 'in him' or 'in Christ Jesus'.
      (b) Sometimes it is 'in the one he loves' (AV 'in the beloved').
   3. *The Greek is* en Christo *but sometimes translated 'by' or 'with' in some translations.*

B. **'In Christ': the guarantee of the believer's security with all its privileges.**
   1. *It refers to our union with Christ – before and after we have come to faith.*
   2. *It means that we are as secure in Christ as he himself is secure in the Godhead and the Father's love.*
      (a) We were chosen before the foundation of the world.
      (b) We are being kept – apart from our works.
   3. *It embraces the privilege of being at one with Christ, which promises not only security but also intimacy with the Father..*

C. **Why is this teaching important?**
   1. It focuses on the heartbeat of the gospel.
   2. It focuses on the heartbeat of the apostle Paul.
   3. The phrase 'in Christ' is not accidental but is a carefully worked out scheme.
   4. It brings us face to face with one of the most neglected teachings of our day – the sovereignty of God.
   5. It brings us to the doctrine of justification by faith alone.
   6. It shows us that salvation is by grace and not of works.
   7. It reveals the basis of true intimacy with God.
   8. It gives us a wonderful security (something all of us hope is true, but so often are afraid to believe).

D. **The phrase 'in Christ' does not have one single sense, but refers to a variety of relationships.**

## 1 THE SOURCE OF OUR UNION WITH CHRIST: THE ELECTION OF GOD THE FATHER

A. **Election (being chosen) flows from God's blessing:** 'Praise be to the God and Father of our Lord Jesus Christ, who has blessed us in the heavenly realms with every spiritual blessing in Christ' (Ephesians 1:3).
   1. The Greek word is *eklegomai* and it means 'to choose something for oneself', 'to make one's choice'.
   2. The term is used 21 times in the New Testament and 108 times in Septuagint; among them: Psalm 78:70; Isaiah 42:1; Mark 13:20; John 15:16; 1 Corinthians 1:27; Ephesians 1:4.

B. **Being appointed, which flows from God's choice of some:** 'When the Gentiles heard this, they were glad and honoured the word of the Lord; and all who were appointed for eternal life believed' (Acts 13:48).
   1. The Greek word is *tasso*, meaning 'to appoint', 'to order', 'to arrange'.
   2. Used 8 times in the New Testament, among them: Matthew 28:16; Luke 7:8; Acts 15:2; Romans 13:1.

C. **Being predestined, which flows from God's secret will:** 'And those he predestined, he also called; those he called, he also justified; those he justified, he also glorified' (Romans 8:30).
   1. The Greek word is *proorizo*, meaning 'to set beforehand'.
   2. Used 6 times in the New Testament: Acts 4:28; Romans 8:29,30; 1 Corinthians 2:7; Ephesians 1:5,11.

D. **In some cases none of the Greek words noted above are used but the meaning comes to the same thing.**
   1. 'All things have been committed to me by my Father. No-one knows the Son except the Father, and no-one knows the Father except the Son and those to whom the Son chooses to reveal him' (Matthew 11:27).
   2. 'All that the Father gives me will come to me, and whoever comes to me I will never drive away' (John 6:37).
   3. '... who has saved us and called us to a holy life – not because of anything we have done but because of his own purpose and grace. This grace was given us in Christ Jesus before the beginning of time' (2 Timothy 1:9).

E. **According to Paul we were chosen in Christ from the foundation of the world:** 'For he chose us in him before the creation of the world to be holy and blameless in his sight. In love he predestined us to be adopted as

his sons through Jesus Christ, in accordance with his pleasure and will'
(Ephesians 1:4-5).
1. *The choice was made by God the Father* (cf. John 6:37).
2. *The choice was made before the world began* (cf. 2 Timothy 1:9).
.3. *We were regarded as 'in Christ' at that time!*
    (a) This is not only before we believe (cf. Ephesians 2:1-4).
    (b) This was before we were born (Romans 9:11).
    (c) The late John Murray writes:
       'Union with Christ has its source in the election of God the Father
       before the foundation of the world and has its fruition in the
       glorification of the sons of God. Why does the believer entertain
       the thought of God's determinate counsel with such joy? Why
       can he (or she) have patience in the perplexities and adversities
       of the present? Why can he (or she) have confident assurance
       with reference to the future and rejoice in the hope of the glory
       of God? It is because he (or she) cannot think of past, present,
       or future apart from union with Christ.'
    (d) This is why Luke said: 'and all who were appointed for eternal
       life believed.'
    (e) As Wayne Grudem puts it:
       'Since we did not exist before the foundation of the world... God,
       looking into the future and knowing that we would exist, thought
       of us being in a special relationship with Christ. He did not first
       choose us and later decide to relate us to Christ. Rather, while
       choosing us, he at the same time thought about us as belonging to
       Christ in a special way, as being 'in Christ'. Therefore, he thought
       about us as eventually having the right to share in the blessings of
       Christ's work.'

## 2  THE ACTUALISING OF OUR UNION WITH CHRIST: BEING JUSTIFIED BY FAITH

### A. This began with Christ's life on earth (Romans 5:10).
1. *During Christ's earthly ministry God thought of us as being 'in*
   *Christ'.*
    (a) Not that we were consciously present in Christ, since we did not
       exist then.
    (b) Not that we were present in Christ's body in some way.
2. *Rather, we were present in Christ only in God's thoughts.*

### B. The reason for this:  Jesus was our substitute even as he lived.
1. *He came to fulfil the Law* (Matthew 5:17).
2. *This he did!* (John 19:30). *And he did it for* us.

(a) When Jesus perfectly obeyed God for the whole of his life, God thought of us as having obeyed too: 'Through the obedience of the one man the many will be made righteous' (Romans 5:19).

(b) So Christ is our source of righteousness: 'It is because of him that you are in Christ Jesus, who has become for us wisdom from God – that is, our righteousness, holiness and redemption' (1 Corinthians 1:30; cf. Philippians 3:9).

C. **Because God thought of us as being 'in Christ', he also regarded our sins as belonging to Christ.**
1. *'God made him who had no sin to be sin for us, so that in him we might become the righteousness of God'* (2 Corinthians 5:21).
2. *The Lord 'laid on him the iniquity of us all'* (Isaiah 53:6).
   (a) These were sins we had not yet committed.
   (b) But God knew about them in advance.
3. *God also thought of us, as well as our sins, as belonging to Christ.*
   (a) When Christ died, God thought of us as having died.
      (1) Our old self was 'crucified with him' (Romans 6:6).
      (2) 'I have been crucified with Christ' (Galatians 2:20).
   (b) One died for all; 'therefore all died' (2 Corinthians 5:14).
      (1) Likewise we have been buried with Christ (Romans 6:4-11).
      (2) We have been raised with him (Ephesians 2:6).
4. *When Jesus returned to heaven, all the blessings of salvation were earned for us.*
   (a) God thought of these blessings as rightfully ours.
   (b) As though we earned them ourselves.

D. **All that Jesus did for us is ours – by faith (Romans 3:22-26).**
1. *Justification by faith: to be declared righteous by God.*
   (a) The Greek word is *dikaioo*, meaning 'to make righteous', 'to establish as righteous', 'to validate'.
   (b) Used 60 times in the New Testament, for example, Matthew 11:19; Romans 3:4, 20, 24, 26, 28, 30; Galatians 2:16; 5:4; Titus 3:7.
   (c) It is a legal transaction (Romans 4:5).
   (d) It may not be what we 'feel'; it is the way God reckons us (Romans 4:6-8).

2. *There are two sides to justification:*
   (a) Forgiveness of sins (Romans 3:25).
   (b) The imputation of Christ's righteousness (Romans 4:1-8).
      (1) To impute: put to the credit of.
      (2) The Greek word *logizomai*, meaning 'to charge with', is used 41 times in the New Testament, among them: Romans 4:3, 4, 5, 6, 8, 9; 6:11; Galatians 3:6.

3. *As a result: we are 'in Christ Jesus'* (Romans 8:1; 1 Corinthians 1:30).
   (a) We are regarded as a new creation: 'Therefore, if anyone is in Christ, he is a new creation; the old has gone, the new has come!' (2 Corinthians 5:17).
   (b) Such blessings are available only to those who are 'in Christ'; but if we are in Christ, these blessings are ours.

4. *John held to the same truth:* 'And this is the testimony: God has given us eternal life, and this life is in his Son' (1 John 5:11).

## 3   OUR SECURITY AS A RESULT OF OUR UNION WITH CHRIST

### A. Faith puts us in the family of God (1 John 3:1).
1. *Faith is the result of the Holy Spirit's work* (Ephesians 2:1-8).
2. *Those who are led by the Spirit are called sons of God* (Romans 8:14).
   (a) This sonship is the result of two things:
      (1) Receiving Christ by faith: 'Yet to all who received him, to those who believed in his name, he gave the right to become children of God – children born not of natural descent, nor of human decision or a husband's will, but born of God' (John 1:12-13).
      (2) Adoption by the Father: 'For he chose us in him before the creation of the world to be holy and blameless in his sight. In love he predestined us to be adopted as his sons through Jesus Christ, in accordance with his pleasure and will' (Ephesians 1:4).

### B. Question: What are the rights of the sons of God? Answer: the same rights as that of God's 'one and only' Son.
1. *When we are called sons of God the assumption is that we are given the privileges of sonship* (1 John 3:1).
2. *But how can we be called 'sons of God' if God has only one Son? Answer: by adoption into the Family.*
   (a) God has only one 'natural' Son: Jesus Christ (John 1:18; 3:16).
      (1) There can never be 'another' Son of God.
      (2) Jesus Christ of Nazareth is God's only Son.
   (b) But yet we are told that God will bring 'many sons to glory' (Hebrews 2:10).
      (1) Jesus Christ is the 'firstborn among many brothers' (Romans 8:29).
      (2) We are therefore Jesus' little brothers and sisters; he may truly be called our elder brother.

3. *As adopted children into the Family we are made co-heirs with God's one and only Son:* The Spirit himself testifies with our spirit that we are God's children. Now if we are children, then we are heirs – heirs of God and co-heirs with Christ, if indeed we share in his sufferings in order that we may also share in his glory' (Romans 8:16-17).
   (a) We are given a security in Christ which is the same as the Son has with the Father.
       (1) Jesus is 'in' the Father (John 10:38; 14:10).
       (2) How secure do you suppose Jesus is by being 'in the Father'?
   (b) The Bible could not be clearer; by giving us sonship there is the immediate assumption that we are as secure in the Family as Jesus.
       (1) That is the ultimate significance of being 'in Christ'.
       (2) If the Son's security in the Father is one thing, but our security 'in Christ' is another, what value does it have?
   (c) Our adoption was not carried out in the first place on the basis of works (2 Timothy 1:9).
       (1) We were chosen before we were born (Ephesians 1:4).
       (2) We did not adopt God; he adopted us.
   (d) God took us on board not because we were 'good enough' – but because he loved us: 'For he chose us in him before the creation of the world to be holy and blameless in his sight. In love he predestined us to be adopted as his sons through Jesus Christ, in accordance with his pleasure and will – to the praise of his glorious grace, which he has freely given us *in the* One he loves' (Ephesians 1:4-6).
       (1) 'In the One' is one of those 'in Christ' references we already referred to in Ephesians 1:4-13.
       (2) God put us 'in the One he loves' that we might be assured of his love from the beginning.

4. *God never wants us to doubt his love.*
   (a) Doubting parental love is a common experience.
   (b) Many of us know what it is to fear that our parents won't love us if we don't come up to their expectations.
   (c) God wanted to show what unconditional love is.
       (1) This he did when he showed his love for his Son (Matthew 3:17; 17:5).
       (2) Jesus never doubted his Father's love (John 15:9; 17:23-24).

5. *Question: Does God love us as much as he loves Jesus? Yes.*
   (a) We are 'co-heirs' with Christ (Romans 8:17).
   (b) 'I have given them the glory that you gave me, that they may be one as we are one: I in them and you in me. May they be brought

to complete unity to let the world know that you sent me and have loved them even as you have loved me' (John 17:22-23).

(c)   What do you suppose are the possibilities of Jesus being thrown out of the Godhead – and ceasing to be God's Son? Answer: none.
   (1)   That is the security we have.
   (2)   We are loved by the Father as much as he loved Jesus (that's a lot!).
   (3)   We are as secure in the Father's love as Jesus was (if only all of us will believe it!).
   (4)   'I give them eternal life, and they shall never perish; no-one can snatch them out of my hand' (John 10:28).

6.  *This is why Paul loved the phrase 'in Christ'.*
   (a)   Christ is in the Father – eternally secure.
   (b)   We are in Christ – eternally secure.

## 4   OUR GLORIFICATION: THE ULTIMATE PURPOSE OF BEING 'IN CHRIST' (1 John 3:2).

### A.   What is the Father's good pleasure, which he purposed 'in Christ'?

1.  *Answer:* 'In order that we, who were the first to hope in Christ, might be for the praise of his glory. And you also were included in Christ when you heard the word of truth, the gospel of your salvation. Having believed, you were marked in him with a seal, the promised HolySpirit' (Ephesians 1:12-13).

2.  *This takes place when we are glorified:* 'And those he predestined, he also called; those he called, he also justified; those he justified, he also glorified' (Romans 8:30).

3.  *This is when we will reach Stage Four of Augustine's four stages:*
   (a) Able to sin (creation); (b) Not able not to sin (after the Fall); (c) Able not to sin (after being saved); (d) Not able to sin (glorification).

### B.   Our glorification is therefore assured. Why?

(1) Because we have been adopted, (2) because our adoption is 'in Christ', (3) because Christ intercedes for us (Romans 8:34), (4) because he is coming again (1 Thessalonians 4:13-18).

## CONCLUSION

Where will we spend eternity? If we are in Christ then our destiny is heaven. Being 'in Christ' is the guarantee of the believer's security with all its privileges. It is how God thinks about us. It began with predestination; it continues with our being called and justified; it will be finalised at glorification. The related subject of 'Christ in us' is dealt with in the chapter called 'The Christian's Lifestyle'.

# 20

# JUSTIFICATION BY FAITH

## INTRODUCTION

**A. This teaching has a bearing on many other subjects.**
1. *It is at the heart of soteriology (doctrine of salvation).*
2. *It is what God's elect are chosen to* (Romans 8:30).
3. *It is what (given some thought) proves the eternal security of the believer.*
4. *It is the teaching that broke open the Great Reformation of the sixteenth century.*
   (a) It is what largely separates Protestants from Roman Catholics.
   (b) It is an assumed teaching of all Protestants, no matter what denomination.

**B. This teaching is largely associated with the Protestant Reformer Martin Luther (1483-1546).**
1. *Luther did not discover this teaching; he re-discovered it.*
   (a) It was for him a discovery.
   (b) But he got it all from the apostle Paul.
2. *It is hard for us to believe that this teaching largely lay behind a cloud for 1,500 years.*
   (a) It is absolutely clear in the writings of St. Paul.
   (b) It is consistent with the teachings of most of the Church Fathers.
      (1) Eastern Fathers, e.g. Chrysostom and Athanasius.
      (2) Western Fathers, e.g. Ambrose and St. Augustine.
   (c) But the issue did not appear to come up.
      (1) Adolf Harnack wryly observed that Marcion (second century) was the first to understand Paul but that he also 'misunderstood him'.
      (2) Perhaps people so feared Marcion that they stayed away from any teaching that faintly resembled his. Marcion was a Gnostic but also said something that paralleled Luther's re-discovery.

## 1 HISTORICAL BACKGROUND
**A. Soteriology did not emerge in early church history as the issue that needed attention (at least as it appeared at the time). The issues largely were:**

1. *Defending the faith against Caesar.*
   (a) One confessed Christ under fear of death.
   (b) Hence baptism sent a signal that one was prepared to die for Jesus Christ.
2. *Confessing Jesus Christ as Lord was the issue.*
   (a) Caesar was not Lord; Jesus was.
   (b) The theological content of Christ's lordship was not as clear to some as it may be to us now.
3. *Fighting against Gnosticism.*
   (a) Some Gnostics were prepared to affirm Christ's deity but not his humanity.
      (1) They were called Docetists.
      (2) Greek *dokeo*: to appear; Christ only appeared to have a body but it was not really fleshly.
   (b) The Apostles' Creed was drawn up to fight Gnosticism.
      (1) It emphasised the human side of Jesus.
      (2) Christology, not soteriology (e.g. 'forgiveness of sins') was the main issue.
4. *Emerging moralistic Christianity.*
   (a) It has been cogently argued by T F Torrance that there was scarcely a theology of grace at all in the early church.
   (b) The need to be above reproach was seen as the main issue among believers.
5. *Ecclesiology was somewhat dominant.*
   (a) The role of the bishop.
   (b) The ascendancy of the bishop of Rome.
   (c) The place of the Lord's Supper.
6. *Not until the time of St. Augustine (c.400) was there much discussion regarding soteriology.*
   (a) Even then the issue was grace rather than what is given to us by faith alone.
   (b) Nothing in Augustine was inconsistent with what Luther would teach; it only has to be said that Augustine did not perceive the issue clearly.

B. **Prevailing teaching of Rome prior to Luther.**
   1. The Bible should be hidden from ordinary people.
   2. The doctrine of purgatory.
   3. The doctrine of penance.
   4. Faith is assent to the teaching of the church.
   5. Faith plus works is the way of salvation.

## C. Martin Luther

1. *Brief summary of his life.*
   (a) born 1483, Eisleben, Germany; son of a coal miner.
   (b) Thunderstorm experience: 'Help me, St. Anne and I will become a monk.'
   (c) Entered monastery; completed his doctorate.
   (d) Lectured in theology 1512-1516.
   (e) Ninety-five Theses 1517.
   (f) Excommunicated from Rome 1520.
   (g) Married 1525.
   (h) Died 1547.

2. *By faith alone: theological breakthrough.*
   (a) Justice of God in Romans 1:17 means God's 'passive' justice.
      (1) Active justice: what one does in order to get satisfaction.
      (2) Passive justice refers to God doing nothing to get satisfaction.
   (b) God's justice was satisfied not by what he did but by what we do, namely, our faith.
      (1) Later on Calvin would demonstrate God's active justice by God punishing his Son.
      (2) But for Luther the whole matter was settled by our own faith.
   (c) By faith 'alone'.
      (1) Luther saw that God's justice was satisfied by faith plus nothing.
      (2) That faith, to be faith, was faith 'only'.

3. *For Luther this discovery was profound.*
   (a) It meant that Rome's teaching was faulty.
   (b) The doctrine of purgatory was not only unbiblical but led to gross corruption.
   (c) It set ordinary people free.
   (d) Luther himself got married!

## D. John Calvin's clarification

1. *Calvin and Luther never met.*
   (a) Calvin wrote Luther a letter which the latter never saw.
   (b) Calvin agreed with Luther (save on the Lord's Supper) but added clarification to Luther's views.

2. *Calvin's main contributions (on this matter) were these:*
   (a) He emphasised what *Christ* does as going before what we do (i.e. our faith).
   (b) He pointed to three causes of justification:

(1) Meritorious cause (what Christ does).

(2) Instrumental cause (what we do – believe); hence 'faith is the instrument' of our justification.

(3) Efficient cause (the effectual work of the Holy Spirit in producing faith).

(c) He showed that we can have assurance that we have been justified.

(d) He provided greater clarification regarding the imputation of Christ's righteousness when we believe.

## 2 OUTLINE OF JUSTIFICATION BY FAITH (Romans 1:17-4:12).

### A. The righteousness of God revealed.

1. *The Greek word is* dikaiosune *and it has two meanings which are often used interchangeably.*

   (a) 'Righteousness', meaning the righteousness of the Law.

      (1) It includes the moral righteousness that God requires.

      (2) It means the righteousness that Christ provides.

   (b) 'Justice'; what God demands owing to his essential nature.

      (1) It refers to what lies behind his wrath.

      (2) It means that which must be satisfied before his wrath can be appeased.

2. *The gospel (good news) means the unveiling of God's righteousness/justice.*

   (a) When we preach the gospel we are at once declaring two things simultaneously:

      (1) God is angry with sin.

      (2) God's anger has been appeased by Jesus Christ.

   (b) This is why Paul proceeds to talk about God's anger toward sin (Romans 1:18, the NIV left out the Greek word *gar* – 'for').

      (1) When the gospel is preached it should show why good news is good news: that although God is angry with sin there is still hope.

   (c) The full gospel must ultimately include the fact of God's wrath.

      (1) Some today refer to a 'full gospel' as including what the Holy Spirit will do with believers.

      (2) But in actual fact the full gospel means the simultaneous revelation of mercy *and* wrath!

### B. From 'faith to faith'.

1. *Here is the most overlooked teaching today when it comes to the doctrine of justification by faith.*

   (a) It is implicit in Calvin's clarification of Luther.

    (b)  It combines two of the 'causes':
        (1)  Meritorious cause – what Christ did for us.
        (2)  Instrumental cause – what we must do in order to have the benefit of Christ's merit.

2.  *It is in these three words: 'faith to faith'.*
    (a)  The Greek word is *pistis*.
        (1)  The Authorised Version makes it absolutely clear.
        (2)  The New International Version shows it only as a footnote.
    (b)  It is the heart of Paul's teaching and the first statement he makes when introducing this teaching in Romans 1:17.
        (1)  It must not be glossed over. Otherwise Romans 3:22 will make little sense.

3.  *'Faith to faith' means two faiths.*
    (a)  One faith comes first: meritorious cause.
        (1)  It is what Jesus has done for us.
        (2)  It literally refers to his own very faith as a man when he was on this earth.
    (b)  The second faith follows: instrumental cause.
        (1)  It is what we must have to be saved.
        (2)  If Jesus is the only one who believes then we will perish; we too must believe.
    (c)  It is not until Romans 3:22 that this is clear, but only in the literal translation of the Greek.
        (2)  The Authorised Version is correct when it says: 'Even the righteousness of God which is by the faith of Jesus Christ unto all and upon all them that believe'.
    (d)  Romans 3:22 shows:
        (1)  What Paul meant by righteousness of God in Romans 1:17.
        (2)  What Paul meant by 'faith to faith' in Romans 1:17.
    (e)  Romans 3:22 thus demonstrates three things:
        (1)  The first faith is the faith of Jesus Christ.
        (2)  What Christ did is for 'all': 'unto all and upon all'.
        (3)  The benefit of what Christ did is null and void except 'them that believe' (see Romans 3:25).
    (f)  Hence, Christ's faith must be followed by our faith or there will be no *justification*.
    (g)  What is Christ's faith?
        (1)  His perfect faith as a man.
        (2)  His perfect faith as our substitute.
        (3)  His perfect obedience to the Father (keeping the Law).
        (4)  His death on the cross (Romans 3:25-26).

- (h) Paul said, 'I live by the faith of the Son of God' (Galatians 2:20, AV).
  - (1) This was the basis of Paul's own justification.
  - (2) He lived and breathed this faith.
  - (3) Note: it can even be extended to include Christ's perfect faith when interceding for us at God's right hand!

## 3  IMPUTATION OF CHRIST'S RIGHTEOUSNESS

### A. What happens when our faith follows Christ's faith?
1. *It ratifies what Christ did for us.*
   - (a) Ratify: to make officially valid.
   - (b) Until what Christ did is ratified it is of no value to us.
     - (1) 'All that Christ did and suffered for the human race is of no value', said Calvin. That is, until we believe.

2. *This means that all that Christ did for us is ours!*
   - (a) He died for all, believed perfectly for all, fulfilled the Law for all; but it is not ours until we too believe.
   - (b) But *when* we believe, all he did for us is ours. We are instantly granted: (1) forgiveness of sins; (2) imputation of righteousness; (3) eternal life.

3. *The forgiveness of sins* (Romans 3:25; Ephesians 1:7).
   - (a) It is difficult to know which comes first in the order of Paul's thinking:
     - (1) Imputation of righteousness, implied by Romans 3:21.
     - (2) Forgiveness of sins.

4. *What we tend to be most conscious of is the forgiveness of all our sins.*
   - (a) This is because we have been convicted of our sins, and made sorry.
   - (b) Thus the feeling of being forgiven is very wonderful indeed (1 John 1:9).

5. *This too seems to have been most prominent in Luke's theology* (Acts 2:38; 5:31; 10:43; 13:38; 26:18).
   - (a) It anticipates the doctrine of imputation – not only of righteousness but of 'no sin' (Romans 4:6-8).
   - (b) In other words, God instantly puts to our credit 'no sin' – it is just as if I'd never sinned!
     - (1) This is the way it is in God's sight.
     - (2) The 'forgiveness' however is what we feel by assurance of faith in God's promise.

**B. The imputation of righteousness (Romans 4:5).**
1. *The righteousness of Christ is put to our credit.*
    (a) How do we know that?
       (1) He came to fulfil the Law (Matthew 5:17).
       (2) He did everything for us – as our substitute (Romans 5:10).
    (b) Thus everything he did is transferred to us as though we did it ourselves; e.g.:
       (1) Being baptised (Matthew 3:15).
       (2) Believing perfectly (Galatians 2:16).
       (3) Perfect sanctification (1 Corinthians 1:30).

2. *This implicitly proves the eternal security of the believer.*
    (a) For this is the way God sees us from the moment of faith; as righteous as Jesus.
    (b) This means that in the sight of God I am no more righteous fifty years after my conversion than I was the day I was saved.
    (c) Where is boasting then? It is excluded (Romans 3:27; Ephesians 2:8-9).

**C. Eternal life (John 3:16).**
1. *Eternal life in the New Testament is described in four ways:*
    (a) The very life of Jesus – the Eternal Son (1 John 1:1).
    (b) The quality of knowing God (John 17:3; 1 Timothy 6:12).
    (c) Life beyond the grave (Mark 10:30).
    (d) Heaven as opposed to hell (Matthew 25:46).

2. *The life eternal that issues from justification by faith is basically two things, in this order:*
    (a) That we will go to heaven when we die.
    (b) That we may come to know God intimately.

**D. Justification by faith must be understood as being *forensic*.**
1. It is a legal transaction concerned with what is lawful in God's eyes. It is also a double transaction: what happened with regard to the Father and the Son at the cross of Calvary and what happens between God and the believer at the moment of conversion.

## CONCLUSION
Because justification by faith is forensic there is nothing necessarily that we may feel. But although we may not feel righteous – we are; although we may not feel forgiven – we are. Justified is the way God sees us, not the way we see ourselves. But if God sees us as righteous, that is what matters. But when we are *convinced* that God sees us that way, we have *assurance* of our justification.

# 21

## THE ETERNAL SECURITY OF THE BELIEVER

### INTRODUCTION

A. **The doctrine stated: those who truly believe the gospel can never be lost, no matter what they do.**
B. **The purpose of this study is not:**
   1. *To convince those who do not believe this doctrine.*
      (a) Some have made up their minds.
      (b) Some have never been taught anything else.
   2. *To divide sincere Christians.*
      (a) Some of the best of God's people do not believe this doctrine.
      (b) The church has enough divisions already.

C. **The purpose of this study is:**
   1. *To help those who want to believe it but are afraid it isn't true.*
   2. *To show how it fits with the doctrine of predestination.*
      (a) Election goes *before* faith in Christ.
      (b) Eternal security *follows* faith in Christ.
         (1) Those who are called are predestinated.
         (2) Their predestination does not stop with calling but with glorification (Romans 8:30).

D. **Personal testimony.**
   1. *I have not always believed 'once saved, always saved'.*
      (a) I was brought up in a Wesleyan type of Christian background.
      (b) I was deeply biased against this teaching. It was said to have been born in hell.
      (c) My view changed as a result of an experience of God on 31st October, 1955.
      (d) I wasn't prepared for the eventual change of doctrine.
      (e) I felt I alone believed new things I learned from the Bible.
      (f). For what it's worth, I have yet to convince any of my old friends.
      (g) It is revealed only by the Holy Spirit (I hope I'm not being unfair in putting it like this).
      (h) The only ones I have persuaded (that I know of) are:
         (1) Those who wanted to believe it.
         (2) New Christians who didn't have any theological biases.

E. **Why is this teaching important?**
1. *It will give you confidence.*
   (a) It is a wonderful thing to know that you are not *saved* by works (Ephesians 2:8-9).
   (b) It is a wonderful thing to know that you are not *kept* saved by works (Philippians 1:6).
   (c) It is a wonderful thing to know that you will never go to hell – but heaven is your home (John 10:28).

2. *It coheres with the whole of scripture.*
   (a) Some scriptures appear to be against this teaching. However, they are decidedly outweighed by those that support it.
   (b) Those scriptures that appear (at first sight) to contradict this teaching do not refer to being saved at all. They refer to a different theological perspective (e.g., fellowship with God; the Kingdom of God; rewards).

F. **Is not this teaching dangerous?  No.**
1. *No truth is dangerous when it is properly understood and applied.*
2. *This teaching has been made to appear dangerous:*
   (a) By those who are selective with the truth (who don't want to believe *all* of the Bible).
   (b) When this teaching is not set in the context of three important New Testament truths:
      (1) The Kingdom of God.
      (2) God's chastening (disciplining).
      (3) The Judgement Seat of Christ.

G. **There are two sides to this teaching.**
1. Objective side: what the New Testament teaches.
2. Subjective side: does this teaching apply to me?

## 1 THE DOCTRINE REPEATED: THOSE WHO TRULY BELIEVE THE GOSPEL CAN NEVER BE LOST, NO MATTER WHAT THEY DO

A. **One critic of my book *Once Saved, Always Saved* said that what I taught is true but it is too clear!**
1. *He was happy to affirm the first part of the above statement.*
2. *He felt that the second part was inviting problems.*
   (a) I answer: It is either true or it isn't.
   (b) We all want to know the answer to these questions:
      (1) Is eternal security conditional upon my behaviour? If so, we are back to works.

(2) Is eternal security unconditional – regardless of my behaviour? If so, it is by grace (Romans 11:6).

3. *Many believe the doctrine as I have defined it.*
   (a) Yet some of them feel it is dangerous to be so clear.
   (b) They feel it is spiritually healthy for the weaker Christian to be in some doubt – to keep him/her on their toes!
   (c) I regard their approach as:
       (1) Dishonest – what God has unveiled needs to be unveiled.
       (2) Controlling – lest people take advantage of free grace.

4. *I do not know of a single case in which this is not taught in the vestry (assuming the pastor is a Calvinist).*
   (a) When discouraged or backslidden Christians appear, the last thing that will help them is to say, 'You are not saved.'
       (1) If such were true, they may or may not want to be saved.
       (2) If they do, and they repent (as best as they know how), what will happen the next time they sin – say they weren't saved after all?
   (b) It is pastorally the most comforting doctrine there is:
       (1) When one feels so ashamed that he sinned.
       (2) When it comes time to die.

## B. What is saving faith? Trusting Christ alone.

1. *It is the sure confidence that Jesus Christ did all that is required of us by:*
   (a) Who he is – the God-man.
   (b) What he did:
       (1) Lived without sin for us (Romans 5:10).
       (2) Died for (or instead of) us (Romans 5:8).
       (3) Rose from the dead (Romans 10:9).
2. *It is the persuasion that we will go to heaven – not hell – by:*
   (a) His complete work (life, death, resurrection).
   (b) Our faith: transferring our trust from our good works to what he has already done for us.

## C. What is true of the person who has saving faith?

1. *He or she will be given assurance of salvation.*
   (a) This assurance has degrees.
   (b) This assurance may come in stages; it almost always does.
2. *He/she will have a desire to please God.*
   (a) The ability to believe is by the Holy Spirit (John 6:44).
   (b) The Holy Spirit who gives that ability lives in us (Romans 8:9).
   (c) The Holy Spirit guarantees holiness (2 Thessalonians 2:13).

(1) Any holiness below is by degrees (Romans 6:11ff.).

(2) All holiness below is in stages (2 Corinthians 3:18).

(d) The lack of holiness in us means:

(1) The sure chastening of God.

(2) Forfeiting (losing) our inheritance.

(i) In the Kingdom of God below.

(ii) At the Judgement Seat of Christ above.

## 2 THERE ARE SOME ESSENTIAL DOCTRINES THAT GUARANTEE THE ETERNAL SECURITY OF THE BELIEVER

### A. Our position as sons of God (John 1:12-13).

1. *In a word: we are 'born' of God.*

(a) The Greek word *gennao* means to beget, generate, produce, bring forth.

(1) If one is born of God, it is God who has done the bringing forth or producing.

(2) God gave us life (Ephesians 2:5).

(b) It is called the New Birth, being 'born again' (John 3:3).

(1) What is by flesh (natural birth) is called *procreation*.

(2) What is by Spirit (spiritual birth) is called *regeneration*.

2. *Does the New Birth in and of itself guarantee that we will never be lost? Yes.*

(a) Our new creation is engendered by God's own Spirit who, according to Jesus, would abide in us 'forever' (John 14:16).

(1) The new life is called God's Spirit (1 Corinthians 3:16).

(2) The new life is called God's seed (1 John 3:9).

(b) The new life is the life of God himself: God cannot die!

(1) This life was not given according to our works (2 Timothy 1:9).

(2) It is unthinkable that this life would be turned over to us, as if we must now 'keep ourselves alive'.

(c) This is why we have certain promises (Philippians 1:6; John 10:28).

### B. Our adoption into the family (Ephesians 1:4-5).

1. *Whereas the New Birth is God's internal act by which we are* born *into the family, adoption is his external act by which we are* chosen *as members of his family.*

(a) This further demonstrates how predestination and eternal security fit together.

(1) Predestination and adoption lie totally outside our control.

(2) Would God predestine us to faith and then allow us to lose what he predestined?

- (b) Adoption is another term for election.
    - (1) We did not choose God; he chose us.
    - (2) Children don't choose to be adopted; this is only what the parents do.

2. *There is an analogy (comparison) between Jesus' security in the Godhead and our security in the family.*
    - (a) But Jesus is God's 'natural' Son.
        - (1) God has adopted as his sons all who believe in Jesus.
        - (2) Jesus is called 'the firstborn among many brothers' (Romans 8:29).
    - (b) God always had a Son; he is the eternal Son.
        - (1) He waited for the fullness of time before he 'sent' his Son (Galatians 4:4).
        - (2) But he was always God's Son.
    - (c) Our adoption into the family has been known from the foundation of the world (Ephesians 1:4-5).
        - (1) But it did not become known until after we were born – and 'born again'.
        - (2) Behind our being made sons by regeneration was God's choice – called Adoption.
    - (d) This means we are Jesus' little brothers and sisters.
        - (1) Jesus may be called our Elder Brother.
        - (2) He is not ashamed to call us brothers (Hebrews 2:11).
    - (e) What do you suppose is the possibility of Jesus being disenfranchised from the Godhead?
        - (1) We are called 'co-heirs' with Christ (Romans 8:17).
        - (2) We are 'in Christ' (Ephesians 1:4ff.).
    - (f) Bottom line: our security in the family as children of God is as strong as that of Jesus in the Godhead.
        - (1) God loves his Son (Matthew 3:17).
        - (2) God loves his children as much as he loves his Son (John 17:23).

C. **As children of God we are eternally secure:**
    1. From the standpoint of regeneration – the life of God which cannot die.
    2. From the standpoint of adoption – the choice of God which cannot be undone.

D. **As can be seen in the previous chapter, the doctrine of justification by faith in and by itself proves the eternal security of the believer.**

**3   SCRIPTURES THAT SEEM TO OPPOSE THIS DOCTRINE.**

**A. There is not a single verse in the Bible that suggests we can lose our salvation – only our inheritance or reward (Colossians 3:24).**
  1. *There is a difference between being saved and receiving a reward at the Judgement Seat of Christ* (1 Corinthians 3:12-15).
     (a)  All who are saved will go to heaven (John 5:24).
     (b)  Not all who go to heaven will receive a reward (2 Corinthians 5:10).

  2. *It is possible to lose the reward and still be saved* (1 Corinthians 3:15).
     (a)  It depends on how we build on the foundation.
         (1)  Some build wood, hay, straw.
         (2)  Some build gold, silver, costly stones.
     (b)  The fire will expose the quality of each one's work.
         (1)  Wood, hay, straw will be burned up.
         (2)  Gold, silver, precious stones will survive.

  3. *Losing the reward was Paul's concern* (1 Corinthians 9:27).
     (a)  He was not fearful of losing his soul.
     (b)  He was fearful of being rejected for the prize.

**B. Parallel to this is the New Testament understanding of the Kingdom of God.**
  1. *The Kingdom of God is described in several ways.*
     (a)  The reign of Christ, which is future (2 Timothy 4:1).
     (b)  The power of Christ, which is at hand (Luke 11:20).
     (c)  The intimate knowing of Christ, which comes by tribulation (Acts 14:22).
     (d)  The inheritance of Christ, which comes by obedience (Galatians 5:21).

  2. *The Kingdom of God is entered here below in a two-fold manner: like a circle within a circle.*
     (a)  By the New Birth (John 3:3).
     (b)  By obedience (Ephesians 5:5).
         (1)  The larger circle is entered by conversion (Colossians 1:13).
         (2)  The inner circle is entered by tribulation (Acts 14:22).

  3. *It is in this sense that scripture warns against losing our inheritance in the Kingdom.*
     (a)  Sometimes the Kingdom of God and salvation are the same thing (John 3:3). But not always (1 Corinthians 6:9-10).
     (c)  This is the reason the incestuous man of Corinth was presumed to be saved (1 Corinthians 5:5).

## 4  RELEVANCE OF THE DOCTRINE OF CHASTENING  (Hebrews 12:5-11).

A. **What happens to those who abuse their rights as sons?**
   1. *As we have seen, they can be disinherited. Sonship and inheritance are not the same thing.*
      (a)  This refers to the Kingdom of God below (Ephesians 5:5).
      (b)  This relates to the Judgement Seat of Christ above (2 Corinthians 5:10).

   2. *But there is more: they experience God's chastening.*
      (a)  Chastening is enforced learning.
      (b)  It is God's way of ensuring holiness (Hebrews 12:10-11).

B. **There are three stages of chastening:**
   1. *Internal chastening.*
      (a)  By the Word and Holy Spirit within.
      (b)  This is the best way to have your problems solved!

   2. *External chastening (Plan B).*
      (a)  By providence from outside us.
      (b)  This is sometimes the only way God can get our attention.

   3. *Terminal chastening (when all the above fail).*
      (a)  This is being saved by fire at the Judgement Seat of Christ (1 Corinthians 3:15).
      (b)  It is when all works are burned up and no reward is given.

C. **Chastening, or disciplining, is for true believers only.**
   1.  It proves we are sons and daughters.
   2.  The purpose: to make us more like Jesus.

**CONCLUSION**
It is a wonderful thing to know that we can never be lost; that God loves his adopted sons as much as he loves Jesus. But God doesn't like it one bit when we take advantage of this teaching. Those who abuse their rights as adopted sons can lose their reward and experience severe chastening. We must take every care that this does not happen to us.

# 22

# THE GRACE OF TOTAL FORGIVENESS

## INTRODUCTION

A. **Christianity is unique in the religions of the world because of these three truths:**
 1. *Its founder is alive and well.*
    (a) All other leaders are dead.
    (b) Only Jesus Christ is still alive (Revelation 1:18).

 2. *All good that takes place is initiated by God.*
    (a) The truth or falsehood in religion is, who initiates what you do.
    (b) With Christianity alone God takes the initiative (John 6:44; James 1:18).

 3. *Total forgiveness is given to us by sheer grace* (Ephesians 2:8-9).
    (a) Other religions offer forgiveness – but on the basis of good works.
    (b) Christianity alone offers forgiveness by the death of God's Son (Romans 5:8-9).

B. **This subject is to be understood in two ways: objectively and subjectively.**
 1. *Objectively: our forgiveness in Christ.*
    (a) What are the benefits of Christ's death, with particular reference to forgiveness of sins?
    (b) To what extent are we forgiven of all our sins?

 2. *Subjectively: our forgiving others.*
    (a) What is the fruit of our being forgiven, with particular reference to forgiving others?
    (b) To what extent must we forgive others?

C. **Total forgiveness**
 1. *The Lord has totally forgiven us of all our sins.*
    (a) Total forgiveness: as though we had never sinned.
    (b) This forgiveness is given to us on the basis of Christ's death on the cross.

 2. *We must forgive others of all they have done to us.*
    (a) Total forgiveness: as though they had done nothing wrong.
    (b) Our forgiving others is on the basis of God's goodness to us.

D. **Why is this study important?**
 1. It reminds us of God's goodness to us (Psalm 103:10-14).
 2. It reminds us of what God has done through his Son.
 3. It reminds us of the benefits of being justified by faith.
 4. It reminds us of our responsibility to others in the light of God's forgiveness.
 5. The art of forgiving others can provide the greatest spiritual breakthrough you have ever known.

1 **THE OBJECTIVE SIDE: GOD HAS TOTALLY FORGIVEN US IN CHRIST**

A. **The benefits of Christ's death can be summed up like this:**
 1. *Forgiveness of sins* (Colossians 1:14).
   (a) This is the immediate consequence of justification by faith.
     (1) Justification: being made righteous.
     (2) It is 'forensic' – legal – that is the way God sees us in Christ, not the way we may feel.
   (b) This is ours by faith alone (not works) (Ephesians 2:8-9).
     (1) It is available to all (Romans 3:22; 5:15).
     (2) It is applied however by faith (Romans 3:26).

 2. *Imputed righteousness* (Romans 4:3).
   (a) Imputed: put to the credit of.
   (b) All that Jesus was and did for us is transferred to us:
     (1) His sinless life is put to our credit as though we were without sin (Romans 4:8).
     (2) His blood assures us that the Father does not hold our sin against us but sees us 'in Christ' (Ephesians 1:7).

 3. *Eternal life* (John 3:16).
   (a) 'Eternal life' is used more than one way in the Bible.
     (1) It is the very life of Jesus Christ himself (1 John 1:1).
     (2) It is knowing the Father (John 17:3).
     (3) It is endless duration in heaven (Mark 10:30).
   (b) But the main way eternal life is understood in the present study is summed up: we will go to heaven, not hell, when we die.

B. **To what extent are our sins forgiven?**
 1. *Sins of the past* (Romans 3:25; Hebrews 8:12).
   (a) Sins committed before we were converted.
   (b) All of them are washed away (Revelation 1:5).

    2. *Present sin* (1 John 1:7-9).
        (a) The blood continues to cleanse our sins; but on the condition:
            (1) That we walk in the light.
            (2) That we confess them.
        (b) What is forfeited if we don't walk in the light?
            (1) Fellowship with the Father.
            (2) Superstructure of gold, silver, precious stones (1 Corinthians 3:12-15).

    3. *Future sins* (Romans 8:33-39).
        (a) Because we are 'in Christ' by faith our position is as secure as his.
            (1) He cannot lose his place in the Godhead.
            (2) We cannot lose our place in him (John 10:28).
        (b) God loves us as much as he loves Jesus (John 17:23).

## C. What about chastening or being disciplined?

    1. *Chastening/disciplining: enforced learning.*
        (a) Internal chastening: the warning of the Holy Spirit.
        (b) External chastening: when God steps in from without.
        (c) Terminal chastening: when no further repentance is granted (Hebrews 6:4-6); it could mean a premature death (1 Corinthians 11:30).

    2. *Question: if God totally forgives us why does he chasten us? Answer: because he loves us* (Hebrews 12:6).
        (a) Chastening is not God 'getting even' (Psalm 103:10).
        (b) Chastening is God treating us as sons (Hebrews 12:7-8).
            (1) A parent disciplines his child *because* he loves the child, not because he is holding a grudge.
            (2) Disciplining is given to improve us (Hebrews 12:10-11).

    3. *Chastening is given to us not because we haven't been forgiven but because we* have *been forgiven.*
        (a) It is the proof of forgiveness, the proof of sonship.
        (b) Not to be chastened is an ominous sign that we *haven't* been forgiven!

## 2  THE SUBJECTIVE SIDE: OUR FORGIVING OTHERS

## A. There is yet another benefit that comes by Jesus' death on the cross: we are given the Holy Spirit (Romans 8:9).

    1. *The Holy Spirit is a person who, as it were, took the place of Jesus in the lives of the disciples* (John 14:16).

2. *The Holy Spirit is a person who is also very sensitive* (Ephesians 4:30).
   (a) He can be grieved, or quenched (1 Thessalonians 5:19).
   (b) The result of grieving the Spirit is a diminishing of fellowship with God (1 John 1:7).
       (1) The grieving of the Spirit does not forfeit eternal salvation.
       (2) The grieving of the Spirit forfeits clear thinking, presence of mind.

3. *The chief way we grieve the Holy Spirit is by bitterness and an unforgiving spirit* (Ephesians 4:31-32).
   (a) Bitterness always seems justified at the time we feel and show it.
   (b) For this reason we seldom are conscious of grieving the Holy Spirit *when* we do it; we realise it later – to our regret.

B. **What should flow mostly from our being forgiven of all our sins is gratitude (Romans 6:22).**
   1. *Sanctification can be called 'the doctrine of gratitude'.*
      (a) We live lives of holiness not in order to ensure a place in heaven; we've already got that by grace through faith (Ephesians 2:8-9).
      (b) We live holy lives out of gratitude: 'Thank you, Lord, for saving my soul.'

   2. *One of the greatest proofs of gratitude is that we forgive others as we have been forgiven.*
      (a) When I know of how much God has forgiven me I can well afford to forgive you!
      (b) But when I don't forgive you I have shown my ingratitude to God for forgiving me.
          (1) Not to forgive is a sign of self-righteousness.
          (2) Not to forgive is to imply I am better than you; I would never do what you have done.
      (c) And yet when I carefully examine what I have been forgiven of I will see that I have no right whatever to condemn another (Matthew 7:1-2).

   3. *God hates ingratitude* (Romans 1:21).
      (a) When we are conscious that all our sins are forgiven, we will be thankful.
      (b) This forgiveness leaves us without excuse when we don't forgive others.

C. **Our forgiving others moreover is a command (Ephesians 4:32).**
   1. *It is put in the Lord's Prayer* (Matthew 6:12).
      (a)   When we pray it we claim to have forgiven others!
      (b)   Could it be that the Lord's Prayer has made liars out of us?
   2. *It is put as a summary of the Lord's Prayer, as if being the main reason the prayer itself was given:* 'For if you forgive men when they sin against you, your heavenly Father will also forgive you. But if you do not forgive men their sins, your Father will not forgive your sins' (Matthew 6:14-15).
   3. *Forgiving others is the central theme in the Parable of the Unmerciful Servant* (Matthew 18:21-35).
   4. *It is possibly what lies behind praying in faith* (Mark 11:24-25).

3  **THE PROOF OF TOTAL FORGIVENESS: KEEPING NO RECORD OF WRONGS (1 CORINTHIANS 13:5).**

A. **Others are kept from the knowledge of our sins (Genesis 45:1).**
   1. *When God forgives us we are assured that our sins will never be held against us* (Hebrews 8:12).
      (a)   Nobody will ever know what it is we have been forgiven of.
      (b)   God washes our sins away so that at the Judgement Seat of Christ there is no record of our sins.

   2. *We are commanded to forgive others as God has forgiven us!* (Ephesians 4:32).
      (a)   This means we will shield others from knowing what a person has done to us.
         (1)   We protect the identity of that person who has hurt us, just as Joseph kept all in Egypt from knowing what his brothers did to him.
         (2)   We refuse to let anybody know who hurt us – or what it was they did.
      (b)   The proof we *haven't* forgiven: we tell what we know about the person who hurt us.

B. **Others are relieved of any fear due to their sins (Genesis 45:3-4).**
   1. *When God forgives us he wants us to know his love not his wrath* (Romans 5). *He doesn't want us to be afraid and so he puts us at ease* (1 John 1:9).
   2. *When we totally forgive others we will not let them fear us.*
      (a)   We will put them at ease.
      (b)   The proof we *haven't* forgiven: we want them to worry over what they have done – and fear that we might expose them.

C. **One is encouraged to forgive himself as opposed to being forever sorry for what he has done (Genesis 45:5).**
  1. *When God forgives he forgets* (Jeremiah 31:31-34).
     (a) It doesn't mean he doesn't know our past – of course he knows.
     (b) But it is forgotten in the sense of having been dealt with.
D. **One is enabled to save face (Genesis 45:8).**
  1. *When God forgives he gives us a future and says, 'As for the past leave it to me'* (Romans 8:28).
     (a) He causes the past, however bad, to work together for good.
     (b) It can begin to seem as if that is the way it was supposed to be!
        (1) Caution: that something works for good doesn't mean it was right at the time.
        (2) But God can make it seem that way – to let us save face!

  2. *When we have totally forgiven others we will let them save face.*
     (a) We will refuse to let them feel guilty: we will show we are no different from them, given the same circumstances.
     (b) The proof we *haven't* forgiven: we want the person who has hurt us to lose face. Something Christ never does.

E. **The keeping no record of wrongs continues on and on.**
  1. *God gives us an eternal salvation* (Hebrews 5:9).
     (a) He doesn't just forgive us once; he keeps on doing it.
     (b) He doesn't later change his mind and decide, after all, what we did was so bad it must be reported.

  2. *When we have totally forgiven others we will do it on and on and on* (Matthew 18:21-22).
     (a) It is not enough that we do it once. Or twice.
     (b) The proof we *haven't* totally forgiven is that we later give in and break all of the above principles. What if *God* did that?

## 4   WHAT IF WE DON'T FORGIVE OTHERS?

A. **What is not true is that we lose our salvation.**
  1. We are sealed to the Day of Redemption which will occur at the Second Coming (Ephesians 4:30).
  2. To lose one's salvation is not the meaning of Matthew 6:14-15 or Matthew 18:35.

B. **What it does mean:**
  1. *We lose fellowship with the Father.*
     (a) The reason for the Lord's Prayer is precisely that we might enjoy fellowship with the Father.

   (1)   It is not a prayer for salvation; if it were there would be no
         need to repeat it.
   (2)   Why repeat it? For abiding fellowship with the Father.
   (b)   Once we violate the principle of total forgiveness God ceases to
         forgive us – for what we just did!
   (1)   It doesn't mean he resurrects an old skeleton.
   (2)   It means that the very thing we just did, not forgiving – which
         is a sin – is standing between us and God.

2.  *God may turn on us and deal with us in a severe manner* (Matthew
    18:32-34).
    (a)   When you know you have been graciously forgiven and graciously
          dealt with – but refuse to be gracious to another, God may turn
          on you! (James 5:9).
    (b)   His disciplining can be most severe; it could be God will let you
          get caught for something he has protected!

3.  *God may discipline you, to teach you a lesson on self-righteous-*
    *ness and pointing the finger!*

## CONCLUSION

When we as believers totally forgive another believer the consequences are
wonderful and indescribable. The Holy Spirit flows within us (Galatians 5:22-
23) and makes us aware of his ongoing inner purifying of our hearts (1 Timothy
1:5). As this happens, we are becoming more like Jesus (Luke 23:34; 1 Peter
2:23).

However, if we don't totally forgive one another we become spiritually
impoverished, even if we feel good by 'getting even'. In fact, we are only
hurting ourselves when we don't totally forgive. To those of us who do not
forgive but harbour resentment and bitterness, God says, 'Let me handle it'
(Romans 12:19).

# 23

# THE HOLY SPIRIT

## INTRODUCTION

A. **In Chapter 4 we looked at what is meant by the Trinity.**
1. *Such a study of course brings in the Holy Spirit.*
2. *But to try to understand the Holy Spirit via the Trinity is to plunge in at the deep end. However:*
   - (a) We saw that the Holy Spirit is a person.
   - (b) We saw that the Holy Spirit is God.
   - (c) It was not until the Council of Constantinople (380) that the Holy Spirit was given the same recognition that had been given to the Son at Nicea (325).

B. **In this study we are going to introduce the Holy Spirit in an entirely different way.**
1. Instead of plunging in at the deep end, we will wade in shallow water, then move toward the deep.
2. We will try to understand what we mean by the Holy Spirit as though we knew nothing.

C. **There are a few possible approaches to the introduction to the Spirit.**
1. *We could begin with the Holy Spirit and the Old Testament.*
   - (a) The Spirit of God is mentioned in Genesis 1:2.
   - (b) There are other scattered references to the Spirit in the Old Testament, e.g., Isaiah 11:2; 61:1.

2. *We could begin with the Synoptic gospels.*
   - (a) The Synoptic Gospels are Matthew, Mark and Luke. They are so called because of the high degree of similarity between the texts.
   - (b) The first reference to the Holy Spirit in the New Testament is Matthew 1:18, 20. Cf. Luke 1:35.
   - (c) The Synoptics connect Jesus' baptism by John the Baptist to the Holy Spirit's descent like a dove (Matthew 3:16; Mark 1:10; Luke 3:22).

3. *We could begin with the Book of Acts, the first account of church history.*
   - (a) Luke, who wrote Acts, of all the Synoptic writers had the most to say about the Holy Spirit.

(b) Having been told to wait in Jerusalem, the Spirit fell on the Day of Pentecost (Acts 2).
    (1) This is when the disciples understood the Holy Spirit and also the reason why Jesus died on the cross.
    (2) But they had been *introduced* to the Holy Spirit earlier by Jesus.

4. *We could begin with the Apostle Paul.*
    (a) Paul, in his letters, most clearly defines the gospel and helps us to understood the New Testament as a whole.
    (b) But Paul began where Jesus ended (John 16:12).
        (1) Jesus introduced the Holy Spirit (John 14:16).
        (2) Paul continued what Jesus said would be too much for the disciples to bear.

5. *Other New Testament books refer to the Spirit but in them it is assumed that the readers already know something about the Holy Spirit. Some examples*: Hebrews 2:4; 3:7; 6:4; 9:14; 10:29; James 4:5; 1 Peter 1:2,11-12; 3:18; 4:14; 2 Peter 1:21; Jude 20.

D. **The best way to begin to understand the Holy Spirit is the way Jesus himself introduced him to the disciples as recorded in the Gospel of John.**

1 **JESUS' INTRODUCTION OF THE HOLY SPIRIT TO HIS DISCIPLES IMPLIES THAT THE HOLY SPIRIT IS A PERSON JUST AS JESUS IS A PERSON (John 14:16-17)**

A. **In his initial remarks Jesus said seven things about the Holy Spirit.**
    1. *He is 'another Counsellor'. This implies two things*:
        (a) 'Another' refers to one in addition to what Jesus had been.
        (b) Counsellor is the NIV translation of the Greek *parakletos*.
            (1) It is difficult to translate *parakletos* into one word, e.g., Comforter, Advocate.
            (2) It literally means 'one who comes alongside'.
        (c) In short: as Jesus had come alongside, so too would the Holy Spirit.

    2. *The Holy Spirit would be a gift of the Father. 'He will give you...'*
        (a) It was the Father who had sent Jesus into the world (John 8:16).
        (b) One of the differences between the Western church and Eastern Orthodoxy was over the manner in which the Spirit was sent: The Western church says the Spirit came from the Father *and* the Son. The Eastern church says the Spirit came from the Father *through* the Son.

3. *The Holy Spirit would come as a result of Jesus' intercession: 'I will ask...'*
   (a) This may have been implied in Jesus' prayer in John 17.
   (b) It is likely that this was fully carried out after Jesus took his seat at God's right hand (Acts 2:33).

4. *The Holy Spirit would never depart from them: 'To be with you forever'.*
   (a) This promise coincides with Jesus' words (Matthew 28:20; cf. Hebrews 13:5).
   (b) Though the Spirit can be grieved (Ephesians 4:30), he will never depart from us.

5. *The Holy Spirit is the Spirit of truth. 'The Spirit of truth'.*
   (a) Objectively, the Spirit cannot lie since God cannot lie (Hebrews 6:18; Titus 1:2).
       (1) The Holy Spirit witnesses only to the truth.
       (2) The Holy Spirit leads only to the truth.
   (b) Subjectively, we must be honest with the Holy Spirit (Psalm 51:6).
       (1) We must desire above all else to be on good terms with the Spirit.
       (2) It is required that we play no games with him or with ourselves.

6. *The unsaved cannot appreciate the Holy Spirit: 'The world cannot accept him'.*
   (a) Before the world can accept the Spirit three things are required, which Jesus would later make clear (John 16:8):
       (1) To be convicted of sin.
       (2) To be convicted of righteousness.
       (3) To be convicted of judgement.
   (b) Together these constitute conversion and thus translate people from the kingdom of darkness to the kingdom of light.

7. *The Holy Spirit would be in our hearts: 'Will be in you'.*
   (a) Jesus, who came alongside, was 'with' the disciples.
   (b) The Holy Spirit, who would come alongside, would be 'in' us.

B. **The result of this would be that Jesus would be as real by the Spirit within the disciples as Jesus had been real to the disciples outside of them.**
   1. *The disciples knew Jesus at the 'natural' level. This means:*
      (a) They could describe him physically (1 John 1:1).
          (1) They could tell you the colour of his eyes, hair, skin.
          (2) They could tell you how tall he was, how he walked.
          (3) They knew the sound of his voice.

(b)  They had witnessed the whole of his ministry.
   (1)  They heard his sermons, his parables.
   (2)  They saw the signs and wonders.
   (3)  Where Jesus went, they (for the most part) went.

2.  *The Holy Spirit would make Jesus real without having him with them physically.*
   (a)  This was the hardest thing for them to believe.
      (1)  Jesus assured them that his departure was 'for their good' (John 16:7).
      (2)  This did not thrill them (John 16:6).
   (b)  *Jesus promised that they would both not see him and see him* (John 16:16).
      (1)  They would not see him, as they would learn later, because he would ascend to heaven (Acts 1:9).
      (2)  They would see him, as they found out on the Day of Pentecost, by the Spirit.

3.  *Therefore they would not lose Jesus after all.*
   (a)  Through the Holy Spirit they got him back.
   (b)  He was now as real by the Spirit as he had been in the flesh.

## 2  THE HOLY SPIRIT IS OUR TEACHER

### A.  He teaches in basically two ways.

1.  *By reminding us of what we have been taught: 'Will remind you of everything...'*
   (a)  The disciples had received a lot of teaching during the previous three years.
      (1) Sermon on the Mount; (2) Parables; (3) Dialogues with Jews.
   (b)  They had received a lot of training as well, for example:
      (1) How to do ministry; (2) how to answer criticism; (3) how to pray.
   (c)  They may have felt they could not grasp, let alone remember all they had heard and seen. But Jesus reassured them that the Holy Spirit would take care of that.

2.  *By guiding us beyond our present understanding: 'He will guide you into all truth'* (John 16:13).
   (a)  The Holy Spirit begins with us where we are in order to take us to where we have never been.
   (b)  We are all still learning.
      (1)  The disciples were still learning; Jesus did not tell them everything that was knowable (John 16:12).
      (2)  Who knows what the Holy Spirit will show us (1 Corinthians 2:9-10)?

    (c)   The purpose of a guide: to show us what is there.
        (1)   The guide does not invent what is there.
        (2)   So it is with the Holy Spirit: 'He will not speak on his own (John 16:13).
    (d)   As Jesus took orders from the Father (John 5:19, 30) so does the Holy Spirit (John 16:13).
        (1)   There is no 'new truth'.
        (2)   Only fresh revelation of old truth.

## B.  The basic teaching of the Holy Spirit is to glorify Christ (John 16:14).

    1.   *His essential role: to witness to Jesus Christ* (John 15:26).
        (a)   Who Jesus is (John 1:1, 14).
        (b)   What he came to do (John 3:16).
        (c)   Why he came to do it (1 Peter 2:24).
        (d)   Why he rose from the dead (Romans 1:4; 4:25).
        (e)   Where he is now (Acts 2:33).
        (f)   Why he is there (Acts 2:36; Hebrews 7:25).
        (g)   Why he is coming again (2 Timothy 4:1; Hebrews 9:27-28).

    2.   *This does not mean he never calls attention to himself.*
        (a)   The Authorised Version translation of John 16:13 is not correct.
        (b)   Jesus, the First Paraclete, spoke of himself (John 14:6).
        (c)   The Holy Spirit, though self-effacing and heaping praise on the Father and Son, refers to himself all the time.
            (1)   The Holy Spirit wrote the New Testament which tells of the Spirit.
            (2)   The disciples when Spirit-filled referred to the Spirit (Acts 5:32).
            (3)   We are commanded to be filled with the Spirit (Ephesians 5:18).
            (4)   We are told to desire earnestly the gifts – anointings – of the Spirit (1 Corinthians 12:31).

    3   *All that Jesus promised concerning the Holy Spirit is subject to a condition: that he is allowed to be himself.*

## C.  The Holy Spirit is a sensitive person.

    1.   *He can be grieved* (Ephesians 4:30).
        (a)   This refers to our current attitude and lifestyle (Ephesians 4:30-5:7). Here is what grieves the Holy Spirit: (1) bitterness; (2) anger; (3) slander; (4) holding a grudge; (5) sexual immorality; (6) greed; (7) obscene jokes.
        (b)   I grieve the Spirit inwardly if I give in to any of the above. Two cautions:

        (1)    We almost never know we grieve the Spirit at first; we discover later that is what we did (Judges 16:20).

        (2)    Grieving the Spirit does not mean that he utterly leaves us (John 14:16; Ephesians 4:30).

  (c)    What happens when I grieve the Holy Spirit: confusion replaces clarity.

        (1)    Jesus will not be real.

        (2)    The Spirit, since he is grieved, will not remind me of things.

        (3)    The Spirit will not guide me into all truth.

2.  *He can be quenched* (1 Thessalonians 5:19).

  (a)    This primarily refers to the Spirit at work in others, e.g., the church.

        (1)    Grieving the Spirit is an 'inward' malady.

        (2)    Quenching the Spirit is an 'outward' malady.

  (b)    I quench the Spirit when:

        (1)    I hurt a weaker brother (1 Corinthians 8:9ff.).

        (2)    I judge a weaker brother (Romans 14:10).

        (3)    I speak against what God may want to do, especially when revival may be involved.

        (4)    I say or do things that divide God's people. This sin is called schism.

        (5)    I do or say anything that will give an uneasy feeling among God's people.

  (c)    When the Spirit is quenched it means his flow to the church is cut off.

        (1)    Unfortunately it is an easy thing to do.

        (2)    Unfortunately when it occurs, it is not easy to bring back the unquenched Spirit.

        (3)    This is why church unity is to be prized possibly above all other wishes.

## CONCLUSION

Jesus gave the disciples many promises regarding the Holy Spirit, but it was not until Jesus had returned to Heaven after his resurrection and poured out the Holy Spirit on the Day of Pentecost that the disciples understood what he had taught them. All that he promised regarding the Holy Spirit is absolutely true. To experience what he promised means that the Spirit will be at home in us as individuals and in the church.

# 24

## THE BAPTISM OF THE HOLY SPIRIT

**INTRODUCTION**

A. **Jesus is now enthroned at the right of God where he also intercedes for us.**

B. **The realisation of what was going on in heaven came on the Day of Pentecost, when the Holy Spirit fell on the early disciples.**

C. **The coming of the Holy Spirit was the direct consequence of the intercession of Christ in heaven:** 'Exalted to the right hand of God, he has received from the Father the promised Holy Spirit and has poured out what you now see and hear' (Acts 2:33).

D. **What happened on the Day of Pentecost is what we may safely call the 'Baptism of the Holy Spirit'.**
   1. We know this because, in Jesus' final past-resurrection appearance he said, 'For John baptised with water, but in a few days you will be baptised with the Holy Spirit' (Acts 1:5).
   2. What happened at Pentecost was precisely what he had predicted; they were baptised not with water but with the Holy Spirit.

E. **Why is this subject worthy of our study?**
   1. *It is the first great event to follow Christ's ascension.*
   2. *It is what Jesus had been preparing his disciples for during his last days on earth.*
      (a) He introduced the Holy Spirit in John 14:16, calling him 'another counsellor'.
         (1) Greek: *parakletos*, literally 'one who comes alongside'.
         (2) 'Another' implies that Jesus too had been just that to them – he had come alongside for three years.
      (b) He made a number of claims pertaining to the Spirit.
         (1) He would be as real as Jesus had been (John 14:16-17).
         (2) He would be a teacher and a reminder of what Jesus taught (John 14:26).
         (3) He would convince the world of sin, righteousness and judgement (John 16:8-11).
         (4) He would guide into all truth (John 16:13).
         (5) He would make Jesus as real to them at a spiritual level as he had been at the natural level (John 16:17ff.).

3. *It is what in a sense could be called 'the birth of the church'.*
   (a) I say 'in a sense'.
   (b) After all, the church existed long before Pentecost! (Acts 7:38).
       (1) 'Congregation' is from the Greek *ekklesia*: 'called out'.
       (2) The church has always been the 'called out'.

4. *It was a most astonishing experience for those who were blessed by it.*

5. *The subject of the Baptism of the Holy Spirit has been hotly disputed, especially in recent years.*
   (a) Can one experience it today?
   (b) Is it conversion – or after conversion?
   (c) Is it evidenced by speaking in tongues?

F. **Baptism of the Spirit: being drenched by the Spirit.**
   1. The Greek word *baptizo* means to dip, to plunge, usually with reference to water.
   2. Baptism in the New Testament was understood as immersion in water.
   3. Thus when the Spirit fell on the disciples they were 'drenched' – I liken it to a person in a powerful rainstorm without an umbrella!

## 1 THE ORIGINAL EVENT AT PENTECOST

A. **People present: obedient believers.**
   1. *They were the ones who had been obedient to Jesus' command to stay in Jerusalem.*
      (a) 'I am going to send you what my Father has promised; but stay in the city until you have been clothed with power from on high' (Luke 24:49).
      (b) On one occasion, while he was eating with them, he gave them this command: 'Do not leave Jerusalem, but wait for the gift my Father promised, which you have heard me speak about' (Acts 1:4).

   2. *They were almost certainly all eyewitnesses of Jesus after his being raised from the dead.*
      (a) They chose a successor to Judas Iscariot who must become 'a witness with us of his resurrection' (Acts 1:22).
      (b) Five hundred saw him on one occasion (1 Corinthians 15:6).
      (c) Luke mentions one hundred and twenty, presumably the number that stuck it out until Pentecost (Acts 1:15).

B. **Where it happened: 'upstairs' in a room in Jerusalem (Acts 1:13).**
   1. It may have been the same 'upper room' mentioned in Luke 22:12, where Jesus kept the Passover with the Twelve and where the Lord's Supper was instituted.
   2. What we know: 'They were all together in one place' (Acts 2:1).

C. **When it happened: on the Day of Pentecost.**
   1. This was fifty days after Passover.
   2. Their actual time of 'tarrying' was probably seven or eight days.

D. **What happened: an astonishing drenching of the Spirit.**
   1. A sound like the blowing of violent wind suddenly came from heaven.
   2. It filled 'the whole house' where they were sitting – they weren't kneeling but sitting!
   3. A visible phenomenon appeared: 'tongues of fire that separated and came to rest on each of them.'
   4. All of them were filled with the Holy Spirit.
   5. They began speaking in 'other tongues as the Spirit enabled them' (Acts 2:1-4).

E. **How it happened: Jesus' intercession.**
   1. Had Jesus not interceded, the Spirit would never have come down.
   2. This essential ingredient must lie behind every baptism of the Spirit – or one will never experience it; it is what Jesus does, not what we do.

F. **Why it happened: to vindicate Christ (Acts 2:36).**
   1. *It explained why he died.*
      (a) By God's set purpose and foreknowledge (Acts 2:23).
      (b) That we may have forgiveness of sins (Acts 2:38).
   2. *It explained where Jesus went after he was raised from the dead* (Acts 2:33).
   3. *It got the attention of unconverted Jews* (Acts 2:12-13).
   4. *It enabled Peter to preach with unusual power* (Acts 2:14-36).
   5. *It resulted in three thousand conversions.*

## 2  SOME FURTHER OBSERVATIONS

A. **Jesus was very, very real to those who were baptised with the Holy Spirit.**
   1. Psalm 16:8 came to Peter: 'David said about him: "I saw the Lord always before me. Because he is at my right hand, I will not be shaken" ' (Acts 2:25).
   2. We may safely assume that Jesus was no less real to the 120. Acts 2:1-4 stresses that what was true of one was true of 'each' or 'all'.

B. **Old Testament scriptures came together. Peter quoted three passages:**
   1. Joel 2:28-32 in  Acts 2:17-21.
   2. Psalm 16:8-11 in Acts 2:25-28.
   3. Psalm 110:1 in  Acts 2:34-35.

C. **We may safely assume that all else which Jesus promised was true:**
   1. The Holy Spirit was as real as Jesus had been.
   2. They were freshly taught and reminded of Jesus' teaching.
   3. They were being led to more truth.
   4. Jesus was so real that they 'saw him again' (cf. John 16:16).
   5. Those who were subsequently baptised in water had been convicted of sin, righteousness and judgement.

D. **The 'tongues' were languages.**
   1. *The Greek word* glossa *means language.*
   2. *That these tongues were known languages is evidenced by various foreigners who heard them speak in recognisable languages* (Acts 2:7-12).
      (a) It is highly possible if not probable that those who actually spoke in tongues did not know what they were saying.
         (1) Hence the tongues were 'unknown' to those speaking.
         (2) They were 'known' by those who heard.
      (b) It is also possible if not probable that there was a miracle of 'hearing' present.
         (1) This meant that the Holy Spirit simultaneously gave the interpretation.
         (2) With at least fifteen locations (and possibly as many tongues) represented the only way all of them could understand would be by the gift of interpretation of tongues in some way being carried out.

E. **The result was evangelistic.**
   1. The baptism of the Spirit was not merely a subjective experience (what those felt who were 'drenched') but an objective effect on bystanders.
   2. The result was three thousand conversions.
   3. Thus those baptised with the Spirit were witnesses (Acts 1:8).

F. **For Peter the result was enormous power.**
   1. What Peter was enabled to say is what the 120 were enabled to do. The same word is used in Acts 2:4 (infinitive) and Acts 2:14 (aorist).
      (a) Greek *apophtheggesthai*: 'enabled' (NIV); 'utterance' (AV) (Acts 2:4).
      (b) Greek *apephthegxato*: no translation has ever (to my knowledge)

translated this word in Acts 2:14 to show the kind of power that Peter had: 'addressed' (NIV); 'said' (AV).
2. The truth is, Peter had the same power speaking in his own language (presumably Aramaic) as the 120 had to speak in 'other' languages.
3. The gift of interpretation of tongues may have been what gripped his hearers even more!

G. **Luke's initial comment after this event reveals their priorities:** teaching; fellowship; breaking of bread; prayer (Acts 2:42).

## 3   DID IT HAPPEN AGAIN?

A. **A number of persecuted believers apparently experienced something very similar:** 'After they prayed, the place where they were meeting was shaken. And they were all filled with the Holy Spirit and spoke the word of God boldly' (Acts 4:31).
1. *Absent on this occasion:*
   (a) Tongues of fire; speaking in tongues. This is not to say for certain that speaking in tongues did not take place, but it is not mentioned.
   (b) The place being shaken *may* have been the result of wind but this is speculative.
2. *Present:* speaking the word boldly; unity (Acts 4:32).
3. *This proves that those who have been baptised by the Spirit can possibly experience it again!*
   (a) The original experience at Pentecost may be in a sense 'one off'.
   (b) But renewal is possible.

B. **A receiving of the Spirit is described in Acts 8.**
1. *This was in those who had not yet received the Spirit* (Acts 8:16).
2. *'Then Peter and John placed their hands on them, and they received the Holy Spirit'* (Acts 8:17).
   (a) No evidence of further phenomena is described.
   (b) They may or may not have spoken in tongues.
   (c) A new development: the Spirit came after an apostolic laying on of hands.

C. **Paul's conversion and receiving the Spirit.**
1. *His conversion was clearly* followed *by his being filled with the Holy Spirit* (Acts 9:1-9,17).
2. *He was filled with the Spirit and got his sight back* (Acts 9:18).
   (a) He was immediately baptised (Acts 9:18).
   (b) This would have been water baptism.
   (c) He may or may not have spoken in tongues, although it is odd that Luke would omit this for one as significant as Paul had he done so.

## D. The conversion of Cornelius.
1. *Cornelius was baptised with the Spirit at conversion!* (Acts 10:45).
2. *He spoke in tongues as well* (Acts 10:46).
   (a) The speaking in tongues was essential in this case or Peter could not have been convinced that the conversion of a Gentile was authentic.
   (b) And yet this example shows that one *can* (if God chooses) be baptised with the Spirit at conversion.
   (c) This should make all of us pause lest we build a dogmatic, inflexible theology that attempts to make everybody fit into one mould!

## E. And the disciples were filled with joy and with the Holy Spirit (Acts 13:52).
Note: this is another example of the *renewal* of the Spirit in believers.

## F. Some disciples at Ephesus.
1. *They had received 'John's baptism' but had never heard of the Holy Spirit* (Acts 19:2-3).
2. *After Christ was preached they were baptised in water* (Acts 19:4-5).
3. *'When Paul placed his hands on them, the Holy Spirit came on them, and they spoke in tongues and prophesied'* (Acts 19:6).
   (a) This came from Paul laying his hands on them.
   (b) A new phenomenon: they prophesied!
   (c) Yet we are not to require that all who are baptised by the Spirit evidence it by prophesying.

## G. Summary:
1. *The baptism of the Spirit obviously recurred after Pentecost.*
   (a) But it was never called 'baptism of the Spirit'. It was only called that in Jesus' prediction in Acts 1:5.
2. *No uniform sign invariably proved the filling of the Spirit.*

## 4    CAN IT HAPPEN TO US TODAY?

## A. Biblical terms
1. *There is more than one term for the baptism of the Holy Spirit.*
   (a) If anything, the term 'Baptism of the Spirit' is not always very satisfactory. Why?
       (1) It is used mostly by John the Baptist and Jesus to promise what *would* happen (Matthew 3:11; John 1:33; Acts 1:5).
       (2) Only twice is the term 'baptise' used as a description of the Spirit as to what *happened:* 1 Corinthians 12:13 which clearly refers to conversion and *not* to what many people

really mean by a baptism of the Spirit; and in Acts 11:16ff.,
which suggests the same thing.
- (b) The experience is described in other ways:
    - (1) Sealing of the Spirit (2 Corinthians 1:22; Ephesians 1:13).
    - (2) Receiving the Spirit (Galatians 3:2; 4:6).
    - (3) Being filled with the Spirit (Ephesians 5:18).
    - (4) Renewal of the Spirit (Titus 3:5).
    - (5) God's rest (Hebrews 4:10).
    - (6) Receiving the promise (Hebrews 6:12; 10:36).

2. *The terms for this teaching ultimately only make sense to the one who has experienced it..*
    - (a) If we were to build a theology entirely on Acts 11:16 and 1 Corinthians 12:13 we would have to conclude that all Christians are given the fullness of the Spirit at conversion.
    - (b) If we were to build a theology on the fact that the experience at Pentecost came on *believers* (cf. Acts 19:2), we would have to conclude that the fullness of the Spirit will be post-conversion.

## B. What was true in the early church is true today:
1. *Some may receive the fullness of the Spirit at conversion, like Cornelius.*
2. *Some may receive the fullness of the Spirit after conversion, even many years later.*
    - (a) We must never forget this principle: all Christians have the Holy Spirit (Romans 8:9).
    - (b) But it is also true: not all Christians have been filled with the Spirit.
3. *Some may speak in tongues.*

## C. The purpose of the baptism of the Spirit.
1. *To make Jesus real; it is the highest form of assurance.*
    - (a) One 'knows that he knows'; it is sheer certainty.
    - (b) It may refer to more than on thing; e.g.:
        - (1) Full assurance of salvation (2 Corinthians 1:22).
        - (2) Full assurance of understanding (Colossians 2:2).
        - (3) Full assurance of answered prayer before it happens (Mark 11:24; 1 John 5:14-15).

2. *To give power for service* (Acts 1:8).
    - (a) This was D. L. Moody's essential teaching.
    - (b) It sets a person free and gives fearlessness.

D. **How do we know we have been baptised with the Holy Spirit? I
   answer:**
   1. You will know that you have: if you have to ask you probably haven't
      experienced it.
   2. The clear evidences are (a) great peace and joy and (b) fearlessness.
   3. Yet if one experiences speaking in tongues he or she should not im-
      pose this on others as 'the' evidence of the Spirit.


**CONCLUSION**

The Baptism of the Spirit was originally experienced by the disciples on the
Day of Pentecost to fulfil the promises made by Jesus. The disciples were
given power, great joy and boldness in witnessing that could not be explained
from 'natural' causes.

Believers today may also have this experience of the Spirit. Martyn Lloyd-
Jones stated that it is the greatest need of the church at the present time. We
should tarry before the Lord and plead that it will happen to us – even if we
have experienced it before!

# 25

# THE GIFTS OF THE SPIRIT

## INTRODUCTION

A. **Interest in the gifts of the Holy Spirit is largely a feature of the twentieth century.**
   1. *In the earliest church, Montanus (c.200) brought in an emphasis on the Spirit.*
      (a) Montanism, as it became known, was the ancient 'Charismatic Movement'!
      (b) This movement would probably have gone unnoticed by church historians were it not for one 'convert' to the Montanist Movement: Tertullian.
         (1) For this reason there was no 'St Tertullian'; Montanism was regarded as too far outside the camp.

   2. *The doctrine of the Spirit flourished in the Reformation and Great Awakening but not with reference to the gifts of the Spirit.*
      (a) Calvin emphasised the inner testimony of the Spirit, by which we know the Bible is true.
      (b) Wesley, Whitefield and Edwards were witness to unusual manifestations of the Spirit, such as people being struck down under preaching.

   3. *The Pentecostal Movement really took off following a phenomenal outpouring of the Spirit in Azusa Street, Los Angeles, in 1906.*
      (a) The Baptism of the Spirit tended to be equated with speaking in tongues.
      (b) Alongside this there emerged an emphasis on healing.

   4. *The Charismatic Movement really appeared in the 1960s, and was an inter-denominational phenomenon.*
      (a) Pentecostalism became denominational, the main offsprings in Britain being the Elim Church and the Assemblies of God.
      (b) But the Charismatic Movement has probably touched every denomination.
         (1) Some equate tongues with the Baptism of the Spirit, others do not.
         (2) The emphasis in most cases is on the gifts of the Spirit.

B. **Why deal with this matter here?**
1. The Charismatic Movement has forced the whole of the Christian world to look at the Holy Spirit in a new way.
2. God has raised up the Charismatic Movement and we are all the better for it.
3. We need to look at what the Bible teaches and not get our opinions on this matter second hand.

## 1 THE DIFFERENCE BETWEEN HAVING SPIRITUAL GIFTS AND BEING SPIRITUAL

A. **It is possible to have spirituality and not have spiritual gifts.**
1. *This is what many do not seem to understand.*
   (a) It is largely assumed that if you have a gift of the Spirit, especially tongues, you are spiritual.
   (b) The assumption is wrong: the Church of Corinth had those who spoke in tongues and Paul called them 'children' and 'carnal' (1 Corinthians 3:1-4).

2. *Spirituality does not necessarily relate to spiritual gifts..*
   (a) Spirituality is being tuned in to the Holy Spirit.
   (b) This is having the fruit of the Spirit, which is more important than the gifts of the Spirit.
      (1) The fruit of the Spirit is love (Galatians 5:22ff.).
      (2) Paul called this the 'most excellent way', having just described the gifts of the Spirit (1 Corinthians 12:31).

B. **It is, alas, possible to have spiritual gifts and yet not be spiritual (Romans 11:29).**
1. *This fact was what led Paul to discuss gifts of the Spirit in the first place* (1 Corinthians 12:1-7).
   (a) There were those in Corinth who felt possessing gifts was not only important but the most important thing. They mainly emphasised tongues as proof of their spirituality (1 Corinthians 14:1-20).

2. *One does not necessarily need to be 'spiritual' to receive any gift of the Spirit.*
   (a) It comes without repentance. Once given, it is irrevocable.

3. *It seems that gifts of the Spirit, especially tongues, tend to camouflage one's true spiritual state.*
   (a) This is what happened in Corinth.
   (b) It is true today when people tell you that, unless you speak in tongues, you are not spiritual.

    (1) You can be spiritual and not speak in tongues.

    (2) You can speak in tongues and not be spiritual.

C. **One proof that you have the Holy Spirit is that you confess Jesus is Lord (1 Corinthians 12:3).**

  1. Many Corinthians were regarded as spiritually inferior because they did not speak in tongues.

  2. Paul comments that no-one is inferior who has the Spirit; all who say 'Jesus is Lord' have the Spirit (1 Corinthians 12:3).

## 2 THERE IS AN OVERLAPPING BETWEEN THE NATURAL AND THE SUPERNATURAL (1 Corinthians 12:4-7).

A. **All of us have gifts by 'common grace'.**

  1. *Common grace is God's goodness to all whether or not they are Christians.*

    (a) Calvin called it 'special grace within nature'.

    (b) This means that one may have an unusual ability which is natural, yet it was uniquely given by God.

  2. *Some who have never been converted have unusual talents or intellects, just as some who are converted have unusual talents and intellects.*

    (a) But this is owing to common grace, not saving grace.

      (1) After all, God is our Creator.

      (2) All gifts by virtue of creation come from the same God who saves us.

B. **When we are converted we should expect that the gifts that are ours by virtue of creation should be used of the Lord.**

  1. *We then might call them 'spiritual', although they are quite natural.*

  2. *This comes out in 1 Corinthians 12:4-7.*

    (a) The Greek word is *diairesis* which means differences, distinctions, distributions or dealings out.

    (b) The word in this context refers to the gifts being distributed among different *individuals* rather than to the distinctions between the gifts themselves.

      (1) It is not the *gifts* God uses; it is *you*.

      (2) Every Christian is unique.

    (c) How many gifts of the Spirit are there?

      (1) Nine? Cf. 1 Corinthians 12:8-10.

      (2) Three or four more? Cf. 1 Corinthians 12:28-30.

      (3) What about Romans 12:7-8?

      (4) What about Ephesians 4:7-13?

    (d) There are as many gifts of the Spirit as there are Christians!

C. **1 Corinthians 12:4-7 flattens the distinction between the charismatic and non-charismatic gifts.**
  1. *Charismatic: spiritual gift. It means 'grace gift'.*
  2. *Non-charismatic: natural gift, as in ability or talent.*
      (a) One may be endowed with a charismatic gift (e.g., tongues or healing) and be somewhat weak in natural gifts.
      (b) One may have a superabundance of natural gifts (we tend to refer to this as talent) and be somewhat devoid of spiritual gifts.
          (1) An apostle needed to have both.
          (2) Not all Christians have a lot of both.
      (c) We are *all* required to have the fruits of the Spirit.

D. **I prefer the word 'anointing' to 'gift'.**
  1. *This word combines the natural and supernatural.*
      (a) One may have an anointing to teach, to play an instrument.
      (b) This combines the natural gift with the Spirit's power.
  2. *Anointing: what comes easily.*
      (a) If you struggle, your anointing is wanting.
      (b) To the spiritual person the supernatural seems natural.

## 3  ANOINTINGS OF 1 CORINTHIANS 12

A. **The anointing of wisdom (verse 8).**
  1. *Wisdom: the intelligent use of knowledge (what you know).*
      (a) It is the intelligent use of three things in particular:
          (1) Tongue (what to say).
          (2) Tact (how to say it).
          (3) Timing (when to speak).
      (b) It is 'presence of mind'.
          (1) Nobody has this all of the time else he/she will be conceited.

  2. *The anointing of wisdom: presence of the mind of the Spirit.*
      (a) It is being impartial. It is unbiased.
      (b) It is knowing what to say next!

B. **The anointing of knowledge (verse 8).**
  1. *The Greek is 'word of knowledge'.*
      (a) At bottom of any anointing is revelation.
      (b) This is why anointing is without struggling; either you have it or you don't.

  2. *What is knowledge? Answer: information.*
      (a) But the anointing of knowledge in 1 Corinthians 12:8 is with reference to *spiritual* knowledge.

(1)  It does not refer to arts or science.
(2)  It is divine information to help us spiritually as Christians.
(b)  This anointing may be either general or particular.
  (1)  General – through teaching or preaching.
  (2)  Particular – through a specific word given to one person, and for him/her only.

## C.  The anointing of faith (verse 9).

1.  *This is not (obviously) a reference to saving faith.*
    (a)  Neither does it refer to living by faith, which every Christian is required to do.
    (b)  It is special faith, given under unusual circumstances:
        (1)  Extreme trial (James 1:2, 12).
        (2)  Satanic attack (Ephesians 6:10-20).
2.  *It is spectacular faith to perform extraordinary work* (Hebrews 11).
    (a)  Like all anointings, it is sovereignly given.
    (b)  Like all anointings, it is given to those who need it.

## D.  The anointing of healing (verse 9).

1.  *This is in a sense a perpetuation of the ministry of Jesus – who healed people.*
    (a)  Early Pentecostals (and some Charismatics) put healing in the Atonement: 'God saves, sanctifies, heals'.
    (b)  It is in the atonement as a provision but not as the chief reason Jesus died.
        (1)  All who trust Christ's death are saved.
        (2)  Not all who trust Christ's death are healed.

2.  *Healing: when disease or defect in the physical body is removed and the natural process of cure is restored; sometimes gradually, sometimes suddenly.*
    (a)  The anointing of healing is distinguished from ordinary medical skill.
    (b)  Value of healing: relief of pain and/or the prolonging of life that demonstrates the power of God's Name.

## E.  The anointing of miracles (verse 10).

1.  *Miracle: the extraordinary that cannot be explained naturally.* There are three Greek words: (1) *semeion* meaning 'signs', used 77 times; (2) *teras* meaning 'wonders', used 16 times; (3) *dunamis* meaning 'miracles', used 120 times.

2.  *A miracle may be anything from an answer to prayer to awesome providence to God's raw power.*

(a)   A healing is usually gradual whereas a miracle is usually sudden.
(b)   A miracle may refer to an exorcism as well as healing.

F.  **The anointing of prophecy (verse 10).**
  1. *Prophecy: immediate revelation from God, or knowledge that is beyond sense perception.*
     (a)   In the Old Testament there were two levels:
           (1)   Ordinary gifts, as with King Saul (1 Samuel 10:10).
           (2)   Extraordinary prophets, such as  Samuel or Elijah.
     (b)   Some believe that apostles succeeded the extraordinary Old Testament prophets.

  2. *There are two levels of prophecy, generally speaking.*
     (a)   Preaching, when God uses the Word in an unusually relevant manner.
     (b)   Word of knowledge, when God gives an accurate word for a specific person or situation.

G.  **The anointing of discernment (verse 10).**
  1. *This refers to the ability to make a distinction between the spirits, for example:*
     (a)   The demonic.
     (b)   What is of the flesh.
     (c)   When it is the Holy Spirit.

  2. *This is a most valuable gift, whether in a revival atmosphere or a revolutionary age.*
     (a)   In a time of revival there is the likelihood of the counterfeit.
     (b)   In a revolutionary age we need discernment for the times (Matthew 16:1-4).
     (c)   Above all, one needs to be able to recognise the Holy Spirit himself.

H.  **The anointing of speaking in tongues ( verse 10).**
  1. *The Greek word is* glossa. *They used to speak of the Glossolalia Movement in the 1960s and 1970s.*
     (a)   Tongues: unintelligible inspired speech in a language one has never learned and which one does not understand.
     (b)   It may be an angelic language or a human language.

  2. *It is often called a prayer language* (1 Corinthians 14:1ff.).
     (a)   It is an anointing to worship God.
     (b)   It is an anointing to intercede (Romans 8:26, 27; Ephesians 6:18).

(c)  It heightens communion with God, and may be the only time Satan does not know what we are saying.

I.  **The anointing of interpretation of tongues (verse 10).**
1.  *This assumes two things of the tongue which one was speaking (but unknown to him or her):*
    (a)  That it has a meaning.
    (b)  That it can be accurately interpreted.

2.  *This is perhaps a very rare gift and is a real test of whether or not God is supernaturally at work.*
    (a)  It is used publicly.
    (b)  It could be a great evangelistic tool, and is tantamount to prophecy.

J.  **The anointing of helping others (verse 28).**
1.  This is the forgotten anointing.
2.  It refers to a special grace or ability to help people in need.

K.  **The anointing of leadership or 'gifts of administration', NIV (verse 28).**
1.  It comes from a Greek word that means piloting a ship through dangerous waters.
2.  It refers both to a natural ability and to a presence of mind of the Spirit.

**CONCLUSION**
The gifts of the Spirit are given to believers to further God's work, both within us and in witnessing to him. There are as many gifts of the Spirit as there are believers. Paul, however, encourages us to desire the greater gifts.

# 26

## WHAT IS SPIRITUALITY?

**INTRODUCTION**

A. **Spirituality is a general term which may not even refer to the Christian faith, nor to the Holy Spirit.**
   1. *Illustration: Oprah Winfrey asked Michael Jackson, 'Are you a spiritual man?' His answer was generally affirmative because he believes in God 'absolutely'. He said he was a 'chosen instrument of nature' to bring his gift to the world.*
   2. *The New Age Movement regards spirituality as essential to all it stands for.*
   3. *One could be into cultic religion and stress spirituality.*
      (a) Some churches are into science of the mind and spiritualism.
      (b) Anything occultic could be regarded as spiritual if by that term it refers to what is non-material.
   4. *By some definitions a person could be an atheist and be spiritual.*
      (a) Spirituality is sometimes defined as belief in man's spirit and the need to affirm humanity or plants or animals.
      (b) Some think that any retreat from materialism is spiritual.
         (1) Those who talk to plants may be regarded as spiritual by this definition.
         (2) Those who want to preserve nature – for example, whales and seals – may likewise be regarded as being spiritual.

B. **True spirituality is an affirmation of three things: (1) the Christian faith; (2) the Trinity; (3) the Bible as the inspired and infallible Word of God.**
   (a) We stress the person of Jesus Christ.
   (b) We stress the person of the Holy Spirit.

C. **Spirituality: being tuned in to the Holy Spirit.**
   1. *This definition implies four things:*
      (a) The ungrieved Spirit (cf. Ephesians 4:30).
         (1) You cannot be tuned in to the Spirit unless you are in conscious contact with the Spirit as he wants to be in us.
         (2) The only way the Spirit is at home in us is when he is ungrieved.

(b) A relationship with the Holy Spirit, otherwise one could not be 'tuned in to the Holy Spirit.'
  (1) This means that you know him.
  (2) This means a reciprocal relationship, that is, he has a relationship with you too.
(c) A living, present-moment relationship.
  (1) It is not enough to have experienced this in the past.
  (2) Spirituality is a present relationship with the Spirit; it is what is real right now!
  (3) It is not merely knowing *about* the Spirit; it is knowing the Holy Spirit – now.
(d) Spirituality is a work of the Spirit.
  (1) Being 'tuned in' is the result of the Spirit at work.
  (2) Thus one cannot 'work it up'

2. *Spirituality, then, refers to the Christian's relationship with the Holy Spirit in the here and now.*

## D. Why is this study important?
1. Because of the wide misconception as to what spirituality is, especially since it may not even refer to Christianity at all.
2. Because the church today as an institution may not necessarily be spiritual at all.
3. Because a Christian may not necessarily be a spiritual person.
4. Because a church leader may not necessarily be a spiritual person.
5. Because a person with certain natural gifts may not necessarily be a spiritual person.
6. Because a person can have spiritual gifts and yet not be a spiritual person.
7. Because as Christians we are called to be spiritual.

## 1 SPIRITUALITY IS BEING SPIRIT-FILLED (Galatians 5:22-23).

## A. Not all Christians are necessarily filled with the Spirit.
1. *Otherwise, there is no need for Paul's command:* 'Be filled with the Holy Spirit' (Ephesians 5:18).
  (a) This implies that they may not have been filled with the Spirit.
  (b) This suggests clearly that we too need to keep this in mind as we are not that different from the early Christians.

2. *The Galatian Christians were obviously not Spirit-filled.*
  (a) They had given in, at least to some extent, to the Judaizers (Galatians 3:1-3).

          (1)  'Judaizers' is the nickname given by scholars to describe legalistic Jewish Christians who wanted to bring believers back under the Law. They particularly emphasised that Gentiles should be circumcised.

     (b)  Paul prayed that Christ would be 'formed' in them (Galatians 4:19).

          (1)  This implies that Christ was far from being formed in them.

          (2)  It meant they had given in to the flesh.

   3.  *The Corinthian Christians were obviously not all Spirit-filled.*

     (a)  Paul calls them 'worldly', not spiritual (1 Corinthians 3:1).

     (b)  They were more interested in the spiritual gifts then in being spiritual (1 Corinthians 12).

     (c)  This is why we have the 'love chapter' – 1 Corinthians 13 – which Paul calls 'the most excellent way' (1 Corinthians 12:31).

## B. Being Spirit-filled results in the fruit of the Spirit (Galatians 5:22-23).

   1.  *There is a difference between the gifts of the Spirit and the fruit of the Spirit.*

     (a)  The gifts are sovereignly bestowed and are irrevocable (Romans 11:29).

          (1)  Repentance does not guarantee them.

          (2)  Once bestowed, they remain.

     (b)  The fruit of the Spirit comes as the result of obedience, which is:

          (1)  Walking in the Spirit (Galatians 5:16).

          (2)  Walking in the light (1 John 1:7).

   2.  *The fruits of the Spirit therefore flow out of obedience.*

     (a)  This means resisting the flesh (Galatians 5:19-20).

          (1)  It is hating the works of the flesh.

          (2)  It means not thinking about how you can gratify sinful desires (Romans 13:14).

     (b)  This means openness to the Spirit.

          (1)  Being willing to accept his rebukes and new ways of obedience.

          (2)  Following every bit of light God gives you.

## 2 SPIRITUALITY IS TUNING IN TO GOD'S LOVE (1 John 4:16-18).

## A. It begins by relying on his love (1 John 4:16).

   1.  *We will not become spiritual by relying on our love.*

     (a)  Trusting our love for God leads to self-reliance, which in turn leads to smugness and self-righteousness.

2. *Relying on God's love is faith.*
   (a) We don't go from our love to faith; we go from faith to love.
       (1) If we look at our love we will become introspective – which
           Calvin described as the way of 'sure damnation'.
       (2) Spurgeon said: 'I looked to Christ and the dove flew in; I
           looked to the dove and it disappeared.'
   (b) God wants us literally to believe his love (1 John 4:16, AV).
       (1) We therefore rest on his love.
       (2) Not that we love God but that he loves us (1 John 4:10).

## B. God is love; spirituality is therefore manifesting God.

1. *1 Corinthians 13 is the sheer love of God.*
   (a) It is what Jesus was (and is).
   (b) Substitute 'Jesus' for 'love' in 1 Corinthians 13 and you can see
       two things:
       (1) What Jesus is like.
       (2) What God is like.
   (c) Therefore when we are truly spiritual we will display *God* to
       others.

2. *The key to love is 'keeping no record of wrongs'* (1 Corinthians 13:5).
   (a) This is the essence of forgiveness.
       (1) It is how God acts towards us (Psalm 103:12).
       (2) He no longer remembers our sins.
   (b) The first step towards love then is refusing to dwell on any hurt
       we may feel, keeping no record of it in our minds.
   (c) Once that transaction has taken place in our hearts, here is what
       follows:
       (1) The Spirit enters us in fuller measure.
       (2) The feeling of bitterness is gone (Ephesians 4:30).
       (3) The need to point the finger disappears (see Isaiah 58:9).
       (4) We begin to think more clearly (2 Timothy 1:7, AV).
       (5) Peace takes charge (Philippians 4:7).

## 3  SPIRITUALITY IS DISCERNMENT OF THE TRUTH (1 Corinthians 2:9-15).

## A. Jesus called the Holy Spirit the 'Spirit of truth' (John 14:17).

1. *This means that the Spirit is absolutely free of error.*
   (a) The more we have of the Holy Spirit, the more we will recognise
       truth, the less we will have of error.
   (b) Two promises guarantee this (John 7:17; 2 Peter 1:8).

2. *It follows that the Holy Spirit leads to truth* (John 14:26; 16:13).
   (a) This is what guarantees that the Spirit is wholly Christian.
       (1) He only glorifies Jesus Christ.
       (2) He hates anything that is cultic (false doctrine) or occultic (directly of the devil).
   (b) Spirituality therefore not only touches our life-style, but also our thinking.
       (1) We must demonstrate the love of Jesus.
       (2) We must be theologically sound in our minds.

B. **Spirituality dips into the 'deep things of God' (1 Corinthians 2:10).**
   1. *It begins with the ABC's, the 'elementary teachings'* (Hebrews 6:1-2).
      (a) Repentance and faith, which presuppose:
          (1) Christ's death on the cross.
          (2) Faith in Christ's blood.
      (b) Elementary teaching:
          (1) Baptism.
          (2) Laying on of hands.
      (c) Eschatological things:
          (1) Final resurrection.
          (2) Final judgement.

   2. *It leads to the things of the Spirit.*
      (a) Insight (1 Corinthians 2:9-10).
          (1) This refers to things beyond what we know.
          (2) It includes what is knowable now, things revealed by the Spirit.
      (b) God's thoughts (1 Corinthians 2:11).
          (1) Only the Holy Spirit perfectly knows God's thoughts.
          (2) Our only link with his thoughts is the Holy Spirit.
      (c) God's thoughts are to be seen in two ways:
          (1) Understanding what has been given to us (1 Corinthians 2:12).
          (2) Understanding what the Spirit continues to show us (1 Corinthians 2:13).

   3. *What the Spirit will show us, insofar as theological truth is concerned, will only be that already found in the Bible.*
      (a) When we get to heaven we may discover truths that are not explicit (as far as we know) in the Bible. But nothing that will be learned will contradict the Bible.
      (b) In the meantime, all that will be revealed to us this side of glory will be found right in our Bibles.
          (1) There may be truths we have not yet discovered. When we do it will be but a re-discovery of what was always in the Bible.
      (c) There are no new truths, only fresh revelation of old truths!

## 4 SPIRITUALITY IS SANCTIFICATION (2 Thessalonians 2:13)

### A. Sanctification: process of being made holy.
1. The Greek word is *hagiazo*: to set apart; that which is treated with awe.
2. Latin is *sanctus* (holy) and *facere* (to make).
3. Sanctification and holiness are used interchangeably.

### B. We are called with a 'holy' calling (2 Timothy 1:9).
1. *The work of sanctification is the inevitable effect of regeneration (being born again).*
   (a) One is not converted to remain the same (Ephesians 4:22-23).
   (b) We are not saved 'in' our sins but 'from' our sins (Matthew 1:21).

2. *The appearance of holiness varies in degrees and from person to person.*
   (a) One must consider the background of the new convert.
      (1) His education, culture, intellect.
      (2) His emotional and psychological make-up.
      (3) His pre-Christian exposure to the Bible and preaching.

### C. All New Testament commands to new Christians, implicitly or explicitly, call for sanctification or holiness.
1. That we will be moral (1 Thessalonians 4:3).
2. That we will demonstrate a change of life (Romans 6).
3. That we will receive a reward at the Judgement Seat of Christ (1 Corinthians 3:12-15; 2 Corinthians 5:10).
4. That we will not gratify the desires of the flesh (Galatians 5:16).

### D. Any true spirituality flows from the Holy Spirit.
1. *Worldly 'spirituality' (as with New Age) could be immoral. But not true spirituality.*
2. *True spirituality flows from the Holy Spirit.*
   (a) Not from the human spirit, which is naturally opposed to holiness.
   (b) Not from the demonic, which absolutely hates holiness.
3. *What flows from the Holy Spirit will therefore be* holy.
   (a) This does not mean we are perfect.
      (1) Sanctification is the *process* of being made holy.
      (2) We will not be perfect until glorification (Romans 8:30).
   (b) What it means is that the bent of our lives will be in the direction of pleasing God which involves:
      (1) Keeping his commands (John 14:15).
      (2) Wanting to please God in all we do (1 Thessalonians 2:12).

## 5 SPIRITUALITY IS SENSITIVITY TO OTHERS' NEEDS AND FEELINGS (1 John 4:20).

A. **Spirituality involves caring for the underdog** (James 1:27).
1. *It is demonstrating faith by works (James 2:14ff.).*
   (a) This is not done to get assurance of salvation.
   (b) This is done to demonstrate faith to others.

2. *The love of God in us will cause us to demonstrate pity* (1 John 3:17).
   (a) Tuning in to God's love then is not limited to the absence of bitterness.
   (b) It is showing that we care by what we do for others.

B. **Spirituality includes caring for the backslider with humility (Galatians 6:1).**
1. *Spirituality has as a goal to restore the brother or sister who is 'caught in a sin'.*
   (a) This task is assigned only to the 'spiritual.'
   (b) The spiritual person will therefore be all the above!

2. *But Galatians 6:1 reveals another dimension to spirituality: morality that is not self-righteous.*
   (a) This is a rare quality.
      (1) Many who are moral are self-righteous.
      (2) Those who are moral but not self-righteous are wanted.
   (b) Spirituality can be summed up at this point:
      (1) The care to restore a fallen brother or sister.
      (2) The approach that must be followed is one of meekness, knowing that what you sadly observe in another could happen to you.

## CONCLUSION

True spirituality describes the state of closeness to the Holy Spirit – being tuned in to him. It is a relationship where the Holy Spirit is not grieved; a living, present moment relationship.

Spirituality is being Spirit-filled, the fruit of the Spirit evident in our lives.

Spirituality is what Jesus was. He was without sin. But there was nothing 'wet' or self-righteous about him. Sinners felt welcome in his presence. Do they in ours?

There is only way forward for us: more of the Holy Spirit in our lives!

# 27

# INTRODUCING ECCLESIOLOGY

## INTRODUCTION

A. At first glance the doctrine of the church may not seem so interesting. But it deals with some very edifying and important matters.

B. Ecclesiology: things pertaining to the nature of the church, church government and the sacraments.
1. *The Greek word translated 'church' is* ekklesia, *and it literally means 'called out'.*
    (a)    The word 'church' actually comes from a Scottish word *kirk.*
    (b)    But in the Greek language (the language of the New Testament) it merely means 'the called out'.
        (1)    It does not refer to a building but to a people.
        (2)    Those people have been 'called out' by God's electing grace.
    (c)    The doctrine of election is really inseparable from the doctrine of the church.
        (1)    *Eklektos* (Greek) means the 'elect' or 'chosen' (Matthew 20:16; 22:14; Romans 8:33).
        (2)    Hence 'the called out' are those whom God has chosen and called out of darkness into light.

2. *Ecclesiology therefore embraces most of the discussions pertaining to:*
    (a)    The nature of the church.
    (b)    The issue of church and state.
    (c)    Church government.
    (d)    The sacraments.

C. Why is this subject important?
1. *We should come to see the difference between the visible church and the invisible church.*
2. *We should see the difference between the church 'militant' and the church 'triumphant'.*
3. *We ought to have a good perspective on the issues of church and state.*
    (a)    Should the state and the church be one?
    (b)    Or should they be separate?

4. *We ought to be aware of the forms of church government that are implied in scripture and those which govern a particular group or denomination.*
5. *We ought to have a good understanding of the history of the sacraments and of what is biblical.*
6. *Church history gives us an appreciation and understanding of how certain views emerged.*

## 1. EARLY CHURCH HISTORY
### A. The Apostolic Fathers.
1. *The first church history was written by Luke; it is called the Acts of the Apostles (covering events from the Ascension of Jesus to Paul's arrival in Rome, before 65 AD).*
2. *The Apostolic Fathers begin with influential church leaders or thinkers after the time of the apostles, some of whom were said to be converted by certain apostles.*
   - (a) Clement of Rome (c.96), sometimes said to be the third Bishop of Rome.
   - (b) Ignatius (c.35-c.107), the second Bishop of Antioch, who became a legend because of his looking forward to martyrdom – to be the 'wheat of Christ' by being torn to bits by the lions.
   - (c) Polycarp (c.69-c.155), Bishop of Smyrna, possibly a convert of John, made legendary by his martyrdom.
   - (d) The Didache, a short Christian manual on morals and Christian practice. It calls for baptism by immersion if possible, otherwise by threefold affusion (sprinkling or pouring water).
   - (e) Hermas (second century), author of *The Shepherd.*

### B. The Apologists.
1. *This is the name given to certain Christian writers who set themselves to the task of defending the faith to outsiders.*
2. *They aimed to make converts among the educated.*
   - (a) Justin Martyr (c.100-c.165).
   - (b) Tatian (c.160), probably a Gnostic.
   - (c) Tertullian (c.160-c.220), a great theologian.
   - (d) Irenaeus (c.130-c.200), opponent of Gnosticism.

### C. Some Church Fathers.
   - (1) Origen (d.254), a great scholar.
   - (2) Cyprian (d.258), Bishop of Carthage.
   - (3) Ambrose (d.397), Bishop of Milan.
   - (4) Augustine (d.430), Bishop of Hippo.

D. **The mounting influence and power of the Church of Rome.**
1. *Irenaeus gave weight to the tradition that it was founded by Peter and Paul.*
2. *Widespread belief that Peter and Paul were martyred in Rome under Nero (c.64 AD).*
3. *The fact that the church in Rome held up with great vigour under persecution by Nero.*
4. *Paul's epistle to the Romans served to thrust the church there into some prominence.*
5. *The prestige of being situated in the capital of the empire, 'the eternal city'.*
6. *Apparently by AD 100 it was the largest church in Christendom.*
7. *Its successful resistance of Gnosticism and other forces strengthened its reputation.*
8. *It is thought that the Apostolic Creed (c.150-170) was formed there.*
9. *It was looked to for leadership and orthodoxy by opponents of Gnosticism, especially Irenaeus.*
    (a)    He said, 'It is a matter of necessity that every church should agree with this church,' meaning the church at Rome.
    (b)    It was apparently the only church in the West with which any of the apostles was associated.
10. *It continued to have a number of strong and gifted men as its bishops.*
11. *There was a decline of Christian influence in Asia Minor and elsewhere where one might have expected great leadership. Note: Jerusalem was destroyed in AD 70 and again in 135.*
12. *The influence of the Epistle of Clement of Rome.*
13. *The Edict of Valentinian III (445), Emperor, affirming the primacy of the Pope.*
14. *The Chalcedonian Formula (451), drawn up by Leo, Bishop of Rome. It was acclaimed, 'Peter has spoken through the mouth of Leo.'*

E. **Baptism, as it was understood.**
1. *Symbolic view; that baptism is a symbol of several things:*
    (a)    Christ's death, burial and resurrection.
    (b)    The believer's spiritual participation in Christ's death, burial and resurrection.
    (c)    A wholly new relationship to Christ.
    (d)    A cleansing from sin.
    (e)    The reception of the Holy Spirit.
    (f)    The result: admission to the church.

2. *Sacramental view:* it is a rite which actually cleanses from sin whereby the grace of God is mediated to the recipient and regeneration is effected.

3. *Changes in the meaning of baptism*:
   (a)  It came to be regarded as indispensable. 'Whoever believes and is baptised will be saved, but whoever does not believe will be condemned' (Mark 16:16).
   (b)  Hermas regarded it as the very foundation of the church; for it washes away all previous sins.
   (c)  Justin said that baptism effected separation and illumination; washing away all previous sins.
   (d)  Tertullian believed it conveyed eternal life itself.

4. *Infant baptism.*
   (a)  First mentioned by Irenaeus in an obscure way.
   (b)  Tertullian discouraged it, holding that character should be formed first.
   (c)  Constantine (d.337), who made the Roman Empire officially 'Christian', felt one should not be baptised until one was sure one would not sin again. (He waited until just before his death.)
   (d)  Origen (d.254) said it was an apostolic custom.
   (e)  Cyprian (d.258) favoured its earliest possible reception.
   (f)  Probable reasons for the rise of infant baptism:
      (1)  Original sin, articulated by Augustine (d.430).
      (2)  Outside the church 'there is no salvation' (Cyprian), and baptism is the entrance requirement.
      (3)  Interpretation of Christ's words, 'I tell you the truth, no-one can enter the kingdom of God unless he is born of water and the Spirit' (John 3:5).
   (g)  Became universal in the sixth century.

5. *Mode of baptism.*
   (a)  The New Testament seems to assume immersion.
      (1)  The Greek word is *baptizo* (to plunge in water).
      (2)  Calvin, who did not immerse, granted that it was so in the New Testament.
   (b)  Immersion prevailed until the late Middle Ages in the West; it is still practised in the East.
   (c)  The Didache stated immersion was preferable, where there is 'running water'.
   (d)  Affusion (sprinkling water) eventually replaced immersion owing to convenience.

6. *By Tertullian's time an elaborate ritual had developed:*
   (a)  First, a formal renunciation of evil by the candidate.
   (b)  A threefold immersion.

    (c)    The newly baptised tasted a mixture of milk and honey, symbolising a newborn babe.

    (d)    He or she was then anointed with oil.

    (e)    Hands were laid on him or her, in token of the reception of the Holy Spirit.

    (f)    Tertullian is the first to reveal the existence of sponsors, or godparents.

## F. The Lord's Supper.

1. *The New Testament setting.*
    - (a)    The New Testament seems to refer to two meals observed by early Christians.
        - (1)    The Supper instituted by Christ in the Upper Room (Luke 22:19-20).
        - (2)    An *agape* meal or love feast; a 'breaking of bread'; a common meal which was a bond of fellowship and a means of support for the needy (Acts 2:46; cf. Jude 12).
    - (b)    In many instances they seem to have been practised jointly (1 Corinthians 11:20ff.).
    - (c)    In the second century the two were separate and the *agape* meal was later dropped.

2. *The use of the term 'eucharist' (thanksgiving, from* eucharistia – *1 Corinthians 11:24 and Matthew 26:27ff.), by Justin Martyr referred to the supper and was retained largely by Catholicism.*

3. *Ignatius used two metaphors to describe the Supper:*
    - (a)    'Medicine of immortality'.
    - (b)    'Antidote to death' which gives eternal life in Jesus Christ.

4. *By the late second century, the conception of a 'real presence' of Christ in the Supper was widespread.*
    - (a)    The Supper was looked upon as a sacrifice by Irenaeus and Tertullian.
    - (b)    Of course, a sacrifice demands a priest.
        - (1)    With Cyprian, the Supper is regarded as a sacrifice offered to God by a priest.
        - (2)    By 253 the Supper was seen as a sacrament, in which Christ is really present.

5. *The emergence of the Mass (fourth century).*
    - (a)    It was composed of two parts:

(1)   The sacrifice of the Mass.

(2)   The eucharist, or communion; the prayer of thanks which preceded the Supper.

(b)   Ambrose (d.397) applied to the eucharist the Latin expression *missam facere* ('to perform the Mass').

    (1)   It comes from *missa* and *mittere* (to send).

    (2)   The word was apparently used to dismiss the unbaptised from the part of the service when the Supper was observed.

6.  *By the Middle Ages the Roman Catholic Church turned the eucharist into a refined dogma, known as transubstantiation.*

(a)   With a wave of the priest's hand and the words, 'Hoc est corpus meum' (this is my body), the bread is said to become the body of Christ.

(b)   The same sort of thing was done to the wine, making it to become the blood of Christ.

## G. The church.

1.  *Apostolic succession, wherein it is held that the ministry is derived from the apostles by a continuous succession.*

(a)   Bishops are said to be successors to the apostles because:

    (1)   They perform the functions of apostles.

    (2)   Their commission goes back to the apostles.

    (3)   Their continuity can be traced back to the apostles.

(b)   This was first emphasised by Clement of Rome.

(c)   It was elaborated on by Irenaeus and Cyprian.

(d)   This is the foundation for the Episcopalian form of church government.

    (1)   The church's authority lies with the bishop.

    (2)   Apostolic succession is assumed.

2.  *The Church and salvation.*

(a)   Cyprian is the first to use the phrase, 'No salvation outside the church.' He also said, 'He cannot have God for his Father who has not the Church for his mother.'

3.  *The Church and State.*

(a)   In 313 the Emperor Constantine saw a vision of the cross and the words, 'With this sign you will conquer.'

(b)   This led to his conversion and decree to identify the Roman Empire with the Church.

    (1)   Until then the Church was without any connection to the State.

(2)    After then the Church under Constantine became iden-
tified with the State.

4. *The sacraments eventually evolved to seven:* baptism, the eucharist, holy
orders, marriage, extreme unction, confirmation, penance.

## 2. THE PROTESTANT PERSPECTIVE IN THE LIGHT OF MORE RECENT CHURCH HISTORY

**A. The nature of the church, as generally understood by the Reformers.**
1. *The visible church and the invisible church.*
   (a)    The visible church are those who have been baptised and who
          partake of the sacraments; they may or may not have been regen-
          erated.
   (b)    The invisible church are those who have been regenerated by
          the Holy Spirit; God's true elect.

2. *The church militant and the church triumphant.*
   (a)    The church militant: the church here below which wages war-
          fare against the world, the flesh and the devil.
   (b)    The church triumphant: those who have gone on to be with the
          Lord; the perfected saints.

3. *'The church' is where three things are taking place:*
   (a)    The Word of God is preached.
   (b)    The sacraments are faithfully administered.
   (c)    Discipline is exercised; that is, ungodliness in the church's
          membership is dealt with.

4. *The church is to be separate from the state.*
   (a)    There are varying degrees of this view when actually carried
          out in practice.
   (b)    Various countries in the sixteenth century tended to retain a
          national church of a sort, even if their ecclesiologies varied:
          (1)    The church in Germany tended to be Lutheran.
          (2)    The church in Switzerland tended to be Reformed.
          (3)    The church in England tended to be Episcopal.

5. *The main point that emerged from the Great Reformation is that the
   visible church was no longer seen as exclusively Roman Catholic.*
   (a)    This is why the concept of the invisible church and the church
          militant came into being.
   (b)    What mattered: not that you are in the visible church (which does

not prove that you are born again), but in the invisible church and church militant.

(1)    The invisible church included all who were saved.
(2)    The church militant included those who were active and committed in their faith.

**B. Three forms of church government followed the Reformation:**
1. *Episcopal, the church governed by bishops.*
   (a)    the Greek word *episkopos* means 'overseer' (Acts 20:28; Philippians 1:1; 1 Timothy 3:2).
   (b)    the Greek word *presbuteros* means 'elder'. It is sometimes used interchangeably with *episkopos* (cf. Acts 20:17, 28).
   (c)    The main bodies which retain the episcopalian form of church government are:
          (1)    The Roman Catholic Church.
          (2)    The Church of England.
          (3)    The Methodist Church.

2. *Presbyterian, the church governed by a presbytery, or board of elders.*
   (a)    Based partly on scriptures like Acts 15 (the Jerusalem Council) and 1 Timothy 4:14.
   (b)    This form of government emerged under the teaching of John Calvin, who claimed that it was the apostolic model.
   (c)    There are two kinds of elders, generally speaking, which form the presbytery.
          (1)    Ruling elder, who may be a layman.
          (2)    Teaching elder, the pastor (or clergyman).
   (d)    The main bodies holding to this form of government include:
          (1)    The Presbyterian Church.
          (2)    Reformed churches.

3. *Congregationalism, which rests on the independence and autonomy of the local congregation.*
   (a)    The Greek term *ekklesia* is taken to mean not a wider body of churches but only a local meeting together of believers.
   (b)    This view emerged under Puritan separatism in England through men like Robert Brown (d.1633) and John Owen (d.1683).
   (c)    The main bodies which hold to congregationalism include:
          (1)    Congregational churches.
          (2)    Baptist churches.
          (3)    Brethren assemblies.

## C. Baptism

1. *Most Episcopalian and Presbyterian churches retained the practice of infant baptism.*
    (a)    John Calvin held that baptism was a sign of the covenant.
           (1)    Baptism replaced circumcision.
           (2)    All children born into believing families (if at least one parent was a Christian) should be baptised.
    (b)    There are two views as to whether those who are baptised are saved:
           (1)    With most episcopal churches baptism is regarded as effecting regeneration.
           (2)    With Reformed churches there are two further options:
                  (a) Consider them saved until the opposite appears.
                  (b) Consider them unsaved until the positive appears.

2. *Believer's baptism.*
    (a)    Whether by sprinkling or immersion, the only suitable candidate for baptism is a believer.
    (b)    Men like John Smyth (d.1612) became convinced that infant baptism was not baptism at all, though sprinkling was the mode with early Baptists.
    (c)    The mode of immersion came to England from Holland (where it was practised by 'Anabaptists') in 1641.
    (d)    Most Baptist churches hold to believer's baptism by immersion.

## D. The Lord's Supper (see chapter on the Lord's Supper).

1. Martin Luther rejected transubstantiation and came up with consubstantiation: the bread and wine become Christ's body and blood by faith.
2. Ulrich Zwingli (d.1531) said that the Lord's Supper is merely a memorial: 'This do in remembrance of me.'
3. John Calvin believed in the 'spiritual presence' of Christ at the Supper – by faith grace is imparted by 'feasting on Christ'.

## E. The sacraments.

1. *Most Protestant churches retain only two of the seven aforementioned sacraments:* (a) baptism, (b) the Lord's Supper.
2. *Some churches, especially some Baptists, are uneasy with the term 'sacrament' and prefer 'ordinance'.*
    (a)    'Sacrament' implies something necessarily happens whether or not the person believes for himself or herself.
    (b)    Using the term 'ordinance' sets one free to believe for himself.

## Conclusion

When it comes to ecclesiology, Christians hold different views, especially on baptism, the Lord's Supper, and Church Government. Historical perspectives on these and other topics will stimulate our thinking about them. However, it is important to check these perspectives with what the Bible says.

Often we will find ourselves in churches with whose practices we personally disagree. It is important in such situations to realise that the fundamentals of the faith are more important that those issues on which we may disagree.

# 28

# THE WORSHIP OF GOD

**INTRODUCTION**

A. **The subject of the worship of God deals with the very nature of the true God.**
   1. *The God of the Bible is admittedly and unapologetically a jealous God* (Joshua 24:19).
      (a) He will tolerate no rivals (Isaiah 42:8).
      (b) He is very 'possessive' (1 Corinthians 6:20).

   2. *The God of the Bible wants to be worshipped* (Exodus 20:2-6).
      (a) He wants praise and adoration (Psalm 8:1).
      (b) He wants to be feared and served (Psalm 34:9).

B. **Why is this subject important?**
   1. *Worship touches the heart of God; he is moved when we worship him.*
   2. *In learning about worship we are learning how to please God.*
      (a) We will learn that God wants to be worshipped.
      (b) We will learn how to worship him.

   3. *There is widespread interest in 'worship' these days in many Christian circles.*
      (a) 'Worship' is often a euphemism for chorus singing.
      (2) 'Worship' is often a euphemism for almost anything in church other than preaching.

   4. *I suspect that the widespread interest in worship is also matched by a widespread ignorance as to the true meaning of worship.*
      (a) Worship is not that which one does only at church – or even in his private quiet time.
      (b) Worship should involve the whole of our lives, seven days a week.

C. **In the New Testament there are two Greek words that translate as worship:**
   1. Proskuneo *(used 60 times) means 'to adore', 'to give reverence to'.*
      (a) This word refers to the condition of the heart.
      (b) It is used by Jesus to the woman of Samaria: 'God is a spirit, and his worshippers must worship in spirit and in truth' (John 4:24).

2.  Latreuontes *(used as a noun or verb 26 times) means 'service'.*
    (a)  This is the word which is used to refer to public worship.
    (b)  It is used by Paul in Philippians 3:3: '....who worship by the Spirit of God'; and in Romans 12:1: 'Therefore, I urge you, brothers, in view of God's mercy, to offer your bodies as living sacrifices, holy and pleasing to God – this is your spiritual act of worship.'

3.  *Both words, then, are used to refer to attitudes and actions that are Spirit-led and Spirit-controlled worship.*

D.  **Worshipincludes our preparation for hearing the preached Word, our response as we are listening to the preached Word, and further responses in changing our lifestyles because of the preached Word.**
    1.  *Worship, properly understood, makes preaching central.*
    2.  *We can only worship to the degree we have heard from God.*
        (a)  God's chief means of speaking is through preaching (1 Corinthians 1:21; Titus 1:3).
        (b)  Our ability to show God how we feel is the result of having heard him speak.
    3.  *But worship can also be preparation for the preached Word.*
        (a)  Singing his praise and reading his Word prepares our hearts to receive from God. It puts us in the right frame of mind.
    4.  *Preaching in any case is paramount.*

E.  **Design (aim) of worship: to glorify God and edify the soul.**
    1.  A W Tozer in his book *Whatever Happened to Worship?* says there are two levels in the worship of God.
        (a)  *Gratitude: when we express sincere thanks.*
        (b)  *Excellence: when we worship God for what he is.*
            (1)  Most people never get beyond the level of gratitude.
            (2)  Few, very few, worship God for his excellence – for all that he is in himself – for his transcendence and immanent glory.
                (1)  Transcendence: the glory of God that is beyond the level of ordinary human experience (Exodus 33:18-23).
                (2)  Immanence: the nearness of God, whereby we cry, 'Abba, Father' (Galatians 4:6).

## 1   GOD HAS HIS OWN IDEA HOW HE WANTS TO BE WORSHIPPED

A.  **When it comes to worship, we must ask this question: Who are we aiming to please – God or ourselves?**
    1.  Is our worship actually doing something for God himself?
    2.  Or is it a case of worship doing more for us than for him?

B. **If we really want to please God by our worship we will seek his face as to how he wants to be worshipped.**
1. *It is like when you buy someone a present – who do you want to please?*
    (a) Do you want to please the person you buy for?
    (b) Or do you seek preeminently to please yourself when you give another a present?
2. *True worship will aim to please God entirely, without any view to pleasing ourselves in the process.*
    (a) The wonderful irony is, the more we please God the more we enjoy it!
    (b) It is the most wonderful feeling in the world to discover you really are pleasing God!

C. **There is only one way worship pleases God: when we worship 'by the Spirit of God' (Philippians 3:3).**
1. *What we do in the flesh turns him off* (John 6:63).
2. *What we do in the Spirit gets his attention* (Zechariah 4:6).
    (a) Objectively, we get God's attention by affirming what it is he wants of us. For example,
        (1) To know him as he is.
        (2) To explore the truth about him.
        (3) To honour his Son.
        Note: these three items largely pertain to his *excellence*.
    (b) Subjectively, we get God's attention by allowing his ungrieved Spirit to lead us. For example,
        (1) To feel God's presence.
        (2) To thank him for what he has done.
        (3) To praise him.
        Note: these three items largely pertain to *gratitude*.
    (c) The big assumption in the above is that we are worshipping by the *ungrieved* Spirit.
        (1) The Holy Spirit is a sensitive person and can therefore be grieved (Ephesians 4:30), or quenched (1 Thessalonians 5:19).
        (2) For the Spirit to be ungrieved assumes that our personal lives have been put right.
    (d) The Holy Spirit *ungrieved* means that the Holy Spirit is utterly himself.
    (e) For the Spirit to be himself means that we are rid of whatever displeases God: bitterness; unforgiving spirit; gossip; slander; lust (Ephesians 4:31 -5:5).

3. *It does not follow therefore that any 'worship' must be pleasing to God; whether:*
   (a) Traditional worship; which may do more for us than for God.
   (b) Lively worship; which may do more for us than for God.
   (c) Good preaching; which may do more for us than for God.

4. *Worshipping by the Spirit means:*
   (a) By his help.
   (b) By his impulse.
   (c) Worshipping God so that it does everything for him.

## 2 PREACHING AND WORSHIP

**A. The greatest worship service in the New Testament was on the Day of Pentecost.**
   1. *It was spontaneous and yet the whole event was directed from heaven by 'remote control'.*
      (a) All that took place in Jerusalem was 'by the Spirit of God'.
         (1) The Holy Spirit fell on the people of God in the upper room (Acts 2:1ff.).
         (2) Their response – speaking in tongues – and strange behaviour attracted widespread attention (Acts 2:4ff.).
      (b) Peter preached the Inaugural Sermon of the Church.
         (1) It is likely it was spontaneous; unplanned and without notes.
         (2) It happens that the sermon was 'expository preaching': Peter gave the meaning of certain Old Testament scriptures: Joel 2:28-32; Psalm 16:8-11 and Psalm 110:1 (Acts 2:1-36).

   2. *Luke describes the immediate result for the church following 3,000 people being baptised* (Acts 2:42):
      (a) Teaching of the apostles. (Does this surprise us?)
         (1) One would have to say that, if ever there was an 'optimum level' of the Holy Spirit in the church, it was at this time.
         (2) When the Spirit was present in greatest measure the result was: teaching.
      (b) Fellowship. This was a spontaneous by-product of what God did through anointed people.
         (1) The new converts loved one another.
         (2) They shared in common their new faith and the ostracism (rejection) of their fellow Jews.
      (c) Breaking of bread. This was what we call the Lord's Supper.
         (1) The fact that it is recorded here shows the high priority of the Spirit upon this ancient institution.
         (2) This would be a way they experienced intimacy with Jesus.

(d)  Prayer. The more the Spirit is present, the more we will pray (and want to pray).
   (1)  This may have been largely spontaneous.
   (2)  But Acts 3:1 suggests they developed a corporate time of prayer.

3.  *What are we to learn from the above so far?*
   (a)  The high priority the Holy Spirit placed on preaching.
      (1)  It is how Peter explained what had happened.
      (2)  Luke takes time to show some of *what Peter preached* (instead of saying 'After Peter explained what happened 3,000 asked for baptism').
   (b)  The response to preaching:
      (1)  3,000 converts.
      (2)  The church at worship.

## B. Preaching: the Word of God through human personality.

1.  *There is a parallel between true preaching and the Incarnate Word.*
   (a)  Jesus was God as though he were not man, and yet man as though he were not God.
   (b)  Preaching is the Word of God as though no man delivered it, and yet it is a man speaking according to his own gift, intellect, accent and personality.

2   *The chief thing about preaching is that it must bring a real sense of God.*
   (a)  Not just the Word of God, but of God himself.
   (b)  We will never truly worship if this does not happen.
      (1)  'My message and my preaching were not with wise and persuasive words, but with a demonstration of the Spirit's powei' (1 Corinthians 2:4).
      (2)  'Our gospel came to you not simply with words, but also with power, with the Holy Spirit and with deep conviction' (1 Thessalonians 1:5).

3.  *Preaching that precipitates true worship will be characterised by these things:*
   (a)  Sound doctrine. Good theology!
   (b)  Urgency – when the preacher ostensibly fears that his hearers will remain unmoved.
   (c)  Relevance – touching the lives of the listeners.
   (d)  Gripping – when it gets past defensive barriers.
   (e)  Effectual – when the hearer loses sight of everything but God's voice.

      (1)  Effectual preaching leads to change of mind and change of life.

      (2)  The inevitable effect of this kind of preaching will be worship.

**C. The preacher may be involved in one of three ways while he is preaching:**
1. He may feel nothing at all, yet the people feel the presence of God.
2. He may enjoy preaching but no-one else does!
3. Sometimes both preacher and hearers are simultaneously filled with a sense of God.

**D. Worship and listening.**
1. *We only worship to the degree we hear God speak.*
   - (a) Jesus frequently said, 'He who has an ear let him hear.'
   - (b) 'For he is our God and we are the people of his pasture, the flock under his care. Today, if you hear his voice, do not harden your hearts as you did at Meribah, as you did that day at Massah in the desert' (Psalm 95:7-8).

2. *We worship to the degree we recognise and respond to the Spirit's impulse.*
   - (a) A. W. Tozer said: 'We can have as much of God as we want.'
   - (b) One way we can get more of God is to come with expectancy with reference to the preaching.

3. *There are two kinds of listening:*
   - (a) Active listening: when we listen with eagerness. This leads to worship and is characterised by:
     - (1) An open mind.
     - (2) Willingness to be vulnerable.
     - (3) Willingness to be chastened.
     - (4) Obedience in dealing with any defect the Spirit exposes in us.
   - (b) Passive listening: when we barely listen but God manages to break through unexpectedly.

## 3 WHAT WE PERCEIVE OBJECTIVELY WILL DETERMINE HOW WE WORSHIP SUBJECTIVELY

**A. If lively music and a beautiful tune turn us on, we may feel good.**
1. *That good feeling may be sheer nostalgia*
2. *A good feeling that comes during the worship services may have nothing to do with worship whatever; it may be:*
   - (a) We like the sight of the place where we are supposedly worshipping God.

(b)  We like the sound of the organ or the music.

(c)  We like the preacher's voice or accent.

(d)  We like the ethos of the place: Anglican, Pentecostal, Reformed, and so on.

## B. There are three kinds of doubtful worship.

1. *Emotional worship.*
   (a)  Often this is nostalgic.
   (b)  Often this is provincial or parochial.

2. *Elitist worship.*
   (a)  When a sophisticated style is sought, often appealing to the intellect rather than to the soul.
   (b)  This is sometimes found in a liturgical church.

3. *Entertainment worship.*
   (a)  This is when singing is a performance.
   (b)  The very glory of God is often forgotten.

## C. True worship comes only to the degree we see and love the glory of God.

1. *The glory of God is the sum total of all his attributes.*
   (a)  It is the nearest you come to the 'essence' of God.
   (b)  To see God's glory is to see God.
      (1)  Not literally, that is, face to face.
      (2)  But yet truly, as though you saw him!

2. *True preaching in the Spirit will be God-centred and cause one to feel God.*
   (a)  This is what leads to worship.
   (b)  It is when we have been challenged, rebuked, encouraged, thrilled – because the Word of God cut through our hearts (Hebrews 4:12).

## D. A pattern of worship is seen not only on the Day of Pentecost but also in Isaiah 6:1-8.

1. Isaiah saw the glory of God objectively (verses 1-4).
2. Isaiah then responded to this subjectively (verses 5-8).

## CONCLUSION

Our aim in worship is to glorify God and edify ourselves. While everything in our lives is to be involved in our worship, it is important to realise the prominence given to the preaching of the Word. Yet it is not enough to have only preaching; what is wanted is worship by the Spirit. This way our worship pleases God (which is what worship is designed to do!).

# 29

# THE LORD'S SUPPER

## INTRODUCTION

A. **One of the least understood, yet most practical, events in church life is the Lord's Supper.**
1. Many Christians privately admit to a lack of understanding of what happens when the Lord's Supper takes place.
2. Many equally admit (reluctantly) to a lack of real enjoyment and edification when the Lord's Supper takes place.

B. **Why this study?**
1. *To explain the Lord's Supper, as though you knew nothing about it.*
   (a) It is often good to begin at Square One.
   (b) This way all understand, and even those who know a lot often learn new things.

2. *To come to terms with something that was very special to the early church.*
   (a) On the Day of Pentecost it was the third thing that Luke mentioned which they did (Acts 2:42).
   (b) This was when the church was at 'optimum power'.

3. *To understand why Jesus himself instituted the Lord's Supper.*
   (a) This was his idea, not that of the early church.
   (b) Why did Jesus introduce this before his death?

4. *To see why it is special to God.*
   (a) It must be, as it has been used by the Lord to prepare people for revival. This was true with both of America's two Great Awakenings: in New England (c.1740) and Kentucky (c.1800).

5. *To trace its development in church history, especially since the Great Reformation.*

C. **Definition of terms.**
1. *Eucharist:* from the Greek word *eucharisto* meaning 'giving of thanks'. The Lord's Supper has often been called the Eucharist.

2. *Ordinance;* a rule made by authority, a decree.
3. *Sacrament:* an outward and visible sign of an inward and spiritual grace given to us as a pledge from Christ.
4. *Some Protestants have objected to the term 'sacrament', both with reference to the Lord's Supper and baptism.*
   (a) They feel it is a misleading carry-over from Roman Catholicism.
   (b) They are keen to establish that nothing 'happens' at baptism or the Lord's Supper.
       (1) This could be an over-reaction.
       (2) Just because nothing 'automatic' happens, e.g., baptismal regeneration, it does not mean something cannot still take place that is very precious indeed if we approach either, especially the Lord's Supper, in faith. 'According to your faith, be it unto you.'
5. *Transubstantiation:* the conversion of the whole substance of the bread and wine into the whole Body and Blood of Christ, only the 'accidents' remaining. Connected to this is the idea of the Real Presence, that the bread and wine literally become the body and blood of Christ once the priest says, 'Hoc est corpus meum (This is my body)'. This is the Roman Catholic view.
6. *Consubstantiation:* the co-existence of the substance of the bread and wine with the Body and Blood of Christ. This was Martin Luther's view.
7. *Memorial Supper:* the view of Ulrich Zwingli, that the Lord's Supper is but a memorial, or remembrance, of Christ's death.
9. *Spiritual Presence:* the view of John Calvin's, that Christ is *spiritually* present at the Supper of the Lord when he is discerned by faith.

## 1   BRIEF HISTORY OF THE LORD'S SUPPER

### A. Jesus introduced the Lord's Supper (Matthew 26:17-30; Mark 14:12-26; Luke 22:7-23).

1. *The occasion is noteworthy for two things:*
   (a) It was the Passover (Matthew 26:17).
   (b) It was the night Jesus was betrayed (1 Corinthians 11:23).

2. *Jesus introduced the Lord's Supper with an ominous prophecy and also a glorious promise.*
   (a) Prophecy: one of the twelve would betray him (Matthew 26:21).
   (b) Promise: he would drink the fruit of the vine with us in the Kingdom of God (Matthew 26:29).

3. *The Lord's Supper would be in two parts.*
   (a) The eating of bread.
   (b) The drinking of the fruit of the vine.
   (c) Prayer of thanks was given before the partaking of *both* the bread
       and the wine (Matthew 26:26-27).

4. *Both the bread and wine were said to be 'his'.*
   (a) As for the bread: 'This is my body' (Matthew 26:26).
   (b) As for the wine: 'This is my blood' (Matthew 26:28).

5. *Both the bread and wine were said to be for us.*
   (a) The body is 'given for you' (Luke 22:19).
   (b) The blood is 'poured out for you' (Luke 22:20). Matthew adds 'for
       many for the forgiveness of sins' (26:28).

6. *The reason we call it an institution is because Jesus said, 'Do this in
   remembrance of me'* (Luke 22:19).
   (a) It was therefore a command.
   (b) It was also an assumption that they would keep it up; 'I will not
       drink of this fruit of the vine from now on until I drink it anew with
       you in my Father's kingdom' (Matthew 26:29).

### B. Paul's contribution (1 Corinthians 11:23-34).

1. *The Lord's Supper was possibly preceded by a common meal, sometimes called the 'Agape Feast'.*
   (a) It was much like today's 'pot-luck supper'; all ate each other's food.
   (b) After all had eaten (they were supposed to do it together, and
       each having equal access to the same food), they carried out the
       Lord's Supper.
   (c) However, this had been abused by some Corinthian Christians (1
       Corinthians 11:17-22).
       (1) The more affluent Christians went ahead of others.
       (2) The slaves could not arrive until later – when all the better
           food and wine was gone.

2. *Paul passed on what he had received regarding the Lord's Supper.*
   (a) The Lord's Supper was a proclamation of the Lord's death, with a
       lovely reference to the Second Coming (1 Corinthians 11:26).
   (b) The grave warning concerning partaking 'in an unworthy manner'
       (1 Corinthians 11:27).
   (c) The need to examine oneself (1 Corinthians 11:28).
   (d) The possibility of drinking judgement on oneself by not recognis-
       ing the Lord's body (1 Corinthians 11:29).

## C. Subsequent developments.

1. *Ignatius, a disciple of John and famous Christian martyr, referred to the Lord's Supper as 'the medicine of immortality', which sadly may have given rise to a superstitious trend.*

2. *The rise of the Mass.*

    (a) The early Christian worship in certain places was in two parts: public and private (in that order).

    (b) The private part was for believers only, the rest being 'sent' on their way.

        (1) Some think the Latin *missa* (meaning 'to send') is what gave rise to the second part of the service being called 'mass' because of the similarity of the sound of *missa* and mass.

        (2) In any case, Mass became a word used to refer to the celebration of the Lord's Supper for Christians only.

3. *Radbertus (c.785-c.860) came up with a theological rationale to explain how Christ's body and blood were present in the bread and wine.*

    (a) What 'appeared' was 'accidents'.

    (b) What was real was the 'substance'.

    (c) This led to referring to the body and blood of Christ as *substantially* in the bread and wine.

    (d) The doctrine of transubstantiation follows from this; it became official Roman Catholic dogma (teaching).

4. *Martin Luther (1483-1546) objected to transubstantiation but came up with consubstantiation which appeared to mean that the bread and wine became the body and blood of Christ when eaten.*

5. *Ulrich Zwingli (1484-1532) objected both to Roman Catholic teaching and to Luther's attempt to compromise by saying that the Lord's Supper has nothing whatever to do with the body and blood of Christ but that the Supper is merely a 'memorial' to Christ in honour of his death.*

    (a) This became standard orthodoxy for a number of Protestants, especially Baptists.

    (b) This may also be why the Lord's Supper has been relatively meaningless to many Christians.

6. *Calvin felt that all the above missed the point.*

    (a) He said Christ is *spiritually* present in the bread and wine; as if 'set before our very eyes'.

    (b) He felt that grace *is* imparted to us in the Supper if we have faith.

    (c) For this reason Calvin could speak of 'feasting on Christ' when we take the Supper.

7. *One of the sadder developments in church history is that of 'fencing the table', which became a practice in some places.*
   - (a) This meant that spiritual leaders sat in judgement on fellow Christians as to who could or could not partake of the Supper.
   - (b) They 'fenced' the table, that is, kept certain people from partaking who did not appear worthy.

8. *Another questionable development (it seems to me) is that of restricting participants to being a member of the particular local church that offers the Supper.*
   - (a) If you are not a member of their own local church (even if you are a Christian), you are not allowed to partake.
   - (b) It is thus limited not to believers only but to members of the particular church that has the Lord's Supper.
   - (c) My reply to this: it is not 'our' table but the Lord's table.
   - (d) We are surely put on our honour to examine ourselves (1 Corinthians 11:28).

## 2 THE PURPOSE OF THE LORD'S SUPPER

**A. To make us face continually the real reason God sent his Son to die on a cross for our sins (1 Corinthians 11:26).**
   1. Were it not for the Lord's Supper, who knows how much further removed from the gospel the church would be than it already is!
   2. Partaking of the Lord's Supper is one way of bringing us to the ABC's – why Jesus came.

**B. To bring us to intimacy with Christ (see John 6:53-58).**
   1. To eat someone's flesh, or drink their blood, is to show an intimacy that is ordinarily unthinkable!
   2. But we are to love Christ so much that, by partaking of the bread and wine, we affirm him to the most extreme degree.

**C. To enjoy the Lord's presence in a special manner (Matthew 26:29).**
   1. *There are various manifestations of the Lord's presence, e.g.:*
      - (a) Healing presence (Luke 5:17).
      - (b) Judgement presence (Acts 5:1-11).

   2. *The fact is, when we meet around the Lord's table, Jesus is there.*
      - (a) The Corinthians forgot him entirely and drank judgement upon themselves.
      - (b) This is why we must recognise the Lord's body.
         - (1) When we do, anything can happen!
         - (2) We ought to come with this kind of expectancy.

**D. To have more of him in us! (John 6:53ff.).**

1. In the Middle Ages people superstitiously thought they were eating Jesus when they came to Mass daily – to have Jesus in their bodies all the time.

2. But if we adopt Calvin's view, that grace is imparted because of Christ's spiritual presence in the Supper, we do well to wish that Christ will become more a part of us.

**E. To affirm both the body and the blood.**

1. *'A body you have prepared for me'* (Hebrews 10:5).
   (a) When we partake of the bread we should remember that the Son of God literally has a body.
   (b) Remember that that body suffered for us because of our sins.

2. *The Lord's Supper is in two parts, the latter being especially devoted to Christ's own blood.*
   (a) This mirrors the ancient Day of Atonement which was in two parts:
       (1) The sacrifice of the body of the animal on the altar.
       (2) The carrying of the blood by the high priest inside the curtain where it was sprinkled on the Mercy Seat.
   (b) We can never go wrong in honouring Christ's blood – not just his 'death' but his very blood.

**F. To affirm the Church.**

1. *The term 'body' in 1 Corinthians 11:29 is an intentional ambiguity: referring both to Christ's body on the cross and also to his body – the church.*

2. *This means at least two things:*
   (a) Every person at the Supper is equally recognised (no second class Christians).
   (b) We are at peace with one another.

## 3  THE SERIOUSNESS OF THE LORD'S SUPPER

**A. We are to partake in a worthy manner.**

1. *This does not mean we are worthy in the sense of being 'good' enough. We would be most unworthy indeed!*

2. *Partaking in a worthy manner consists of these things:*
   (a) Examining yourself (1 Corinthians 11:28).
   (b) Affirming those partaking of the Supper with you.
   (c) Remembering the reasons for the Supper.
   (d) Coming with expectancy that Christ will be real to you.

**B. Partaking unworthily is inviting judgement upon ourselves.**
  1. *In Corinth, judgement had come; they experienced:*
     (a) External chastening: some were sick.
     (b) Terminal chastening: some were dead.

  2. *Remember, they were in a revival situation.*
     (a) If revival comes, a return of God's presence of judgement may well be experienced.
     (b) In the meantime, we are without excuse if we take the Supper lightly.

**C. We can prevent chastening by judging ourselves.**
  1. *That means we come to terms with God's Word.*
  2. *We can spare much needless disciplining* (1 Corinthians 11:31).
     (a) Being chastened proves we are saved (Hebrews 12:6).
     (b) But certain kinds of chastening can be avoided!

**CONCLUSION**
Jesus instituted the Lord's Supper on the night of the Passover, shortly before his death. It was designed as a remembrance of his sacrifice on the Cross: his life for ours. Through partaking in the Lord's Supper we affirm Christ and enjoy his presence in a special manner.

# 30

## OUR RESPONSIBILITY TO THE LOST

**INTRODUCTION**

**A. Our responsibility to the lost.**
  1. *'Am I my brother's keeper?'*
     (a) That was Cain's self-justifying rationale when asked, 'Where is your brother Abel?' (Genesis 4:9).
     (b) This is often our rationale for our irresponsible attitude and actions toward the lost.
         (1) D L Moody was once told, 'We don't like the way you evangelise.' He replied, 'I don't like the way you don't do it.'

  2. *We answer Cain's question with a resounding 'Yes'.*
     (a) In my first interview after becoming the minister of Westminster Chapel I was asked, 'What weaknesses do you see in British evangelicalism?' I replied quite spontaneously – without giving it much thought – two things:
         (1) British evangelicals, generally speaking, don't tithe.
         (2) They tend to be passive in evangelism.
     (b) I fear that many are 'evangelistic' with other things:
         (1) Converting others to their own point of view.
         (2) Rivalry between churches.
         (3) Fishing in the Christian pond.

**B. In this chapter I want to put forward the case for rugged evangelism.**
  1. *I want to put the case in a two-fold manner:*
     (a) The church's responsibility to be evangelistic.
     (b) Your own responsibility to be a soul-winner.

  2. *There will be no soul-winning in heaven.*
     (a) You may regret many things with regard to your use of time and money on earth.
     (b) When you face God at the Judgement Seat of Christ there are two things you won't regret:
         (1) The amount of money you gave to God.
         (2) The amount of time spent in trying to be a soul-winner.

## C. Why is this subject important?

1. *The doctrine of eternal punishment ought to be one of the greatest motivations to evangelise.*
   - (a) There are two things that will militate against evangelism:
     - (1) The doctrine of universalism (all will be saved regardless of our efforts).
     - (2) The doctrine of annihilation (that the lost ultimately cease to exist as persons).
   - (b) When we are convicted that there really is a hell in the old-fashioned and classic sense, it should shame us for our lack of evangelistic fervour.
     - (1) None of us can save everybody.
     - (2) But we can save some (1 Corinthians 9:22).

2. *Among Jesus' final words on earth were his commands to evangelise.*
   - (a) 'Therefore go and make disciples of all nations, baptising them in the name of the Father and of the Son and of the Holy Spirit' (Matthew 28:19).
   - (b) 'He said to them, "Go into all the world and preach the good news to all creation' (Mark 16:15).
   - (c) 'But you will receive power when the Holy Spirit comes on you; and you will be my witnesses in Jerusalem, and in all Judea and Samaria, and to the ends of the earth' (Acts 1:8).
     - (1) The missing note with regard to the baptism of the Holy Spirit nowadays is its connection with evangelising.
     - (2) One could argue from Acts 1:8 (and other places) that one isn't really filled with the Spirit if one isn't evangelising.

3. *Some don't evangelise because they haven't been taught.*
   - (a) This is one of the reasons people don't tithe.
   - (b) This is also why some don't evangelise.
     - (1) They haven't been taught – or motivated.
     - (2) They haven't been trained.
   - (c) This chapter may not give you much training, but perhaps it may motivate you:
     - (1) To want to evangelise.
     - (2) To get training.

4. *Britain is ripe for the gospel.*
   - (a) Many feel the secular age is against us – wrong!
   - (b) When John Wesley saw the appalling conditions in Newcastle in the eighteenth century he wrote in this journal, 'This place is ripe for the gospel.'

(c)  Many may feel offended when they are confronted with the gospel
     – true.
     (1)  But what should we expect?
     (2)  We should not evangelise only because it's easy!

5.  *Evangelism is a vital link with the very reason God sent his Son
    into the world:*
    (a)  To die on a cross – to save us.
    (b)  That we might point people to the cross (Romans 10:14-15).
    (c)  When we are evangelising we *know* we are doing something right!

## 1   WHAT HOPE IS THERE FOR THE LOST?

### A.  The lost (unsaved) are of two kinds:
1.  Those who are living.
2.  Those who are dead.

### B.  What hope have the lost while they are living?
1.  *None, if they have not heard the gospel.*
    (a)  The Bible makes it clear: all men by nature are damned.
        (1)  We are born in sin: 'Surely I have been a sinner from birth,
             sinful from the time my mother conceived me' (Psalm 51:5).
        (2)  We are born dead: 'As for you, you were dead in your
             transgressions and sins' (Ephesians 2:1).
        (3)  We are born condemned: 'Whoever believes in him is not
             condemned, but whoever does not believe stands condemned
             already because he has not believed in the name of God's
             one and only Son' (John 3:18).
    (b)  The gospel is the only thing that can help them.
        (1)  The gospel isn't what damns people.
        (2)  They are damned anyway.
        (3)  The gospel is their only hope.

2.  *Some claim that people will be saved if they haven't heard the gospel.*
    (a)  If so, let us stop evangelising; we are sending more people to
         hell than we are saving by our gospel.
        (1)  Most people will not believe.
        (2)  The number of believers has always been small.
    (b)  If hearing but not responding to the gospel damns people, we are
         cruel monsters to preach the Word!

3.  *We must never forget: we are the instruments of salvation.*
    (a)  We have the only word that can rescue people from sin, the wrath
         of God and eternal death.

(b)  This is what motivated missionaries to leave Britain for heathen nations in the first place.

(c)  William Carey, the first modern foreign missionary, went to India because he knew the people were lost.

C.  **The work of Jesus Christ on the cross must be applied.**
  1.  *It wasn't enough that Jesus died.*
      (a)  He died for all ( 2 Corinthians 5:15; Hebrews 2:9).
      (b)  But not all are saved; otherwise there would be no doctrine of hell.
          (1)  Jesus' death did not automatically save the world.
          (2)  If it did, Jesus' words in Mark 16:15 are nonsense.

  2.  *The promise of eternal life was given on a condition* (John 3:16).
      (a)  Jesus died for the whole world (1 John 2:1-2).
      (b)  But only believers will be saved; God presented his Son as a 'sacrifice of atonement through faith in his blood' (Romans 3:25).
          (1)  Those who believe in Christ are saved.
          (2)  Those who don't are lost.

D.  **The good news is: lost people can be found and saved.**
  1.  *There is hope for the lost.*
      (a)  Millions are lost at this moment.
      (b)  There is hope for every one of them.

  2.  *But on this condition: that they believe the gospel.*
      (a)  This gospel offers them hope.
      (b)  It not only changes destinies; it changes lives.
          (1)  You aren't ready to live until you are ready to die.
          (2)  The gospel is designed primarily to help a person face death.
      (c)  Some say: if there were no heaven or hell, I would still be a Christian. Not Paul!
          (1)  'If only for this life we have hope in Christ, we are to be pitied more than all men' (1 Corinthians 15:19).
          (2)  We must not be ashamed to talk about heaven and hell; it is what lay behind Jesus dying on the cross.

E.  **The lost who have died are also of two kinds:**
  1.  *Those who have heard the gospel.*
  2.  *Those who have not heard the gospel.*
      (a)  Those who have heard the gospel are obviously without excuse (Ezekiel 33:1-6).
      (b)  Those who have not heard the gospel are also without excuse:

'For since the creation of the world God's invisible qualities –
his eternal power and divine nature – have been clearly seen, being
understood from what has been made, so that men are without
excuse' (Romans 1:20).

3. *It would seem that those who have not heard the gospel will be
judged by a different standard* (Romans 2:12-16).
   (a) Those who sin without the knowledge of the Law will perish.
   (b) Those who sin with the knowledge of the Law will perish.
   (c) Those who had no knowledge of the Law still have consciences,
       and the requirements of the Law are on their consciences.
   (d) Their consciences bearing witness, with their thoughts, will be
       doing two things:
       (1) Accusing.
       (2) Defending.
   (e) Note: there is no indication that such will be saved, and yet they
       will be judged by a different standard.

4. *There are principles that emerge that do not answer all our questions but which shed some light:*
   (a) As there are degrees of rewards for the saved, so too there are
       degrees of punishment for the lost. Luke 12:48 says this: 'But
       the one who does not know and does things deserving punishment
       will be beaten with few blows. From everyone who has been given
       much, much will be demanded; and from the one who has been
       entrusted with much, much more will be asked.'
   (b) From this we may conclude:
       (1) From whom much is given much will be required;
           consequently, from whom less is given less is required.
       (2) The lost who never heard the gospel will not be punished as
           severely as those who heard it.
   (c) Remember, 'Will not the Judge of all the earth do right?' (Genesis
       18:25).

## 2   GOD'S MEANS OR METHOD TO REACH THE LOST

### A.  The application of redemption (salvation) is two-fold.

1. *'Redemption' and 'salvation' may often be used interchangeably
   (see Chapter 18).*
   (a) Redemption: 'buying back' by Christ's blood those who are lost
       (1 Peter 1:18-19).
   (b) Salvation: being 'saved' from God's wrath (Romans 5:9).

2.  *What Jesus did on the cross is applied by way of God's calling, which must be understood in two ways (but in this order):*
    (a)  The general calling – the work of the church.
         (1)  This is what all of us are called to do (Mark 16:15).
         (2)  'As the Father has sent me, I am sending you' (John 20:21).
    (b)  The particular calling – the work of the Holy Spirit.
         (1)  'The Spirit and the bride say, "Come!"' (Revelation 22:17).
         (2)  'Many are invited' (the general calling), 'but few are chosen' (the particular calling) (Matthew 22:14).
    (c)  Before the particular calling can take place the general call must come. 'How, then, can they call on the one they have not believed in? And how can they believe in the one of whom they have not heard? And how can they hear without someone preaching to them?' (Romans 10:14).
         (1)  People cannot receive the gospel unless they have heard it.
         (2)  This is our job; to see that all around us hear the Word.

3.  *And yet the general call is not enough.*
    (a)  There must be the particular, special or inner call.
         (1)  This is the work of the Holy Spirit.
         (2)  This is what happens inside a person's heart.
    (b)  There is a saying: 'A man convinced against his will is of the same opinion still.'
         (1)  We may do our best to persuade another person.
         (2)  Only the Holy Spirit can 'open' a person's heart (Acts 16:14).
    (c)  Before the lost can be saved, then, two things must come together:
         (1)  The work of the Christian and the work of the Spirit.
         (2)  If the Spirit does not come alongside our efforts the person we witness to will not be saved.
    (d)  Many references to the 'called' presuppose that the Spirit has done his own work:
         (1)  'And you also are among those who are called to belong to Jesus Christ' (Romans 1:6).
         (2)  'And those he predestined, he also called; those he called, he also justified; those he justified, he also glorified' (Romans 8:30).
         (3)  'Brothers, think of what you were when you were called. Not many of you were wise by human standards; not many were influential; not many were of noble birth' (1 Corinthians 1:26).

B.  **The general call is given another name as well: preaching.**
    1.  *The word 'preaching' refers both to the message and the method by which God works.*

(a)  'For since in the wisdom of God the world through its wisdom
     did not know him, God was pleased through the foolishness of
     what was preached to save those who believe' (1 Corinthians
     1:21).
(b)  'And at his appointed season he brought his word to light through
     the preaching entrusted to me by the command of God our
     Saviour' (Titus 1:3).
     (1)  The message: Jesus Christ who was crucified (1 Corinthians
          2:2).
     (2)  The method: tell this event by our lips (1 Peter 4:11).

2. *Preaching is done basically in two ways:*
   (a)  By the person who has had a 'call' to be a full-time preacher.
        (1)  This is sometimes called teaching. 'The elders who direct
             the affairs of the church well are worthy of double honour,
             especially those whose work is preaching and teaching' (1
             Timothy 5:17).
        (2)  This may be the pastor, vicar or curate, and so on.
   (b)  By every person. All except the apostles were scattered through-
        out Judea and Samaria. Those who had been scattered preached
        the word wherever they went (Acts 8:1, 4)!
        (1)  Preaching therefore is not limited to the pulpit.
        (2)  You and I *are* called to be our brother's keeper!

3. *All Christians, then, are in some sense called to preach.*
   (a)  Are you a Christian? Then you are a preacher.
   (b)  How much preaching have you done lately?
        (1)  This need not be done by the 'clergy' to hundreds at a time.
        (2)  It is easier to speak to hundreds than to one other person!

C. **Preaching includes speaking the truth about the person and work
   of Jesus.**
   1. *This is done by the 'professional' clergyman or church leader who
      will have been trained and equipped for this.*
   2. *And yet preaching is that which all Christians should do.*
      (a)  They may not have had professional training.
           (1)  Some new converts giving their testimonies can do great
                preaching!
           (2)  Saul of Tarsus started this immediately (Acts 9:20).
      (b)  Those who tend to do this best are those who have sought further
           teaching or training.
           (1)  This can take place by sitting under public teaching or
                preaching.

(2) Spurgeon said that the best way to learn how to preach is to sit under good preaching.

(c) Those who find difficulty in leading another person to Christ should take one of the many courses available today.

3. *Speaking personally, God has dealt with me along these lines.*
   (a) For years I felt I had sufficiently fulfilled my calling because I preached evangelistic sermons!
   (b) I began to see that what I asked others to do I had to do myself.

## CONCLUSION

There is hope for the lost – while they are still alive and well. That hope is summed up in one word: the gospel. The gospel is not that all are saved because Jesus died for them. The gospel is the good news that Jesus died in our place and that by hearing of his sacrifice we may believe and be saved. It is our responsibility to tell this good news to the lost.

# 31

## THE PRIESTHOOD OF ALL BELIEVERS

### INTRODUCTION

A. **This subject is one of the contributions, or rediscoveries, of the Great Reformation of the sixteenth century.**
   1. *The Great Reformation was the movement for reform of certain doctrines and practices of the Church of Rome, resulting in the establishment of the Reformed or Protestant Church.*
      (a) Reform: to make or become better by removal or abandonment of imperfection or faults.
      (b) Reformed churches: those churches that accepted the principles of the Reformation, especially those that were more Calvinistic in doctrine.

   2. *The Reformation generally had four streams:*
      (a) Those that followed the teachings of Martin Luther (1483-1546), mainly found in Germany and Scandinavia.
      (b) The Reformed wing, largely in Switzerland and Scotland, who in varying degrees followed:
         (1) Ulrich Zwingli (1484-1532) of Zurich.
         (2) John Calvin (1509-1564) of Geneva.
      (c) The English wing, influenced largely by:
         (1) William Tyndale (d.1536).
         (2) Archbishop Thomas Cranmer (1489 - 1556).
      (d) The 'Radical Reformers', usually called Anabaptists.

   3. *The teachings of the Reformation can be summarised in this manner:*
      (a) *Sola scriptura* (the scriptures alone), with the emphasis on the Bible being the only basis of faith and practice.
      (b) *Sola fidei* (faith alone), the emphasis being on justification by faith alone – not works.
      (c) *Sola gratia* (grace alone), the emphasis being largely on Christ's substitutionary work on the cross and predestination.
         (1) Most of the Reformers were generally agreed on the above, although Calvin was more explicit on the doctrines of grace than Luther or the English Reformers were.
         (2) However, the Anabaptists were sometimes anti-predestinarian in their soteriology (doctrine of salvation).

4. *Parallel with the above were these assumptions and practices by the Reformers and their followers:*
   (a) The centrality of preaching (as opposed to the centrality of the eucharist – the Lord's Supper).
   (b) Opposition to the Mass (especially to the idea that Christ's body and blood were literally present in the bread and wine).
   (c) Opposition to the teaching of purgatory (a place or condition in which souls undergo purification by temporary punishment).
   (d) Opposition to praying to the virgin Mary and to saints.
   (e) The priesthood of the believer, as opposed to the need for an earthly person to serve as a mediator between us and God.

B. **Priesthood of the believer: immediate and direct influence and communion with God without an earthly mediator.**
   1. Immediate: nearest, next, with nothing between.
   2. Direct: with nothing or no-one in between, in an unbroken line.
   3. Mediator: one who acts as go-between or peacemaker between opposing sides in a dispute.
   4. Influence: the power to produce an effect.
   5. Communion: fellowship, or two-way relationship with one another.
   6. God: the Creator, the true God (the God of the Bible), who has been offended by sin and whose justice must be satisfied.

C. **Why is this study important and why is it relevant?**
   1. It forces us to examine a bit of church history.
   2. It helps us to see why there was a need for the Great Reformation and why we should be happy that it came about.
   3. It requires that we look at the emergence of the priesthood in the Bible.
   4. It gives us a needed glimpse of the Old Testament, a part of the Bible sadly so unknown to so many today.
   5. It gives us a wonderful view of Christ's priesthood.
   6. It shows us our privilege and responsibility as Christians.
   7. It should bring us closer to God.
   8. It affirms the importance of all Christians, regardless of age, sex or background.

## 1    THE RISE OF THE PRIESTHOOD

A. **The priesthood has its origins in the Old Testament.**
   1. *The word 'priest' occurs over 700 times in the Old Testament.*
      (a) The Hebrew is *kohen*.
      (b) It is sometimes qualified by 'chief' or 'high'.

2. *The priest was one who stood before God as his servant or minister.*
   (a) The posture of standing, rather than sitting, is inherent in the Hebrew:
       (1) *Kohen* is derived from *kahan.*
       (2) The latter appears to have the same meaning as *kur*, 'to stand'.
   (b) The priest's function was to stand before God, not unlike being that of a bridge between God and the people.

3. *There was moreover a threefold hierarchy of officials: (1) High priest, or chief priest; (2) priest; (3) Levite. Each order was distinct with its own distinctive functions and privileges.*

4. *The priesthood was made up of men from the tribe of Levi.*
   (a) This seems to have been somewhat of a reward to the tribe for their response to Moses after the Israelites worshipped the golden calf (Exodus 32).
       (1) 'So he stood at the entrance to the camp and said, "Whoever is for the LORD, come to me." And all the Levites rallied to him' (Exodus 32:26).
       (2) 'Then Moses said, "You have been set apart to the LORD today, for you were against your own sons and brothers, and he has blessed you this day"' (Exodus 32:29).
       (3) 'At that time the LORD set apart the tribe of Levi to carry the ark of the covenant of the LORD, to stand before the LORD to minister and to pronounce blessings in his name, as they still do today' (Deuteronomy 10:8).
       (4) Moses never forgot this and they were given special recognition in Moses' final blessing (Deuteronomy 33:8-11).
   (b) Although they received no inheritance in terms of land, they were the most prestigious of the tribes (Deuteronomy 18:1-2).

## B. The theological significance of the priesthood.

1. *The priesthood represented Israel's union with God.*
   (a) Under the Mosaic covenant (see the chapter on the Covenant) the whole nation was to be:
       (1) 'A kingdom of priests' (Exodus 19:6).
       (2) 'A holy nation' (Leviticus 11:44ff.; Numbers 15:40).
   (b) The priesthood became the mediator of the covenant.
       (1) It therefore had a representative character.
       (2) Corporate responsibility was delegated to representative persons, who discharged it on behalf of the community as a whole.

    (c)  The priests therefore acted as representatives of the people.
- (1) Likeness to God in character was essential for those who would serve him.
- (2) This state of sanctity was symbolised in the Levitical priesthood.

    (d)  The result was twofold:
- (1) The true requirements of serving God were continually kept before the eyes of his covenant people.
- (2) This covenant relationship was vicariously maintained by the priesthood on behalf of the nation as a whole.

2. *The three-fold hierarchy: high priest, priests, Levites.*
    (a)  Levi had three sons: Kohath, Gershom and Merari.
- (1) The Kohathite clan was set apart for special service; this was the family of Aaron, the brother of Moses.
  - (i) He and his descendants were appointed priests.
  - (ii) Only the priests could offer sacrifices; other Levite families did the more menial tasks.
  - (iii) They were the most 'holy' group within Israel.
- (2) The Gershonites carried the curtains and coverings in the desert.
- (3) The Merarites carried and set up the tabernacle itself.

    (b)  The lowest grade were known as Levites, who were set apart for the service of the sanctuary.
    (c)  Above them were the descendants of Aaron – priests.
    (d)  The man in charge of the priests was the chief or 'high' priest.
- (1) He had one privilege, allowed to no-one else.
- (2) He alone could enter the 'holy of holies' once a year, on the Day of Atonement.

3. *Duties of priests and Levites.*
    (a)  Although mostly connected with the tabernacle, temple sacrifice and worship, they had other duties.
- (1) A group of men from each of the three Levite clans formed the temple chorus; they may have composed several of the psalms (e.g., Psalms 85 and 87).
- (2) They also had to answer in God's name to questions that could not otherwise be decided (e.g., when to go out to battle); they used sacred stones called Urim and Thummim, which were kept in a pouch worn on the high priest's chest (Deuteronomy 33:8-11).
  - (i) If the priest pulled out the Urim stone, the answer was 'no'.

(ii) If the priest pulled out the Thummim stone, the answer was 'yes'.
(b)  More important: teaching the Law of God (Malachi 2:7).
  (1)  When Moses blessed the tribes of Israel he said that the Levites would first teach the 'precepts to Jacob and your law to Israel' (Deuteronomy 33:10).
  (2)  Then they would present offerings (Deuteronomy 33:10).
(c)  Sadly, the prophets often had to take the priests and Levites to task for failing in these duties (Ezekiel 34).

## 2  THE PRIESTHOOD IN THE NEW TESTAMENT

### A.  In Israel, priesthood was hereditary in the tribe of Levi.
1.  *A priest was born, not made.*
  (a)  No matter how able a person:
    (1)  An Israelite not of the tribe of Levi need not apply!
    (2)  A Gentile of course was also out of the question.
  (b)  A priest was regarded as possessing special knowledge of God.
    (1)  He was the director, if not the performer, of sacrifices offered to God.
    (2)  He was the dispenser and interpreter of any claim to a message from God.
  (c)  John the Baptist was of priestly lineage (Luke 1:5-17).

2.  *Jesus himself was not of priestly stock but a humbly born Galilean carpenter.*
  (a)  Jesus was of the tribe of Judah (Matthew 1:2).
  (b)  'Others said, "He is the Christ." Still others asked, "How can the Christ come from Galilee?"' (John 7:41).
  (c)  Jesus was hated by the Sadducean priesthood generally and the chief priests particularly (Matthew 22:23-33; 27:1).

3.  *Some priests however were converted to the Christian faith* (Acts 6:7).

### B.  Christianity contains a radical development of the concept of priesthood.
1.  *The transferral of the role of high priest to Jesus.*
  (a)  The doctrine of the priesthood of Christ is a major contribution of the Epistle to the Hebrews.
    (1)  'Therefore, holy brothers, who share in the heavenly calling, fix your thoughts on Jesus, the apostle and high priest whom we confess' (Hebrews 3:1).

(2) 'Therefore, since we have a great high priest who has gone through the heavens, Jesus the Son of God, let us hold firmly to the faith we profess' (Hebrews 4:14).

(b) He is seen as the perfect fulfilment of the Old Testament priesthood.
   (1) He brought the priesthood to a definitive end in history.
   (2) He established a once-for-all eternal mediatorship between God and man.

(c) The writer of Hebrews knew he had his work cut out for him.
   (1) 'For it is clear that our Lord descended from Judah, and in regard to that tribe Moses said nothing about priests' (Hebrews 7:14).
   (2) But it was the priesthood of Melchizedek which is fulfilled (Psalm 110; Hebrews 7:1-25).

2. *The transfer of priesthood generally to all believers.*
   (a) A corollary of the priesthood of Christ is the New Testament application of the priesthood to the whole company of the faithful in the church.
      (1) Corollary: a natural consequence or result, something that follows logically after something else is proved.
      (2) The believer is made one with his or her Saviour (see the previous study on 'The believer's position in Christ') and so shares in the dignity of Christ.

   (b) This does not mean we no longer need a mediator.
      (1) 'Jesus answered, "I am the way and the truth and the life. No-one comes to the Father except through me" ' (John 14:6).
      (2) 'For there is one God and one mediator between God and men, the man Christ Jesus' (1 Timothy 2:5).

   (c) It means we don't need an *earthly* mediator!
      (1) 'You also, like living stones, are being built into a spiritual house to be a holy priesthood, offering spiritual sacrifices acceptable to God through Jesus Christ' (1 Peter 2:5).
      (2) 'But you are a chosen people, a royal priesthood, a holy nation, a people belonging to God, that you may declare the praises of him who called you out of darkness in to his wonderful light' (1 Peter 2:9).

(3) 'And has made us to be a kingdom and priests to serve his God and Father – to him be glory and power for ever and ever! Amen' (Revelation 1:6).

(4) 'You have made them to be a kingdom and priests to serve our God, and they will reign on the earth' (Revelation 5:10).

(d) In no instance does any New Testament writer ascribe the title of priest to any individual member or order of ministry in the church.

3. *The transfer of the status of Jewish believers to Gentiles.*
   (a) This was prophesied eight hundred years in advance. 'I revealed myself to those who did not ask for me; I was found by those who did not seek me. To a nation that did not call on my name, I said, "Here am I, here am I"' (Isaiah 65:1).
   (b) Jesus also prophesied this: 'Therefore I tell you that the kingdom of God will be taken away from you and given to a people who will produce its fruit' (Matthew 21:43).
   (c) Peter was among the first to grasp this: 'Then Peter began to speak: "I now realise how true it is that God does not show favouritism but accepts men from every nation who fear him and do what is right"' (Acts 10:34-35).
      (1) 'After much discussion, Peter got up and addressed them: "Brothers, you know that some time ago God made a choice among you that the Gentiles might hear from my lips the message of the gospel and believe"' (Acts 15:7).
      (2) 'He made no distinction between us and them, for he purified their hearts by faith. Now then, why do you try to test God by putting on the necks of the disciples a yoke that neither we nor our fathers have been able to bear? No! We believe it is through the grace of our Lord Jesus that we are saved, just as they are' (Acts 15:9-11).
   (d) Paul became the Apostle to the Gentiles (Galatians 2:7). 'Consequently, you are no longer foreigners and aliens, but fellow-citizens with God's people and members of God's household' (Ephesians 2:19).

4. *The transfer of an exclusively male priesthood to either sex:* 'You are all sons of God through faith in Christ Jesus, for all of you who were baptised into Christ have clothed yourselves with Christ. There is neither Jew nor Greek, slave nor free, male nor female, for you are all one in Christ Jesus' (Galatians 3:26-28).

## 3 THE RISE OF A VICARIOUS PRIESTHOOD IN CHURCH HISTORY

A. **An aberration (a deviation from the New Testament norm) developed from towards the end of the first century.**
1. Clement ((c. 95) employed the three-fold hierarchy of high priest, priests and Levites as an analogous (similar) type of the Christian ministry.
2. The *Didache* (150) called prophets 'your high priests', and spoke of the eucharist as a 'sacrifice'.
3. Tertullian ((c. 200) used the term 'priest' and 'high priest' of the church's ministers.
4. Jerome (345-419) translated the Greek *mysterion* by 'sacramentum' in the Vulgate (Latin translation of the Bible).
5. St Augustine (354-430) defined a sacrament as 'a visible sign of a divine thing'.

B. **The 'sacramental system' was fully developed in the Middle Ages by theologians known as 'Scholastics', such as Thomas Aquinas (1225-1274).**
1. *The sacraments were seven in number:*
    (a) baptism, (b) eucharist, (c) confirmation, (d) extreme unction (prayer for the dying), (e) penance (confession, absolution and act of imposed penitence), (f) ordination, (g) marriage.
2. *Only a priest could administer the sacraments.*

C. **Confession of sins.**
1. *An outgrowth of the above development, especially of penance, in church history was confessing sins to a priest. The biblical support was:*
    (a) 'If you forgive anyone his sins, they are forgiven; if you do not forgive them, they are not forgiven' (John 20:23).
    (b) 'Therefore confess your sins to each other and pray for each other so that you may be healed' (James 5:16a).

2. *The Lateran Council of 1215 made regular confession an absolute law of the Church.*
    (a) The form of absolution (the priest's formal declaration of the forgiveness of the penitent's sins) was: 'I absolve thee.'
    (b) The penitent (the one who is sorry for sins) was assured of the secrecy of the priest.

3. *Martin Luther wrote in 1519, 'There is nothing in the Church which needs reform so much as confession and penance.'*

## 4  THE RELEVANCE OF ALL THE ABOVE FOR US TODAY

### A.  We have one Great High Priest (Hebrews 4:14).

1. *This function is carried out by Jesus at God's right hand* (Hebrews 3:1-4; 7:25).
2. *The nature of his prayer is seen partly in John 17.*
   (a) We confess our sins only to God (1 Timothy 2:5).
   (b) He absolves those who confess to him (1 John 1:9; 2:1-2).

### B.  We are all priests (1 Peter 2:5, 9).

1. *All that is said of the Levite's relationship with God may be generally transferred to us.*
   (a) We do not let another live a holy life vicariously; we must do it ourselves (1 Peter 1:16).
   (b) We do not let another perform worship for us; we must do it ourselves (Hebrews 13:15).
   (c) We do not let a priesthood of men sing for us; we – male and female – sing for ourselves (Galatians 3:28; Ephesians 5:19).
   (d) We do not require that another answer questions pertaining to God; we are required to do it ourselves (1 Peter 3:15).
   (e) We do not ask another to get God's will for guidance; we must seek God's guidance for ourselves (Ephesians 5:17).

2. *This does not mean there are not special functions that are largely required of those called for particular ministry* (1 Corinthians 12:28; Ephesians 4:11ff.).
   (a) There is some overlap between the ancient priesthood and New Testament ministry (cf. 1 Timothy 5:17-18).
   (b) But they do not have a 'head start' in fellowship with God because of their special calling.

## CONCLUSION

In the worship system of Israel, priests were born not made and had this privilege because they belonged to the tribe of Levi. In the new covenant, however, Jesus is the High Priest and all believers are priests because of their faith in him. Believers still need Jesus as the Mediator, but he alone fulfils that function. Because they are priests, all believers can have equal intimacy with God. As A. W. Tozer said, 'You can have as much of God as you want.'

# 32

# THE ROLE OF WOMEN IN MINISTRY

## INTRODUCTION

A. This is an area 'where angels fear to tread'.

B. Not all the questions we may want to ask are clearly answered in the Bible.
   1. *Scriptures that do refer to women are of two sorts:*
      (a) Those that touch on eternal, unchanging principles (1 Timothy 2:13-14).
      (b) Those that are obviously culturally related (1 Corinthians 11:5ff.).

   2. *It is not always easy to tell the difference between the two the eternal and the cultural.*
      (a) Eternal: what must not change, regardless of the times or the culture.
      (b) Cultural: what may have been relevant for Corinth may not fit in Zambia for example, or other places.

C. We all have our biases, and have a fairly shrewd idea (if we are really honest) where we want to end up!
   1. *There are those who want to give women a higher role or profile – they will be selective with the biblical material.*
   2. *There are those who want to give women low (if any) role or profile – they will be selective too with the biblical material.*
   3. *It is very difficult to be objective and unbiased, especially when:*
      (a) It is an emotive issue.
      (b) We want to please certain people.

D. My approach: to go from the general to the particular as openly as we know how to be, in answering the question:  what does the Bible teach on the role of women in ministry?
   1. *The general: the role of women in marriage and the family.*
      (a) Before the Fall; (b) After the Fall.
   2. *The particular: the role of women in the church.*
      (a) In worship; (b) In ministry.

E. Why is this study important?
   1. Women are now being ordained to the Anglican priesthood; is this a good or bad thing?

2. The rise of the Feminist Movement has made an impact of great proportion on the church; is this a good or bad thing?
3. Is there a difference between a woman being a preacher and being a pastor?
4. What does the term 'head' mean: 'the head of the woman is man' (1 Corinthians 11:3)?
5. Does it matter if women 'take over' the ministry, and outnumber the men?
6. What the Bible says about these issues surely matters.
7. We need to focus ourselves to think clearly about painful issues.

F. **There are many single women who wonder what their role is.**
1. The principles that follow, however, remain the same whether the person is married or single.
2. It is the spirit which lies behind the general principles which shows the biblical pattern that may be followed.
3. 1 Corinthians 7:34 affirms singleness.

## 1   THE ROLE OF WOMEN IN MARRIAGE AND THE FAMILY

A. **The first thing we must do is to see the distinction between women's role before the Fall and after the Fall.**
1. *Fall: the event in history when Adam and Eve sinned in the Garden of Eden and took the whole human race with them.*
2. *Is the woman being a 'weaker partner' (1 Peter 3:7, AV 'weaker vessel') the consequence of:*
    (a) The way she was created being unfallen?
    (b) Sin, that is, Eve being deceived?

B. **What can be clearly concluded about Adam and Eve before the Fall:**
1. *God made male and female in his image equally.* 'So God created man in his own image, in the image of God he created him; male and female he created them' (Genesis 1:27).
2. *God made man first, then Eve as a helper.* 'The LORD God said, "It is not good for the man to be alone. I will make a helper suitable for him"' (Genesis 2:18).
3. *Man was given the primary responsibility in creation.* 'Now the LORD God had formed out of the ground all the beasts of the field and all the birds of the air. He brought them to the man to see what he would name them; and whatever the man called each living creature, that was its name. So the man gave names to all the livestock, the birds of the air and all the beasts of the field. But for Adam no suitable helper was found' (Genesis 2:19-20).

4. *Woman was made from the man.*
   (a) 'So the LORD God caused the man to fall into a deep sleep; and while he was sleeping, he took one of the man's ribs and closed up the place with flesh. Then the LORD God made a woman from the rib he had taken out of the man, and he brought her to the man' (Genesis 2:21-22).
   (b) 'For man did not come from woman, but woman from man' (1 Corinthians 11:8).

5. *Woman was made for the man.*
   (b) 'The LORD God said, "It is not good for the man to be alone. I will make a helper suitable for him"' (Genesis 2:18).
   (c) 'Neither was man created for woman, but woman for man' (1 Corinthians 11:9).

6. *Man named her 'woman'.* The man said, "This is now bone of my bones and flesh of my flesh; she shall be called 'woman', for she was taken out of man"' (Genesis 2:23).

7. *Marriage was a divine institution.* 'For this reason a man will leave his father and mother and be united to his wife, and they will become one flesh' (Genesis 2:24).

## C. What can be concluded about Adam and Eve after the Fall?

1. They were conscious of their nakedness, and sewed fig leaves together to cover themselves (Genesis 3:7).
2. Fear emerged. 'He answered, "I heard you in the garden, and I was afraid because I was naked; so I hid"' (Genesis 3:10).
3. Self-justification emerged in both of them. 'And he said, "Who told you that you were naked? Have you eaten from the tree from which I commanded you not to eat?" The man said, "The woman you put here with me – she gave me some fruit from the tree, and I ate it." Then the LORD God said to the woman, "What is this you have done?" The woman said, "The serpent deceived me, and I ate"' (Genesis 3:11-13).
4. Bearing children would be painful. 'To the woman he said, "I will greatly increase your pains in childbearing; with pain you will give birth to children' (Genesis 3:16ab).
5. The woman's desire will be for her husband. 'Your desire will be for your husband....' (Genesis 3:16c).
6. Man would rule over her: '....and he will rule over you' (Genesis 3:16d).
7. Man must take the responsibility for the cursed ground: 'Cursed is the ground because of you; through painful toil you will eat of it all the days of your life' (Genesis 3:17b).
8. Man would work by the sweat of his brow. 'By the sweat of your brow

you will eat your food until you return to the ground, since from it
you were taken; for dust you are and to dust you will return' (Genesis
3:19).

## D. Why is the distinction between Adam and Eve *before* the Fall and *after* the Fall important?

1. *Because Paul makes such a distinction.*
   (a) 'A woman should learn in quietness and full submission. I do not
       permit a woman to teach or to have authority over a man; she
       must be silent. For Adam was formed first, then Eve. And Adam
       was not the one deceived; it was the woman who was deceived
       and became a sinner. But women will be saved through child-
       bearing – if they continue in faith, love and holiness with
       propriety' (1 Timothy 2:11-15).
   (b) Paul gives two reasons for his position:
       (1) The order of creation: 'Adam was formed first, then Eve' (1
           Timothy 2:13).
       (2) Eve's deception and sin (1 Timothy 2:14).

2. *Because Christian feminists believe that redemption in Christ ef-
   fectively puts one back to a pre-fallen state.*
   (a) If a woman becomes a Christian, they say, she may be assured of
       being as Eve was before the Fall.
   (b) It is pointed out that the husband's 'rule' over the woman is after
       the Fall.
       (1) But if the husband and wife are Christians, this 'rule' is done
           away with.
       (2) Therefore the equality implied (in the woman being made
           from man – Genesis 2:21) is restored, according to this
           view.

3. *We therefore must come to terms with this issue:*
   (a) Do we base our position on the pre-fallen situation which, some
       say, shows an equality?
   (b) Or do we base our position on the post-fallen situation, which
       seems to accentuate the rule of man over the woman?

## 2  PAUL'S USE OF *KEPHALE*, 'HEAD' IN 1 CORINTHIANS 11:3

## A. The way we understand 1 Corinthians 11:3 is key to our understanding of the role of women:
'Now I want you to realise that
the head of every man is Christ, and the head of the woman is man, and the
head of Christ is God.'

1. *This is the* locus classicus, *the battleground for:*
   (a)  The role of women vis-a-vis men.
   (b)  The role of women in the home.
   (c)  The role of women in the church.

2. *The Greek word* kephale *translated 'head' is crucial..*
   (a)  One may say, 'Isn't that enough? What more evidence do I need?'
   (b)  The problem is, does *kephale* mean head as 'source', or head meaning 'authority'?

3. *The academic literature on this word alone is vast. For example, see* Recovering Biblical Manhood and Womanhood *edited by Wayne Grudem and John Piper.*

**B. One soon discerns that it is hard to remain objective on this subject.**
   1. *Those who are known as Evangelical Feminists want* kephale *to mean 'source'.*
      (a)  The rise of the Feminist Movement has influenced many in the church.
      (b)  Evangelical Feminists have their scholars to prove their point.

   2. *Those who take the more traditional point of view say that* kephale *means 'authority'.*
      (a)  This would suggest the premiss that 'leadership is male', as David Pawson puts it in his book with that title.
      (b)  If so, the man has 'authority' over the woman:
         (1)  In the home.
         (2)  In the church.

   3. *If* kephale *means 'source' the question of leadership is not so relevant.*
      (a)  'Source' means only that woman came from man, as a river flows from a lake, etc..
      (b)  Equality would therefore be the order of the day.

   4. *Wayne Grudem has done a computer study, showing 2,236 examples of* kephale *in Greek literature. He has become convinced that* kephale *overwhelmingly means 'authority'.*

**C. In the LXX (Septuagint), the Greek translation of the Old Testament, with which Paul was familiar, *kephale* means 'authority' every time.**
   1. Kephale *does mean 'source' in a few passages in Hellenistic literature. But never does it take that meaning in the LXX.*

2. *This would have influenced Paul's use of the word:*
   (a) 'Wives, submit to your husbands as to the Lord. For the husband is the head of the wife as Christ is the head of the church, his body, of which he is the Saviour. Now as the church submits to Christ, so also wives should submit to their husbands in everything' (Ephesians 5:22-24).
      (1) Here the word obviously means 'authority'.
      (2) Wives do not derive their life from their husbands.
      (3) Eve was made from Adam's rib (cf. 1 Corinthians 11:8), but in Ephesians 5:22-24 'authority' is the obvious meaning.
   (b) 'And God placed all things under his feet and appointed him to be head over everything for the church, which is his body, the fullness of him who fills everything in every way' (Ephesians 1:22-23).
      (1) The context shows that Christ has been exalted 'far above all rule and authority, power and dominion' (verse 21).
      (2) Here it can only mean 'authority'.

## D. What does *kephale* mean in 1 Corinthians 11:3?

1. Kephale *could mean 'source' in the light of 1 Corinthians 11:8 (woman came from man).*
   (a) But if it only means 'source' in 1 Corinthians 11:3 it makes no sense.
      (1) The most jumbled, muddled explanations are needed.
      (2) If it means 'source', then no-one is in charge – the very issue Paul confronted.
   (b) 1 Corinthians 11:3 means that someone is in charge.

2. *We conclude that 1 Corinthians 11:3 means:*
   (a) Christ is the authority over every man.
      (1) This is what Paul means by 'head'.
      (2) Jesus Christ is in charge.
      (3) Therefore every man must submit to Jesus Christ.
   (b) Jesus Christ is the head of every man because:
      (1) He has been given all authority and power (cf. Matthew 28:18).
      (2) He knows the will of the Father and demands submission.
   (c) Man is the authority over the woman.
      (1) This does not mean 'chain of command', that woman submits to man rather than to Christ.
      (2) She submits directly to Christ.
      (3) But part of her submission to Christ will be the affirmation that man is the head of the woman.

E. **This is the way it was in Eden before the Fall.**
   1. *This says nothing about after the Fall.*
   2. *Evangelical Feminism argues that God created man and woman as equals in a sense that excludes male headship.*
      (a) They say that male leadership was imposed on Eve as a penalty for her part in the Fall and that redemption in Christ releases her from the punishment of male headship.
      (b) This ignores the implications (seen above) of Adam and Eve before the Fall.

## 3  WOMEN IN THE CHURCH AND IN THE HOME

A. **In worship**
   1. *Paul requires their submission and humility.*
      (a) 'A woman should learn in quietness and full submission' (1 Timothy 2:11).
      (b) The appearance will be feminine.
         (1) A covering was required: 'Long hair is given to her as a covering' (1 Corinthians 11:15).
         (2) Mediterranean culture dictated that a woman with an appearance otherwise was not properly dressed.

   2. *They were allowed to pray and prophecy* (1 Corinthians 11:5).
      (a) It was an assumption that they could pray in public worship, as long as their appearance was godly.
      (b) That a woman could prophecy was also assumed.
         (1) This was promised in Joel 2:28 (cf. Acts 2:18).
         (2) Philip had four unmarried daughters who prophesied (Acts 21:9).

   3. *They were not allowed 'to teach or to have authority over a man'* (1 Timothy 2:12).
      (a) This would not refer to a woman teaching generally.
         (1) She could surely teach children.
         (2) She could teach alongside her husband (Acts 18:26).
      (b) It refers to taking the place of those entrusted with the formation of apostolic doctrine.
         (1) Only men were called to this (1 Timothy 3:1-7).
         (2) The cultural factor has to be answered in the light of the eternal principles of 1 Timothy 2:13-14.
      (c) The prohibition of a woman speaking in 1 Corinthians 14:34-35 probably refers to her interpreting a tongue.
         (1) It does not rule out her speaking at all (cf. 1 Corinthians 11:5).

(2)  Interpreting a tongue was seen as handling divine revelation
that fell to an apostolic function.

## B.  In the home.

1.  *Submission to the husband is the order of the day.* 'Wives, submit to
your husbands as to the Lord. For the husband is the head of the wife
as Christ is the head of the church, his body, of which he is the Saviour. Now as the church submits to Christ, so also wives should submit to their husbands in everything' (Ephesians 5:22-24; cf. Colossians 3:18).

2.  *This was not merely a Pauline bias as can be seen from 1 Peter 3:1-6.*
    (a)  This was seen as a way a Christian woman could win her husband
    to Christ.
    (b)  This behaviour was seen as 'purity and reverence' (1 Peter 3:2).

## C.  Women in ministry.

1.  *If one adheres to the Word as the sole basis for belief and practice:*
    (a)  A woman could not be the senior pastor of a church; she could
    possibly be part of a team.
    (b)  A woman could be a prophetess, like Deborah in Judges 4.

2.  *The whole tenor of scripture suggests there is a difference between
    the sexes.*
    (a)  Creation before the Fall is sufficient for this.
    (b)  The woman's role following the Fall is decidedly one of
    submission.

3.  *Positions of leadership in the church are not assumed for women.*
    (a)  Phoebe, a deaconess, was not seen as a deacon, which was to be a
    man (Acts 6:3).
    (b)  One of the problems of Corinth appears to be that certain women
    thought they were more spiritual because of their gift of tongues
    (1 Corinthians 14:34ff.).
    (c)  The view that redemption by Christ puts woman in the pre-fallen
    state is ruled out by 1 Timothy 2:15: 'But women will be kept
    safe through childbirth – if they continue in faith, love and holiness
    with propriety.'

## D.  What are our responsibilities?

1.  *For men:*
    (a)  To be loving, caring and sensitive.
        (1)  Male chauvinism has done more to contribute to the lack of
        balance than many would care to admit.

        (2) Had men over the years followed Paul's words, 'Husbands love your wives, just as Christ loved the church' (Ephesians 5:25), there never would have been a Feminist Movement.

        (3) Men must be *more* concerned that they themselves are loving than they are that women be submissive.

    (b) To be strong.

        (1) It is not always easy to be strong; a revival of manhood is needed.

        (2) Strength consists partly in remembering that women by nature are 'weaker' (1 Peter 3:7).

        (3) Women basically want men to be strong, which is not the same thing as being dictatorial.

2. *For women:*

    (a) To accept humbly the biblical position, which has not changed.

        (1) This will be harder for some (especially for those who are high-powered and in places of authority in the secular world) than for others.

        (2) This will test one's devotion to Christ and the Scriptures.

    (b) To accept themselves as, by nature (order of creation), *weaker.*

        (1) This will lead to peace.

        (2) Real peace is found only in submission to Christ.

## CONCLUSION

This study has had little to say about the view that the New Testament is culturally conditioned and does not reflect unchanging principles. We accept that the New Testament writers were people of their times and cultures. But we reject the suggestion that the Word is irrelevant for later generations, regardless of changing cultures.

There may be some exceptions to the above. Deborah was an exception; she was needed because no strong men were present at the time. And yet Deborah was an example of a submissive woman; she tried to persuade Barak to get on with it (Judges 4:9).

Let us humbly bow before scripture, no matter how difficult it is for us to do.

# 33

# ANGELS: THEIR PURPOSE AND EXISTENCE TODAY

## INTRODUCTION

### A. Why do a theological study on angels?
1. It is a biblical subject, with far more references in scripture than many people suppose.
2. It is an edifying subject, far more thrilling than is often imagined.

### B. The word 'angel' appears 186 times in the New Testament and over 100 times in the Old Testament.
1. *The Greek word* angelos *means 'messenger'.*
2. *On many occasions beings appear which are in fact angels, but the word 'angel' is not actually used:*
   (a) Cherubim (Genesis 3:24).
   (b) Seraphim (Isaiah 6:2).
   (c) a 'man' (Genesis 32:24; Joshua 5:13).
   (d) 'Chariots of fire' (2 Kings 6:17).
   (e) 'Powers' (Colossians 1:16).

## 1 ANGELS ARE CREATURES (Nehemiah 9:6; Colossians 1:16)

### A. They are not (strictly) eternal but are everlasting.
1. The word 'eternal' means there was no beginning.
2. Only God is eternal.

### B. Angels therefore had a beginning – they were created.
1. *We do not know at what point after Genesis 1:1 they were created.*
   (a) They may well have been included in the word 'heavens', a word also used to mean stars, planets, etc..
   (b) They were probably created before the world and mankind.
      (1) Genesis 1:1-2:4 does not mention angels.
      (2) They appear first in Genesis 3:24, after the Fall.

2. *It is likely that angels were the first of created beings.*
   (a) This means that at some point there existed only the Godhead (the Trinity) and angels.
   (b) However, as we are edging perilously close to speculation, we do well to remember two things:

(1) Where the scriptures speak we speak, where the scriptures are silent we are silent.

(2) When we are speculating we must say so – and admit we cannot speak with authority.

C. **What we know: angels were created by God.**
1. They are therefore not to be worshipped (Revelation 19:10; 22:8-9).
2. They themselves are subject to the one and only God.

## 2 THERE ARE TWO SORTS OF ANGELS: FALLEN AND UNFALLEN

A. **Fallen angels (2 Peter 2:4; Jude 6).**
1. *Some angels sinned.*
  (a) It is thought that the chief angel was called Lucifer (AV), 'morning star, son of the dawn' (Isaiah 14:12).
    (1) Isaiah may have been given unprecedented insight into the fall of the chief angel whom we know as Satan.
    (2) Jesus may have referred to the same event when he said, 'I saw Satan fall like lightning from heaven' (Luke 10:18).
  (b) Revelation 12:4 may have mirrored Satan's fall.
    (1) If so, it would seem that a revolt led by Satan succeeded with one third of the angelic creation.

2. *Some angels 'kept not their first estate'* (Jude 6 AV).
  (a) They were thus created unfallen.
    (1) This would have been their initial 'position of authority'.
    (2) We can assume they could have kept this authority.
  (b) What they did they did voluntarily and deliberately.
    (1) We can only speculate as to their motive – pride.
    (2) How evil emerged originally is unprofitable speculation – always!
  (c) What is also speculation:
    (1) How many angels fell.
    (2) How long they existed in their unfallen state.
    (3) Augustine's idea that the number of God's elect will match the number of fallen angels!

3. *They have not been finally punished yet.*
  (a) 2 Peter 2:4 says they were sent to *tartarus*. Many translate this Greek word (only here in the New Testament) as 'hell'.
  (b) *Tartarus* probably does not mean the place of final punishment.
  (c) There are at least two ways of interpreting 2 Peter 2:4:
    (1) That Tartarus is a name for the fallen spirit world which is yet alive and active within the limits God has set.

           (2) That only some fallen angels were sent to Tartarus.

    (d) Satan's punishment is in some ways parallel to man's punishment.

           (1) Satan was cast out of heaven but still awaits his final doom (Revelation 12:12; 20:10).

           (2) Man was punished by death but still awaits his final doom (Romans 6:23; Revelation 20:15).

           (3) There is no promise of redemption to fallen angels, only to man!

  4. *Fallen angels are also known as demons, evil spirits or authorities and powers* (Ephesians 6:12).

    (a) They exist to torment and to oppress (2 Timothy 2:26).

    (b) They sometimes inhabit God's creatures (Mark 1:23).

## B. Unfallen angels. What this study is mainly about.

  1. *These are those who 'kept' their first position of authority. (They are experienced in spiritual warfare.)*

  2. *They are also called 'elect' angels* (1 Timothy 5:21).

  3. *They are powerful* (2 Thessalonians 1:7; 2 Peter 2:11).

  4. *They are given various roles; there are apparently some that have more authority or prominence, e.g.:*

    (a) Gabriel (Daniel 9:21; Luke 1:19).

    (b) Michael the archangel (Jude 9).

    (c) The cherubim (Genesis 3:24).

    (d) The seraphim (Isaiah 6:2).

  5. *One of the more difficult questions: in what way are angels any different from the Holy Spirit?*

    (a) In what way they are alike:

        (1) They strengthen (1 Kings 19:5-8).

        (2) They give insight (Daniel 9:22).

        (3) They protect (Psalms 34:7; 91:11).

        (4) They are self-effacing (Revelation 19:10).

    (b) In what way they are different:

        (1) Angels are created (Colossians 1:16).

        (2) Angels are not to be worshipped ( Colossians 2:18).

        (3) Angels do not possess people; only the Holy Spirit does (Ephesians 5:18).

        (4) Angels are not omniscient (Ephesians 3:10; 1 Peter 1:12).

        (5) Angels will be judged (1 Corinthians 6:3).

        (6) Angels can only be at one place at a time (Psalm 34:7).

  6. *They behold the Father's face* (Matthew 18:10).

## 3 THE PURPOSE OF ANGELS

### A. They are perfect worshippers of God (Isaiah 6:2-3).
1. *They refuse any worship of themselves* (Revelation 19:10).
2. *They have already resisted Satan's recruitment.*
   (a) For these are angels that 'kept' their positions.
   (b) Very likely Satan tried to recruit every single one of them.
3. *They worship Jesus Christ (*Hebrews 1:6).
4. *They can teach us a lot about worship!* (Psalm 148:2).

### B. They serve God
1. *God calls them his servants* (Hebrews 1:7).
   (a) They are perfectly obedient (Psalm 103:20).
   (b) What God sends them to do, they do (Daniel 6:22; Acts 12:7).

### C. They guard God's people (Psalm 34:7; 91:11).
1. This could well have begun before we were even converted (Hebrews 1:14).
2. When we get to heaven God may let us see the very angel he despatched to our side in this world.

### D. They have more to do in the future.
1. *They escort us to heaven when we die* (Luke 16:22).
2. *They figure prominently in the Last Day.*
   (a) An archangel will announce the Second Coming (1 Thessalonians 4:16).
   (b) They will gather God's elect from all over the earth (Matthew 24:31).
   (c) They will accompany Jesus at his Second Coming (Matthew 16:27; 25:31; 2 Thessalonians 1:7).

## 4 THE MINISTRY OF ANGELS
### A. They protected the Garden of Eden (Genesis 3:24).
### B. They surrendered individuality.
1. They are called 'flames of fire' (Psalm 104:4).
2. They can become winds (Psalm 104:4).
3. The burning bush Moses saw was an angel (Acts 7:30; see Exodus 3:2).
4. They appear as strangers (Hebrews 13:2).

### C. They inaugurated the Law (Acts 7:38; Galatians 3:19; Hebrews 2:2).
### D. One or more carried out God's will on behalf of God's people at various times:

1. Passover and the crossing of the Red Sea (Exodus 12; 14:19).
2. Appeared to Gideon (Judges 6:12).
3. Appeared to Samson's parents (Judges 13:3-21).
4. Appeared to Elijah (1 Kings 19:5).
5. Rescued Elisha (2 Kings 6:16ff.).
6. Defeated Sennacherib (Isaiah 37:36).
7. Delivered Daniel (Daniel 6:22).
8. Appeared to Zechariah (Luke 1:11).
9. Appeared to Joseph (Matthew 1:20).
10. Appeared to Mary (Luke 1:26ff.).
11. Appeared to the shepherds (Luke 2:8-14).
12. Appeared to Peter in prison (Acts 12:7ff.).
13. Appeared to Paul on the ship (Acts 27:23).
14. Appeared to John on Patmos (Revelation 1:1).
15. They ministered to Jesus.
    (a) After his temptation in the wilderness (Matthew 4:11).
    (b) In the garden of Gethsemane (Luke 22:43).

E. **They interact with us.**
1. *They rejoice when a sinner repents (Luke 15:7).*
2. *They learn from us (Ephesians 3:10).*
   (a). As Joseph Ton says, there are 'hidden reasons for suffering'.
   (b) Angels watch us to learn more about God (1 Corinthians 4:9).
3. *They seem to intervene mostly in times of severe stress.*

## CONCLUSION

It would be a mistake to become too conscious of angels or emphasize them too much. They work to bring glory to God, not to attract attention to themselves.

It would also be a mistake to underestimate them. God has used angels in many ways over the course of history to further his purposes in the world. We should thank God for them and for all the ways he uses them to help us in our lives as Christians.

# 34

# THE DEVIL

## INTRODUCTION

**A. This is not a subject I look forward to teaching.**
1. *Partly because there is a danger in giving the devil unwarranted profile.*
2. *Partly because it plays into the interests of some who have an undue fascination with this sort of subject.*
3. *Mostly because I fear the revenge that the devil himself will certainly attempt as a result of this study.*
   (a) The devil loves attention (e.g. from the occult or through sensational films).
   (b) He *doesn't* want to be uncovered for what he is – or how he will end up.

**B. There are two extremes when it comes to this subject.**
1. *To give the devil sensational attention.*
   (a) He loves the profile he gets in films that are occultic or which dramatise demon possession.
   (b) He welcomes the occultic, especially any worship of him.
      (1) Occult: what is hidden except from those who have access to it, e.g., fortune telling, witchcraft, etc.
      (2) The more explicit the better since it encourages unbelief in his arch-enemy the Lord Jesus Christ.
   (c) One may think (at first) that his obvious existence and power could logically lead to belief in God.
      (1) This will never happen unless God is sovereignly at work.
      (2) Satan's grip on those who are fascinated with this realm keeps them from clear thinking.

2. *To avoid the subject entirely.*
   (a) The devil would prefer that you do not believe in him at all.
      (1) Unbelief in the devil is the devil's work.
      (2) If a person says 'I don't believe in the existence of a personal devil,' we can answer, 'The devil has succeeded with you.'
   (b) On the whole the devil prefers a low profile lest he overreach himself and be exposed.

C. **Why deal with this subject?**
1. *The Bible speaks of Satan and the subject necessarily becomes an essential part of theology.*
2. *We need to know something of the 'schemes' of our Lord's arch-enemy – who is also our own arch-enemy.*
3. *By understanding his ways we can prevent unnecessary trouble.*
   (a) The best way to deal with a crisis is to anticipate it and avoid it.
   (b) Knowing Satan's devices will help us.
4. *We need to see that the devil is a conquered foe.*
   (a) Many, with their preoccupations with the devil, seem to ascribe more power to him than to God!
   (b) They are wrong. 'You, dear children, are from God and have overcome them, because the one who is in you is greater than the one who is in the world' (1 John 4:4).
5. *We need to realise that the devil is doomed to ultimate defeat and endless punishment.*
   (a) He knows his time is short (Revelation 12:12).
   (b) He knows his end (Matthew 8:29; Revelation 20:10).
6. *We should also know that Satan is behind (and will help along) every belief or religion that is not honouring to Jesus Christ.*
   (a) This includes the cults (e.g., Jehovah's Witnesses, Mormons, the Church of Christ).
   (b) This includes all non-Christian religions.
   (c) This is manifestly true with the New Age Movement.

## 1   THE ORIGIN OF THE DEVIL

A. **The Bible is not as clear as we may wish as to the origin of the devil.**
1. *For that reason we must be content with what we have and remember that God has told us all we need to know.*
   (a) Never forget the axiom: 'Where the scriptures speak we speak, where the scriptures are silent, we are silent.'
   (b) We must avoid unprofitable speculation.
2. *We will state what is undoubtedly clear and then admit what 'seems' to be true.*

B. **God created the devil (Colossians 1:16-17).**
1. *The devil therefore had a beginning and that beginning is from God – indeed, from Christ.*
2. *This is essential to remember if we are ever charged with dualism: eternal parallels of good and evil.*
   (a) We are not dualists.
   (b) The devil had a beginning.

3. *The devil however was not created by God as he now is but as he was before he became evil.*
   (a) But this borders on speculation.
   (b) We don't know for sure how the devil became evil.

## C. What appears to be true:

1. Satan was once known as 'Lucifer, son of the morning' (AV) or 'morning star, son of the dawn' (Isaiah 14:12).
2. He revolted against God: 'I will ascend to heaven; I will raise my throne above the stars of God;... I will make myself like the Most High' (Isaiah 14:13-14).
3. He was turned out of heaven and cast down to Tartarus ( Isaiah 14:15; 2 Peter 2:4).

## D. What is certainly true.

1. *Satan is now to be seen as a fallen angel.*
2. *He took a number of angels with him* (2 Peter 2:4; Jude 6).
   (a) Revelation 12:4 may mirror the fall of the devil.
3. *Satan has been given certain limited powers from God.*
4. *Satan is not in hell now.*
   (a) His being cast down to 'hell' ( Greek *tartarus*) does not mean his final doom (which is future, and to which Revelation 20:10 refers).
   (b) *Tartarus* probably means the spiritual realm in which the devil operates, so that he is called: (1) 'The ruler of the kingdom of the air' (Ephesians 2:2); (2) 'The prince of this world' (John 12:31); (3) 'The god of this age' (2 Corinthians 4:4).
5. *Satan is second to God in power and wisdom, but can do nothing without God's permission!* (Job 1).
   (a) Jonathan Edwards reminds us that Satan was trained in the heaven of heavens!
   (b) He therefore knows theology backwards and forwards and knows the Bible from cover to cover, which is why he can quote it so freely (Matthew 4:6).

## 2 NAMES AND DESCRIPTIONS OF THE DEVIL

## A. Names:

1. Satan, which means accuser, or adversary (1 Chronicles 21:1; Job 1:6-12).
2. Abaddon (Hebrew) or Apollyon (Greek) meaning the destroyer; the angel of the abyss (Revelation 9:11).
3. Beelzebub, meaning the prince of demons (Matthew 12:24).
4. Belial, meaning worthless (2 Corinthians 6:15).

## B. Descriptions:

1. The prince of demons (Matthew 12:24).
2. The ruler of the kingdom of the air (Ephesians 2:2).
3. The prince of this world (John 12:31; 14:30).
4. The god of this age (2 Corinthians 4:4).
5. The tempter (1 Thessalonians 3:5; cf. 1 Corinthians 7:5).
6. The accuser of our brothers (Revelation 12:10).
7. A liar and the father of lies (John 8:44).
8. A serpent (Genesis 3:1; cf. 2 Corinthians 11:3).
9. An angel of light (2 Corinthians 11:14).
10. A roaring lion (1 Peter 5:8).

## 3 THE CHARACTER AND PURPOSE OF THE DEVIL

### A. The essential character of the devil is wicked, evil, and stands against God and us with an icy hatred that is beyond any earthly analogy.

1. *He feels contempt for us to the greatest extreme.*
2. *Never feel sorry for the devil; never underestimate his dedication to destroy you by whatever means he can.*
   (a) temptation; (b) breaking up your marriage; (c) dividing your church; (d) destroying friendships; (e) disease (sometimes).

### B. He has his own personality.

1. He is presumptuous (Job 1:6; Matthew 4:5-6).
2. He is proud (1 Timothy 3:6).
3. He is powerful (Ephesians 2:2; 6:12).
4. He is evil (1 John 2:13).
5. He is clever (2 Corinthians 11:3).
6. He is deceitful (2 Corinthians 11:4; Ephesians 6:11).
7. He is fierce and cruel (Luke 8:29; 9:39, 42; 1 Peter 5:8).

### C. He exists to fight God and us.

1. He brought about the Fall of man (Genesis 3:1ff.).
2. He lied to Eve (Genesis 3:4).
3. He tempted Jesus, hoping to destroy him (Matthew 4:1-11; cf. Luke 4:29).
4. He desired to destroy Peter (Luke 22:31).
5. He perverts the scriptures (Matthew 4:6; cf. Genesis 3:1).
6. He opposes God's work (1 Thessalonians 2:18).
7. He hinders the gospel (2 Corinthians 4:4).
8. He works lying wonders (2 Thessalonians 2:9).
9. He moved David to count the people (1 Chronicles 21:1).
10. He stood against Joshua the high priest (Zechariah 3:1).

D. **Hierarchy of demonic powers.**
   1. *This part is a bit speculative but we conclude:*
      (a) There are archangels (Jude 9) and special angels (Luke 1:19) in God's holy realm.
      (b) It seems not unlikely that such exist in the evil realm.

   2. *This assumes that when Satan recruited followers in his revolt against God he persuaded some leading angelic beings.*
      (a) If so, it is possible that some angels are more powerful than others.
      (b) This seems to have been the case on one occasion at least (Mark 9:29).

## 4  HOW THE DEVIL OPERATES

A. **One of the evidences that we are growing in grace and getting to know God is that we become aware of Satan's manner and ways.**
   1. Paul stresses the importance of mutual forgiveness, 'In order that Satan may not outwit us. For we are not unaware of his schemes' (2 Corinthians 2:11).
   2. We therefore need to be aware of his ways, lest we be taken by surprise.

B. **Here are some of Satan's best known ways to hinder God's purpose and to work against us:**
   1. *To blind the unsaved to ensure they remain lost* (2 Corinthians 4:4).
   2. *To tempt* (Matthew 4:1).
      (a) There are two sources of temptation:
         (1) The flesh (James 1:13ff.).
         (2) The devil (1 Thessalonians 3:5).
      (b) When the devil tempts he will play into our own weakness; for example: sex; love of money; love of prestige; unbelief; fears; deep hurt; lack of theological knowledge; ambition; inability to forgive; personality or cultural differences.
      (c) Satan causes events, people and time to come together that things look 'providential' – so that it seems to be God's doing!

   3. *To put obstacles in our path that we may think it is God at work:* 'For we wanted to come to you – certainly I, Paul, did again and again – but Satan stopped us' (1 Thessalonians 2:18).

   4. *He poses as a man of God:* 'And no wonder, for Satan himself masquerades as an angel of light' (2 Corinthians 11:14).

(a) This could be a minister of the gospel.
(b) This could be a person with an unusual gift.
(c) This could be a person who appears to be spiritual.

5. *He quotes scripture* (Matthew 4:6).
   (a) Satan knows the Bible thoroughly. So do not be surprised if a verse comes to mind when you are tempted to do what is questionable!

6. *He comes in like a lion* (1 Peter 5:8).
   (a) The lion's roar is a bluff!
   (b) The lion roars to make you think you are already defeated, that it's too late.
   (c) How this might work out in day to day experience:
      (1) He plays into a weakness (it may be when you are physically tired, or you've already had a bad day, or have lost your keys!), causing you to make the unguarded comment. This sets off a chain reaction in another.
      (2) (a) A feeling of panic sets in; (b) A fear that you've already 'blown it' sets in (so you really will blow it!); (c) Another's feelings are hurt and he or she will not talk with you now.

C. **The difference between possession and oppression.**
   1. *Demon possession is when Satan gets control 'inside' of a person.*
      (a) It is when the person cannot control himself.
         (1) It may be several demons (Luke 8:30; cf. Mark 16:9).
         (2) It may be one demon (Mark 1:23).
         (3) It may be very strong demons (Luke 9:40).
      (b) It is partly what lay behind Judas betraying Jesus.
         (1) Judas had a weakness for money (Mark 14:10ff; John 12:3-6).
         (2) But Satan actually took control of Judas (Luke 22:3).
      (c) Although rare, it can happen to a professing Christian (Acts 5:3).

   2. *Demonic oppression is when Satan seems to take control but does it 'outside' of us* (2 Timothy 2:26).
      (a) It is when Satan plays into one's weakness and makes a suggestion we take on board.
      (b) All the weaknesses referred to above are vulnerable to oppression, especially that of fear.

## 5   SOME GENERAL OBSERVATIONS ABOUT THE DEVIL

A. **Hell was created for him (Matthew 25:41).**
B. **His approach is to attack us, which Paul calls the 'day of evil' (Ephesians 6:13), then leave for a while (Luke 4:13).**
C. **The devil overreaches himself (1 Corinthians 2:8).**
   1. Overreach: to fail by being too ambitious.
   2. Satan unwittingly advances God's kingdom by his onslaughts (2 Corinthians 12:7-10).

D. **One of the petitions of the Lord's Prayer is 'Lead us not into temptation, but deliver us from the evil one.'**
   1. By 'evil one', Jesus meant the devil.
   2. We should pray to be spared from Satan's attack but remember: if God allows it, it means you are up to it (1 Corinthians 10:13).

E. **The devil is resistible (James 4:7; 1 Peter 5:8-9).**
   1   When a suggestion comes that goes against the revealed will of God (the Bible), refuse to cater to it.
   2   When you are agitated don't speak further (it will almost certainly come out wrong and you will be sorry).
   3   When you are tempted, remind yourself
      (a)   *Resist him and you will feel good.*
      (b)   *Give in to him and you will feel awful.*
   4   A word of advice from William Perkins (d.1602): 'Don't believe the devil even when he tells the truth.'

## CONCLUSION

The devil is a defeated foe. He knows God is victor and he knows that his time is running out. In the meantime, however, his goal is to tempt believers into sin and to blind the lost so that they cannot see God. There is one thing we should never forget: the devil moves only as far as God lets him.

# 35

## SPIRITUAL WARFARE

### INTRODUCTION

A. **This chapter obviously follows and connects with the previous chapter on the Devil'. A number of points are very relevant to the subject of spiritual warfare.**
   1. *Satan is alive and well although his downfall is assured and his doom absolutely certain.*
   2. *In the meantime he exists to do all the damage he can possibly do to thwart God's purpose and work.*
   3. *Although he is a conquered foe he has been given limited scope to work – by God himself.*
   4. *We therefore need to keep constantly in mind these truths:*
      (a) Satan only moves as far as God allows.
      (b) His freedom to attack is limited.
      (c) 1 Corinthians 10:13 is *always* relevant when it comes to spiritual warfare: 'No temptation has seized you except what is common to man. And God is faithful; he will not let you be tempted beyond what you can bear. But when you are tempted, he will also provide a way out so that you can stand up under it.'
   5 *If we learn how to engage in spiritual warfare, when Satan attacks we will find:*
      (a) He will overreach himself.
      (b) He will unwittingly advance the very purpose he hoped to hinder.
      (c) We ourselves will be better off than ever – and further along spiritually.

B. **Spiritual warfare: our reaction in the Spirit to Satan's attacks.**
   1. *It is called spiritual warfare because it is not natural but supernatural, and therefore spiritual.*
      (a) This is not merely the attack of the flesh – which is natural.
      (b) The devil's attack is supernatural (that is, beyond the natural realm) and the only defence we have must be supernatural (that is, by the Holy Spirit).
   2. *Spiritual warfare is our reaction to the devil, not our initiating an attack on him.*

## C. Why should we study spiritual warfare?

1. *Because what we learned in the previous chapter about the devil must be applied in our daily Christian living.*
2. *We must not become experts on the devil but complacent in our Christian lives when Satan attacks – which he will certainly do.*
3. *There is a widespread (even unhealthy) interest in this subject, almost paralleling that in signs and wonders.*
   (a) We must beware of the idea of merely 'doing spiritual warfare'.
   (b) I fear many 'do' spiritual warfare who are no more competent than the seven sons of Sceva (mentioned in Acts), who promoted themselves to the level of their incompetence.
       (1) They went around driving out demons.
       (2) They used the name of the Lord Jesus to do this alongside Paul's name.
       (3) Once the evil spirit answered, 'Jesus I know, I know about Paul, but who are you?'
       (4) They were overpowered and ran away 'naked and bleeding' (Acts 19:13-16).
4. *There is a valid enterprise that can justly be called 'spiritual warfare'.*
   (a) It must be looked at carefully.
   (b) Wrongly understood and applied, 'spiritual warfare' (so called) will leave people 'naked and bleeding' and worse off than before they got involved in it all.
5. *A proper understanding of this subject will leave us stronger than ever and more equipped as believers.*

## 1 SPIRITUAL WARFARE IS ALWAYS AND ONLY DEFENSIVE (Ephesians 6:10-18).

## A. It is never, never, never taking the initiative or even trying to 'prevent' the devil working.

1. *If Satan does not attack, we are to leave the supernatural realm of Satan alone.*
2. *If we go looking for problems, we will find them!*
   (a) The worst thing we can do is to go about 'picking a fight' with the devil.
   (b) Those who engage in spiritual warfare, whether through a prayer meeting, a march, or when they begin to rebuke the devil before he is stirred up, *will* stir him up and find themselves tragically out of their depth.
       (1) A march for Jesus is a wonderful and glorious thing.
       (2) But a march that attacks Satan's forces – even if it is retaliatory – will be counter-productive.

    (3)  I fear some people underestimate how powerful and vindictive Satan is.

    (4)  I know of one international leader's ministry that has been virtually destroyed because he went on the attack before he got attacked.

B.  **Ephesians 6:13 confirms the defensive nature of spiritual armour: 'Therefore put on the full armour of God so that *when* the day of evil comes, you may be able to stand your ground, and after you have done everything, to stand.'**

    1.  *Armour is strictly defensive clothing.*
        (a)  One does not wear armour, or a helmet, unless there is the fear of being attacked.
        (b)  We are to be dressed like this all the time but not because we take the initiative in spiritual warfare.

    2.  *One is equipped 'so that when the day of evil comes' we may stand our ground.*
        (a)  One hopes that the day of evil will be postponed as long as possible.
           (1)  It will come soon enough.
           (2)  We won't have to go looking for it.
        (b)  One therefore stays ready.
           (1)  The devil will come sooner or later.
           (2)  It is then we take the defence.

    3.  *Some say, 'The best defence is a good offence.'*
        (a)  This is true with sports, or games, for in such both are equals.
        (b)  But it is not true with spiritual warfare.
           (1)  But we are no match for the devil – not a single one of us.
           (2)  There is only one time when we are a match for Satan: when he attacks, because Christ comes alongside to help us. Then, and only then, can we emerge as victors.
        (c)  Attack him when he is relatively 'quiet', as it were, and he will make complete fools of us.
        (d)  Christ may leave us to ourselves when we proceed on the attack.

    4.  *Some may say, 'If we have to wait for the devil to attack before we engage in spiritual warfare, we may wait and wait for a long while.'*
        (a)  I answer: I only wish! This is why Jesus told us to pray, 'Lead us not into temptation but deliver us from evil' (Greek, 'the evil one').
           (1)  We should hope to be spared indefinitely!
           (2)  Unfortunately it isn't like that; the devil will turn up sooner rather than later.

(b) There are essentially two ways of growing in grace:
  (1) How we respond to God.
  (2) How we respond to the devil's attacks.
(c) If we devote ourselves to the former we will be ready for the latter!

## 2 RULES FOR SPIRITUAL WARFARE.

A. **Be strong in the Lord:** 'Finally, be strong in the Lord and in his mighty power' (Ephesians 6:10).
  1. *Paul introduces this section with the positive.*
    (a) This means that we will know God so well that we recognise his/ our own arch-enemy when he appears.
    (b) Some think the best way to combat the devil is to know more about the occult.
      (1) No; the best way to combat Satan is to be ready by knowing God so well.
      (2) The more you study the occult the more vulnerable to it you might be.
  2. *How to be strong in the Lord.*
    (a) Study of the scriptures.
    (b) Intimacy with the Holy Spirit.

B. **Spiritual warfare is always defensive:** 'Put on the full armour of God so that you can take your stand against the devil's schemes' (Ephesians 6:11).
  1. *We do not go on the attack; we 'take our stand'.*
    (a) This should not surprise us; twice we are told to 'resist' the devil (James 4:7; 1 Peter 5:8-9).
    (b) You only 'resist' when being attacked; you cannot resist when you are taking the initiative.

  2. *The devil's 'scheme', or strategy, is to attack us where we are weak.*
    (a) Satan main means of attack is our weakness, e.g.:
      (1) An unforgiving spirit (perhaps the easiest means the devil uses with people).
      (2) Fear (he is an expert in playing into fears or a negative spirit).
      (3) Uncontrolled sexual tendencies (a way to bring the church's name into disrepute).
      (4) Pride, which for example may relate to easily hurt feelings or unfulfilled ambition, and so on.
      (5) Unbelief, which will centre mainly on God's existence and the reliability of the scriptures.

(b)  Parallel to this he will work through those who are near you who
also have their weaknesses.
(1)  Your husband/wife.
(2)  Your flatmate.
(3)  Your pastor, or the one who is over you.
(4)  Fellow Christians.
(c)  Note:  Satan attacks through people and circumstances that relate
to our own weaknesses.

C.  **Remember, our only enemy is the devil; not those people who attack
us:** 'For our struggle is not against flesh and blood, but against the rulers,
against the authorities, against the powers of this dark world and against
the spiritual forces of evil in the heavenly realms' (Ephesians 6:12).
1.  *The devil loves it when we retaliate by attacking the individual who
gets at us.*
(a)  This is exactly his aim.
(1)  The devil won't leave his footprints (if he can help it).
(2)  He wants you to attack a person (who the devil may well use
to get at you).
(b)  If we retaliate by pointing the finger we give in to the devil
himself.
(1)  He will make you blame your wife, your friend, your pastor
– or your 'enemy'.
(2)  The devil's purpose: to break up your marriage, split your
fellowship, cause dissension.

2.  *Spiritual warfare is not with 'flesh and blood'.  This means:*
(a)  It is not fighting people.
(b)  It is not battling against the flesh.
(c)  The devil *uses* either of the above, yes; but the essence of spiritual
warfare is to see who the real enemy is – the devil.

3.  *Too many Christians never move past seeing the enemy as mere
flesh and blood.*

D.  **We need to develop a strategy:** 'Therefore put on the full armour of
God, so that when the day of evil comes, you may be able to stand your
ground, and after you have done everything, to stand' (Ephesians 6:13).
1.  *Satan has a strategy of his own.*
(a)  Time.  It is called 'the day of evil', although he never sleeps.
(1)  This may or may not be a twenty-four hour day.
(2)  It may be an era that spreads over days or months!
(3)  It is a vicious attack which you will never forget.

(b) Manner:
- (1) He earmarks you for an attack (you of course don't know this at first).
- (2) He plays into your weakness, when the right person or situation emerges.
- (3) He may come 'quietly' as an angel of light (2 Corinthians 11:14), so you will think God is speaking.
- (4) He may come 'noisily' as a roaring lion (1 Peter 5:8), so you will think a victory is hopeless.

2. *Our strategy must be divinely approved (found only in the Word). We can never improve upon God's ways.*
   - (a) The right clothing, wearing the full armour of God. I myself pray daily to be covered by the blood of Jesus.

   - (b) The right posture: to 'stand'.
     - (1) Don't run or even walk – just stand.
     - (2) Don't go backwards or fall down – just stand.

   - (c) The right theology: 'Stand firm then, with the belt of truth buckled round your waist, with the breastplate of righteousness in place' (Ephesians 6:14).
     - (1) The waist partly refers to the seat of 'feelings'. So here we are being warned against emotional weaknesses.
     - (2) The heart is the seat of 'faith', so this is a warning against unbelief in Christ's blood and righteousness.

   - (d) The right conduct: 'And with your feet fitted with the readiness that comes from the gospel of peace' (Ephesians 6:15).
     - (1) 'The feet' partly means walking in the light.
     - (2) 'Readiness' comes from having been faithful.

   - (e) The right reaction: 'In addition to all this, take up the shield of faith, with which you can extinguish all the flaming arrows of the evil one.' (Ephesians 6:16).
     - (1) Note: the shield refers to defence!
     - (2) This mainly refers to *resisting* the devil.

   - (f) The right mentality: 'Take the helmet of salvation and the sword of the Spirit, which is the word of God' (Ephesians 6:17).
     - (1) The helmet protects the mind.
     - (2) What is the most important doctrine? Salvation.
     - (3) The sword of the Spirit is the right use of the Bible when being attacked (cf. Matthew 4:7).

E. **Praying in the Spirit:** 'And pray in the Spirit on all occasions with all kinds of prayers and requests. With this in mind, be alert and always keep on praying for all the saints' (Ephesians 6:18).
   1. *There are basically two kinds of praying in the Spirit.*
      (a) Consciously, when we know we are praying according to God's will (1 John 5:14-15).
      (b) Unconsciously, when we are praying but we aren't sure what God's will is (Romans 8:26-27).
   2. *It is in any case the enterprise of intercessory prayer, which includes praying 'for all the saints'.*

## 3 FIVE R'S OF SPIRITUAL WARFARE

A. **Remember.**
   1. *'Be alert'* (1 Peter 5:8).
   2. *It is easy to forget that the devil, who never sleeps, is always looking for an opportunity to disrupt our peace.*
   3. *When things are going smoothly:*
      (a) It is the easiest time to forget.
      (b) It is the best time for the devil to catch us by surprise.
   4. *The nearest we are allowed to come in taking the initiative in spiritual warfare is to* remember *that we are earmarked for a satanic attack.*

B. **Be ready.**
   *1. Again, 'Be alert'* (1 Peter 5:8).
   1. *If we remember, then we can be ready.*
   2. *To be ready, then, means:*
      (a) We will not be the slightest bit surprised when attacked!
      (b) We will be sure to have the proper clothing, posture, theology, conduct, and all the things previously discussed in this chapter.

C. **Recognise.**
   1. *The sooner we can recognise the devil, the better.*
      (a) Otherwise, we may get personal and point the finger (which Satan wants).
      (b) When we recognise it is the devil we are without excuse if we point the finger at anyone else.
   2. *A definition of spirituality is closing the time gap between the onslaught of the attack and recognising it for what it is.*
      (a) Some may take years, or months.
      (b) Some may take minutes, or seconds.

**D. Refuse.**
1. *This is extremely crucial; refuse to take seriously the devil's suggestion.*
   (a) But what if it is true? Answer: 'Don't believe the devil even when he tells the truth.'
   (b) But what if there is a fault in us that needs to be dealt with? Answer: Admit to the fault without letting Satan demoralise you.
      (1) One must learn to accept criticism without retorting or being totally defeated.
      (2) Remember: 'A gentle answer turns away wrath' (Proverbs 15:1).

2. *The essence of refusal is to refuse to dignify the devil's suggestion:*
   (a) By not being drawn in.
   (b) By not being demoralised.

**E. Resist (James 4:7; 1 Peter 5:8-9).**
1. *This means 'keeping at it'.*
2. *The devil will keep it up; you keep resisting.*
   (a) When he sees you mean business, he will leave you alone.
   (b) As long as you appear weak, he will keep it up.
3. *Resisting: refusing the devil's suggestion with persistence.*
4. *When we resist, the result is very gratifying.*
   (a) It shows we are growing in grace.
   (b) It always results in a blessing of its own.

**CONCLUSION**
Spiritual warfare, then, is our reaction to the devil's schemes to thwart God's purposes in this world and to lead us into sin. The initiative for this warfare is always the devil's, not ours. Our part is to resist him, using the full armour of God, and to be prepared for the attack. We do not face the struggle in our own strength but in the strength of our Saviour, Jesus Christ, who has the victory.

# 36

## THE CHRISTIAN LIFESTYLE

### INTRODUCTION

**A. The implications and consequences of being 'in Christ'.**

1. *Being 'in Christ' focuses on two things (in the main):*
   - (a) Our security and all the privileges of being a Christian.
   - (b) Union with Christ (see chapter, The Believer's Position 'In Christ'.

2. *We therefore want to show what else this means.*
   - (a) What does being 'in Christ' imply?
   - (b) What are the results of being 'in Christ'?

3. *We therefore will focus on the Christian lifestyle.*
   - (a) Lifestyle: way of life.
   - (b) What, then, is the way of life of the person 'in Christ'?

**B. In order to come to terms with the Christian lifestyle one must see the 'other side of the coin': Christ in us.**

1. *'In Christ' has largely to do with our objective relationship rather than a subjective experience.*
   - (a) There may be some exceptions:
     - (1) 'In Christ' may refer to one's conversion. See Romans 16:7: 'They were in Christ before I was.'
     - (2) 'In Christ' may refer to a heightened spiritual experience. 'I know a man in Christ who fourteen years ago was caught up to the third heaven' (2 Corinthians 12:2).
   - (b) But generally 'in Christ' refers to the way God thinks about us: he sees us 'in Christ'.
     - (1) This began with predestination (Ephesians 1:4).
     - (2) It continued with our being called and justified (2 Corinthians 5:21).
     - (3) It will be finalised at glorification (Romans 8:30).

2. *'Christ in us' has to do both with our objective and subjective relationship.*
   - (a) For Christ is in us objectively: 'To them God has chosen to make

known among the Gentiles the glorious riches of this mystery, which is Christ in you, the hope of glory' (Colossians 1:27).

    (1) By 'objective' we mean 'having reality outside a person's mind'.

    (2) Christ is in us objectively – he is there, in us – whether or not we 'feel' him.

  (b) And yet Christ is also in us subjectively: 'Being confident of this, that he who began a good work in you will carry it on to completion until the day of Christ Jesus' (Philippians 1:6).

    (1) By 'subjective' we mean what we consciously perceive and feel.

    (2) Christ is in us subjectively – he is to be felt and experienced in us, by his Spirit.

## C. Why is this study important?

1. We need to bring the 'intellectual' and 'experiential' together.
2. Many only enjoy what is forensic (legally true) about justification by faith, but never come to grips with what is knowable at the level of experience; we need both.
3. We need to see the difference between 'imputed' righteousness (what is objective) and 'imparted' righteousness (what is subjective).
4. Too much emphasis on what is objective about being 'in Christ' may lead to dry intellectualism – even careless living.
5. The Bible has as much to say about our experience of being 'in Christ' as it does with regard to our objective position.
6. Being 'in Christ' is not only a privilege but it also carries with it an enormous responsibility.
7. Knowing that Christ is in us opens the way for an ever-increasing intimacy with God and the limitless possibilities of manifestations of his glory.

## 1 CHRIST IN US IS BOTH OBJECTIVE AND SUBJECTIVE

## A. Objectively Christ is in us from the moment of regeneration.

1. Keep in mind that what is 'objective' is not felt – but is true none the less.
2. Much of the Christian life is coming to grips with what is already true of us, even though we do not always 'feel' it.

## B. Objectively, then, our union with Christ is both our being 'in him' and his being 'in us' – simultaneously.

1. *This is the way God considered us in eternity before we were born and then at conversion the moment we were justified.*

2. *This means that we have union with Christ's death, being buried, raised and ascended.*
   (a) When Christ died, God thought of us as having died. Our old self was 'crucified with him' (Romans 6:6).
       (1) 'I have been crucified with Christ' (Galatians 2:20).
       (2) 'One died for all, and therefore all died' (2 Corinthians 5:14).
   (b) God thought of us as having been buried with Christ; raised with him, and taken up to heaven with him in glory (Romans 6:4-11).
       (1) 'And God raised us up with Christ and seated us with him in the heavenly realms in Christ Jesus' (Ephesians 2:6).
       (2) 'Having been buried with him in baptism and raised with him through your faith in the power of God, who raised him from the dead. When you were dead in your sins and in the uncircumcision of your sinful nature, God made you alive with Christ. He forgave us all our sins' (Colossians 2:12-13).

3. *Paul's references to baptism and faith indicate that our dying and being raised with Christ occur in this present life, at the time we become Christians.*
   (a) This is objectively true, whether or not we 'feel' it.
   (b) It is a mistake to think it hasn't happened merely because this aspect of our faith has not gripped us.

C. **However, the fact that it *is* true that we have been crucified and raised with Christ is what lies behind the change that the Holy Spirit brings about in our character, personality, experience, understanding and conduct as Christians.**
   1. *This is true because we are in Christ.*
   2. *It is true because Christ is in us. 'Christ lives in me'* (Galatians 2:20).
      (a) In ever-increasing measure, the Holy Spirit reproduces Jesus' death and resurrection in our lives.
      (b) Little by little, more and more we become so unresponsive to the pressures and attractions of our former life that:
          (1) Paul can say we have died to these influences (Romans 7:6).
          (2) It is because we died with Christ (Colossians 3:3).
      (c) We are wanting to serve God more and more.
          (1) We are able to serve him with greater power and success.
          (2) Paul calls this being 'alive' to God (Romans 6:11).
      (d) We have power to overcome personal sin more and more (Romans 6:12-14, 19).

## 2 CHRIST IN US OBJECTIVELY IS WHY WE MAY FEEL HIM IN US SUBJECTIVELY

A. **In short: Christ is already in us if we are in Christ.**
  1. *For that reason we do not have to pretend that he is there; he is truly in us.*
  2. *However, there is a case for 'stirring up' the gift in us.*
     (a) 'I think it is right to refresh your memory as long as I live in the tent of this body' (2 Peter 1:13).
     (b) 'For this reason I remind you to fan into flame the gift of God, which is in you through the laying on of my hands' (2 Timothy 1:6).
     (c) 'Dear friends, this is now my second letter to you. I have written both of them as reminders to stimulate you to wholesome thinking' (2 Peter 3:1).
  3. *One of the reasons for the Lord's Supper is to partake 'in remembrance' of Christ* (1 Corinthians 11:24).

B. **There are biblical ways by which we come to experience subjectively what is already true objectively.**
  1. *Our lives are inseparably connected to Christ himself.*
  2. *The Holy Spirit works through means by which we come to enjoy 'every spiritual blessing in Christ'* (Ephesians 1:3).
     (a) In Christ we 'do not lack any spiritual gift' (1 Corinthians 1:7).
     (b) And yet in the same letter Paul said we should 'eagerly desire the greater gifts' (1 Corinthians 12:31).
        (1) This shows that what is one's in Christ is not experienced by all 'automatically'.
        (2) The Holy Spirit therefore uses means by which we come to enjoy what is ours in Christ – and because Christ is in us.

C. **What are the means by which we come to enjoy what we have by Christ being in us? In a word: sanctification.**
  1. *Faith.* 'So then, just as you received Christ Jesus as Lord, continue to live in him, rooted and built up in him, strengthened in the faith as you were taught, and overflowing with thankfulness' (Colossians 2:6-7).
     (a) Faith is what justified us (Romans 5:1).
     (b) There is saving faith (which justifies) and achieving faith (by which we come to see glorious possibilities).
        (1) Faith is what produces works (Ephesians 2:10; 1 Thessalonians 1:3).
        (2) Achieving faith is that which is mainly described in Hebrews 11: 'These were all commended for their faith' (verse 39).

- (c) In short: we must *believe* that:
  - (1) We are in Christ.
  - (2) Christ is in us.
  - (3) We may consciously enjoy what is ours by our being in Christ and he in us.

2. *Abiding in Christ.* 'Remain in me, and I will remain in you. No branch can bear fruit by itself; it must remain in the vine. Neither can you bear fruit unless you remain in me' (John 15:4).
   - (a) This refers to our actualising what is true by faith.
     - (1) This means experiencing what is true.
     - (2) This does not mean that we are dislodged from the family if we don't remain in him; we lose the intimacy, the possibility of fruit and assurance of answered prayer if we do not abide in Christ. 'If you remain in me and my words remain in you, ask whatever you wish, and it will be given you' (John 15:7).

   - (b) We remain in Christ by obedience and love. 'As the Father has loved me, so have I loved you. Now remain in my love. If you obey my commands, you will remain in my love, just as I have obeyed my Father's commands and remain in his love' (John 15:9-10).
     - (1) 'If you love me, you will obey what I command' (John 14:15).
     - (2) 'My command is this: Love each other as I have loved you' (John 15:12).

3. *Not grieving the Holy Spirit.* 'And do not grieve the Holy Spirit of God, with whom you were sealed for the day of redemption' (Ephesians 4:30).
   - (a) The Holy Spirit is a very sensitive person (cf. 1 Thessalonians 5:19).
     - (1) When the Spirit is grieved, we lose 'presence of mind'; confusion and the absence of clear thinking follows.
     - (2) When the Holy Spirit dwells in us *ungrieved*, we are in the best position to experience Christ in us.
   - (b) Grieving the Holy Spirit does not forfeit salvation: we are 'sealed for the day of redemption'.
     - (1) 'And I will ask the Father, and he will give you another Counsellor to be with you for ever' (John 14:16).
     - (2) 'God's seed remains in him' (1 John 3:9).
   - (c) What causes the Spirit to be grieved? Ephesians 4:31-32 tells us:
     - (1) Bitterness (cf. James 2:14; Hebrews 12:15).
     - (2) Rage and anger (see Colossians 3:8).

(3) Brawling and slander (see Galatians 5:20).

(4) Holding a grudge or refusing to forgive totally (see Colossians 3:13).

4. *Putting to death what belongs to our 'earthly nature'* (Colossians 3:5).
   (a) Putting to death means:
       (1) Refusing to give in to temptation to sin (Romans 13:12-13).
       (2) Avoiding temptation (Romans 13:14).
   (b) What exactly belongs to our 'earthly nature'?
       (1) Sexual immorality ( Colossians 3:5; 1 Thessalonians 4:3).
       (2) Greed (1 Timothy 6:10).
       (3) Filthy language (Colossians 3:8).
       (4) Lying (Colossians 3:9).
       (5) Drunkenness (Romans 13:13).
       (6) Dissension and jealousy (Romans 13:13).
       (7) Idolatry and witchcraft (Galatians 5:20).
       (8) Selfish ambition (James 4:14).
   (c) Love is the fulfilment of the Law. The commandments, 'Do not commit adultery', 'Do not murder', 'Do not steal', 'Do not covet', and whatever other commandment there may be, are summed up in this one rule: 'Love your neighbour as yourself' (Romans 13:9-10).

5. *Dignifying the trial* (James 1:2-4).
   (a) This is one of the most forgotten avenues toward actualising what we have in Christ.
       (1) The most natural reaction to trial: to complain.
       (2) The other reaction: to hasten its end prematurely.
   (b) How do we dignify the trial?
       (1) Regard it as God's act: 'Consider it pure joy, my brothers, whenever you face trials of many kinds' (James 1:2).
       (2) Let it run its full course; every trial has a sovereignly built-in time scale by God. 'Perseverance must finish its work so that you may be mature and complete, not lacking anything' (James 1:4).

6. *Walking in love* (1 Corinthians 13).
   (a) This is the heart of 'remaining in Christ'.
       (1) Walking in love fulfils the Law (Romans 13:10).
       (2) Walking in love eliminates envy, boasting, pride, rudeness, selfish ambition, losing your temper and keeping a record of wrongs (1 Corinthians 13:4-5).

    (b)  This is also the best way to obtain the greater gifts.
        (1)  'But eagerly desire the greater gifts' (1 Corinthians 12:31).
        (2)  'For if you possess these qualities in increasing measure, they will keep you from being ineffective and unproductive in your knowledge of our Lord Jesus Christ' (2 Peter 1:8).
    (c)  In the husband-wife relationship.
        (1)  The wife's gracious submission to her husband (Ephesians 5:22).
        (2)  The husband's unselfish love to his wife (Ephesians 5:25).

7.  *Walking in the light* (1 John 1:7).
    (a)  This means accepting and obeying the fresh Word that is illuminated by the Holy Spirit.
        (1)  It will always be what is already revealed in God's Word – the Bible.
        (2)  But often it comes as 'fresh' – pointed and gripping – that leaves no doubt what the Word really meant.
    (b)  This requires transparent openness to whatever God may drive home to us.
        (1)  Often our reaction to the plain teaching of the Word is to say, 'It surely can't mean *that*'.
        (2)  But once God's sobering searchlight focuses on our inner struggle, we know in our hearts what it is we have to do.
    (c)  Speaking personally, some of the things about which God has dealt with me most are:
        (1)  Tithing.
        (2)  Dignifying the trial.
        (3)  Totally forgiving.
        (4)  Personal witnessing.
        (5)  Being willing to change my mind on previously held opinions.

8.  *Being filled with the Spirit* (Ephesians 5:18).
    (a)  All Christians have the Holy Spirit (Romans 8:9).
    (b)  But not all Christians are always filled with the Spirit, or Paul would not have commanded this.
    (c)  How are we filled with the Spirit? Answer:
        (1)  All of the above being carried out.
        (2)  Praying daily for this (Luke 11:9-13).
        (3)  Seeking God's face (his approval), not his hand (his gifts) (Psalm 27:8).
        (4)  Being open to the immediate filling of the Spirit.

## 3 WHAT WILL WE 'FEEL' WHEN WE HAVE RESPONDED AS ABOVE?

A. **What we *have* in Christ (Ephesians 1:3).**
  1. Adoption, justification, sealing (Ephesians 1:4-13).
  2. New life and that 'to the full' (2 Corinthians 5:17; John 10:10).
  3. The indwelling Spirit (Romans 8:9).
  4. Intimacy with the Father (1 John 1:3-7).
  5. Praying in God's will (John 15:7).

B. **Dying and rising with Christ (Philippians 3:10).**
  1. *The fellowship of his sufferings.*
     (a) Re-living what Jesus went through.
        (1) Shame (Acts 5:41).
        (2) Silence (Isaiah 53:7).
        (3) Sacrifice (Romans 12:1).
        (4) Solitude (Matthew 26:56).
     (b) We develop an intimacy with Jesus.

  2. *Resurrection power.*
     (a) Internal vindication (1 Timothy 3:16).
     (b) Deliverance from the trial (Hebrews 12:2).
     (c) Ministering to those who forsook you (John 20:19).

C. **Ever-increasing Christ-likeness (1 Peter 2:20ff.; 1 John 2:6).**
  1. *If Christ is in us, it stands to reason: we will be more like him.*
  2. *We will be like him:*
     (a) In attitude (Philippians 2:5).
     (b) In accepting others (Matthew 8:1-4; John 8:1-8).

**CONCLUSION**
To be 'in Christ' basically means to have his 'imputed' righteousness put to our account and so giving us a perfect standing before God. 'Christ in us' means 'imparted' righteousness, the development of his likeness within each believer (Galatians 5:5). The ultimate proof to others that we are in Christ is that Christ in us is clearly seen.

# 37

## BEARING THE CROSS

### INTRODUCTION

A. **This study is concerned with our response to the Cross of Christ. You may find it helpful at this stage to re-read Chapter 13, 'The Cross of Christ'.**
  1. *What Jesus did on the cross was for us.*
      (a) He was our substitute (2 Corinthians 5:21).
      (b) He did for us what we could not do for ourselves: he satisfied the justice of God.

  2. *The cross of Christ demands a response from us.*
      (a) All that Jesus did in suffering for the human race is of 'no value' until we believe.
      (b) We are not saved by Jesus' death apart from faith (Romans 3:26).

B. **There are two levels of response to the cross of Christ:**
  1. *The response of faith, which assures us of a home in heaven.*
      (a) It is acknowledging that our works cannot save us.
      (b) It is affirming that Jesus' death is the only way we can be saved.
      (c) Baptism is accepting the stigma (offence) that Jesus Christ is our Lord and Saviour.

  2. *The response of bearing the cross.*
      (a) Having received Christ as Lord and Saviour we need the second level of the stigma: bearing the cross.
          (1) Bearing the cross: accepting the sufferings of Christ with dignity.
          (2) Bearing the cross is a symbol of suffering for the honour and glory of God.
          (3) This is to fulfil Jesus' own words: 'If anyone would come after me, he must deny himself and take up his cross and follow me.'

C. **Why are Christians enamoured with this symbol of the cross?**
  1. *It is central to our faith.*
      (a) It is why Jesus came into the world – to die on a cross (John 3:16).

      (b) It is the emblem we embrace as proof we are in love with Jesus Christ (Galatians 6:14).

  2. *What bearing the cross is not:*
     (a) Wearing a cross on a chain around your neck.
     (b) Worshipping where the cross is affixed to the church's architecture.
     (c) Suffering that has nothing to do with the honour and glory of God.

  3. *Bearing the cross is accepting the suffering God has put on you.*
     (a) It is because you are a Christian.
     (b) It is designed for a specific purpose.

## D. Why is this study important?
  1. *It is at the heart of Christian discipleship.*
     (a) Jesus said if we are to follow him we must take up our own cross.
     (b) Bearing the cross is inevitable if we are going to follow Christ.

  2. *We need to know exactly what it means to bear our cross.*
     (a) Could we be bearing the cross without knowing it?
     (b) How would we recognise it if we were bearing the cross?

  3. *It is the most plausible explanation of the question, Why does the Christian suffer?*
     (a) Many suggest that Christianity promises an easy way of life – a life of 'health and wealth'. Really?
     (b) The truth is, all Christians will suffer (2 Timothy 3:12).

  4. *We should see that bearing the cross is not for nothing!*
     (a) 'For just as the sufferings of Christ flow over into our lives, so also through Christ our comfort overflows' (2 Corinthians 1:5).
     (b) All that Jesus experienced we too will experience.
       (1) The attitude of Christ in us means both the cross and the crown (Philippians 2:5-11).
       (2) 'Let us fix our eyes on Jesus, the author and perfecter of our faith, who for the joy set before him endured the cross, scorning its shame, and sat down at the right hand of the throne of God' (Hebrews 12:2).

## 1  THE ESSENCE OF BEARING THE CROSS:  THE WILLINGNESS TO BE MISUNDERSTOOD

### A.  Being misunderstood was part of Jesus' own pain.

1. *He was not allowed to explain everything to his own disciples* (John 16:12).
   (a)  They did not know why he let wicked men crucify him.
   (b)  He could not explain to those nearest to him what was happening.

2. *The pain of being misunderstood is relieved by knowing God alone understands.*
   (a)  This is why Jesus asked the question, 'How can you believe if you accept praise from one another, yet make no effort to obtain the praise that comes from the only God?' (John 5:44).
   (b)  Jesus got his joy from knowing that the Father was pleased with him.

3. *Jesus was willing to look like a fool.*
   (a)  He was adorned with a purple robe (Luke 23:11).
   (b)  He wore the crown of thorns (Matthew 27:29).
   (c)  These made him look utterly stupid and foolish and was designed to bring embarrassment to him and those who were his followers.

### B.  Being misunderstood for the sake of the cross.

1. *By preaching its message:* 'For I resolved to know nothing while I was with you except Jesus Christ and him crucified' (1 Corinthians 2:2).
   (a)  It seemed foolish to put forward a message at Corinth that, humanly speaking, made no sense at all.
   (b)  It was a 'stumbling block' to Jews, 'foolishness' to Gentiles.
       (1)  Stumbling block: Greek is *skandalon*, 'scandal'.
       (2)  It was designed to play right into the prejudices of those who would not believe.
   (c)  When we preach the gospel we must beware of trying to explain it so that it becomes logical or respectable.
       (1)  It has a theological explanation, yes.
       (2)  But we must let the Holy Spirit take the offensive and apply it, instead of attempting sophisticated explanations of our own.

2. *By receiving its message.*
   (a)  Receiving Jesus Christ as Lord and Saviour will make no sense to our friends.

       (1)  Those who are not saved will laugh us to scorn.

       (2)  The greater the offence, the greater honour it is to God.

  (b)  If we try to make it too 'reasonable' we will de-stigmatise the gospel – something Paul would never do.

       (1)  De-stigmatise: to take away the shame.

       (2)  We must gladly bear the stigma of the cross, knowing full well that it will never make sense to the unconverted unless the Holy Spirit creates faith in them as well.

  (c)  The greatest proof that the health and wealth gospel is false is that those who uphold it necessarily de-stigmatise the gospel.

**C. When we reach the second response level of bearing the cross we truly begin to experience something of what Jesus suffered.**

  1.  What God puts us through will make no sense to those around us.

  2.  Even those closest to us will question us, as in the case of Job.

## 2  THE PAIN OF BEARING THE CROSS: ITS QUALITY AND QUANTITY

### A.  The quality

  1.  *Bearing the cross isn't fun.*

    (a)  Jesus scorned the shame (Hebrews 12:2).

    (b)  The ancient crucifixion was the most painful death ever known.

       (1)  We may not have to experience pain like this; the Hebrew Christians did not (Hebrews 12:4).

       (2)  But we may none the less know an awful lot of pain.

  2.  *The pain may be of the following sorts:*

    (a)  *Physical.* God may put us through physical suffering.

       (1)  It could be the loss of health.

       (2)  It could be through an accident.

    (b)  *Emotional.* God may allow us to go through mental anguish.

       (1)  It should not surprise us if Christians experience emotional difficulties.

       (2)  All of us experience a nervous condition to some degree.

    (c)  *Financial.* God could lead us through a state of severe financial insecurity.

       (1)  We could lose our job.

       (2)  We could be allowed to experience great expense overnight.

    (d)  *Losing face.* God may take all self-esteem from us.

       (1)  We may be allowed to appear as fools.

       (2)  Vindication, what we may covet most, can be withheld indefinitely.

(e) *Spiritual.* God may hide his face from us.
  (1) This has been called 'the midnight of the soul'.
  (2) It can last a long time – when God seems to have betrayed us.

(f) *Persecution.* We may suffer at the hands of others for what we uphold.
  (1) This could mean losing face or losing our job.
  (2) It could mean being treated with contempt.

## B. The quantity

1. *The quantity of the pain is often increased because there is no hint that the end of the suffering is near.*
   (a) If we knew how long it would last, we could cope more easily.
   (b) Often we fear it will never end.
2. *When things go 'from bad to worse'.*
   (a) Sometimes things have to get worse before they get better.
   (b) We should not be surprised at anything: 'Dear friends, do not be surprised at the painful trial you are suffering, as though something strange were happening to you. But rejoice that you participate in the sufferings of Christ, so that you may be overjoyed when his glory is revealed' (1 Peter 4:12-13).

## 3 THE CAUSES OF BEARING THE CROSS

### A. The underlying cause: that we are Christians.

1. *We are not our own; we are bought with a price* (1 Corinthians 6:19-20).
   (a) We are owned – totally – by God. He paid for us in full – by the blood of his Son. He therefore has a right to do with us as he pleases.

2. *This means that at any time – without notice – God may put a cross in front of us that he wants us to carry.*
   (a) The underlying cause means that there is never a time, from the moment of conversion to the present, that God cannot require us to bear the cross.
   (b) The experience need not be related to anything we have done.

### B. The precipitating cause: what we do may bring on the cross.

1. *Precipitating: causing to happen suddenly.*
   (a) The bearing of the cross may unexpectedly be thrust upon us.
   (b) As we saw in the previous section God can require us to bear the cross at any time, but we can precipitate it by what we do.

2. *There are two sorts of precipitating cause:*
   (a)  For doing good: 'It is better, if it is God's will, to suffer for doing good than for doing evil' (1 Peter 3:17).
      (1)  Suffering for doing good is the ideal manner in which to bear the cross.
      (2)  Joseph was put in the dungeon because he did the right thing, not the wrong thing (Genesis 39:10,20).

   (b)  For disobeying God (1 Peter 4:15; cf. 2 Samuel 12:10).
      (1)  God will thrust the cross upon believers who fall into sin.
      (2)  How one responds to this chastening can determine whether one will truly bear his cross.

3. *For those who bear the cross of self-inflicted pain there are still rewards and dividends, both in this life and in the age to come.*
   (a)  This gives hope to those of us who have slipped and fallen (and who hasn't?).
   (b)  The bearing of the cross can be the way God brings us back and enables us to forgive ourselves.

## C. The teleological cause: the design God has in mind for us.
1. *Teleological: the hidden purpose, or aim (in bearing the cross).*
   (a)  There is always a reason why God thrusts the cross upon us.
   (b)  It is never without meaning; the cross always has a purpose: 'If you are insulted because of the name of Christ, you are blessed, for the Spirit of glory and of God rests on you' (1 Peter 4:14).

2. *The purpose of the cross is five-fold:*
   (a)  To make us more like Jesus.
      (1)  This is the main reason why God calls us bear the cross.
      (2)  It prepares us to be more and more what we shall be (Romans 8:30).
   (b)  To increase our anointing.
      (1)  God wants us to have more of his Spirit.
      (2)  The degree to which we dignify the cross in our lives will be the degree to which we experience more anointing (1 Peter 1:7).
   (c)  To enable us to cope with success.
      (1)  Most of us in fact handle failure better than we do success!
      (2)  That we can be trusted with success requires that we suffer with dignity (Luke 16:10; cf. Joseph).
   (d)  To cause us to see ourselves as we are.
      (1)  Job was 'blameless and upright; he feared God and shunned evil' (Job 1:1).

(2) After his intense suffering – during which he was totally misunderstood by his 'friends' – he saw how self-righteous he had been (Job 42:6).

(e) To make us stop pointing the finger.

(1) It is natural but never justifiable to point the finger: 'Do not judge, or you too will be judged' (Matthew 7:1).

(2) If we learn this lesson we are promised that, 'A good measure, pressed down, shaken together and running over, will be poured into your lap. For with the measure you use, it will be measured to you' (Luke 6:38).

## 4  HOW DO WE BEAR THE CROSS WITH DIGNITY?

### A. We bear the cross with dignity by what we don't do:

1. *Refusing to complain.*

   (a) Murmuring is one of the chief causes of rejecting the cross God puts on us.

   (1) If we knew how intensely God hates murmuring we would more likely stop it! (1 Corinthians 10:10).

   (2) Grumbling is proof we aren't fit for a greater anointing.

   (b) Jesus never grumbled because of what they did to him.

   (1) This is our aim: to come to the end of complaining.

   (2) When we cease complaining it is a sign we are being refined.

2. *Refusing to defend ourselves.*

   (a) Job postponed the end of his ordeal by being so defensive (Job 27:5-6).

   (b) Joseph did the same thing (Genesis 40:15).

   (c) Remember that vindication is what God does best! (Romans 12:19).

3. *Refusing to blame God.*

   (a) God, in fact, has put the cross on us – by what he has allowed:

   (1) The sickness.

   (2) The persecution.

   (3) The injustice.

   (4) The delayed answered prayer.

   (b) But when we are angry with him we only delay the end of the trial.

   (1) First of all, our anger toward God doesn't work: 'The wrath of man worketh not the righteousness of God' (James 1:20, AV).

   (2) God will not honour us with a greater anointing when we faint in the day of adversity.

## B. We bear the cross with dignity by what we do:

1. *Counting the cross a thing of joy* (James 1:2; 1 Peter 4:13).
   - (a) It is our invitation to greater things.
   - (b) God seldom promotes us to a greater measure of glory without suffering.

2. *Get our joy from knowing that God alone understands.*
   - (a) When we know he knows, that is enough.
   - (b) He takes great delight in us when we don't tell others our pain – only him.

3. *Waiting on God to step in.*
   - (a) 'Therefore judge nothing before the appointed time; wait till the Lord comes. He will bring to light what is hidden in darkness and will expose the motives of men's hearts. At that time each will receive his praise from God' (1 Corinthians 4:5).
   - (b) There can be no greater joy than the realisation that we waited and didn't give in (Isaiah 25:9).

## CONCLUSION

There are some elementary rules regarding bearing the cross:

1. The greater the cross, the greater the anointing.
2. Persecution for being a Christian is the highest form of bearing the cross: 'If you are insulted because of the name of Christ, you are blessed, for the Spirit of glory and of God rests on you' (1 Peter 4:14).
3. The highest level of Christ-likeness is praying for your enemies: 'But love your enemies, do good to them, and lend to them without expecting to get anything back. Then your reward will be great, and you will be sons of the Most High, because he is kind to the ungrateful and wicked' (Luke 6:35).
4. While we live on this earth we will have to bear the cross, although the specific trials God thrusts upon us usually come to an end.
5. The reward is worth waiting for.

Bearing the cross God puts on us is the greatest privilege in the world. We will be sorry if we cave in beneath the load, but we will be blessed if we hold on until the end.

# 38

# WHATEVER HAPPENED TO HOLINESS?

**INTRODUCTION**

A. **We are living in the 'What's in it for me?' generation.**
   1. *Theology, generally speaking, has become anything but God-centred.*
      (a) There are two ways of doing theology:
         (1) From man's point of view.
         (2) From God's point of view.
      (b) Very little theology today is explored from God's point of view which is why few have any concept of the sovereignty of God. In fact, many Christians are horrified at the doctrine of election.

   2. *People are far more interested in what excites them rather than asking, 'What gives God pleasure?'*
      (a) For example, people are more interested in the Holy Spirit than in Jesus or God the Father.
         (1) This is not because they really care about the person of the Holy Spirit.
         (2) It is because they are interested in the gifts of the Spirit – in miracles, signs and wonders.
      (b) The other issues that seem to turn people on also are, for example:
         (1) Women in the ministry.
         (2) Health and wealth.
         (3) Exciting worship.
         (4) Relationships.

   3. *This is not to say that all the above are unimportant, irrelevant or do not deserve exploration.*
      (a) We must be ready to give an answer on all these issues.
      (b) But are they the things that God wants us to be excited about?

   4. *Last on our own list is probably the matter of holiness.*
      (a) It is hardly our priority.
      (b) It is not what excites us.
      (c) It is not what we usually want to know more about.

### B. Holiness: what God is like.

1. It is what he is in himself; it is the nearest we get to his 'essence'.
2. It is what he wants us to be.

### C. Why is this subject important?

1. It brings us face to face with the character of the true God – the God of the Bible.
2. It confronts us with the kind of lives we as Christians are called to lead.
3. It helps balance the interests that excite most people today with an emphasis that is clearly God-centred.
4. It lets us see afresh what Jesus was truly like.
5. It should sober us to get our priorities right.
6. It also will hopefully enable us to see that true holiness is not the unattractive, legalistic life-style that has given holiness a needlessly bad name.

## 1 HOLINESS: WHAT GOD IS LIKE

### A. There is no earthly frame of reference by which we can fully understand God.

1. We must begin with his word about himself: 'I am holy' (Leviticus 11:44).
2. We then look at the descriptions of his dealings with men, in contrast with what man is (Exodus 19).
3. We then turn to what man is like and conclude: God is the opposite of that!

### B. God is 'wholly other', as some theologians have put it.

1. *This means that God is utterly different from what man is and does.*
    (a) This would include all creation.
        (1) The universe.
        (2) Things on earth – the sky, plants, earth, animals.
    (b) This also includes angelic beings.
        (1) Although unfallen angels come closer to mirroring God's holiness, even they are not as holy as God.
        (2) The proof of this: 'In the year that King Uzziah died, I saw the Lord seated on a throne, high and exalted, and the train of his robe filled the temple. Above him were seraphs, each with six wings: With two wings they covered their faces, with two they covered their feet, and with two they were flying. And they were calling to one another: "Holy, holy, holy is the Lord Almighty; the whole earth is full of his glory"' (Isaiah 6:1-3).

2. *God's 'otherness' is seen in his words:* ' "To whom will you compare me? Or who is my equal?" says the Holy One' (Isaiah 40:25).
   (a) There is no earthly comparison by which we can conclude what God is like.
   (b) Even though we were created in God's image (Genesis 1:26, 27), the image of God in us has been defaced.
   (c) We therefore do not have the intelligence to comprehend God's essence.

## C. God is light (1 John 1:5).

1. *He is what I can only call brilliant brightness.*
   (a) He 'lives in unapproachable light, whom no-one has seen or can see' (1 Timothy 6:16).
   (b) The brightest light – the noon-day sun, or lightning – are mere hints of God's brightness.
2. *This brightness is reflected in what Saul of Tarsus witnessed.*
   (a) 'As he neared Damascus in his journey, suddenly a light from heaven flashed around him' (Acts 9:3).
   (b) 'Saul got up from the ground, but when he opened his eyes he could see nothing. So they led him by the hand into Damascus' (Acts 9:8).
   (c) 'About noon, O King, as I was on the road, I saw a light from heaven, brighter than the sun, blazing around me and my companions' (Acts 26:13).
3. *This brightness is also seen in John's vision of Jesus' face:* 'His face was like the sun shining in all its brilliance' (Revelation 1:16).
4. *To put it another way, all that is fallen, due to sin, is the very opposite, it is darkness.*
   (a) In God 'there is no darkness at all' (1 John 1:5).
   (b) 'This is the verdict: Light had come into the world, but men loved darkness instead of light because their deeds were evil' (John 3:19).
5. *Hell is described as 'darkness'* (Matthew 8:12).
6. *Satan is called the prince of darkness* (cf. Ephesians 6:12).
7. *We have been turned from darkness to light* (Acts. 26:18).

## D. God is truth (Deuteronomy 32:4).

1. *It is impossible for God to lie* (Hebrews 6:18; Titus 1:2).
2. *Jesus is truth* (John 1:14; 14:6).
3. *The Holy Spirit is the Spirit of truth* (John 14:17).
4. *From God's truthfulness flows his faithfulness* (Lamentations 3:23).
   (a) He keeps his Word (Psalm 91:4).
   (b) He can always be depended upon (1 Corinthians 1:9; 10:13).

## E. God hates sin (Habakkuk 1:13; Zechariah 8:16-17).

1. *The giving of the Law, which reflects his holiness, was because of his hatred of sin* (Galatians 3:21-22).
    (a) The Ten Commandments reflect his attitude toward sin (Exodus 20).
    (b) The Ten Commandments show us the minimum standard of living that is required among God's people.

2. *God will in no way clear the guilty* (Exodus 34:7).
    (a) This means God must punish sin (Romans 2:16).
    (b) The only way anybody could ever be saved is by sin being punished in a substitute (2 Corinthians 5:21).

## 2 JESUS CHRIST PERFECTLY MIRRORS THE HOLINESS OF GOD

### A. Jesus is this in his person (John 14:9).
1. *Jesus was utterly without sin* (Hebrews 7:26).
2. *In his very person was perfect holiness* (1 Peter 2:22).
    (a) His deity was veiled in human flesh, so that his divine holiness was not usually openly manifested.
    (b) When he chose to manifest his glory, none could argue with him.
        (1) 'When they kept on questioning him, he straightened up and said to them, "If any one of you is without sin, let him be the first to throw a stone at her." Again he stooped down and wrote on the ground. At this, those who heard began to go away one at a time, the older ones first, until only Jesus was left, with the woman still standing there' (John 8:7-9).
        (2) 'When Jesus said, "I am he," they drew back and fell to the ground' (John 18:6).

### B. Jesus showed God's holiness in his deeds (Hebrews 4:15).
1. He never once committed a sin (1 Peter 2:22).
2. All he did and said mirrored the Father's wishes (John 12:49) and demonstrated the perfection of the Law (Matthew 5:17).

### C. He therefore became the perfect substitute.
1. By his life (Romans 5:10).
2. By his death (1 Peter 2:24).

## 3 THE PEOPLE OF GOD ARE CALLED TO HOLINESS (Hebrews 12:14).

### A. Holiness: the Greek word is *hagiasmos* and is used ten times in the New Testament. It means to reflect what God is: clean, or pure.

B. **The word 'holy' (Greek *hagios*) is used 229 times in the New Testament. It is used as the main adjective for the Spirit; it is sometimes translated 'saints'.**

C. **The word 'sanctified' in Greek is *hagiasmos*, the same word as above. The verb, *hagiazo*, means to sanctify: to make holy. It is used 29 times in the New Testament.**

D. **'Holiness' and 'sanctification' are words that are often used interchangeably.**
   1. *Holiness, pertaining to God, is what he has or is in himself.*
   2. *Holiness, pertaining to us, is derived, that is, it does not come from us but comes to us from God.*
      (a) In ourselves we are vile (Romans 3:10-18).
      (b) The heart is 'deceitful above all things and beyond cure' (Jeremiah 17:9).
   3. *Sanctification would refer to us more than to God.*
      (a) We would not tend to speak of God's sanctification but rather the believer's sanctification.
      (b) However, sanctification, or holiness, is ascribed to Christ, that is, what we have in him (1 Corinthians 1:30).

E. **Sanctification is that to which we are called.**
   1. *We are called with a 'holy' calling, which means that our effectual calling by the Holy Spirit is a call to holiness* (2 Timothy 1:9).
   2. *This is why Paul said we are chosen 'to be saved through the sanctifying work of the Spirit'* (2 Thessalonians 2:13).
      (a) In other words, in our being saved sanctification is equally assumed.
      (b) There is no such thing as faith that saves which does not also sanctify (Romans 6:22).

F. **Sanctification: the process of being made holy.**
   1. *It is a process, not a crisis.*
      (a) If it were a crisis then all could profess to being sanctified in the same way they are saved.
         (1) It is true that all believers are also sanctified (Hebrews 2:11; 10:10).
         (2) But not in the same sense that all believers are saved.
      (b) Being saved is a once for all event.
         (1) We are no more 'saved' ten years after we are converted than at the moment we were converted.
         (2) But this is *not* true with sanctification.

2. *Being saved, that is, justified by faith, is a once for all happening.*
   (a) The imputed righteousness of Christ is a completed act.
   (b) Thus 'in Christ' I am no more righteous ten years after I am justified than at the moment I believed!

3. *Sanctification, however, is a process and admits to degrees.*
   (a) Nobody (that I have yet met) is thoroughly sanctified in thought, word and deed in this life. Not even the apostle Paul claimed to have 'arrived' (Philippians 3:12ff.).
   (b) Sanctification is not perfected in this life.
   (c) Glorification (when Jesus comes) will be a once for all event which will make us like Christ.
   (d) Some good and godly scholars teach two works of grace:
       (1) We are saved – when our sins are forgiven.
       (2) We are afterwards sanctified – some say 'sanctified wholly' (cf. 1 Thessalonians 5:23) – when we are cleansed (some say 'eradicated') from 'inbred sin'.
       (3) Some of them regard the baptism with the Holy Spirit as synonymous with sanctification.
       (4) To my mind, this is a theological error. I believe the baptism of the Holy Spirit is often after conversion, but it does not equate to sanctification.

## 4 WHAT ARE THE ACHIEVABLE GOALS OF HOLINESS IN THIS LIFE?

### A. Morality.

1. *We rightly tend to think of holiness as morality – why?*
   (a) Peter's quotation of Leviticus 11:44, 'Be holy, because I am holy', follows his admonition, 'As obedient children, do not conform to the evil desires you had when you lived in ignorance' (1 Peter 1:14).
   (b) Paul's injunction was with sexual immorality in mind: 'It is God's will that you should be holy: that you should avoid sexual immorality; that each of you should learn to control his own body in a way that is holy and honourable' (1 Thessalonians 4:3-4).
       (1) God warns that sexual immorality will surely be punished . It follows, then: 'For God did not call us to be impure, but to live a holy life' (1 Thessalonians 4:6, 7).
       (2) Nothing will bring shame or disgrace upon the church like sexual sin. The TV evangelists' scandal in recent years is proof of that. Whatever else may be true of us as Christians, 'there must not be even a hint of sexual immorality, or of

any kind of impurity, or of greed, because these are improper
for God's holy people' (Ephesians 5:3).

## B. Honesty.

1. *In our financial dealings:*'He who has been stealing must steal no
   longer, but must work, doing something useful with his own hands,
   that he may have something to share with those in need' (Ephesians
   4:28).
   (a)  There must never be a hint of mishandling money in the church.
   (b)  We must not omit the matter of tithing here either! 'Will a man
        rob God?' How? 'In tithes and offerings' (Malachi 3:8).

2. *Telling the truth.*
   (a)  By nature we are all liars (Psalm 58:3).
   (b)  One proof of sanctification is that we tell the truth!
   (c)  'All liars – their place will be in the fiery lake of burning sulphur'
        (Revelation 21:8).

## C. A sweet spirit.

1. *The forgotten phrase of Hebrews 12:14 is 'make every effort to live
   in peace with all men'.*
2. *This means an attitude devoid of bitterness.*
   (a)  One of the chief ways we grieve the Holy Spirit is by bitterness
        (Ephesians 4:30ff.).
   (b)  The proof that we are bitterness-free is that we have totally
        forgiven those who have hurt us. A good example is Joseph in
        Genesis 45:
        (1)  We protect the identity of those who mistreated us (verse 1).
        (2)  We put them at perfect ease (verse 4).
        (3)  We let them be at peace with themselves (verse 5).
        (4)  We let them save face (verses 5-8).
        (5)  We refuse to blackmail them (verse 13).
        (6)  We keep on forgiving (Genesis 50:20-21).

## D. A controlled tongue in ever-increasing measure (James 3).

1. *This means no judging* (Matthew 7:1-2).
   (a)  In what we say to people.
   (b)  In what we say *about* people.
2. *A legalistic spirit often governs people who, say, are moral and
   honest, but who destroy all the good the aforementioned do by being judgemental.*
3. *A controlled tongue also excludes 'obscenity, foolish talk or coarse
   joking, which are out of place'* (Ephesians 5:4).

4. *Here's a verse many Christians wish was not in the Bible:* 'But I tell you that men will have to give account on the day of judgment for every careless word they have spoken' (Matthew 12:36).

E. **Walking in the light (1 John 1:7).**
   1. *This means that we must stay open to the Holy Spirit.*
   2. *As we 'press on to take hold of that for which Christ Jesus took hold of' us, we discover things along the way:*
      (a) Areas of sin which must be confessed (1 John 1:8-9).
      (b) Areas of fresh obedience which God puts his finger on.
   3. *When in doubt God will make clear if we are off the rails when earnestly seeking his will* (Philippians 3:15).

**CONCLUSION**

Holiness is God's essential character. His holiness is perfectly mirrored in Jesus Christ, the perfect example for Christians. In fact, holiness in believers comes to one thing: being like Jesus. None of them, however, perfectly comes up to his standard for none of them is without sin (1 John 1:8). God , however, begins the work of sanctification in each believer at the time each believes, and it is a work he will continue until they get to heaven. In the meantime, all believers should be able to say with John Newton: 'I am not what I ought to be. I am not what I want to be. I am not what I hope to be. But thank God I'm not what I used to be.'

# 39

## THE FEAR OF GOD

**INTRODUCTION**

**A. This is a subject that has been forgotten today by most Christians.**

1. *There is perhaps no other concept that is so biblical and yet is so far removed from the general consensus of Christian thinking today.*

2. *Yet it is a concept that we come across again and again in the Bible.*

   (a) Abraham was commended for his fear of God (Genesis 22:12).

      (1) Abraham is a prototype of the Christian (Romans 4:16; Galatians 3:8).

      (2) When he was tested to the extreme it was to show that he really feared God. ' "Do not lay a hand on the boy," he said, "Do not do anything to him. Now I know that you fear God, because you have not withheld from me your son, your only son"' (Genesis 22:12).

   (b) The immediate consequence of the law being given at Sinai was trembling and fear (Exodus 20:18).

      (1) God later said that this was by design (Deuteronomy 4:10).

      (2) Indeed, this was to be learned: 'Oh, that their hearts would be inclined to fear me and keep my commands always, so that it might go well with them and their children for ever!' (Deuteronomy 5:29).

   (c) The fear of the Lord was to be taught (Psalm 34:11).

      (1) By nature men do not fear God (Romans 3:18).

      (2) It follows that we must somehow learn it

   (d) The bottom line of the Book of Ecclesiastes is this: 'Fear God and keep his commandments, for this is the whole duty of man' (12:13).

   (e) The initial message of the angel with the everlasting gospel was the fear of God: 'He said in a loud voice, "Fear God and give him glory, because the hour of his judgment has come. Worship him who made the heavens, the earth, the sea and the springs of water"' (Revelation 14:7).

**B. Fear of God: Deepest reverence for his person, his Name and his ways; being afraid of displeasing him.**

1. *The fear of God generally means the combination of four things:*
   (a) Deepest reverence (respect).
   (b) A feeling of awe (respect combined with fear or wonder).
   (c) Being sincerely afraid.
   (d) Careful obedience.

2. *Being afraid of God.*
   (a) Afraid: an unpleasant emotion caused by the nearness of danger or pain; being anxious about consequences.
   (b) There may be a strong element of this in the genuine fear of God. 'I feared the anger and wrath of the LORD, for he was angry enough with you to destroy you. But again the LORD listened to me' (Deuteronomy 9:19). There is no doubt this is what Moses felt (Hebrews 12:21).

3. *There seems to be a tendency in our generation to dismiss any notion of being 'scared' of God.*
   (a) I suspect this is why there is no fear of God around at all.
   (b) What some mean by the fear of the Lord is so diluted that none respect God at all.

4. *The first message of the New Testament was this:* 'Who warned you to flee from the coming wrath?' (Matthew 3:7).
   (a) Why would people 'flee' – run – from God's wrath?
   (b) Answer: they were scared to death.

## C. Why is this study important?

1. *There is no fear of God in the land today.*
   (a) The attitude of government, the media, educators, entertainment, business and the church shows there is no fear of God.

2. *There is little fear of God among Christians generally.*
   (a) The standards of morality have degenerated so that little warning is given from church leaders as to how we should live.
   (b) We are too often not unlike Lot whose compromise led him to unthinkable solutions (Genesis 19:7-8). True, Lot was a righteous man (2 Peter 2:7). But he shows how a true Christian can backslide.

3. *Our concept of God generally has been altered by a lack of solid teaching about the God of the Bible.*
   (a) The absence of the preaching of hell has contributed to this.
   (b) The idea of annihilation is manufactured largely because men cannot bring themselves to believe that God is as terrible as he is often depicted in the Bible.

4. *In Bible times God often revealed himself in such a way that men 'trembled'.*
   (a)  Were people different then?
   (b)  Has God changed?
   (c)  I believe that if God were unveiled as he truly is – through teaching and preaching – the trembling of people would reappear.

5. *The fear of God alone will restore integrity to life generally.*
   (a)  The true fear of God would change society.
   (b)  This study is a drop in the bucket – but may none the less point to the kind of God we need to uphold whenever we have opportunity.

6. *This study coheres with other studies in this book on signs and wonders generally and the prophetic particularly.*
   (a)  Signs and wonders do not only bring great joy and happiness (e.g. healing), they also bring fear (Acts 2:43).
   (b)  Peter's prophetic ministry with Ananias and Sapphira resulted in 'great fear' (Acts 5:11).

7. *Joy and laughter are valid responses of the presence of God* (Nehemiah 8:10).
   (a)  But they are not the only responses.
   (b)  We need to have a balanced view of God's presence: his majesty and awesomeness as well as 'Abba Father' intimacy.

## 1   THE FEAR OF GOD AND MANIFESTATIONS OF HIS GLORY

### A. According to his good pleasure, God may make himself known in more than one way.

1. *There may be a 'healing presence':* 'And the power of the Lord was present for him to heal the sick' (Luke 5:17).
   (a)  This is a sovereign manifestation of the Holy Spirit.
   (b)  When this manifestation is there, one should, if needing healing, do anything to be near this presence. 'Some men came carrying a paralytic on a mat and tried to take him into the house to lay him before Jesus. When they could not find a way to do this because of the crowd, they went up on the roof and lowered him on his mat through the tiles into the middle of the crowd, right in front of Jesus' (Luke 5:18-19; cf. Acts 5:15).

2. *There may be a 'worship presence':* Jesus blessed the disciples as he was taken up to heaven. 'Then they worshipped him and returned to Jerusalem with great joy. And they stayed continually at the temple, praising God' (Luke 24:52, 53).

    (a)   This also followed the outpouring of the Spirit (Acts 2:47).
    (b)   This obviously came upon Paul and Silas (Acts 16:25).

3.  *There may be laughter:* 'Our mouths were filled with laughter, our tongues with songs of joy. Then it was said among the nations, "The LORD has done great things for them"' (Psalm 126:2).
    (a)   'With praise and thanksgiving they sang to the LORD: "He is good; his love to Israel endures for ever." And all the people gave a great shout of praise to the LORD, because the foundation of the house of the LORD was laid' (Ezra 3:11).
    (b)   'Nehemiah said, "Go and enjoy choice food and sweet drinks, and send some to those who have nothing prepared. This day is sacred to our Lord. Do not grieve, for the joy of the LORD is your strength"' (Nehemiah 8:10).

4.  *There may be a spirit of intercessory prayer:* 'So Peter was kept in prison, but the church was earnestly praying to God for him' (Acts 12:5).
    (a)   This preceded Pentecost (Acts 1:14).
    (b)   This also followed Pentecost (Acts 4:24-31).

5.  *There may be a judgement presence.*
    (a)   This was certainly the case when Peter confronted Ananias and Sapphira: 'You have not lied to men but to God' (Acts 5:1-11).
    (b)   This was true with Peter and Simon Magus. 'You have no part or share in this ministry, because your heart is not right before God' (Acts 8:21).

6.  *There is a time for deliverance* (Mark 5:1-21).
    (a)   One should wait on the right timing, and not be too anxious to find a 'demon behind every bush'.
    (b)   Paul waited 'for many days' before casting out the demon (Acts 16:16-18).

## B.  With many of the above there is a presence of the fear of God.

1.  *This is the opposite of a spirit of fear which sadly motivates some Christians* (cf. 2 Timothy 1:7).

2.  *Rather it is the feeling of holy awe.*
    (a)   'When Zechariah saw him, he was startled and was gripped with fear' (Luke 1:12).
    (b)   'Everyone was amazed and gave praise to God. They were filled with awe and said, "We have seen remarkable things today"' (Luke 5:26).

(c) 'They were all filled with awe and praised God. "A great prophet has appeared among us," they said. "God has come to help his people" ' (Luke 7:16).

(d) 'Then all the people of the region of the Gerasenes asked Jesus to leave them, because they were overcome with fear. So he got into the boat and left' (Luke 8:37).

(e) 'Everyone was filled with awe' (Acts 2:43).

(f) 'Great fear seized all who heard what had happened' (Acts 5:5).

(g) 'Great fear seized the whole church and all who heard about these events' (Acts 5:11).

(h) 'When this became known to the Jews and Greeks living in Ephesus, they were all seized with fear, and the name of the Lord Jesus was held in high honour' (Acts 19:17).

## C. Often the first thing God has to say is, 'Do not be afraid' (Matthew 28:10).

1. *This shows that his presence is often so awesome that people are afraid.*

   (a) But the angel said to him: 'Do not be afraid, Zechariah; your prayer has been heard. Your wife Elizabeth will bear you a son, and you are to give him the name John' (Luke 1:13).

   (b) But the angel said to them, 'Do not be afraid. I bring you good news of great joy that will be for all the people ...' (Luke 2:10).

   (c) 'When I saw him, I fell at his feet as though dead. Then he placed his right hand on me and said: 'Do not be afraid. I am the First and the Last ...' (Revelation 1:17).

2. *And yet sometimes the effect of what God is doing is simultaneous joy, weeping and fear.*

   (a) 'No-one could distinguish the sound of the shouts of joy from the sound of weeping, because the people made so much noise. And the sound was heard far away' (Ezra 3:13).

   (b) 'So the women hurried away from the tomb, afraid yet filled with joy, and ran to tell his disciples' (Matthew 28:8).

3. *Whenever we pray for a manifestation of God's glory (and we should) we must be open to the manner in which he chooses to show himself.*

   (a) Some believe it will be always joy and praise.

   (b) Some believe it will be always fear and awe.

   (c) We must let God be himself and respect him for the way he sovereignly chooses to work.

   (d) But at the end of the day the result of his presence will be to fear him more and more.

(1) Much familiarity with some people often results in loss of respect.

(2) The more familiar with God we are, the more we fear him.

## 2 HOW THE FEAR OF GOD IS TAUGHT (Deuteronomy 4:10).

**A. We do not come to the fear of God naturally. 'An oracle is within my heart concerning the sinfulness of the wicked. There is no fear of God before his eyes' (Psalm 36:1).**

1. *It is God's grace that teaches us.*

(a) Many wrongly assume that the fear of God is in contradistinction to the love of God.

(b) Wrong. It is through God's love in operation that we come to fear him.

(1) If there is no fear of God it is an ominous sign that God is not showing his love (Ephesians 2:3-4).

(2) When God pours out his wrath on the earth the result is not fear but the opposite: 'They were seared by the intense heat and they cursed the name of God, who had control over these plagues, but they refused to repent and glorify him' (Revelation 16:9).

(c) The worst thing God can do is to leave us alone.

(1) The wrath of God is seen as God giving people up to their own ways (Romans 1:24, 26).

(2) The wrath of God upon the wicked is seen even as his 'icy blast' (Psalm 147:17).

(3) Such is God's 'cold shoulder' – when he takes no notice.

## B. The fear of God is taught three ways:

1. *By hearing*

(a) This refers primarily to the Word. 'Consequently, faith comes from hearing the message, and the message is heard through the word of Christ' (Romans 10:17).

(b) This was the ancient manner of teaching the fear of God. 'Fix these words of mine in your hearts and minds; tie them as symbols on your hands and bind them on your foreheads. Teach them to your children, talking about them when you sit at home and when you walk along the road, when you lie down and when you get up' (Deuteronomy 11:18-19).

(c) The preaching of the gospel is received by hearing (Romans 10:14).

(1) It assumes God's wrath (John 3:36).

(2) The need to be convicted of sin (John 16:8-9).

        (3)  The need to be forgiven (Acts 2:38).
        (4)  The need for faith (Romans 3:25).
        (5)  The good news of Christ's atonement (Romans 5:8).
   (d)  When the gospel is preached with power those who hear will be asking, 'What shall we do?' (Acts 2:37).
        (1)  It is because what they 'heard' has 'cut to the heart'.
        (2)  The sense of fear lay behind Peter's words, 'Save yourselves from this corrupt generation' (Acts 2:40).

2.  *By seeing:* 'But it was your own eyes that saw all these great things the LORD has done' (Deuteronomy 11:7).
   (a)  This refers largely to signs and wonders (Hebrews 2:4).
   (b)  Fear followed Jesus' miracles: 'Everyone was amazed and gave praise to God. They were filled with awe and said, "We have seen remarkable things today"' (Luke 5:26).
   (c)  This fear followed the solemn demonstration of the Spirit concerning Ananias and Sapphira (Acts 5:5, 11).
   (d)  This fear spread to the unbelieving community through what was seen and it brought honour to God: 'When this became known to the Jews and Greeks living in Ephesus, they were all seized with fear, and the name of the Lord Jesus was held in high honour' (Acts 19:17).

3.  *By obeying* (Deuteronomy 11:8; Romans 1:5).
   (a)  Obedience leads to the proper fear of God: 'And now, O Israel, what does the LORD your God ask of you but to fear the LORD your God, to walk in all his ways, to love him, to serve the LORD your God with all your heart and with all your soul, and to observe the LORD's commands and decrees that I am giving you today for your own good?' (Deuteronomy 10:12-13).
   (b)  The fear of God and the love of God come to exactly the same thing! 'Love the LORD your God and keep his requirements, his decrees, his laws and his commands always' (Deuteronomy 11:1).
   (c)  Therefore Jesus said, 'If you love me, you will obey what I command' (John 14:15).
   (d)  The lost are punished for disobedience: 'He will punish those who do not know God and do not obey the gospel of our Lord Jesus' (2 Thessalonians 1:8; cf. 1 Peter 4:17).

4.  *All the above are the consequences of the gracious calling of the Holy Spirit* (Acts 2:39).

## C. Motivations by which people come to fear God.

1. *The non-Christian.*
   - (a) The preaching of God's wrath (Matthew 3:7).
   - (b) Any preaching with power (Acts 2:37).
   - (c) Authoritative teaching (Matthew 7:28-29; 22:33).
   - (d) Signs and wonders (Acts 4:16).

2. *The Christian.*
   - (a) The fear of God's chastening (Psalm 6:1).
   - (b) The fear of displeasing God (Psalm 19:7-14).
   - (c) The fear of not entering God's rest (Hebrews 4:1).
   - (d) The fear of continued disobedience (Hebrews 10:26-31).

## 3   THE RESULT OF FEARING GOD

### A. Wisdom and understanding.
1. It is the beginning of knowledge (Proverbs 1:7).
2. It leads to understanding (Proverbs 9:10).

### B. It saves us from a lot of trouble.
1. It is a 'fountain of life' and it turns one from the 'snares of death' (Proverbs 14:27).
2. It keeps one from immorality (Proverbs 6:24).

### C. It leads to intimacy with God.
1. God confides in those who fear him (Psalm 25:14).
2. The fear of God motivates us to walk in the light and the consequence is not only the cleansing blood of Christ but also fellowship with the Father  (1 John 1:7).

### D. Untold blessings.
1. God stores up goodness for those who fear him (Psalm 31:19).
2. His continuous hand is on such (Psalm 33:18).

### E. He fulfils our desires (Psalm 145:19; cf. Psalm 37:4).
1. It promises long life (Proverbs 10:27).
2. It promises happiness (Psalm 112:1; Proverbs 22:4; cf. Ecclesiastes 8:12).

## 4   HOW WILL WE KNOW THAT WE TRULY FEAR THE LORD?

1. *When we truly seek the glory that comes from him and not the honour of man* (John 5:44).
   - (a) The easiest thing in the world is to want man's approval.
   - (b) A true fear of God will lead us to seek the honour that comes from him only.

2. *A reverence for his Name* (Deuteronomy 28:58).
   (a) God wants us to fear his Name (Psalm 86:11).
   (b) This means that we are jealous for God's reputation and the way people speak of his Name.

3. *A care to please him* (1 John 1:7).
   (a) When we truly really care to please him in everything (2 Corinthians 5:9).
   (b) This means faithfulness in the 'very little' (Luke 16:10).

## CONCLUSION

The fear of God may well be a forgotten concept, but we forget it at our peril. Truly to fear God will transform our lives and our relationship with him. Remember Martin Luther's words: 'We must know God as an enemy before we know him as a friend.' Yet it is important that we keep a balance in our attitude towards God. Therefore, having read about the fear of God, you may now wish to read the chapter entitled 'Letting God Love Us'.

# 40

# INTERCESSORY PRAYER

## INTRODUCTION

A. **Over forty years ago I read a tract entitled 'Where are the Intercessors?'**
   1. It was a tract on intercessory prayer.
   2. It made an impact on me, showing me in particular that intercessory prayer is greatly needed but seldom done.

B. **This study builds on what was taught in the chapter on the priestly work of Christ.**
   1. *Jesus is the Chief Intercessor!*
      (a) He prays for us at the Father's right hand.
      (b) The essence of his work can safely be called 'intercessory prayer'.

   2. *We are likewise called to be intercessors for the Kingdom of God generally and for one another particularly.*
      (a) The purpose of this study is to introduce the concept of intercessory prayer.
      (b) Most of all, it is hoped that each of us will begin now, if we haven't already, to engage in this tremendous enterprise called 'intercessory prayer'.

C. **Intercessory prayer: pleading with God on behalf of another.**
   1. *Why 'plead'?*
      (a) Is this necessary?
      (b) Yes. Our first request to God is always for 'mercy' (Hebrews 4:16).

   2. *To intercede is to be a go-between.*
   3. *Intercessory prayer is standing in the gap between God and another in need; it may include:*
      (a) Praying for one other person.
      (b) Praying for several people in need.
      (c) Praying for the church.
      (d) Praying for the nation.
      (e) Praying for any aspect of God's kingdom.

D. **There are generally two Greek words for prayer:**
  1. *Proseuche*, used 37 times in the New Testament.
     (a) It is the general term for prayer and is a word used when one addresses God.
     (b) This is a word that could include any kind of praying:
         (1) Communion with God (Luke 6:12).
         (2) Asking God to act (Matthew 21:21).
         (3) Corporate praying (Acts 2:42; 3:1).
         (4) The task of all ministers (Acts 6:4).
         (5) Intercessory prayer (Acts 12:5).

  2. *Deesis*, used 19 times in the New Testament.
     (a) It is a more specific word and while it is usually translated 'prayer' it is also translated 'petition': 'Do not be anxious about anything, but in everything, by prayer and petition, with thanksgiving, present your requests to God' (Philippians 4:6).
     (b) It is a word that might be used if one took a petition to the Prime Minister, or City Hall.
         (1) Implicitly it suggests humility, since it is an inferior going to a superior.
         (2) It is like going on bended knee to a higher authority (Hebrews 5:7).

  3. *Either of the above words is relevant to intercessory prayer, although the latter provides a healthy attitude for us to adopt when praying.*

E. **The Greek word *entungchano* is the word 'to intercede' (Romans 8:27,34; Hebrews 7:25).**
  1. It means 'to solicit' or 'to petition'.
  2. The noun form is used in 1 Timothy 2:1: 'I urge, then, first of all, that requests, prayers, intercession and thanksgiving be made for everyone.'

F. **Why is intercessory prayer necessary?**
  1. Can't God step in without us?
  2. Yes – but he chooses to use vessels of prayer.
  3. Prayer is an infinite mystery.

G. **When is an intercessor needed?**
  1. In a crisis.
  2. When an enormous task is forthcoming.
  3. In a time of indecision.
  4. When one is a likely satanic target.
  5. When one has a strategic ministry.

## H. Why is this study important?

1. It focuses on what is perhaps the greatest need of the church at the present time – to plead with God.
2. It is a lesson in unselfishness; intercessory prayer, while it can refer to praying for yourself, mainly focuses on others.
3. It lets us see how God turns over to us a measure of authority – to see things achieved through prayer.
4. It is a way of being more like Jesus – he intercedes not for himself but for others.
5. It could be the turning point in our spiritual lives, should we be gripped by this lesson.
6. It will give us warm hearts.
7. It is a terrific threat to Satan's interests.

## 1   WE LEARN BEST BY LOOKING AT THE CHIEF INTERCESSOR

## A. He sympathises with our weaknesses (Hebrews 4:15).

1. *This is the way he feels about us when he prays for us.*
2. *If we are to be true intercessors we must sympathise with those for whom we pray.*
   (a) This will keep us warm and non-judgemental.
   (b) If we are disgusted with the person we are praying for, our attitude will be wrong; we should thus question if we really are 'pleading' with God on behalf of another.
   (c) An essential ingredient in intercessory prayer is the *feeling* we have toward those for whom we pray.

3. *We cannot play games with God when we are engaged in intercessory prayer.*
   (a) He knows what is in our hearts: 'Nothing in all creation is hidden from God's sight. Everything is uncovered and laid bare before the eyes of him to whom we must give account' (Hebrews 4:13).
   (b) To say one thing with our mouths but feel another way in our hearts is an insult to God if we truly claim to intercede for another!

## B. Jesus prayed for those who crucified him; he said, 'Father, forgive them, for they do not know what they are doing' (Luke 23:34).

1. G Campbell Morgan asked, 'Was that prayer answered?' and then replied by saying he expected to see in heaven the very men who hammered in the nails!
2. The heart of an intercessor should be free of bitterness.

C. **Jesus took on board the case of others: 'Christ did not please himself'**
   **(Romans 15:3).**
   1. His life was devoted to others.
   2. His intercession at God's right hand is devoted to others.

D. **He is faithful: Jesus is a 'merciful and faithful high priest' (Hebrews**
   **2:17).**
   1. He not only sympathises but also is constant in his care for us.
   2. He 'always lives to intercede' (Hebrews 7:25).

E. **Jesus was heard because of his 'reverent submission' (Hebrews 5:7).**
   1. Jesus always lived to please the Father (John 5:30).
   2. He therefore could not intercede with the Father if he did not have a
      good relationship with him!

## 2  THE NEED FOR INTERCESSORY PRAYER

A. **One no less than the apostle Paul felt the need for it.**
   1. *'Pray also for me, that whenever I open my mouth, words may be*
      *given me so that I will fearlessly make known the mystery of the*
      *gospel, for which I am an ambassador in chains. Pray that I may*
      *declare it fearlessly, as I should'* (Ephesians 6:19-20; cf. Colossians
      4:3-4).
   2. *'Brothers, pray for us'* (1 Thessalonians 5:25).
   3. *How would you like to have been Paul's intercessor? Could you*
      *have kept quiet about it?*
      (a) When Paul interceded for himself he got a rather different answer
          from what he wanted. 'But he said to me, "My grace is sufficient
          for you, for my power is made perfect in weakness." Therefore I
          will boast all the more gladly about my weaknesses, so that Christ's
          power may rest on me' (2 Corinthians 12:9).
      (b) When Paul was undergoing his greatest trial ever he attributed
          his deliverance to two things:
          (1) God's sovereign intervention (2 Corinthians 1:10).
          (2) Others' intercessory prayer (2 Corinthians 1:11).

B. **Paul himself was an intercessor.**
   1. *He interceded for his own race:* 'Brothers, my heart's desire and
      prayer to God for the Israelites is that they may be saved' (Romans
      10:1).
      (a) Do you intercede for Israel? 'Pray for the peace of Jerusalem'
          (Psalm 122:6).
      (b) Do you bring big requests to God daily?  For example:

  (1) A breakthrough in the Moslem world.

  (2) Peace in Northern Ireland and the Middle East.

  (3) The government; MPs; the royal family: 'I urge, then, first of all, that requests, prayers, intercession and thanksgiving be made for everyone – for kings and all those in authority, that we may live peaceful and quiet lives in all godliness and holiness' (1 Timothy 2:1-2).

2. *He interceded for churches in which he had a vital interest.*

 (a) For their illumination and growth:

  (1) 'I keep asking that the God of our Lord Jesus Christ, the glorious Father, may give you the Spirit of wisdom and revelation, so that you may know him better' (Ephesians 1:17).

  (2) 'For this reason I kneel before the Father, from whom his whole family in heaven and on earth derives its name. I pray that out of his glorious riches he may strengthen you with power through his Spirit in your inner being, so that Christ may dwell in your hearts through faith. And I pray that you, being rooted and established in love, may have the power, together with all the saints, to grasp how wide and long and high and deep is the love of Christ, and to know this love that surpasses knowledge – that you may be filled to the measure of all the fullness of God' (Ephesians 3:14-19).

 (b) Thanking God for their progress:

  (1) I thank my God every time I remember you. In all my prayers for all of you, I always pray with joy because of your partnership in the gospel from the first day until now, being confident of this, that he who began a good work in you will carry it on to completion until the day of Christ Jesus (Philippians 1:3-6).

  (2) We always thank God for all of you, mentioning you in our prayers. We continually remember before our God and Father your work produced by faith, your labour prompted by love, and your endurance inspired by hope in our Lord Jesus Christ (1 Thessalonians 1:2-3).

 (c) Even before he met them:

  (1) 'God, whom I serve with my whole heart in preaching the gospel of his Son, is my witness how constantly I remember you in my prayers at all times; and I pray that now at last by God's will the way may be opened for me to come to you' (Romans 1:9-10).

3. *He interceded for one person:* Night and day I constantly remember you in my prayers. Recalling your tears....' (2 Timothy 1:3).
   (a) Timothy was a timid soul (cf. 2 Timothy 1:7).
   (b) Yet Paul was about to die! (2 Timothy 4:6).

## C. Moses was a great intercessor.

1. *Note: There are, generally speaking, two types of intercessors:*
   (a) Leaders, who pray for followers as well as for others.
       (1) I fear that many leaders today are not intercessors.
       (2) Moses was one of the greatest leaders in history, but he may also have been the greatest earthly intercessor ever.
   (b) Followers, who pray for leaders as well as for others.
       (1) It may be that the greatest rewards in heaven will be given to 'low profile' Christians who laboured in prayer behind the scenes.
       (2) There is no greater ministry on earth than a person who is willing to be nameless and who prays on behalf of others.

2. *Moses interceded for the Israelites by holding up his hands.*
   (a) 'As long as Moses held up his hands, the Israelites were winning, but whenever he lowered his hands, the Amalekites were winning. When Moses' hands grew tired, they took a stone and put it under him and he sat on it. Aaron and Hur held his hands up – one on one side, one on the other – so that his hands remained steady till sunset' (Exodus 17:11-12).
   (b) This story demonstrates the profound mystery of prayer:
       (1) When we wrestle and labour in prayer, God works.
       (2) When we relax, God backs off!

3. *Moses interceded for his rebellious followers* (Exodus 32:11-14).
   (a) God was angry with the Israelites; he said two things to Moses:
       (1) 'Leave me alone so that my anger may burn against them and that I may destroy them.'
       (2) 'Then I will make you into a great nation' (Exodus 32:10).
   (b) Moses interceded:
       (1) He 'sought the favour of the LORD his God' (Exodus 32:11).
       (2) He reminded God of his reputation: 'Why should the Egyptians say, "It was with evil intent that he brought them out, to kill them in the mountains and to wipe them off the face of the earth"? Turn from your fierce anger; relent and do not bring disaster on your people" ' (Exodus 32:12).
   (c) How many of us would intercede for people like that?

### D. Some other Old Testament intercessors:
1. Ezra (Ezra 9:5-15).
2. Daniel (Daniel 9:3-19).
3. Samuel (1 Samuel 7:5ff.).
4. Elijah (James 5:17-18).
5. Abraham (Genesis 18:16-33).

### E. Corporate intercessory prayer: 'They all joined together constantly in prayer' (Acts 1:14).
1. *Part of spiritual warfare consists of intercessory prayer* (Ephesians 6:10-18).
   - (a) This admonition was addressed to the church generally (Ephesians 1:1).
   - (b) The last request was: 'And pray in the Spirit on all occasions with all kinds of prayers and requests. With this in mind, be alert and always keep on praying for all the saints' (Ephesians 6:18).

2. *The early church interceded for Peter.*
   - (a) Peter was put in prison (Acts 12:3-4).
     - (1) This followed the martyrdom of James, John's brother (Acts 12:2).
     - (2) The church feared that Peter would be next – which was unthinkable!
   - b) Peter was kept in prison, 'but the church was earnestly praying to God for him' (Acts 12:5).
     - (1) Peter was given a miraculous deliverance (Acts 12:6-17).
     - (2) This was an answer to corporate intercessory prayer!

3. *The church under stress is best served by corporate intercessory prayer.*
   - (a) The first major miracle led to persecution (Acts 3:7; 4:3).
   - (b) After being threatened, 'they raised their voices together in prayer to God' (Acts 4:24).
   - (c) The result: 'After they prayed, the place where they were meeting was shaken. And they were all filled with the Holy Spirit and spoke the word of God boldly' (Acts 4:31).

## 3  THE CONTENT OF INTERCESSORY PRAYER

### A. Praise: We pray 'with thanksgiving' (Philippians 4:6).
1. *Affirming God for who he is:* 'You made the heaven and the earth and the sea, and everything in them' (Acts 4:24).
2. *Affirming God for his Word:* 'You spoke by the Holy Spirit through the mouth of your servant, our father David' (Acts 4:25).

    3. *Affirming God for his sovereignty:* 'They did what your power and
    will had decided beforehand should happen' (Acts 4:28).

    4. *Paul couched intercessory prayer in praise:*
      (a) 'First, I thank my God through Jesus Christ for all of you, because
         your faith is being reported all over the world' (Romans 1:8).
         Then Paul interceded (Romans 1:9-10).
      (b) 'And in their prayers for you their hearts will go out to you,
         because of the surpassing grace God has given you. Thanks be to
         God for his indescribable gift!' (2 Corinthians 9:14-15).
      (c) 'I thank my God every time I remember you. In all my prayers for
         all of you, I always pray with joy' (Philippians 1:3-4).

B. **Acknowledging the immediate problem:** 'Indeed Herod and Pontius
   Pilate met together with the Gentiles and the people of Israel in this city
   to conspire against your holy servant Jesus, whom you anointed' (Acts
   4:27).
    1. *God clearly knows the need before we ask* (Matthew 6:8).
    2. *But we are none the less invited to bring our requests to God's at-*
      *tention* (Philippians 4:6).
    3. *Paul asked the church to be specific:* 'Pray also for me, that when-
      ever I open my mouth, words may be given me so that I will fearlessly
      make known the mystery of the gospel' (Ephesians 6:19).

C. **Intercessory prayer may include prayer for healing.**
    1. *The early church prayed, 'Stretch out your hand to heal and per-*
      *form miraculous signs and wonders through the name of your holy*
      *servant Jesus'* (Acts 4:30).
    2. *James said, 'Pray for each other that you may be healed'* (James
      5:16).
      (a) This followed the request for the anointing of oil (James 5:14ff.).
      (b) 'The prayer of a righteous man is powerful and effective', an
         implicit reference to intercessory prayer for healing (James 5:16).

D. **That the will of God will be known:** 'Epaphras, who is one of you and
   a servant of Christ Jesus, sends greetings. He is always wrestling in prayer
   for you, that you may stand firm in all the will of God, mature and fully
   assured' (Colossians 4:12).

E. **That Christ will be known better in us (Ephesians 1:16ff; 3:17ff.).**

4  **PRAYING FOR YOUR ENEMIES**

A. **A most neglected but valuable ingredient in the enterprise of intercessory prayer is: praying for those whose conduct you don't like.**

1. *We have seen above how Moses treated this matter.*
   (a) God told Moses to get out of the way so he could destroy the Israelites.
   (b) 'So he said that he would destroy them – had not Moses, his chosen one, stood in the breach before him to keep his wrath from destroying them' (Psalm 106:23).

2. *This is exactly what God hoped Moses would do.*
   (a) The result: God became nearer and dearer to Moses then ever.
   (b) The scenario of total forgiveness seen in Exodus 32 is followed by Moses' seeing God's glory in Exodus 33:21ff.

## B. Not holding anything against anyone when we pray.

1. *Most of us know about Jesus' words:* 'I tell you the truth, if anyone says to this mountain, "Go throw yourself into the sea," and does not doubt in his heart but believes that what he says will happen, it will be done for him' (Mark 11:23).
2. *What is often overlooked:* 'And when you stand praying, if you hold anything against anyone, forgive him, so that your Father in heaven may forgive you your sins' (Mark 11:25).
3. *We must never overlook:*
   (a) The petition in the Lord's Prayer, 'Forgive us our debts, as we also have forgiven our debtors' (Matthew 6:12).
   (b) The possible reason we were given the Lord's Prayer in the first place: 'For if you forgive men when they sin against you, your heavenly Father will also forgive you. But if you do not forgive men their sins, your Father will not forgive your sins' (Matthew 6:14-15).

## C. We may know about Job's ordeal, but how many realise what changed everything in the end?

1. *Job had 'friends' – persecutors of the worst sort!*
2. *In the end Job was required to intercede for the very people that added to his pain!* 'After Job had prayed for his friends, the LORD made him prosperous again and gave him twice as much as he had before' (Job 42:10).

## D. It is a most sublime but serious matter to intercede for your enemies (Acts 7:50).

1. *It is serious stuff indeed; but if you pray for your enemies, be sure that you mean it.*
2. *Be totally prepared for God to answer your prayer:*
   (a) That they will be blessed, not judged.

(b)  That you want God to bless them as you would want him to bless you (and overlook your faults).

3.  *This sets God free – and he can take you at your word.*

## 5  THE IDEAL INTERCESSOR:  ONE WHO INTERCEDES LIKE JESUS

### A.  He sympathises with our weaknesses: 'Merciful' (Hebrews 2:17).
1.  An effective intercessor will not be a judgemental person.
2.  He or she will be understanding of human frailty.

### B.  He prays for his enemies (Luke 23:34).
1.  You don't want an intercessor who is uncritically 'on your side'; he or she will be impartial and will pray for one's enemies.
2.  After all, don't you want to be heard by God?

### C.  He is faithful (Hebrews 2:17).
1.  An intercessor must be committed to pray regularly – daily at least.
2.  Are you prepared to intercede for others as a commitment?

### D.  He is self-effacing: 'Gentle and humble' (Matthew 11:29).
1.  An intercessor will not want 'profile' or attention.
2.  Like the Holy Spirit, who is self-effacing and who intercedes behind the scenes (Romans 8:26-27), a good intercessor is willing never to be 'known'.

### E.  He is available: 'He always lives to intercede' (Hebrews 7:25).
1.  An intercessor is one who has the time to pray – or will take the time.
2.  Even if the intercessor is a busy person, he or she will make intercessory prayer a priority in a busy schedule.

## CONCLUSION

Intercessory prayer is a mystery. We often wonder why it is necessary. Cannot God step in without us? The answer is yes, but he chooses to use our prayers.

Jesus Christ is the chief intercessor and is our example. Remember the tract I mentioned at the start of the chapter: 'Where are the intercessors?' Are you one? Will you be one? God will do great things when we pray in this way.

# 41

# PRAYER AND FASTING

**INTRODUCTION**

**A. We looked at the subject of prayer in the previous chapter.**
1. *I am convinced that we can never emphasise prayer too much.*
   (a) 'God does nothing but in answer to prayer.' *John Wesley.*
   (b) 'The less I pray, the harder it gets; the more I pray, the better it gets.' *Martin Luther.*
   (c) 'I have a very busy day today; must spend not two but three hours in prayer.' *Martin Luther.*
   (d) 'When I pray, coincidences happen, and when I don't, they don't.' *William Temple.*
   (e) 'Pray harder when it is hardest to pray. Prayer is a powerful thing, for God has bound and tied himself thereto.' *Martin Luther.*

2. *All that will be mentioned in this chapter assumes that we bear in mind what has been learned about prayer in the previous chapter.*
   (a) Prayer is a great mystery; why God doesn't act without waiting for us first, I do not know; I only know he has tied himself to prayer.
   (b) The same God who predestines the end has also predestined the means; this includes prayer.

**B. Fasting is no less desirable than praying.**
1. It is easier to watch television than to pray.
2. It is easier to pray than to fast – and pray.

**C. Fasting: doing without.**
1. *Normally this means doing without food for a period of time.*
   (a) One may fast one meal (no big deal but it is a beginning if you are doing it to the glory of God).
   (b) One may fast for a whole day, or twenty-four hour period.
   (c) One may fast for several days.
2. *Fasting may take in other things:*
   (a) Going without sleep.
   (b) Doing without certain legitimate pleasures.
   (c) Sheer obedience to the matters we may tend to overlook. 'Is not this the kind of fasting I have chosen: to loose the chains of

injustice and untie the cords of the yoke, to set the oppressed free and break every yoke? Is it not to share your food with the hungry and to provide the poor wanderer with shelter – when you see the naked, to clothe him, and not to turn away from your own flesh and blood?' (Isaiah 58:6-7).

D. **This study will largely concentrate on the matter of going without food.**
  1. Any of the above may have their place.
  2. But for most of us, to begin to seek God's face in conjunction with going without food will be a major breakthrough.

E. **The New Testament assumption is that believers will fast.**
  1. Jesus did not say 'if' but 'when' we fast (Matthew 6:16).
  2. Jesus predicted that his own followers would fast: 'Jesus answered, "How can the guests of the bridegroom mourn while he is with them? The time will come when the bridegroom will be taken from them; then they will fast" ' (Matthew 9:15).

F. **Why is this study important?**
  1. *It is almost entirely neglected – in theology and practice.*
  2. *It provides a new dimension for many people with regard to a discipline that is needed from time to time.*
  3. *It is a valid exercise in sheer discipline.*
     (a) Many of us are undisciplined generally in our lives.
     (b) This is something we can do about that, perhaps a beginning to becoming more disciplined.
  4. *It could provide a great spiritual breakthrough:*
     (a) For your church.
     (b) For you as a Christian.
  5. *It is a way by which we can begin to experience intimacy with God:*
     (a) To know his mind.
     (b) To experience his power.
  6. *For someone who is experiencing dulness in his or her Christian life, this may well be the way forward.*
  7. *It may set one on to a way of tackling life's problems of which you have not thought.*
  8. *It could be a key to survival:*
     (a) For the nation.
     (b) For a church in grave difficulty.
     (c) For you as a discouraged believer.

**G. All that follows below should be combined with prayer.**
1. We are not talking just about fasting.
2. All fasting should be accompanied by praying as much as possible.

# 1   BIBLICAL EXAMPLES OF FASTING

## A. For the nation.

1. *It was required for Israel on the Day of Atonement* (Leviticus 23:27,29).
   - (a) Israel was of course a theocracy.
     - (1) Theocracy: a nation under a covenant of God by which they are governed solely by the Law of God.
     - (2) There is no biblical doctrine of church and state that suggests this should continue beyond the Cross (Romans 13:1-5; Colossians 2:14-17).
   - (b) No theocracy exists today but we can still learn from the way it was done in ancient Israel.
     - (1) It would do our nation no harm if our leaders would call the nation to a day of prayer and fasting (Proverbs 14:34).
     - (2) This used to be done in Britain – the last time being during World War II.
2. *Fearful of the encroaching enemy, King Jehoshaphat called for a time of fasting for Judah* (2 Chronicles 20:3).
3. *The king of Nineveh proclaimed a fast in the light of Jonah's prophecy of doom* (Jonah 3:5).
4. *Under the threat of the Philistines the people of Israel fasted under Samuel's leadership* (1 Samuel 7:6).
5. *The prophet Joel called for a fast in the light of a recent calamity* (Joel 2:15).

## B. For the believing community.

1. *Ezra made great claims for God's power and care for Israel, then felt the need to call people to fast* (Ezra 8:21).
   - (a) 'I was ashamed to ask the king for soldiers and horsemen to protect us from enemies on the road, because we had told the king, "The good hand of our God is on everyone who looks to him, but his great anger is against all who forsake him." So we fasted and petitioned our God about this, and he answered our prayer' (Ezra 8:22-23).
   - (b) This shows how human Ezra was and yet he had abiding faith in God – but not without fasting.

2.  *In connection with confession of sin* (Nehemiah 9:1).
    (a)  This is possibly the rarest kind of fasting of all.
    (b)  It is when God's people are *so sorry* for their waywardness that
         they accentuate their sorrow – as if to show God their sincerity –
         by fasting.

3.  *When Queen Esther saw the validity of Mordecai's burden, and
    agreed to do the unthinkable by approaching the king without his
    initiative, she said, 'Go, gather together all the Jews who are in
    Susa, and fast for me. Do not eat or drink for three days, night or
    day. I and my maids will fast as you do. When this is done, I will go
    to the king, even though it is against the law. And if I perish, I per-
    ish' (Esther 4:16).*
    (a)  This shows how desperate the situation was.
    (b)  This shows how desperate Esther felt.

4.  *The early church appears to have combined worship with fasting.*
    (a)  The result was that God spoke: 'While they were worshipping
         the Lord and fasting, the Holy Spirit said, "Set apart for me
         Barnabas and Saul for the work to which I have called them" '
         (Acts 13:2).
    (b)  This appears to have been God's means to launch the strategic
         ministry of Paul and Barnabas.

5.  *Appointing church leaders and sending them out seems to have
    been done 'with prayer and fasting'* (Acts 14:23).
    (a)  One gets the impression that this was almost a routine.
    (b)  One asks: Is this ever done today?

## C.  **When it is by the person alone.**

1.  *Moses fasted for forty days and forty nights* (Exodus 34:28).
    (a)  This was not merely for himself but 'because of all the sin you
         committed, doing what was evil in the LORD's sight and so
         provoking him to anger... But again the LORD listened to me'
         (Deuteronomy 9:18-19).
    (b)  It has been said also that this was without a doubt a *supernatural*
         fast: 'I ate no bread and drank no water' during that forty days
         (Deuteronomy 9:18).
         (1)  One should never fast without drinking water.
         (2)  Humanly speaking, Moses would have died had not God
              supernaturally sustained him.
    (c)  Moses' fast was intercession for God's people.

2. *Jesus fasted forty days and forty nights* (Matthew 4:1-2).
   (a)  This may or may not have included drinking water.
   (b)  In any case it followed his baptism and coincided with the beginning of his public ministry.

3. *David fasted after Nathan's prophecy – 'The son born to you will die' – and the immediate illness of his son.*
   (a)  'David pleaded with God for the child. He fasted and went into his house and spent the nights lying on the ground' (2 Samuel 12:16).
   (b)  When the child died, he ate. He explained, 'While the child was still alive, I fasted and wept. I thought, "Who knows? The LORD may be gracious to me and let the child live." But now that he is dead, why should I fast? Can I bring him back again? I will go to him, but he will not return to me' (2 Samuel 12:22-23).

4. *Elijah was apparently fasting during the time of his greatest trial* (1 Kings 19:1-8).
   (a)  Elijah feared for his life owing to Queen Jezebel's threat (1 Kings 19:2-3).
   (b)  He was ordered to eat – which he did (1 Kings 19:5, 8).

5. *Daniel had a habit of fasting when he lacked understanding.*
   (a)  Apparently he did not understand as much as he desired to know regarding Jeremiah's prophecy. 'So I turned to the Lord God and pleaded with him in prayer and petition, in fasting, and in sackcloth and ashes' (Daniel 9:3).
   (b)  He fasted when he did not even understand his own vision (Daniel 10:1-3).

6. *The apostle Paul seems to have fasted often* (2 Corinthians 6:5; 11:27).
   (a)  It is difficult to know if these fasts were always voluntary.
   (b)  In any case, he seems not to have enjoyed them!
   (c)  Note:  fasting is no fun.
      (1)  If it's fun it's not a spiritual discipline.
      (2)  If it is truly a fast it will probably take a lot of effort; that is what makes a fast a fast.

## 2  THE PURPOSE OF FASTING

### A.  To get God's attention (Isaiah 58:1-11).

1. *This may seem strange to us – surely God already knows everything* (Hebrews 4:13).

    (a) Nothing is hidden from God (Psalm 139:1-2).

    (b) The greatest folly we can engage in is to say, 'The LORD does not see; the God of Jacob pays no heed' (Psalm 94:7).

2. *But that fasting is done with the explicit purpose of trying to get God's attention is borne out by these words: ' "Why have we fasted," they say, "and you have not seen it? Why have we humbled ourselves, and you have not noticed?" '* (Isaiah 58:3a).

    (a) They clearly were trying to get God's attention.

    (b) But in this case it didn't work! Why?

        (1) Their fasting was fun: 'On the day of your fasting, you do as you please' (Isaiah 58:3b).

        (2) In other words, their humbling themselves, bowing their heads and lying in sackcloth and ashes was what they loved doing.

    (c) Note: self-righteous people are vulnerable to loving godliness more than God.

3. *However, there is no doubt that the reason for* all *the biblical examples of fasting is to get God's attention.*

## B. To show God that we mean business.

1. *'He already knows that,' the sophisticated person may say.*

2. *I reply: Does he? Show it by doing that which is not so easy for you to do!*

    (a) This is why Joel called for a fast; the calamity of locusts was a sign of God's judgement (Joel 2).

    (b) Fasting was almost certainly a condition attached to whether or not Samuel interceded for Israel (1 Samuel 7:5-6).

## C. To show God that we are really sorry.

1. *This is what lay behind the fasting in Ezra's day (Ezra 9:1-3).*

2. *When we have been exposed for our folly – and are really sorry – we should also want to know that God is pleased with our repentance.*

    (a) This does not mean we should fast every time we sin or confess our sins (1 John 1:9).

    (b) But in some cases, if we have truly grieved the Lord in an acute manner, fasting is not out of order to show God:

        (1) That you see your sin.

        (2) That you are truly sorry.

        (3) That you are truly changing.

## D. **To plead with God to change his mind.**

1. *There are verses that say God doesn't change his mind* (1 Samuel 15:29).
   - (a) This almost certainly is restricted to God's oath.
   - (b) For example, when God swore that Israel would not enter into his rest, the decision was irrevocable.

2. *There are verses that show God does change his mind.*
   - (a) Concerning Hezekiah's illness (2 Kings 20:1-6).
      - (1) Isaiah told him he would not recover.
      - (2) Hezekiah wept and prayed – it worked!
   - (b) Nathan's initial word to David regarding building the temple (2 Samuel 7:1-17).
      - (1) At first Nathan said, 'Go for it.'
      - (2) But God spoke to Nathan who then had to go back the next day with a totally different perspective.
      - (3) One can therefore see why David fasted during his son's illness; it was the same Nathan who had given the fatal word about his son.
   - (c) The king of Nineveh, hearing of Jonah's message of doom, said, 'Who knows? God may yet relent and with compassion turn from his fierce anger so that we will not perish' (Jonah 3:9).
      - (1) The king of Nineveh was on to something.
      - (2) God did change his mind – to Jonah's chagrin!
   - (d) Elijah gave King Ahab a devastating word: 'I am going to bring disaster on you. I will consume your descendants and cut off from Ahab every last male in Israel – slave or free. I will make your house like that of Jeroboam son of Nebat and that of Baasha son of Ahijah, because you have provoked me to anger and have caused Israel to sin' (1 Kings 21:21-22).
      - (1) 'When Ahab heard these words, he tore his clothes, put on sackcloth and fasted. He lay in sackcloth and went around meekly' (1 Kings 21:27).
      - (2) Then God said to Elijah, 'Have you noticed how Ahab has humbled himself before me? Because he has humbled himself, I will not bring this disaster in his day, but I will bring it on his house in the days of his son' (1 Kings 21:29).

3. *This is a most encouraging possibility.*
   - (a) We are wise if we climb down from our inflexible views of God and become more like the king of Nineveh who said, 'Who knows?'
   - (b) Remember, ' "For my thoughts are not your thoughts, neither are your ways my ways," declares the LORD. "As the heavens are higher

than the earth, so are my ways higher then your ways and my thoughts than your thoughts" ' (Isaiah 55:8-9).

### E. For clarification of God's will.

1. *We are instructed to know God's will* (Ephesians 5:17).
   - (a) However, this is not always so clear.
   - (b) Fasting is an indication of how seriously we want to know.
2. *This is what Daniel wanted regarding the future* (Daniel 9:3; 10:3).

### F. For God's continued blessing.

1. This is what lay behind the launching of the disciples for specific ministry (Acts 13:2; 14:23).
2. This lay behind Ezra's burden (Ezra 8:21ff.).

### G. For power (Matthew 17:20; Mark 9:29).

1. The disciples wanted to know why they couldn't cast out a powerful demon.
2. The answer, according to some manuscripts: 'This kind does not go out except by prayer and fasting.'
3. Note: many of God's greatest men in church history have spent time in prayer and fasting when they felt a need for more power.

### H. Because of unanswered prayer.

1. David said, 'I put on sackcloth and humbled myself with fasting. When my prayers returned to me unanswered I went about mourning as though for my friend or brother' (Psalm 35:13-14).
2. This is the way Psalm 109 is introduced; in it David said, 'My knees give way from fasting' (Psalm 109:24).

## 3  SOME CAUTIONS REGARDING FASTING

### A. Do not fast without drinking plenty of liquids.

1. Unless it is a supernatural fast (like that of Moses), do not give place to the devil by not drinking lots of water.
2. Ezra 'ate no food and drank no water' for an unspecified time (Ezra 10:6), but I would not counsel people to go this far; don't regard your fast as supernatural!
3. The human body can go a lot longer without food than without water; we need water daily to survive.

### B. Do not fast when there is a health problem.

1. Unless given specific instructions by your doctor, do not fast when you are ill!
2. A person with diabetes should not consider fasting from food (there are other kinds of fasting).

C. **Don't be deceived by a euphoria after a day or two of fasting; the feeling is probably more physical than spiritual.**
   1. A certain amount of fasting is often good for the body, if only to get rid of poisons in the system.
   2. This often makes us feel better and probably has little, if anything, to do with a special manifestation of God's presence.

D. **Remember that you are vulnerable to the devil when you are fasting.**
   1. It is not fun; you may feel weak, even irritable.
   2. The devil will play into this weakness; be aware of his ways (2 Corinthians 2:11).

E. **Do not expect a lot to happen during the actual time of fasting.**
   1. You may feel God near; you may not.
   2. The results of fasting are often more long-term than immediate.
   3. The blessing will probably come later.

F. **Beware of the temptation to self-righteousness.**
   1. *All of us are self-righteous by nature.*
   2. *Fasting may make us more vulnerable to self-righteousness:*
      (a) In our own eyes (Luke 18:11-12).
      (b) In the eyes of others (Matthew 6:16-18).

   3. *Rule of thumb: never tell people if you are fasting alone; it is between you and God* (John 5:44).
      (a) In the case of a church fasting together, this is different.
      (b) Even then, nobody needs to know for sure whether you yourself fasted; be careful not to judge those who don't wish to enter in.

G. **Beware of fasting beyond three days.**
   1. Have a very good reason for going longer than three days.
   2. If you do, share it with a trusted person who will be aware of what you are doing; and be sure you are in good health!

## CONCLUSION

Fasting, combined with prayer, is a way of getting God's attention and showing that we are in earnest. Many people in the Bible fasted at times of crisis and experienced God's hand at work in a mighty way.

Fasting is often neglected today but it is still a relevant discipline, especially in situations when we feel a great need of God. It is God-honouring and it works!

# 42

## LETTING GOD LOVE US

### INTRODUCTION

A. **A wrong understanding of the fear of God can result in the fear that God doesn't love us.**
   1. *All theology must be balanced; there are almost always 'two sides of the coin'.*
      (a) The fear of God stems from his majesty and awe.
      (b) That, if left utterly alone, can lead to despair.

   2. *This study therefore is a practical application of that lesson.*
      (a) Some of us are more at home with the majesty and sovereignty of God.
      (b) Some of us are more at home with the sweetness and tenderness of God – the 'Abba Father' side of God.

B. **Whatever our theological background, most of us wrestle with the problem that God loves 'ME'.**
   1. *Those who lay stress on God's glory have the problem.*
   2. *Those who lay stress on God's tenderness have the problem.*
   3. *As a pastor I can safely state that it is often the hardest thing in the world for Christians to believe – 'that God really loves ME'.*
      (a) It is in a sense harder to believe than believing that there is a God – or that Jesus died and rose from the dead.
      (b) It is sometimes not too difficult to believe that God will take care of us or that 'in all things God works for the good of those who love him' (though we may not believe that they are for our good at the time!).
   4. *The question is, are we ready to let God love us?*
      (a) Sometimes we are afraid to let him love us, even with all the evidence before us.
      (b) This is especially true of those who have never felt love; they don't honestly know how to respond to or accept love.

C. **What lies behind this difficulty in letting God love us?**
   1. *Some Christians have what is called an 'overly scrupulous conscience', a phrase that comes from Puritan studies.*

     (a)   Scrupulous: being very conscientious (too careful) even in small matters.

     (b)   Some go beyond this: being overly scrupulous leads to constant worry over matters that have nothing to do with sin.

2. *Some have a 'perfectionist' mentality.*
    (a)   They are not content with trying, trying harder, doing your best, getting a 'pass', getting 90 per cent or even 99.9 per cent.
    (b)   They feel they must produce 100 per cent in order to feel accepted; but nobody ever does.

3. *It may be a psychological problem.*
    (a)   Some cannot call God 'Father' and think it is a spiritual problem.
    (b)   It is usually a mental block, something they cannot help, possibly because their only relationship with a father in this life was so poor.
        (1)   They may have had an abusive or over-strict father.
        (2)   They may have had a father who was so busy he was never there when needed; the 'absent' father.

4. *It may be due to a faulty theology.*
    (a)   It may be because they have had a spiritual or theological diet with a one-sided emphasis on the fear, justice, wrath and/or sovereignty of God.
    (b)   It may be because they are still living under the Old Covenant, under the Law, not unlike some Puritans.
        (1)   Such virtually live under the promise of heaven, or assurance you are saved, by works of the Law.
        (2)   Such people often have little or no assurance of their own salvation, even if they have been professing Christians for years and years.
        (3)   Note:it is sadly true that many of the Puritans had no assurance of salvation even at the time of death.

5. *It may be because of personal failure, or sin.*
    (a)   If we have let God down, especially if we've done it more than once, it is often difficult to believe God *still* loves us.
    (b)   Rather than claim 1 John 1:9 – 'If we confess our sins, he is faithful and just and will forgive us our sins and purify us from all unrighteousness' – we often feel the need to 'perform' for him.
    (c)   The result often is that we don't feel he loves us; if anything, we don't think he *should* love us.

## D. Why is this study important?

1. *Because our confidence and sense of well-being are at stake.*
2. *If we can each really and truly believe – and know – that 'God loves ME' we can face difficulties more easily – no doubt about it!*
3. *Our assurance of being saved is at stake.*
   (a) Assurance is a part of saving faith.
   (b) It is absolutely wrong not to know you are saved if you have put all your hope in Jesus' death on the cross.
4. *The devil doesn't want us to believe that God loves us.*
   (a) The less we believe that God loves us, the easier it is for Satan to lead us to despair.
   (b) The more we believe that God loves us, the harder it is for Satan to cast us down.
5. *We are of more use to God in the world when we proceed under the conviction that we are truly and tenderly and everlastingly loved by God.*
6. *We please God most when we feel and affirm his love.*
   (a) He doesn't want us to doubt his love.
   (b) Any parent worth his or her salt *wants* their child to feel secure in their love.
   (c) God is the perfect Father.

## 1   ASSUMPTION: GOD LOVES US

## A. We begin with the general promise of John 3:16: 'For God so loved the world that he gave his one and only Son, that whoever believes in him shall not perish but have eternal life.'

1. Martin Luther said, 'I'm glad that it does not say "For God so loved *Martin Luther* that if *Martin Luther* believed he will not perish but have eternal life".'
2. Why? 'Because I'd be afraid it referred to another *Martin Luther*!'

## B. What are the general promises?

1. *They refer not only to the world but to 'us'.*
   (a) 'But God demonstrates his own love for us in this: While we were still sinners, Christ died for us' (Romans 5:8).
   (b) 'We love because he first loved us' (1 John 4:19).
   (c) 2 Peter 3:9 in the Authorised Version refers to 'us-ward' and 'us'; the New International Version puts it as 'you': 'The Lord is not slow in keeping his promise, as some understand slowness. He is patient with you, not wanting anyone to perish, but everyone to come to repentance.'

2. *Jesus died for everybody.*
    (a) 'For Christ's love compels us, because we are convinced that one died for all, and therefore all died. And he died for all, that those who live should no longer live for themselves but for him who died for them and was raised again' (2 Corinthians 5:14-15).
    (b) 'But we see Jesus, who was made a little lower then the angels, now crowned with glory and honour because he suffered death, so that by the grace of God he might taste death for everyone' (Hebrews 2:9).
    (c) 'My dear children, I write this to you so that you will not sin. But if anybody does sin, we have one who speaks to the Father in our defence – Jesus Christ, the Righteous One. He is the atoning sacrifice for our sins, and not only for ours but also for the sins of the whole world' (1 John 2:1-2).

3. *The promise is to those who believe.*
    (a) 'This righteousness from God comes through faith in Jesus Christ to all who believe. There is no difference' (Romans 3:22).
    (b) 'He did it to demonstrate his justice at the present time, so as to be just and the one who justifies the man who has faith in Jesus' (Romans 3:26).
    (c) 'This is a trustworthy saying that deserves full acceptance (and for this we labour and strive), that we have put our hope in the living God, who is the Saviour of all men, and especially of those who believe' (1 Timothy 4:9-10).

C. **Once we meet the condition of faith in the general promises, the following absolutely apply to us:**
    1. *We are loved with an 'everlasting love'* (Jeremiah 31:3).
    2. *We are loved by Jesus himself:* 'A new command I give you: Love one another. As I have loved you, so you must love one another' (John 13:34).
    3. *We are loved by the Father with the same love that the Father loves Jesus himself.*
        (a) The Father *loves* his Son.
            (1) 'And a voice from heaven said, "This is my Son, whom I love; with him I am well pleased"' (Matthew 3:17).
            (2) 'While he was still speaking, a bright cloud enveloped them, and a voice from the cloud said, "This is my Son, whom I love; with him I am well pleased. Listen to him!"' (Matthew 17:5).
        (b) The Father loves us as much as he loves Jesus.
            (1) This is the heart of the meaning of being 'in Christ'.

    (2)  We are 'co-heirs with Christ' (Romans 8:17).

    (3)  Jesus prayed, 'I in them and you in me. May they be brought to complete unity to let the world know that you sent me and have loved them even as you have loved me' (John 17:23).

## D. Why should we let God love us?

1. *Because he does.*
2. *Because he wants us to enjoy his love.*
   - (a) When I am closer to God, I feel his love more.
   - (b) Many who have experienced the 'Toronto Blessing' have testified to *feeling* for the first time how much they are loved.
   - (c) When I tell another 'I love you', I am thrilled when they feel how much I mean it.

3. *Because he chose us.*
   - (a) He chose us before we were born (Romans 9:11; Ephesians 1:4).
   - (b) We love because he first loved us (1 John 4:19).

4. *Because of God's grace.*
   - (a) His grace and plan for us have *already* taken into account our weaknesses:
     - (1) Failure.
     - (2) Unbelief.
     - (3) Self-righteousness.
     - (4) Fears.
   - (b) The sacrifice of Calvary assures us that our sins are washed away.
     - (1) Jesus didn't die for us because he saw that we were going to turn out all right.
     - (2) He died for us because he knew in advance we weren't going to come up to his standard.
     - (3) He died for us *because* we were utterly unworthy.

5. *Because he is God:* 'God is love' (1 John 4:16).
   - (a) Only God can love like he loves.
   - (b) There is no earthly frame of reference (parent, grandparent or close friend) who can match the way God really feels about his own.
   - (c) We desperately need the kind of love he has.

## 2  HOW WE LET GOD LOVE US

### A. Many of us won't let him love us.

1. *We are so used to rejection that we have a built-in defence mechanism that rejects him before he has a chance to show us how much he loves us.*

2. *I have watched people reject love the more you try to show it. Why?*
   - (a) They are afraid it isn't really true.
   - (b) They are afraid it won't last.
   - (c) They basically mistrust any overture of love.

### B. What are the ways we block God's love?

1. *By trying to perform.*
   - (a) This is what we do when we don't accept ourselves or believe his love toward us (1 John 4:16).
   - (b) It is our way, consciously or unconsciously, of trying to get his approval by our good works.
     - (1) Lord, I will follow you; 'I will lay down my life for you' (John 13:37).
     - (2) 'Lord, you know that I love you' (John 21:15).

2. *By refusing to feel good in his presence unless we are sure we have been 'making the grade'.*
   - (a) This means we are going to feel pretty awful most of the time! (Jeremiah 17:9).
   - (b) We need to be careful here, for when we feel 'good' in his presence in this manner we are vulnerable to self-righteousness – which he *doesn't* like!

3. *By not believing his love* (1 John 4:19).
   - (a) In other words, it is sheer unbelief at work when we don't believe he loves us.
   - (b) God says, as it were, 'Stop it!' But we often don't let that unbelief worry us – it should.
   - (c) God is unhappy with us when we don't believe his own Word.

4. *By not believing we are forgiven even after we have confessed our sins:* 'If we confess our sins, he is faithful and just and will forgive us our sins and purify us from all unrighteousness' (1 John 1:9).
   - (a) This is a word to Christians.
   - (b) God goes to great lengths to show what it means if we have truly confessed our sins; he is two things:
     - (1) Faithful – he will keep his Word.
     - (2) Just – his justice is intact when he forgives.

    5. *By deliberate disobedience* (1 John 1:7).
       (a)  If we don't walk in the light we forfeit two things until we re-commence walking in the light:
           (1)  Fellowship with the Father – intimacy.
           (2)  The cleansing of Christ's blood – a good conscience.
       (b)  When we deliberately disobey we cut off the lines of communication whereby we feel his love.
           (1)  We are refusing to feel his love when we are in disobedience.
           (2)  We are not letting God pour out his love if we are not sincerely wanting to please him.

## C. How do we feel his love?

    1. *By confessing our sins once we realise we have sinned* (1 John 1:9).
       (a)  This means walking in the light (1 John 1:7).
       (b)  Walking in the light will reveal sin we hadn't been aware of.
           (1)  It too was cleansed until now.
           (2)  When we then become aware of it, we confess it then and there!

    2. *By accepting ourselves.*
       (a)  Some say, 'I know God forgives me but I can't forgive myself.'
       (b)  This is sheer self-righteousness.
           (1)  Are we wiser or better then God?
           (2)  If we have confessed our sins we are obliged to accept our forgiveness and accept ourselves.
       (c)  Not to accept ourselves is self-pity and unbelief, both very displeasing to God.

    3. *By quitting trying to 'perform'.*
       (a)  The greatest liberty is 'having nothing to prove'.
       (b)  When I believe that the blood of Jesus covers me, I will enjoy that to the full!
       (c)  God paid the supreme price when he gave his Son to die on the cross.
       (d)  The most pleasing thing to God is to believe that his Son's blood cleanses us.

    4. *By disciplining ourselves to* believe his love (1 John 4:16).
       (a)  At the beginning of the day I draw my own mind to two verses:
           (1)  'Let us then approach the throne of grace with confidence, so that we may receive mercy and find grace to help us in our time of need' (Hebrews 4:16).
           (2)  'And so we know and rely on the love God has for us. God is

love. Whoever lives in love lives in God, and God in him' (1 John 4:16).

5. *By remembering that if our hearts condemn us,* 'God is greater than our hearts' (1 John 3:20).
   (a) God who is 'love' is *bigger* than our faulty, deceptive hearts.
   (b) If I look at my heart I am going to feel awful most of the time!
   (c) God is big-hearted – magnanimous and gracious.
      (1) 'For he knows how we are formed, he remembers that we are dust' (Psalm 103:14).
      (2) He is not 'on the war-path' looking for every fault in us he can find.
      (3) 'He does not treat us as our sins deserve or repay us according to our iniquities' (Psalm 103:10).
   (d) It doesn't take so much faith to believe God loves us when we are 'on top of the world'; but when we are at 'rock bottom' and affirm his love, God likes that very, very much.

## D. When should we affirm God's love?

1. *When we are depressed.*
   (a) If we are able to affirm God's love when we are in this state it will be a great victory. It will show we really believe him!
   (b) Depression is largely overcome when we refuse to believe anything other than God's love for us.

2. *When we have sinned.*
   (a) This is when we need God's love most.
   (b) Affirm his love by employing 1 John 1:9 – and believe it!

3. *When we are happy.*
   (a) People often forget to be thankful when all is going well.
   (b) Whereas people find it easier to weep with those who weep, only God can truly rejoice with those who rejoice (Romans 12:15).

## E. How to accept God's love?

1. *Accept the friendship of people who will accept you.*
   (a) Don't isolate yourself from people who want to be friendly.
   (b) They may be 'angels without knowing it' (Hebrews 13:2) whom God has put in your path.
   (c) If you have been caught in a sin (Galatians 6:1), accept the person who challenges you with a meek spirit.

2. *Ask for more of the Holy Spirit* (Luke 11:13).
   (a) The more you have of the Holy Spirit, the more you will feel God's love.
   (b) Remember: the Spirit *is* God, who is love.

3. *Be loving in every way* (1 John 4:19).
   (a) When we love (e.g., totally forgive those who have hurt us) we will feel loved by God.
   (b) This is why John said, 'We love, because he first loved us.'

4. *Accept his disciplining with dignity* (Hebrews 12:5).
   (a) This is proof of God's love (Hebrews 12:6ff.).
   (b) It is proof of Jesus' own love! (Revelation 3:19).

## CONCLUSION

God loves us as dearly as he loves his own Son, yet many of us have never fully accepted this fact.

We need to remind ourselves of those Scriptures that teach us of God's love and pray that by the Holy Spirit we will be able to allow ourselves to feel the wonder of the reality of God's love for us.

This love is not conditional: we do not need to be perfect. God loves us, no matter how unworthy we feel. Indeed I have known the greatest sense of God's love when I have felt the most unworthy and unlovable. This is the way Peter and the other disciples must have felt (John 13:37-14:1; 20:19).

# 43

# RISING WITH JESUS

## INTRODUCTION

A. **In this chapter we look at one of the fruits of Jesus' resurrection, namely, how we too have a resurrection.**
  1. *I refer not to eschatology, the Last Day, but rather that which we may wish and pray for while we are here.*
  2. *All people will ultimately be raised from the dead* (John 5:28-29).
     (a) This is the ultimate fruit of Jesus' resurrection, of which he was the 'firstfruits' (1 Corinthians 15:20).
     (b) Even the lost owe their being raised from the dead to Christ's resurrection (1 Corinthians 15:22).
        (1) All being 'made alive' is not a reference to being regenerated – for not all will be saved.
        (2) But all will be raised to stand before God (Revelation 20:11-12).

B. **'Rising with Jesus' is that which Paul wanted to experience, at least in measure, while he was yet alive.**
  1. This is what he meant by knowing Christ 'and the power of his resurrection'. He then added that he hoped, 'somehow, to attain to the resurrection from the dead' (Philippians 3:10-11).

C. **Some will want to say that Philippians 3:11 surely refers to Paul's hope that he will be raised on the Last Day.**
  1. *I answer: No-one need pray for that if he or she is a Christian.*
     (a) All Christians will be raised from the dead.
        (1) This is promised and guaranteed (1 Corinthians 15:51-55; 1 Thessalonians 4:16ff.).
        (2) Our faithfulness will have nothing to do with our being raised; Christ's Second Coming will do it – suddenly and without notice!
     (b) Therefore, it would be ridiculous for Paul to wish that, 'somehow' he will attain to that resurrection.
        (1) The 'somehow' implies he isn't sure.
        (2) This view contradicts all he has taught elsewhere.
     (c) He must be referring to something other than the Final Resurrection.

2. *Some would want to inject the view that Paul wasn't sure that he would be finally saved.*
   (a) This would be the line perhaps of those who believe you could be a child of God one day but cease to be his child the next.
       (1) Some good Christians seriously fear that they could lose their salvation.
       (2) Philippians 3:11 might be used by some to substantiate that fear.
   (b) But if Paul is talking about knowing Christ and the power of his resurrection as insurance of being saved:
       (1) 'Knowing Christ' would have a motive that smacks of salvation by works.
       (2) 'Knowing Christ' would be motivated by fear – lest not knowing him may well mean you could be lost.
       (3) This goes against all Paul ever taught about salvation by grace (Romans 8:30; Ephesians 2:8-9; Philippians 1:6).

3. *Some say this verse refers to Christian martyrs who make the grade.*
   (a) It is pointed out that this verse refers to being raised 'from the dead' as opposed to its being the resurrection 'of the dead'.
       (1) This point is correct.
       (2) Jesus' own resurrection was 'from' the dead – thus leaving the rest of the dead behind.
   (b) Some therefore say that there is a resurrection that some Christians, but not all, will enjoy in the Last Day: those who make the grade (the martyrs).
       (1) Is Paul saying 'I hope to be martyred soon?'
       (2) Is this verse relevant for us?

## D. Philippians 3:10-11 is not referring to eschatology at all.
   1. It is not referring to the Final Resurrection of the dead.
   2. It is not referring to the physical resurrection as a reward.
   3. It is not referring to salvation as a reward for faithfulness.
   4. It is not speaking of physical resurrection at all.

## E. David Gooding has put it like this:
   1. *You cannot have a resurrection until you have had a death.*
      (a) If the resurrection is physical, then the death is physical.
      (b) Is Paul doing his best to attain to physical death so he can have a physical resurrection? No.

   2. *The apostle Paul wants 'resurrection power' now.*
      (a) He knows this does not come without suffering.

(1)  There is no resurrection without suffering.
(2)  There is no resurrection without crucifixion.
(b)  Paul is willing to die – in order to have resurrection.
(1)  But the resurrection he is after is not of the body.
(2)  It is the person inside of the body.
(c)  There can be no resurrection power without one having been crucified, or, to use other words, to have his ego slain.
(1)  This explains the 'somehow' of Philippians 3:11.
(2)  Paul is prepared to go to extreme measures to experience 'resurrection power'.

## F. Why is this study important?

1.  It is a practical application of the teaching of Jesus' resurrection.
2.  It is a way forward for those who want to be more like Jesus.
3.  It is a way forward for those who want more power in their spiritual lives.
4.  It will help us to understand what has been seen as a difficult verse (Philippians 3:11).

## 1  BEFORE THERE CAN BE A RESURRECTION, THERE MUST BE A DEATH

## A. It is one thing to want 'resurrection power', quite another to want death!

1.  *But Paul says:* 'I want to know Christ and the power of his resurrection and the fellowship of sharing his sufferings, becoming like him in his death' (Philippians 3:10).
(a)  Why does Paul ask to know Christ? Does he not already know him?
(1)  Certainly he knows Christ.
(2)  But he feels he hardly knows him as he could do!
(b)  This is why he adds 'the fellowship of his sufferings'.
(1)  Many of us want to 'rise with Jesus'.
(2)  How many of us want to share in his sufferings?

2.  *Paul wants 'resurrection power'* so much *that he is prepared to go to extreme lengths to experience this.*
(a)  I ask each of us:
(1)  Are we prepared to go all the way to the cross with Jesus? By 'any means'?
(2)  Are we prepared to experience what he suffered?

## B. We must be prepared to *live* as Jesus *died*.

1. *One day all of us will be like Jesus: when we are glorified.*

   (a) 'For those God foreknew he also predestined to be conformed to the likeness of his Son, that he might be the firstborn among many brothers. And those he predestined, he also called; those he called, he also justified; those he justified, he also glorified' (Romans 8:29-30).

   (b) 'Dear friends, now we are children of God, and what we will be has not yet been made known. But we know that when he appears, we shall be like him, for we shall see him as he is' (1 John 3:2).

   (c) The apostle Paul is saying, 'I can't bring myself to wait until then; I want to be like him now.'

      (1) 'I eagerly expect and hope that I will in no way be ashamed, but will have sufficient courage so that now as always Christ will be exalted in my body, whether by life or by death' (Philippians 1:20).

      (2) 'Your attitude should be the same as that of Christ Jesus: Who, being in very nature God, did not consider equality with God something to be grasped, but made himself nothing, taking the very nature of a servant, being made in human likeness. And being found in appearance as a man, he humbled himself and became obedient to death – even death on a cross!' (Philippians 2:5-8).

2. *Jesus was not 'his own man'.*

   (a) Jesus gave them this answer: 'I tell you the truth, the Son can do nothing by himself; he can do only what he sees his Father doing, because whatever the Father does the Son also does' (John 5:19).

   (b) 'By myself I can do nothing; I judge only as I hear, and my judgment is just, for I seek not to please myself but him who sent me' (John 5:30).

## C. What did Jesus suffer on the cross?

1. *Shame.*

   (a) Jesus did not enjoy this, 'but for the joy set before him endured the cross, scorning its shame, and sat down at the right hand of the throne of God' (Hebrews 12:2).

   (b) There was the shame of nakedness.

      (1) Only criminals were crucified.

      (2) They were the scum of the earth; the lowest of the low.

      (3) There was the shame of being classed as a common criminal.

   (c) There was the shame of being regarded as a deceiver (Matthew 27:63).

        (1) He suffered the shame of an apparent failure.

        (2) He suffered the shame of being misunderstood.

2. *Silence.*

    (a) 'He was oppressed and afflicted, yet he did not open his mouth; he was led like a lamb to the slaughter, and as a sheep before her shearers is silent, so he did not open his mouth' (Isaiah 53:7).

        (1) He could only speak as the Father gave him impulse.

        (2) Before Herod: 'He plied him with many questions, but Jesus gave him no answer' (Luke 23:9).

        (3) Before Pilate: 'When Pilate heard this, he was even more afraid, and he went back inside the palace. "Where do you come from?" he asked Jesus, but Jesus gave him no answer' (John 19:8-9).

    (b) Jesus was not allowed to say one word, when:

        (1) Those who hated him got the upper hand.

        (2) Those who followed him were bewildered.

    (c) 'To this you were called, because Christ suffered for you, leaving you an example, that you should follow in his steps... When they hurled their insults at him, he did not retaliate; when he suffered, he made no threats. Instead, he entrusted himself to him who judges justly' (1 Peter 2:21, 23).

3. *Sacrifice.*

    (a) A sacrifice was a wasted animal.

        (1) A forgotten commodity.

        (2) You never expected to see it again.

    (b) This means self-expendability.

        (1) You do not regard yourself as needed, or important.

        (2) You do not love your life so as to 'shrink from death' (Revelation 12:11).

    (c) You sacrifice personal feelings by total forgiveness. 'Jesus said, "Father, forgive them, for they do not know what they are doing"' (Luke 23:34a).

        (1) You continue to minister to those in need.

        (2) 'Jesus turned and said to them, "Daughters of Jerusalem, do not weep for me; weep for yourselves and for your children"' (Luke 23:28).

4. *Solitude.*

    (a) 'All the disciples deserted him and fled' (Matthew 26:56).

    (b) In Gethsemane he suffered alone.

        (1) The disciples slept. 'Then he returned to his disciples and

found them sleeping. "Could you men not keep watch with me for one hour?" he asked Peter' (Matthew 26:40).

(2) 'He went away a second time and prayed, "My Father, if it is not possible for this cup to be taken away unless I drink it, may your will be done." When he came back, he again found them sleeping, because their eyes were heavy. So he left them and went away once more and prayed the third time, saying the same thing' (Matthew 26:42-44).

(c) In the end he was deserted by God. 'About the ninth hour Jesus cried out in a loud voice, "*Eloi, Eloi, lama sabachthani?*" – which means, "My God, my God, why have you forsaken me?"' (Matthew 27:46).

5. *The apostle Paul took all the above into account when he said that he wanted to share in Christ's sufferings.*
   (a) That is how much he wanted resurrection power.
   (b) What about us? Are we willing to share to this extent in Christ's sufferings?

## 2  WHAT IS RESURRECTION POWER?

### A. It is experiencing the power of the same Spirit that raised Jesus from the dead.

1. *There are three Greek words that may be translated 'power':*
   (a) *Exousia*: authority, or right.
      (1) 'Then Jesus came to them and said, "All authority in heaven and on earth has been given to me"' (Matthew 28:18).
      (2) 'Yet to all who received him, to those who believed in his name, he gave the right to become children of God' (John 1:12).
   (b) *Dunamis*: the Holy Spirit's power for witnessing.
      (1) 'I am going to send you what my Father has promised; but stay in the city until you have been clothed with power from on high' (Luke 24:49).
      (2) 'But you will receive power when the Holy Spirit comes on you; and you will be my witnesses in Jerusalem, and in all Judea and Samaria, and to the ends of the earth' (Acts 1:8).
      (3) 'With great power the apostles continued to testify to the resurrection of the Lord Jesus, and much grace was upon them all' (Acts 4:33).
   (c) *Kratos*: might, or strength.
      (1) 'That power is like the working of his mighty strength, which he exerted in Christ when he raised him from the dead and

seated him at his right hand in the heavenly realms'
(Ephesians 1:19b-20).
(2) 'Finally, be strong in the Lord and in his mighty power'
(Ephesians 6:10).

2. *Paul wanted the Ephesians to experience the power of the same Spirit that raised Jesus from the dead.*
   (a) We are talking about unusual power.
   (b) What Paul wanted for others he wanted also for himself.

3. *There are various kinds of power at the natural level.*
   (a) Political power: control over people.
   (b) Social power: control over those you know.
   (c) Financial power: control over what you can purchase.
   (d) Intellectual power: control by outwitting people.
   (e) Ecclesiastical power: control over parts of the church.

4. *Resurrection power defies Satan's power.*
   (a) Satan had the 'power of death' (*kratos*).
   (b) Resurrection power was greater strength than that of the devil.
       (1) We are commanded to have this power when in spiritual warfare.
       (2) This means that we will not be intimidated by the devil.

B. **Resurrection power is experiencing the person of Jesus at the level of the Spirit that makes him as real to us now as he was to those who saw him personally after he was resurrected.**
   1. *There were those who saw Jesus in the flesh after he was raised from the dead:* 'And that he appeared to Peter, and then to the Twelve. After that, he appeared to more than five hundred of the brothers at the same time, most of whom are still living, though some have fallen asleep' (1 Corinthians 15:5-6).
      (a) They saw him with the naked eye.
      (b) This did not require faith.

   2. *Resurrection power makes Jesus as real to us as he was to those who saw him.*
      (a) We may feel deprived because we were not among those who were alive then.
      (b) With resurrection power we should not envy them for a moment!
      (c) This is what Jesus promised: 'In a little while you will see me no more, and then after a little while you will see me' (John 16:16).
          (1) They did not see him at the natural level after his ascension.
          (2) But they did see him after the Spirit came down (Acts 2:25).

3. *What the disciples experienced on the Day of Pentecost is what we too can experience:*
   (a) When the Holy Spirit is utterly himself in us (John 14:16).
   (b) When he is ungrieved, unquenched and unrivalled (Ephesians 4:30).
   (c) When we aspire to the fellowship of his sufferings as much as we desire resurrection power.

## C. **It is being controlled entirely by the Father's will.**

1. *This means there will be no abuse of this power.*
   (a) It is possible to abuse our gift (Genesis 37:6, 9; 2 Kings 2:23ff.).
   (b) Possession of an awesome gift is no sure sign of being Christ-like.
       (1) The gifts of God are irrevocable (Romans 11:29).
       (2) True spirituality is the fruit of the Spirit (Galatians 5:22ff.).

2. *To whom did Jesus appear after his resurrection?*
   (a) To Herod? To Pilate? To the Sanhedrin?
       (1) To have done so would have meant immediate and personal vindication.
       (2) It would have put his chief enemies in their places!
   (b) Instead, however, he appeared only to those who had already believed in him.
       (1) To Mary Magdalene.
       (2) To the rest of the disciples.

3. *Resurrection power will never be exercised for one's personal use.*
   (a) This is a generation in which people have brought disgrace on Christ's name.
   (b) Resurrection power will be totally for the honour of Christ and the Father.
   (c) Jesus demonstrated total forgiveness to the very disciples who had either forsaken him or denied him.
       (1) This is the way Jesus was in his sufferings.
       (2) This is why we must aspire to Christ-likeness in his sufferings as much as we desire resurrection power.

## D. **Resurrection power is the simultaneous combination of the Word and the Spirit.**

1. *We will be true to sound doctrine:* 'If anyone chooses to do God's will, he will find out whether my teaching comes from God or whether I speak on my own' (John 7:17).

2. *One will enjoy the power of the Holy Spirit in enormous measure:* (a) Joy from within (John 7:38); (b) Signs and wonders (Hebrews 2:4).

3. *Up to now, sadly, there has been an emphasis on one or the other.* (a) Some stress the Word. (b) Some stress the Spirit.

4. *May God hasten the day when we can say with Paul:*
   (a) 'My message and my preaching were not with wise and persuasive words, but with a demonstration of the Spirit's power' (1 Corinthians 2:4).
   (b) 'Because our gospel came to you not simply with words, but also with power, with the Holy Spirit and with deep conviction. You know how we lived among you for your sake' (1 Thessalonians 1:5).

## CONCLUSION

Rising with Jesus was Paul's wish expressed in Philippians 3:10-11. He wanted to experience the power of the resurrection in his life, to experience Jesus in a way that is as real as it was to the first disciples, to be controlled by the Father's will. He understood that in order to experience this power he had to be prepared to live as Jesus died, to share in his sufferings and shame.

**44**

# WHEN GOD HIDES HIS FACE

## INTRODUCTION

A. **Sooner or later, every Christian experiences the hiding of God's face.**

B. **The hiding of God's face: a biblical manner of speaking of God withdrawing the sense of his presence from us.**

    1. *It is a biblical phrase.*
       (a) 'Truly you are a God who hides himself, O God and Saviour of Israel' (Isaiah 45:15).
       (b) 'How long, O LORD? Will you forget me for ever? How long will you hide your face from me?' (Psalm 13:1).
       (c) 'Why, O LORD, do you stand far off? Why do you hide yourself in times of trouble?' (Psalm 10:1).
       (d) 'Why do you hide your face and forget our misery and oppression?' (Psalm 44:24).

    2. *It is a manner of speaking.*
       (a) It is an expression that describes a feeling not a reality.
          (1) It is subjective not objective.
          (2) Subjective: what is felt; objective: what is fact.
       (b) The truth, or fact: God never really leaves us.
          (1) 'The LORD appeared to us in the past, saying: "I have loved you with an everlasting love; I have drawn you with loving-kindness' (Jeremiah 31:3).
          (2) 'No-one will be able to stand up against you all the days of your life. As I was with Moses, so I will be with you; I will never leave you nor forsake you' (Joshua 1:5).
          (3) 'And surely I am with you always, to the very end of the age' (Matthew 28:20).

    3. *God withdraws the 'sense' of his presence.*
       (a) He is always with us, whether or not we feel him.
       (b) The hiding of his face is the *apparent* withdrawal of his presence.
          (1) He *seems* to be gone.
          (2) It causes us to re-live the experience of the psalmist in Psalm 77:6-9.

## C. Why is this subject important?

1. *It is the common experience of most Christians at one time or another.*
2. *We need to know what its relevance is for theology – is there a coherent theological principle that lies behind God hiding his face?*
3. *We will want to ask, why does God hide his face?*
   - (a) Is it our imagination? Our lack of faith?
   - (b) Or is it a deliberate act on God's part?
4. *Are there preparations we can make to anticipate it in advance?*
5. *Can it be avoided?*
6. *New Christians often face this without any warning; how can we help those who suddenly experience it?*

# 1 WHAT IS THE HIDING OF GOD'S FACE? WHAT IS IT LIKE?

## A. In the words of the Westminster Confession of Faith, it is when God 'withdraws the light of his countenance'.

1. *It is the opposite of the blessing described in Numbers 6:22-26:*
   The LORD said to Moses, 'Tell Aaron and his sons, "This is how you are to bless the Israelites. Say to them: 'The LORD bless you and keep you; the LORD make his face shine upon you and be gracious to you; the LORD turn his face towards you and give you peace'." '

2. *The 'face' of the Lord became a symbol of his smile, approval or sense of his presence.*
   - (a) The 'face' of the Lord or 'presence' of the Lord are sometimes used interchangeably.
   - (b) Sometimes translations make a judgement whether to translate the word *prosopon* 'face' or 'presence'.
     - (1) 'Face': (Matthew 6:16; 17:2; 2 Corinthians 4:60.
     - (2) 'Presence': (2 Thessalonians 1:9; Hebrews 9:24).

## B. What is the revealing of God's face, or presence, like?

1. *When he turns up and is real.*
   - (a) It is like having Jesus right there with you!
   - (b) It is when he is not only present but doing things. For example, 'The power of the Lord was present for him to heal the sick' (Luke 5:17).

2. *When the Holy Spirit's power is real.*
   - (a) At Pentecost (Acts 2).
   - (b) When we witness someone being healed (Acts 3:1ff.).
   - (c) When his presence is felt. 'After they prayed, the place where

they were meeting was shaken.  And they were all filled with the Holy Spirit and spoke the word of God boldly. ...With great power the apostles continued to testify to the resurrection of the Lord Jesus, and much grace was upon them all' (Acts 4:31, 33).

3.  *The revealing of God's face can happen in many situations:*
   (a)  When worshipping at church.
   (b)  During the preaching (1 Thessalonians 1:5).
   (c)  When alone at home reading the Bible or praying.
   (d)  When you are sharing the gospel:
      (1)  You feel great liberty.
      (2)  People respond positively.

## C.  **The hiding of God's face is when you feel deserted by him.**
   1.  *It has been called 'the midnight of the soul'.*
      (a)  All of the great saints in church history experienced it.
      (b)  Martin Luther experienced it the night before his finest hour.

   2.  *The same God who was so real yesterday seems a thousand miles away today.*
      (a)  You wonder if you were wrong to have felt him yesterday.
      (b)  Was I deceived?  How could God do this?

   3.  *It is as though you are left utterly to yourself.*
      (a)  The 'flesh' in us seems to take over.
      (b)  Unbelief often sets in.

## D.  **It comes without warning.**
   1.  *A difficult question: do we prepare new Christians for this or let them discover it for themselves – as most of us have had to do!*
      (a)  Isaiah simply paused and said, 'Truly you are a God who hides himself, O God and Saviour of Israel' (Isaiah 45:15).
      (b)  It never comes at a good time! 'Why do you hide yourself in times of trouble?' (Psalm 10:1).

   2.  *If only God would warn us in advance, 'Next Tuesday afternoon about three o'clock you will notice that:*
      (a)  You don't feel my presence.
      (b)  You will feel I have let you down.
      (c)  I will appear not to have kept my Word.

   3.  *But no. It just happens – suddenly.*
      (a)  You read your Bible – your mind wanders.

(b)  You pray – your mind wanders.

(c)  You had been filled with such expectancy – now the future seems so bleak.

## 2  GOD'S REASON AND PURPOSE FOR HIDING HIS FACE.

### A.  The reason for it.

1. *He needs no reason of which we are conscious* (Psalm 115:3).
   (a)  He just does it; he may hide his reason from us.
   (b)  It may not be traceable to any cause of which we are aware.

2. *It may be due to our sins:* 'But your iniquities have separated you from your God; your sins have hidden his face from you, so that he will not hear' (Isaiah 59:2).
   (a)  It should not surprise us if God hides himself when we have sinned (Psalm 66:18).
   (b)  Of this possibility we have been warned (2 Chronicles 7:19-22).

### B.  The purpose in God hiding his face.

1. *To show us exactly what we are like:* 'But when envoys were sent by the rulers of Babylon to ask him about the miraculous sign that had occurred in the land, God left him to test him and to know everything that was in his heart' (2 Chronicles 32:31).
   (a)  A good gauge of what we are like is when God appears to desert us.
      (1)  When we are full of the joy of the Lord it is because God is with us in power.
      (2)  But is this really what we ourselves are like?
   (b)  When God hides his face we discover exactly where we are in our spiritual development.
      (1)  This does not mean we are back to Square One; that is not what happens.
      (2)  It shows us how far we had progressed before the time of perceived desertion!
   (c)  The Christian life should find us improving all the time.
      (1)  God doesn't lead us directly from A to Z, but from A to B, B to C, etc.
      (2)  God suddenly deserts us that we might see how far along the way we have come!
   (d)  We therefore should see God's sudden hiding his face as an unscheduled but fair examination.
      (1)  When I was in school there were two kinds of tests: those you knew would take place and those that could be set on any day.
      (2)  God has the right to test us at any time.

> (i) We may find ourselves deeply ashamed – and fail the test – by murmuring or giving up!
>
> (ii) We may (blessed thought) find ourselves pleasantly surprised – by our dignifying the unexpected trial.

2. *The hiding of God's face is the essence of chastening, or disciplining.*
   (a) Disciplining/chastening: enforced learning.
      (1) 'Because the Lord disciplines those he loves, and he punishes everyone he accepts as a son' (Hebrews 12:6).
      (2) God enforces learning on us – to produce 'a harvest of righteousness and peace for those who have been trained by it' (Hebrews 12:11).
   (b) All chastening is, to some extent, characterised by the hiding of God's face.
      (1) I think I could endure almost *anything* as long as I can see God's face – and sense his smile of approval and presence.
      (2) But adversity, combined with the withdrawal of God's countenance, is very hard to endure.
   (c) What makes chastening chastening is God's *absence*.
      (1) We sense we have displeased him.
      (2) We are tempted to unbelief.
      (3) We are tempted to question God's Word.

## C. **Our responsibility when God hides his face.**

1. *Not to give up.*
   (a) This is when we are most vulnerable.
      (1) The devil knows this.
      (2) He will almost certainly show up at the time God hides himself.
   (b) This is when we must do two things (see James 4:7):
      (1) Submit ourselves to God.
      (2) Resist the devil.

2. *Seek God's face more than ever* (Psalm 27:8).
   (a) If we sulk when God hides himself, we show how pitifully low we were already.
      (1) This means we fail the test.
      (2) Some, sadly, never move beyond this.
   (b) If we seek God's face more than ever, we will be doing exactly what God wanted in the first place!
      (1) God only chastens those he loves.
      (2) His purpose is to see how much we love him (John 21:15-17).

3. *Try fasting (see chapter on fasting and prayer).*
   (a) The reason for fasting in this situation is to get God's attention.
   (b) Fasting may be the next step forward for one who is experiencing the hiding of God's face.

4. *To discover whether there is sin that needs to be dealt with.*
   (a) The sin connected with God's hiding of his face is of two kinds:
       (1) The sin that caused him to hide his face in the first place (Isaiah 59:2).
       (2) The sin in us that needs to surface that we will see it clearly and deal with it (1 John 1:8).
   (b) There also exists the possibility that God hides his face not necessarily because of our sin but to affirm that we *are* walking in the light.
       (1) Therefore the hiding of God's face need not be connected with sin.
       (2) God may none the less test us; the Lord leaving us to test us may produce positive results.

## 3   THE HIDING OF GOD'S FACE IS TEMPORARY

### A. This is a principle we must hang on to.

1. *'The* LORD *is compassionate and gracious, slow to anger, abounding in love. He will not always accuse, nor will be harbour his anger for ever'* (Psalm 103:8-9).
   (a) When we have a serious illness, we tend to think at the time that it will never end!
   (b) So with the hiding of God's face; it seems at the time as if it will last for ever.
       (1) It won't: 'As a father has compassion on his children, so the LORD has compassion on those who fear him; for he knows how we are formed, he remembers that we are dust' (Psalm 103:13-14).
       (2) God knows how much we can bear: 'No temptation has seized you except what is common to man. And God is faithful; he will not let you be tempted beyond what you can bear. But when you are tempted, he will also provide a way out so that you can stand up under it' (1 Corinthians 10:13).

2. *There is a built-in time limit to every trial.*
   (a) Every trial is predestined.
       (1) 'So that no-one would be unsettled by these trials. You know quite well that we were destined for them (1 Thessalonians 3:3).

        (2) 'For it has been granted to you on behalf of Christ not only
           to believe on him, but also to suffer for him' (Philippians
           1:29).
     (b) The end of every trial is also predestined.
        (1) I ask you, therefore, not to be discouraged because of my
           sufferings for you, which are your glory' (Ephesians 3:13).
        (2) 'No discipline seems pleasant at the time, but painful. Later
           on, however, it produces a harvest of righteousness and peace
           for those who have been trained by it' (Hebrews 12:11).

## B. The hiding of God's face often coincides with what Richard Bewes calls the 'in-between times'.

1. *The 'times' here would refer to the seeing of God's face.*
   (a) When things are happening.
   (b) When the Lord turns up.

2. *'Between the times' is often where life is.*
   (a) Most of life is 'between the times'.
      (1) This reveals the stuff we are made of.
      (2) This is when real progress takes place.
   (b) The hiding of God's face therefore frequently takes place between
      the times.
      (1) It is when nothing seems to be happening.
      (2) Sometimes a severe trial occurs as well.

## C. But there comes that blessed time when God rolls up his sleeves.

1. *It is when God shows his muscles!* 'The LORD will lay bare his holy
arm in the sight of all the nations, and all the ends of the earth will see
the salvation of our God' (Isaiah 52:10).
   (a) God looks down on his people and says, 'Enough is enough.'
      (1) 'The LORD said, "I have indeed seen the misery of my people
         in Egypt. I have heard them crying out because of their slave
         drivers, and I am concerned about their suffering"' (Exodus
         3:7).
      (2) '"In a surge of anger I hid my face from you for a moment,
         but with everlasting kindness I will have compassion on you,"
         says the LORD your Redeemer' (Isaiah 54:8).

   (b) In a moment he changes everything (cf. 2 Corinthians 7:6).
      (1) 'For his anger lasts only a moment, but his favour lasts a
         lifetime; weeping may remain for a night, but rejoicing
         comes in the morning' (Psalm 30:5).
      (2) 'Those who sow in tears will reap with songs of joy. He who

goes out weeping, carrying seed to sow, will return with songs of joy, carrying sheaves with him' (Psalm 126:5-6).

2. *He usually does this as suddenly as the initial hiding of his face was.*
   (a) He gives no warning when he hides his face – he just does it!
   (b) This is often the case when he intervenes.
       (1) Like Jesus' Second Coming, it comes suddenly (1 Corinthians 15:51ff.).
       (2) The end of the trial is often sudden, without notice, and all over before we can take it in.

## D. In what state will we be found when the trial ends?
   1. *Will it end when we are praising God, dignifying him and not doubting him?*
   2. *Or will it end while we are grumbling, questioning and finding fault?*
      (a) The beginning of the hiding of God's face is a severe test.
      (b) The end of the hiding of God's face is an even greater test.

## CONCLUSION
When God hides his face from a believer, that person experiences one of the darkest times possible. Without warning the 'sense' of God's presence is removed, although from many passages in the Bible we are assured the reality is different – he will never leave us. Sometimes the hiding of God's face is likened to his being asleep (Psalm 35:23). But that is a time when, equally, it is God at work to get us to stir up ourselves instead! Such a time is a time of testing – to make us aware of our sin or to guage how deep our love for God is. God uses the experience to train us to trust him and to deepen our faith.

Jesus mirrored the Father's tendency to hide his face during the forty-day period after his Resurrection. The disciples never knew when Jesus would turn up; he was apparently absent more than he was present!

# 45

## BREAKING THE BETRAYAL BARRIER

**INTRODUCTION**

**A. This study is the practical follow-up to the previous chapter: 'When God hides his face'.**
1. *This chapter has two main aims:*
   (a) To describe what is perhaps the most acute manifestation of God hiding his face – when he *appears* to betray us.
   (b) To make suggestions on what we must do when this happens.

2. *'Breaking the Betrayal Barrier' is a chapter in Dr James Dobson's book* When God Doesn't Make Sense.
   (a) Dr Dobson describes an experience common to all Christians: there are times when God doesn't seem to make sense.
   (b) What is our reaction to this experience?

**B. The 'Betrayal Barrier': when we feel that God has betrayed us.**
1. *It is when God appears to be disloyal and takes the side of the enemy.*
   (a) God is said to be 'for us' (Romans 8:31) and 'on our side' (Psalm 124:1).
   (b) But sometimes he appears to be disloyal: 'Is it not you, O God, you who have rejected us and no longer go out with our armies?' (Psalm 60:10).

2. *It is when God seems utterly to have let us down.*
   (a) When he does not appear to keep his Word.
   (b) When he appears to break his own promise.
      (1) 'My God, my God, why have you forsaken me? Why are you so far from saving me, so far from the words of my groaning? O my God, I cry out by day, but you do not answer, by night, and am not silent' (Psalm 22:1-2).
      (2) 'You know how I am scorned, disgraced and shamed; all my enemies are before you. Scorn has broken my heart and has left me helpless; I looked for sympathy, but there was none, for comforters, but I found none. They put gall in my food and gave me vinegar for my thirst' (Psalm 69:19-21).

3. *Why call it a 'barrier'?*
   (a) A barrier is something that prevents or controls advance, access, or progress.
   (b) A barrier can also be like a gap – in some cases so wide that reaching across is humanly impossible.
   (c) The hiding of God's face, when carried to an extreme, results in a barrier between us and God.
       (1) There appears no way around it.
       (2) The gap cannot apparently be crossed.

4. *It is when the past, present and future appear equally bleak.*
   (a) It seems that the past cannot possibly work together for good, which Romans 8:28 promises.
   (b) It is when the present finds us without any sense of God, presence of mind or reason for living.
   (c) It is when the future is so bleak that there seems absolutely nothing to live for.

5. *It is God hiding his face – with severity.*
   (a) It is one thing not to feel him near.
   (b) It is quite another thing to feel that our only true Friend has been disloyal and can no longer be trusted.

C. **'Breaking the Betrayal Barrier': coming out on the other side to discover how real and wonderful God is.**
   1. *Greater than aeronautics breaking the sound barrier (earlier in this century) is when a believer breaks the betrayal barrier.*
      (a) It was a great accomplishment when supersonic jets were made to fly faster than the speed of sound.
      (b) The result when this happens: sonic boom, a loud noise caused by the shock wave of an aircraft at supersonic speed.

   2. *Breaking the betrayal barrier is a greater and rarer achievement than that breakthrough in aviation.*
      (a) It is a wonderful, spiritual accomplishment.
      (b) It is (sadly) rare.

D. **Why deal with this matter?**
   1. *Sooner or later Christians will feel that God has betrayed them.*
      (a) Ten out of ten Christians feel betrayed by God at some stage.
      (b) Nine out of ten let this experience affect them adversely.

   2. *I reckon that only one in ten breaks the betrayal barrier.*

(a)  Those who break that betrayal barrier are in the spiritual succession of the great people of faith described in Hebrews chapter 11.

(b)  I would like to encourage you to be in the Big League – that to which Hebrews 11 points.

3.  *God appears to betray us as a test – to see whether we can be trusted with greater responsibility.*

(a)  We often do not recognise this experience as a test from God.

(b)  Remember what was said of Hezekiah, 'God left him to test him and to know everything that was in his heart' (2 Chronicles 32:31).

(c)  This study is designed to do two things:

(1)  To help you to recognise the test – as soon as it happens.

(2)  To help you pass the test – by breaking the betrayal barrier.

4.  *Sovereign vessels are those who break the betrayal barrier: men or women raised up by God for a special task (cf. Acts 9:15).*

5.  *When you break the betrayal barrier, you are never quite the same again.*

## 1  EXAMPLES OF THE BETRAYAL BARRIER

### A.  Abraham.

1.  *The promise to him.* 'The LORD had said to Abram,"Leave your country, your people and your father's household and go to the land I will show you. I will make you into a great nation and I will bless you; I will make your name great, and you will be a blessing. I will bless those who bless you, and whoever curses you I will curse; and all peoples on earth will be blessed through you"' (Genesis 12:1-3).

(a)  'By faith Abraham, when called to go to a place he would later receive as his inheritance, obeyed and went, even though he did not know where he was going' (Hebrews 11:8).

(b)  'He gave him no inheritance here, not even a foot of ground. But God promised him that he and his descendants after him would possess the land, even though at that time Abraham had no child' (Acts 7:5).

2.  *The request to sacrifice Isaac* (Genesis 22:1-2).

(a)  This request made no sense whatever.

(b)  Isaac was the only link between Abraham himself and the seed God had promised!

## B. Moses.

1. *The promise to him* (Exodus 3:7-10).
   - (a) God assured Moses, 'I have indeed seen the misery of my people in Egypt.'
   - (b) He added, 'So now, go, I am sending you to Pharaoh to bring my people the Israelites out of Egypt' (Exodus 3:10).
     - (1) 'So I will stretch out my hand and strike the Egyptians with all the wonders that I will perform among them. After that, he will let you go' (Exodus 3:20).
     - (2) 'And I will make the Egyptians favourably disposed towards this people, so that when you leave you will not go empty-handed' (Exodus 3:21).

2. *What happened?*
   - (a) Pharaoh was unimpressed with Moses and the miracles he performed.
     - (1) He accused the people of being lazy (Exodus 5:8).
     - (2) They now had to make the same number of bricks and at the same time get their own straw wherever they could find it (Exodus 5:10-14).
   - (b) The people who had been encouraged by Moses (Exodus 4:31) now turned against him.
     - (1) 'And they said, "May the LORD look upon you and judge you! You have made us a stench to Pharaoh and his servants and have put a sword in their hand to kill us" ' (Exodus 5:21).
     - (2) Moses felt betrayed; he said to God, 'Ever since I went to Pharaoh to speak in your name, he has brought trouble upon this people, and you have not rescued your people at all' (Exodus 5:23).

## C. David.

1. *After his initial anointing (1 Samuel 16:13) and triumph (slaying Goliath) David was continually on the run from a jealous King Saul.*
   - (a) 'As surely as the LORD lives ... there is only a step between me and death' (1 Samuel 20:3).
   - (b) Saul killed eighty-five priests (and others) as a result of kindness shown to David (1 Samuel 22:18ff.).
   - (c) He was so discouraged that he said, 'One of these days I shall be destroyed by the hand of Saul' (1 Samuel 27:1).

2. *Many psalms were written during this period* (cf. Psalms 56, 57, 59, 63.

## D. Elijah.

1. *After his prophecy to Ahab.*
   (a) Elijah prophesied: 'No rain except at my word' (1 Kings 17:1).
      (1) But how would Elijah himself survive?
      (2) Answer: God said to him, 'You will drink from the brook, and I have ordered the ravens to feed you there' (1 Kings 17:4).
   (b) But Elijah became a victim of his own prophecy!

2. *After being taken care of by the widow of Zarepath.*
   (a) All went well for a while (1 Kings 17:13-16).
   (b) But when her own son became ill and died she turned against Elijah. 'She said to Elijah, "What do you have against me, man of God? Did you come to remind me of my sin and kill my son?"' (1 Kings 17:18).

## E. Jeremiah.

1. 'O LORD, you deceived me, and I was deceived; you overpowered me and prevailed. I am ridiculed all day long; everyone mocks me' (Jeremiah 20:7).

2. So discouraged was he that he cursed the day of his birth (Jeremiah 20:14ff.).

## F. The apostle Paul.

1. Between the writing of 1 and 2 Corinthians he underwent the greatest trial of his life.

2. 'We were under great pressure, far beyond our ability to endure, so that we despaired even of life. Indeed, in our hearts we felt the sentence of death' (2 Corinthians 1:8-9).

## G. Those to whom the Letter to Hebrews was originally addressed.

1. *They were discouraged Christians* (Hebrews 10:35ff.).
   (a) Signs, wonders and miracles were probably a memory (Hebrews 2:4).
   (b) Many old friends had left (Hebrews 6:4-6; 10:25).
   (c) The temple was still standing (cf. Matthew 24:34).

2. *They felt that God had let them down* (Hebrews 12:5-11).

## H. Martin Luther put it like this: 'You must know God as an enemy before you can know him as a friend.'

## 2  RESPONSES TO THE BETRAYAL BARRIER

### A. Negative.

1. *Rebellion* (Hebrews 3:7-8).
   (a) Hardened hearts.
   (b) Inability to hear the Holy Spirit's voice.
2. *Not knowing God's ways* (Hebrews 3:9-10).
   (a) Testing God (rather than letting him test us).
   (b) Hearts going astray.
3. *Unbelief* (Hebrews 3:12-19).
   (a) Turning away from God.
   (b) Disobedience.
4. *In short: blaming God; self-justification* (cf. Exodus 32:1).
   (a) The feeling that God owes us something and must prove himself.
   (b) Examples of when this sort of thing happens:
      (1) When we seek to get closer to God – and he lets us down.
      (2) When we witness.
      (3) When we agree to be tithers.

### B. Positive.

1. Obedience, even when we don't understand why we are having this experience (Genesis 22:1-10).
2. Continued seeking of God's face (Exodus 6-14; 1 Kings 17:8-24).
3. Consciously praising God, despite being misunderstood (Psalms 34 and 52).
4. In short: not questioning God but trusting him (Job 13:15; Daniel 3:18).

### C. From God:

1. *To our negative responses to his apparent betrayal.*
   (a) His patience (Psalm 103:8-14).
      (1) He gives a second chance (Jonah 3:1).
      (2) He gives more grace (James 4:5-6).
   (b) Note: we have all failed to some degree at one time or another.
      (1) God knows our weaknesses (1 Kings 8:46).
      (2) He gives renewed opportunities to get it right (Ezra 9:5-15).
   (c) His wrath (Hebrews 3:11).
      (1) There comes a time when God says, 'Enough is enough'.
      (2) The result: the inability to be renewed again to repentance (Hebrews 6:6; 10:26ff.).

2. *To our positive response to his apparent betrayal.*
   (a) His leading us to greater opportunities for grace (James 1:2-4).

        (1) Every trial has its own goal: to lead us to maturity.

        (2) That level of maturity paves the way for more 'glory' (2 Corinthians 3:18).

  (b) He will eventually show his face again – but with a greater glory than we ever thought possible.

        (1) 'In that day they will say, "Surely this is our God; we trusted in him, and he saved us. This is the LORD, we trusted in him; let us rejoice and be glad in his salvation"' (Isaiah 25:9).

        (2) 'But those who hope in the LORD will renew their strength. They will soar on wings like eagles; they will run and not grow weary, they will walk and not be faint' (Isaiah 40:31).

  (c) The ultimate seal of his approval:

        (1) Entering his rest (Hebrews 4:9-10).

        (2) Swearing an oath of grace (Hebrews 6:9-20; cf. Genesis 22:16).

3. *Note: God may swear either in wrath or in grace to us – at the end of the day, depending on our continued response.*

  (a) To our continued unbelief – that we never enter his rest (Hebrews 3:7-11).

  (b) To our continued trust without murmuring – that we will enter his rest (Hebrews 4:1).

        (1) The reward (here below) is worth waiting for (1 Corinthians 2:9).

        (2) The punishment (here below) is an inability to hear God speak powerfully and intimately again (Hebrews 12:15-17).

## 3   HOW TO BREAK THE BETRAYAL BARRIER

## A. Remember six principles of chastening/disciplining (Hebrews 12:6-11).

1. *It is inevitable* (verse 6).
2. *It is proof that you are truly a Christian* (verses 7-8).
3. *It is from a loving Father* (verses 9-10).
4. *It is preparation* (verse 11).
  (a) It is because God has a job for you to do.
  (b) It is not his getting even (Psalm 103:10).
5. *It is not pleasant* (verse 11).
6. *It is worth dignifying* (verse 11).
  (a) It is what God does to get our attention.
  (b) The irony: what God does to get our attention is the very thing that could put us off him.
  (c) There are essentially three kinds of chastening:

(1) Internal – through the Word.
(2) External – through circumstances.
(3) Terminal – when God gives up on us. This is of two kinds:
    (i) No more repentance (Hebrews 6:6; 10:26ff.).
    (ii) Premature death (1 Corinthians 11:30; 1 John 5:16).

## B. Further principles that must be applied.

1. *Remember that God never betrays us; he only appears to do so* (1 Corinthians 10:13).
   (a) It can feel as though God has let us down.
   (b) Even Jesus felt it (Matthew 27:46).
   (c) But God had not deserted Jesus (John 19:30).

2. *Remember that breaking the betrayal barrier is God's idea* (Genesis 22:1).
   (a) It is what he wants for us.
   (b) How can he know we can be trusted if he does not at first test us? (2 Chronicles 32:31).

3. *See every evidence of an apparent betrayal as a hint we are being tested* (James 1:2).
   (a) We are being tested without knowing it.
   (b) Look for God's hints that he is trusting us with such a test.

4. *Remember what pleases him most – faith* (Hebrews 11:6).
   (a) Grumbling is the opposite of faith (1 Corinthians 10:10).
   (b) God's honour is at stake – he rewards those who diligently seek him.

5. *Pray more than ever* (Psalm 27:8; Luke 18:1-8).
   (a) Praying is partly what God is after; he wants to spend more time with us.
   (b) Those who seek him with all their hearts find him (Jeremiah 29:13).

6. *Walk in all the light God gives you* (1 John 1:7).
   (a) He will show you new things (Jeremiah 33:3).
   (b) He will show you sin of which you were unaware.

7. *Remember that breaking the betrayal barrier is the greatest opportunity you will ever have to know God with intimacy* (Psalm 25:14).
   (a) He confides in few.
   (b) The reward is worth waiting for (Hebrews 12:11).

## CONCLUSION

Dealing with the betrayal barrier is one of the hardest of all experiences that Christians face. It is important, however, that we understand the betrayal is apparent not actual. God hasn't forsaken us, rather he is seeking to test his sovereign vessels.

We need then to face this situation in a way that dignifies the trial. To break the betrayal barrier we need to trust God and wait patiently for him, accepting any discipline he gives us without grumbling.

If we persevere we will receive the reward of greater intimacy with God and a 'harvest of righteousness and peace' (Hebrews 12:11).

# 46

# HOW TO OVERCOME SELF-RIGHTEOUSNESS

## INTRODUCTION

**A. To treat this subject as the title implies is not unlike writing on 'Humility – and how I obtained it'.**
1. This has to be one of the most presumptuous ventures anyone has ever heard of. For who has ever overcome self-righteousness, and who is qualified to write on it?

**B. Why then this subject?**
1. *We need to see the subtlety of self-righteousness.*
 - (a) That is, how it is a part of us and we are not aware of it.
 - (b) He who thinks he is not self-righteous has no objectivity (ability to stand above or apart) about himself or herself.

2. *We need to see the danger of self-righteousness.*
 - (a) It is what is most obnoxious in God's sight.
 - (b) Strangely enough, it is very obnoxious in man's sight as well.

3. *We need to see self-righteousness in ourselves.*
 - (a) We must learn the signs, the danger signals.
 - (b) We must narrow the time-gap, as much as possible, between the emergence and discovery of our own self-righteousness.
 - (1) For some it is never discerned at all.
 - (2) For others it may be detected early on, like the beginnings of cancer.

4. *Self-righteousness is what keeps us from becoming Christians in the first place. (Not that we don't let self-righteousness creep in later on.)*
 - (a) Until we climb down from our self-righteous attitude we will never be saved (Romans 10:2-4).
 - (b) What keeps us from true conversion is our need to prove ourselves to God without the benefit of a Mediator.

5. *Self-righteousness is what puts others off Christianity.* We therefore need to discern it in ourselves, and deal with it, if only to remove this as a reason people give for not coming to church.

6. *Self-righteousness is what causes marriage break-down and tension in human relationships, as well as in the church.*
   - (a) It is because both parties 'stick to their guns' and dig in their heels, that trouble gets worse.
   - (b) The one who is willing to climb down is the one who will admit to being self-righteous.

7. *It is the greatest obstacle to true spirituality.*
   - (a) Immorality is no small obstacle to true spirituality.
   - (b) Believe it or not, self-righteousness is in some ways worse!
     - (1) For immorality is an obvious sin.
     - (2) Self-righteousness is the easiest sin to see in others but the hardest to see in ourselves.

C. **Self-righteousness: a feeling of well-being, whether conscious or unconscious, that comes as a result of justifying ourselves.**
1. *The feeling may be conscious or unconscious.*
   - (a) Conscious: when we *know* we feel good about ourselves, the reason being we know we've got it right.
   - (b) Unconscious: when we are not aware that we are smug even though at bottom we are sure we are right.

2. *We justify ourselves by defending our works or actions.*
   - (a) We say, 'I know I'm right,' and we feel very good inside.
   - (b) There are two kinds of justification (being made right or righteous):
     - (1) Justification by faith.
     - (2) Justification by works.
   - (c) When we justify ourselves it is justification by works.

3. *When we justify ourselves it is because we feel our works (or words) were right (or righteous).*
   - (a) That leads to a feeling of well-being.
     - (1) It may be conscious – that leads to gloating.
     - (2) It may be unconscious – that leads to smugness.
   - (b) In either case, it is a dangerous feeling.

D. **Why is self-righteousness so dangerous?**
1. It is divisive.
2. It is difficult to see in ourselves. 'I can't help it if I happen to be right.'
3. We become unteachable.
4. We are defensive.
5. We grieve the Holy Spirit.

# 1. EXAMPLES OF SELF-RIGHTEOUSNESS

## A. Being judgemental (Matthew 7:1).

1. *Self-righteousness is essentially what lies behind the pointing of the finger* (Isaiah 58:9; Matthew 7:3-5).
   - (a) There is a feeling that somehow we are competent to judge.
   - (b) This stems from the feeling that we are OK, others are not.

2. *Being judgemental refers to motives.*
   - (a) It does not mean we should not make a righteous judgement (John 7:24; 1 Corinthians 2:15).
   - (b) We are never allowed by the Holy Spirit to offer opinions on the motives or spiritual state of others, however clear such may seem to us (Luke 6:37).

## B. Being defensive (1 Corinthians 1:12).

1. *The greatest freedom is having nothing to prove* (2 Corinthians 3:17).
   - (a) When we are in the flesh, we instinctively feel a need to prove ourselves.
   - (b) When we are full of the Spirit that need disappears.

2. *Whenever we begin to defend ourselves we inevitably point to the righteousness of our works or conduct.*
   - (a) This violates the promise that God will do the defending (Romans 12:19).
   - (b) When we do it instead we will be pointing to our own works.

## C. Being argumentative (Romans 3:19).

1. *This springs from a hostile spirit, even if it is repressed, that tends to be critical and fault-finding* (James 4:1).
   - (a) Repress: to deny what we really feel, pushing it down into our sub-conscious minds.
   - (b) Many people have innately hostile feelings but manage to cover them up by a smile.

2. *The need to be argumentative in order to prove a point has self-righteousness as its origin.*
   - (a) One has not come to terms with his own feelings.
   - (b) It stems from a need to prove that one's point of view is correct; another is wrong.

## D. Smugness (Revelation 3:17).

1. *Smugness: a feeling of self-righteousness, whereby one doesn't think, he knows(!), he's got it right and is a cut above others.*

(a)     This person takes the above axiom, having nothing to prove, and wears it on his or her sleeve!

(b)     He 'never complains, never explains, never apologises' – and never comes to terms with his own heart.

2.  *The person like this wears the mask to cover up deep fears of being found out.*

(a)     They cover up with everything from the accent to legalism!

(b)     They are difficult to reach and also to work with.

## E.  Holding a grudge (Ephesians 4:30ff.).

1. *An unforgiving spirit betrays that we:*

(a)     Have forgotten our own sins.

(b)     Do not feel forgiven, the result being guilt, which is the feeling            that someone is to blame.

2. *When we hold a grudge it is because we feel right in doing so.*

(a)     We believe that we have not done anything as bad as another person.

(b)     We therefore long for the day they are punished.

## F.  Referring to our good works (Matthew 6:1-8; 16-18).

1. *The need to call attention to what we do or have done for the Lord.*

(a)     How much we give, pray, fast, witness.

(b)     How much we give up for the Lord.

2.  *The need to refer to our spiritual experiences with the view to make others admire us.*

(a)     This may refer to the baptism of the Holy Spirit, or our gifts.

(b)     It may be the need to talk about our severe trials – and how we dignified them.

## G.  Claiming to have no sin (1 John 1:8).

1. *Perhaps the most dangerous thing about self-righteousness is its blinding power.*

(a)     Murderers and adulterers often see nothing at all wrong in what they have done (Proverbs 14:12).

(b)     Equally easy to overlook is our bitterness, the need to gossip, or complaining.

2.  *The closer we are to God, the more sensitive we are to our sin; the further we are the more defensive we are and blind to wrong.*

**H. Self-pity (1 Corinthians 10:10).**
1. *All murmuring, grumbling and complaining is the result of self-righteousness.*
    (a)    It is our way of saying, 'I don't deserve this.' Really?
    (b)    What is it we think we *do* deserve?

2. *Self-pity is an easy trap to fall into, but when it is seen as basically self-righteousness, perhaps we will confess it and run from it.*

**I. Not forgiving ourselves (1 John 1:9).**
1. *Many say, 'I know God forgives me but I can't forgive myself.'*
    (a)    This is a sign of self-righteousness.
    (b)    It implies that we know better than God what is forgivable.

2. *What God affirms, we must affirm; what God forgives we must forgive – or we compete with him!*
    (a)    God *wants* us to forgive ourselves; otherwise it is not worth anything to our morale.
    (b)    Not to forgive ourselves is not taking the blood of Christ seriously enough! (Psalm 103:12).

**J. The feeling that God owes me something (Romans 9:20).**
1. *This is the heart of self-righteousness: God has a lot to answer for and he owes me an explanation.*
    (a)    This is the essence of unbelief.
    (b)    It is the weapon used by Satan.

2. *If we feel God owes us something, especially if it is because of something we have done, we are being pompous and arrogant.*
    (a)    The first thing the sinner asks for is mercy (Luke 18:13).
    (b)    The Christian never outgrows the need of mercy, which means we have no bargaining power (Hebrews 4:16).

**K. The feeling of guilt (Genesis 45:5).**
1. *This is keeping a record of our wrongs.*
    (a)    Love keeps no record of wrongs (1 Corinthians 13:5).
    (b)    When we have not torn up the record of our wrongs it gives the devil an easy opportunity to bring us down.

2. *God does not want us to feel guilty.*
    (a)    When we don't forgive others, we try to punish them by giving them a guilt trip.
    (b)    If God had not forgiven, only then would he want us to feel guilty; but he does forgive us! (Ephesians 1:7).

## 2. TWO LEVELS OF SELF-RIGHTEOUSNESS
### A. The non-Christian.
1. *All people are self-righteous by nature* (2 Corinthians 4:3-4).
  - (a)  The work of the Holy Spirit is to convict of sin (John 16:8-10).
  - (b)  The work of the Holy Spirit is to show the need of a Mediator (1 Timothy 2:5).

2. *The basic reason people do not come to Christ is because of self-righteousness* (Romans 2:1).
  - (a)  They may claim to be atheists, yes.
  - (b)  But behind that claim is sheer smugness (Acts 17:32).

3. *Before one can be saved he or she must see the need of a Saviour.*
  - (a)  The need of forgiveness of sin through the blood of Christ.
  - (b)  The need of Christ's righteousness by faith in him.
    - (1)  This means abandoning hope of salvation in good works or personal merit.
    - (2)  It is putting all our eggs in one basket: Jesus died for me.

### B. The Christian (1 Corinthians 4:8).
1. *In one sense this is an impossibility; for the Christian is a person whose only hope of salvation is Christ's work on the cross.*
2. *But unfortunately Christians can become self-righteous in a different sense* (Galatians 3:3).
  - (a)  I fear that all of the above examples of self-righteousness can at times apply to the Christian.
  - (b)  It is something to be hated – for God hates it.
    - (1)  It is one of the greatest obstacles to Christian growth.
    - (2)  It is one of the chief ways we grieve the Holy Spirit.

## 3. HOW TO OVERCOME SELF-RIGHTEOUSNESS
### A. Recognise it as your own problem (1 John 1:8).
1. *If we do not see it in ourselves, there is obviously no way forward.*
  - (a)  It is one thing to say, 'I know I'm not perfect.'
  - (b)  It is quite another thing to say, 'My problem is that I am self-righteous.'

2. *Look at the above examples; ask yourself whether any of them could describe you. How many?*
  - (a)  The fewer number you admit to probably means the more self-righteous you are!
  - (b)  The greater number you admit to probably suggests you are closer to overcoming it.

**B. Refuse to compute any wrong done to you (1 Corinthians 13:5).**
1. *This means that we refuse to allow any wrong be 'programmed' into our minds.*
   - (a)     We keep records because we intend to use them.
   - (b)     We keep records of wrongs because we intend to use them.

2. *When any wrong done is not recorded, you don't have it to use.*
   - (a)     Total forgiveness is when it is as though no wrong had been committed.
   - (b)     That is the way God forgives us.

**C. Refuse to say anything that is negative (James 1:19).**
1. *All problems that flow from self-righteousness don't really get off the ground until the tongue takes over* (James 3:3-8).
   - (a)     If we don't speak, no hell will have opportunity to break out.
   - (b)     When we speak a word that flows from the bitter fountain of self-righteousness, the devil gets in (James 3:11-15).

2. *Negative is anything that is critical, judgemental and not designed to bring the good feeling.*
   - (a)     Satan is always negative; when we are negative we often unwittingly mirror the devil.
   - (b)     When what we say will not create a good feeling, but it will cause problems (1 John 2:10).

**D. Refuse to clear your name (Romans 12:19).**
1. *Don't even think of doing what God does best.*
   - (a)     Vindicating is one of God's favourite enterprises.
   - (b)     He is the expert, and has ways of doing it you would never dream of!

2. *Leave everything to him.*
   - (a)     Don't raise a little finger to put the record straight.
   - (b)     Watch him work – but in his own time and manner.

**E. Live completely by faith alone (1 Corinthians 4:5).**
1. *Do not try to figure out things in advance.*
   - (a)     Faith is believing without seeing (Hebrews 11:1).
   - (b)     Be willing to understand nothing that is going on at the time (Proverbs 3:5).

2. *Lower your voice; wait and see what God does.*
   - (a)     His ways of bringing things to pass are 'beyond tracing out' (Romans 11:33).
   - (b)     Say nothing, so that what God does will be to his glory alone.

## 4. WHAT IT IS LIKE TO THE DEGREE WE OVERCOME SELF-RIGHTEOUSNESS.

### A. Great peace flows through us.
1. When peace is absent, something is wrong.
2. The ungrieved Spirit is recognisable by peace.

### B. Absence of judgementalism.
1. The reason we judge: we haven't been broken.
2. When we are broken, no judgementalism is left!

### C. Pleasantness.
1. Self-righteous people are basically miserable people.
2. When we let go of self-righteousness, we *feel* pleasant; and we are pleasant to live with!

### D. People seek us out.
1. Self-righteousness repels.
2. Unself-righteous morality attracts – like when people sought out Jesus.

### E. We begin to love people.
1. This does not mean we become extroverts.
2. It does mean we will care.

### F. God will become more real.
1. Self-righteousness really puts him off!
2. When we let it go, he moves in!

### G. Fresh insights into the scriptures emerge.
1. Self-righteousness grieves the Spirit.
2. When the Spirit is ungrieved, he shows us things in his Word we never saw before.

### Conclusion
When we were converted it was because we climbed down from our self-righteousness. This is the way we must continue to live – in all our dealings with people – until we get to heaven. It isn't always easy, but it's the best way to live.

# 47

# APOSTASY AND BACKSLIDING

## INTRODUCTION

A. **The issue of 'once saved, always saved' versus 'falling away' (so as to lose your salvation) is nothing new.**

1. *Augustine (354-430) is the first major theologian to put the case for the security of the believer.*

2. *Arminius (1560-1609) challenged the Reformed doctrine of predestination but left open the question whether a converted person could ever be lost.*

3. *John Wesley (1703-1791) popularised Arminianism and those after him put the case that saved people could be lost if they fell away.*

   (a) However, those who fell away could be restored if they repented.

   (b) But if they did not repent they would be eternally lost.

4. *Those in the Augustinian/Reformed tradition have resolved the issue generally as follows:*

   (a) All those who truly believe will persevere to the end.

   (1) Saved people are eternally secure.

   (2) But if they fall away it shows that they never were truly converted in the first place.

   (b) However, there is a difference between the backslider and the apostate.

   (1) A backslider is a Christian who can be restored.

   (2) An apostate was never a Christian in the first place and cannot be restored.

   (c) This solution does not solve the problem of the believer's assurance of salvation.

   (1) If I fall, am I a backslider or an apostate?

   (2) How can I know I am truly saved?

5. *The problem is further complicated by Hebrews 6:4-6:* 'It is impossible for those who have once been enlightened, who have tasted the heavenly gift, who have shared in the Holy Spirit, who have tasted the goodness of the word of God and the powers of the coming age, if they fall away, to be brought back to repentance, because to their loss they are crucifying the Son of God all over again and subjecting him to public disgrace.'

(a) If Hebrews 6:4-6 refers to *saved* people, then which is true?
  (1) Saved people can be lost.
  (2) Those who fall away cannot be restored to salvation.
  (3) Those who fall away cannot be restored to repentance.
(b) If Hebrews 6:4-6 refers to *unsaved* people, but they are those who professed to be saved, then the following is true:
  (1) Those who experience the Holy Spirit are counterfeit – those who make a false profession.
  (2) When they fall away they forfeit ever being saved.
  (3) Those who fall away show they were never converted.
(c) If, then, I have professed faith and have experienced the Holy Spirit, then, according to Hebrews 6:4-6. one of the following is true:
  (1) If I fall away I was not truly converted.
  (2) If I fall away I can never be restored to salvation.
  (3) If I fall away I can never be renewed to repentance (my own view).
(d) Two crucial questions follow:
  (1) What is falling away?
  (2) What is it to which I cannot be restored?

## B. Why is this study important?

1. We have all been backsliders to some degree; we have all fallen to some degree.
2. We should learn to detect backsliding in ourselves and know how to deal with it.
3. We should know how to deal with it if we see it in others.
4. We ought to know what precisely is the state of the backslidden – are they beyond hope?
5. Is there a difference between backsliding and apostasy? If so, is one more serious than the other?
6. What is an apostate?
7. Can a true believer become an apostate?
8. Is there an apostasy of the church?
9. How do we recognise apostasy?
10. How can either backsliding or apostasy be anticipated and prevented?

# 1. BACKGROUND AND MEANING OF RELEVANT TERMS

## A. The etymological roots in Greek and Hebrew.

1. *This is a case in which the original languages fail to provide consistent theological definitions.*
2. *And yet this is nothing new.*

(a) One must remember that *koine* Greek, in which the New Testament was written, was the secular and common language of the day.

(b) There were no truly theological terms; secular words were brought into the church and have become theological to us, for example:
(1) *Evangelion*, 'good news'; (2) *Pipto*, 'to fall'.

(c) One must never push the original languages too far.
(1) They can help a lot – at times.
(2) But theology must never be built on the ancient language alone.

## B. Defining our terms.

1. *Apostasy: falling away.*

(a) Greek *apostasia*, which means 'falling away' or 'rebellion'.
(1) 2 Thessalonians 2:3 ('falling away', AV; 'rebellion', NIV).
(2) The verb *aphistemi*, meaning 'to fall' or 'to depart', is used in 1 Timothy 4:1 and other places.

(b) Greek *parapipto*, 'to fall away' (Hebrews 6:6).

(c) Greek *pipto*, meaning 'to fall', is used 90 times in the New Testament.
(1) People literally falling down (Matthew 2:11; John 11:32; Acts 5:5).
(2) A spiritual fall (Romans 11:11; 1 Corinthians 10:12; Hebrews 4:11).
(3) Hebrew *nephal*, 'to fall', is used 400 times in the Old Testament.

(d) Greek *ekpipto*, meaning 'to fall', is used 13 times in the New Testament (e.g. Galatians 5:4; Revelation 2:5).

(e) Greek *arneumai*, meaning 'to deny', is used 31 times in the New Testament (e.g. 2 Peter 2:1; 1 John 2:22-23).

2. *Backsliding: to slip back from good behaviour.*

(a) This is an Old Testament term, but Hebrew and Greek words (LXX) are used which are interchangeable with 'falling away'.
(1) Proverbs 14:14 (AV), from a Hebrew word that means 'go back' or 'turn away'.
(2) Jeremiah 2:19; 3:22; the New International Version generally uses the term 'faithless', as in Jeremiah 3:6,8,11,14.
(3) Hosea 4:16 ('stubborn', NIV); 14:4 ('waywardness', NIV).

(b) This term 'backsliding' is not strictly found in the New Testament, although the idea is present again and again (as we will see below).

(c) The Hebrew words *mushuba* and *showbab* (in Jeremiah and Hosea) are used in LXX interchangeably with *apostasia* and *aphestemi*.

(1) Therefore 'backsliding' and 'falling' or 'departing' come to the same thing in the Old Testament.

(2) In short, one must beware of building a theological system on the Hebrew or Greek words.

C. **Clarification of our definitions.** Note: although the words are interchangeable in the ancient languages, it will suit our purpose to make what I hope will be a helpful distinction.

1. *Apostasy refers to a hopeless state.*
   (a) If it happens to a church there is probably no hope for it, at least in its own generation.
   (b) If it happens to a professing Christian, there is probably no hope for him or her to be saved; they were never truly converted.

2. *Backsliding refers to a sad spiritual state but which is not beyond hope.*
   (a) A backslider is a person who has been converted.
   (b) A backslider therefore may be restored.
   (c) In summary:
      (1) The apostate is not a Christian.
      (2) The backslider is a Christian.

3. *Stone-deafness refers to a Christian but one who can no longer hear God's voice.*
   (a) This person has been truly converted.
   (b) But something happened to his or her spiritual state.
      (1) He or she can no longer hear God.
      (2) The hope of being renewed to repentance in this life is gone.
   (c) In short: this is my interpretation of Hebrews 6:4-6.

## 2  GENERAL APOSTASY

A. **The apostle Paul's only use of 'apostasy' (Greek *apostasia*) is with regard to the professing church generally.**
   1. *'Don't let anyone deceive you in any way, for that day will not come until the* rebellion *occurs and the man of lawlessness is revealed, the man doomed to destruction'* (2 Thessalonians 2:3).
   2. *This was a prophecy which had to take place before the Second Coming.*
      (a) It seems initially to have been fulfilled shortly after the turn of the first century.
         (1) There were a few bright spots, notably in the Apostolic Fathers such as Ignatius, Polycarp and Irenaeus.

- (2) The general falling away was due to the encroachment of Gnosticism (see Section D).
- (3) T F Torrance has shown that the church generally during this period had virtually no concept of the grace of God whatever!
  - (b) It has certainly been fulfilled at various times in church history.
    - (1) The Middle Ages saw the corruption of the Roman Catholic Church; this is the reason for the Great Reformation of the sixteenth century.
    - (2) The twentieth century has seen the church generally in theological disarray; the call to affirm the validity of all religions nowadays is proof of that!

## B. We can certainly conclude that 2 Thessalonians 2:3 has been fulfilled many times.

1. The church was never renewed from within (to my knowledge), except in the hearts of a sanctified minority.
2. Almost always, a reformation from without (rather than from within) has been the order of the day.
3. Perhaps an exception will take place before the twentieth century is over – we certainly hope so.

## C. The apostasy of Israel.

1. *The prophets warned again and again of Israel's fallen state.*
   - (a) Jeremiah stood alone in his day in prophesying Jerusalem's destruction and the Babylonian captivity.
   - (b) The people of Israel said, 'It can't happen to us; we are God's chosen people and Jerusalem is the apple of God's eye.'
   - (c) But Jerusalem was taken; the Babylonian captivity lasted seventy years, as Jeremiah prophesied.

2. *Israel's spiritual state at the time of Jesus was at an all-time low.*
   - (a) The proof of this: the Messiah came and they missed it (Luke 19:41-44).
   - (b) The result: God turned to the Gentiles (cf. Acts 18:6).

## D. Gnosticism and the early church.

1. *The first major onslaught against the church was Gnosticism.*
   - (a) It had emerged somewhat in Paul's day (Colossians 1-2).
   - (b) It developed more fully by the time of John, although 2 Peter and Jude suggest that it had begun to affect the church.

2. *Gnosticism: a 'new' way of knowing.*
   - (a) From the Greek word *gnosis* meaning 'knowledge'.

    (b)  A non-Christian philosophy that claimed a superior way of knowing God penetrated the early church.

        (1)  The came in through the back door (Jude 4).

        (2)  They denied the deity of Jesus Christ (1 John 2:22-23).

    (c)  Note: The New Age Movement is ancient Gnosticism in new dress.

  3.  *This intrusion of hypocrites did great damage to the early church.*

    (a)  They made professions of faith (2 Peter 2:20).

        (1)  They returned to the world (2 Peter 2:21-22).

        (2)  They were never converted (2 Peter 2:1).

    (b)  They can truly be called 'apostates', even though they were never converted: 'They went out from us, but they did not really belong to us. For if they had belonged to us, they would have remained with us; but their going showed that none of them belonged to us' (1 John 2:19).

    (c)  But they do *not* fit Hebrews 6:4-6.

        (1)  They never experienced illumination and the participation of the Spirit, the Word and life to come.

        (2)  They had never experienced repentance (change of mind) in the first place.

## 3  BACKSLIDING AND STONE DEAFNESS

### A.  There are degrees of backsliding.

  1.  *There is overt, open backsliding, which is obvious to all and which may bring disgrace upon the name of Christ and upon the church.*

  2.  *There is less obvious backsliding, which may be unknown to those around us, if not to ourselves!*

  3.  *Not all backsliding therefore gets that name!*

    (a)  Adultery is backsliding.

    (b)  An unforgiving spirit is also backsliding.

  4.  *Some fall and can be restored.*

    (a)  'Brothers, if someone is caught in a sin, you who are spiritual should restore him gently. But watch yourself, or you also may be tempted' (Galatians 6:1).

    (b)  'Remember the height from which you have fallen! Repent and do the things you did at first. If you do not repent, I will come to you and remove your lampstand from its place' (Revelation 2:5).

    (c)  'You who are trying to be justified by law have been alienated from Christ; you have fallen away from grace' (Galatians 5:4).

        (1)  Paul clearly hoped for the restoration of those fallen Galatians: 'My dear children, for whom I am again in the

pains of childbirth until Christ is formed in you...' (4:19).
   (2) They therefore were not beyond hope – at least not then.
5. *David, a man after God's own heart (1 Samuel 13:14), was a backslider.*
   (a) He was guilty of heinous, overt sins.
      (1) Adultery (2 Samuel 11:4).
      (2) Murder (2 Samuel 11:14-17).
   (b) God forgave him (2 Samuel 12:13).
   (c) He was renewed to repentance (Psalm 51).
6. *Jonah was a backslider.*
   (a) He disobeyed (Jonah 1).
   (b) He repented (Jonah 2:8-9).
   (c) He was restored (Jonah 3:1-3).
7. *Note: the examples of Jonah and David are proof enough that the worst sins imaginable are not in and of themselves sufficient to qualify for the state described in Hebrews 6:6.*
   (a) Many have thought they were in a Hebrews 6:6 state because of their scandalous sin.
   (b) Many in the early church delayed baptism because they feared backsliding after baptism.
8. *As stated above, all of us have been backsliders to some degree; for example:* self-pity, (b) holding a grudge, (c) being overcome with pride, (d) gossiping, (e) pointing the finger, (f) prayerlessness, (g) not witnessing, (h) lack of commitment, (the list is endless!).
9. *All the above are forgivable sins.*
   (a) They are not sins that lead to death (1 John 5:17).
   (b) There are also sins that lead to death (1 John 5:16).

B. **While there are degrees of backsliding, there are however only two categories of backsliders:**
1. *Those who commit sins that do not lead to death, and are therefore forgivable* (1 John 1:9).
2. *There are those who commit sins that lead to death (Acts 5:1-11; 1 Corinthians 11:30).*
   (a) How do we tell the difference? Answer: it is not easy to tell if *another* has committed a sin that leads to death but I can know that *I* have not so sinned.
   (b) How do I know that I have not so sinned?
      (1) If I am gripped by God's voice.
      (2) If I am 'being transformed into his likeness with ever-increasing glory' (2 Corinthians 3:18) – this is true repentance!

C. **Stone deafness: an inability to hear God speak again, hence the inability to be renewed *again* to repentance (change of mind).**
  1. *Deafness at the natural level normally comes in stages.*
     (a)  First, a person develops a hardness of hearing.
     (b)  Second, he gets a hearing aid – it helps.
     (c)  Thirdly, he finds that a hearing aid doesn't even help.

  2. *Spiritual deafness follows the same pattern.*
     (a)  One becomes 'dull of hearing' (Hebrews 5:11, AV).
     (b)  But there is still hope at this stage! (Hebrews 6:9).
     (c)  The horror of horrors is when one doesn't hear repeated warnings and, eventually, cannot be renewed again unto repentance.
          (1)  Those described in Hebrews 6:4-6 had previously repented; otherwise there would be no reference to being 'renewed again'.
          (2)  Those in Hebrews 6:6 were saved but stone deaf, even if they lived on for a while.

  3. *Note: it is important to walk in the light* (1 John 1:7).
     (a)  Not to do so is to risk an ever-increasing deafness to God's voice.
     (b)  As long as we walk in the light, there is no need to worry!
     (c)  Moreover, as long as we are moved and gripped by God's warnings it is proof that we are not stone deaf – at least not yet.

D. **Our hope: God's promise to the backslider**
  1. *God claims to be married to the backslider:* 'Return faithless people,' declares the Lord, 'for I am your husband, I will choose you – one from a town and two from a clan – and bring you to Zion' (Jeremiah 3:14).
     (a)  'There is hope for your future' (Jeremiah 31:17).
     (b)  'I will heal their waywardness and love them freely' (Hosea 14:4).

**CONCLUSION**
Apostasy and backsliding are complex issues. We have used terms which we hope have been helpful. It is best to to think of categories: those who have never been converted because they deny the deity of Christ and those who are saved but backslide. 'Falling away' is falling from a state of hearing God's voice: it results in spiritual stone deafness. Such cannot be renewed for they cannot hear God speak. Our attitude towards backsliders should be what Paul describes in Galatians 6:1: 'Brothers, if someone is caught in a sin, you who are spiritual should restore him gently. But watch yourself, or you also may be tempted.'

# 48

# SUFFERING

## INTRODUCTION

A. **The theology of suffering is the heaviest and most difficult we have yet embarked upon.**
   1. *Why did God create man when he knew man would suffer?*
   2. *Why does God allow evil?*
      (a) If God is all-powerful, he could put an end to suffering at once.
      (b) If God is merciful and loving, he could surely step in and stop all injustice.

B. **This study will not attempt to solve the problem of evil.**
   1. *No theological mind or system has done this.*
   2. *This matter will be resolved only when we get to heaven, and that* following *the Second Coming and Judgement Seat of Christ.*
      (a) For even the souls 'under the altar', referring to people in the intermediate state, did not have their questions answered (Revelation 6:9-10).
      (b) This means that our questions will not be answered when we die but after God clears his name at the Final Judgement.

C. **What is the purpose of this study?**
   1. *To acquaint us with the theology of suffering.*
      (a) We need to see that this is no easy matter and that no great mind has resolved it.
      (b) It can be comforting to know that the greatest minds have looked into this and have done their best to come up with answers.

   2. *To help towards an answer to the question, 'Why does God allow suffering?'*
      (a) It is not that we will come up with the perfect answer; but if we show that we understand the problem it can disarm the critics.
      (b) We therefore need to show unbelievers that we are not naïve or blind to this ancient problem.

   3. *To help us to focus upon Jesus, the greatest sufferer that ever was.*
      (a) We will not get the complete or perfect answer to the question of suffering in this life.

(b) But we can see that Jesus is God's answer to the problem of suffering in the meantime.
  (1) Never was such injustice carried out.
  (2) Never was such pain endured.
  (3) And Jesus was God!
(c) This enables us to know that God knows the problem very well!
  (1) Sometimes we wonder, 'Does God understand my questions?'
  (2) This study can answer: He does.

D. **Suffering: the unavoidable feeling of pain – hurt, grief or loss.**
  1. *It is being subjected to disadvantage over which we have no control.*
  2. *It is pain which we are unable to do anything about, whatever the cause:*
    (a) Hunger.
    (b) Poverty.
    (c) Cruel dictators or governments.
    (d) Natural disaster: earthquakes, floods, hurricanes.
    (e) Accidents: airplane crashes, motorway pile-ups that result in death or permanent physical damage.
    (f) Sickness and disease, including afflicted children.
    (g) Sexual abuse.
    (h) Crime: murder, theft.
    (i) Being lied about.
    (j) Some people getting away with wickedness.
      (1) Bad things happening to good people.
      (2) Good things happening to bad people.

E. **In philosophical theology there are two ultimate positions: existentialism versus theodicy.**
  1. *Existentialism: emphasis upon the here and now.*
    (a) The father of existentialism was Soren Kierkegaard (1813-1855), the Danish theologian.
    (b) Existentialism has many proponents but, generally speaking, the principles are these:
      (1) There is no rhyme or reason to life.
      (2) No explanation to suffering can be found.

  2. *Theodicy: the governing ways of God; there is purpose in history.*
    (a) This is the historic Christian view.
    (b) The principles, generally speaking, are these:
      (1) There is purpose in history, for God is in control.
      (2) Though we cannot fully understand suffering in the here and now, one day we will understand.

## 1 SUFFERING IS THE CONSEQUENCE OF SIN

A. **Suffering is therefore a theological problem (in more ways than one).**
   1. *For sin is a theological matter.*
   2. *If sin is the cause of suffering, then suffering too is a theological problem.*
      (a) Not merely because we ask, 'Why does God allow suffering?'
      (b) But because suffering is directly related to sin.

B. **There was no suffering prior to the Fall.**
   1. *God created man and woman in a world free from pain.*
      (a) God created man 'able to sin', said Augustine.
      (b) Why this was so is not knowable.
      (c) But there was no pain in Adam's pre-fallen state.

   2. *Man was given warning of the consequences of sin before he fell* (Genesis 2:17).
      (a) Once man sinned, everything pertaining to his being changed.
         (1) The chemistry of his body (e.g., ageing process).
         (2) The inclinations of the soul that were alien to man before the Fall: unbelief; fear; pride; jealousy; greed; insecurity.
      (b) The earth in a sense fell with man. 'Cursed is the ground because of you' (Genesis 3:17).
         (1) This means that nature itself changed and this change is owing entirely to the Fall.
         (2) Hence all natural disaster has its origin not in God but in man who sinned.

C. **This does not mean that our own suffering is necessarily the result of our own sin in this life.**
   1. *There is however a connection between health and holiness* (1 Corinthians 11:30).
      (a) If we live holy lives we can avoid a lot of needless suffering.
      (b) For example, some diseases are traceable to sexual sin.

   2. *But not all sickness is traceable to sin.*
      (a) The proof of this is that not all who needed healing had sinned so as to be ill (James 5:15).
      (b) We all have to die one way or the other, no matter how godly we are.

D. **The point is, suffering would not exist had not sin entered the world via the Fall in the Garden of Eden.**

1. We therefore must take the blame – and not blame God.
2. All of us are responsible for Adam's and Eve's sin.

## 2  SUFFERING IS NO RESPECTER OF PERSONS

### A. Like common grace, it comes to all – whether Christians or not.
1. The sun shines on the just and the unjust.
2. The rain falls on the just and the unjust (Matthew 5:45).

### B. Becoming a Christian is not a way of avoiding suffering.
1. *The greatest sufferer of all was Jesus; we are called to imitate him* (1 Peter 2:21).
2. *Suffering of a different sort is promised to the Christian* (2 Timothy 3:12).
   - (a)  Therefore the Christian is a person who has a double suffering:
     - (1)  The suffering that comes to all generally (Job 5:7).
     - (2)  The suffering that comes to the Christian particularly.
   - (b)  Parallel with this is God's chastening, or disciplining (Hebrews 12:6).
     - (1)  All disciplining is painful (Hebrews 12:11).
     - (2)  And yet it is for the Christian only (Hebrews 12:7-8).

3. *Anyone who tells you that the Bible promises health and prosperity if we meet certain conditions is misleading you.*
   - (a)  We are not called to avoid suffering.
   - (b)  We are called to accept it graciously when it comes.
   - (c)  Charles Coulson said: 'Jesus does not promise to take us out of the fire but promises to get into the fire with us.'

### C. Suffering comes to all, regardless of their stature or place in society.
1. *The rich and famous.*
   - (a)  Mental and emotional suffering.
     - (1)  From pressures; family problems.
     - (2)  From having to compete and live in the fast lane.
   - (b)  Physical suffering: none is exempt from any of the illnesses and maladies of the world.

2. *The poor and unknown.*
   - (a)  All of the anxieties of the rich and famous.
   - (b)  The poor often suppose they would be better off with more material things; however they do not satisfy.

## 3 SUFFERING IS WHAT MAKES FAITH POSSIBLE

A. **The nearest we can come to an explanation of evil is that, were there no evil, there would be no need for faith.**
   1. *God has decreed that those who know him do so by faith* (Habakkuk 2:4; 1 Corinthians 1:21).
      (a) God might have chosen the way of wisdom.
      (b) God might have chosen the way of works.
      (c) God might have chosen the way of wonders.

   2. *Faith to be faith must believe when there is no empirical evidence* (Hebrews 11:1).
      (a) Empirical: knowledge based upon observation or experience. In other words, *proof.*
      (b) If we need evidences our faith is weak.
         (1) Faith is strong faith when there is belief (or persuasion) but no proof.
         (2) The world, however, says, 'seeing is believing' (Mark 15:32).

   3. *God may have allowed evil if only that there may be faith.*
      (a) God wants us to believe his Word.
         (1) It is the highest affirmation of another when you take their word for what they affirm.
         (2) God wants to be believed that way.
      (b) This is why Jesus did not heal Lazarus immediately (John 11:15).
         (1) It seemed at first that he did not care.
         (2) The truth is, he wanted to make room for the possibility of faith!

B. **God may sometimes use suffering to get the attention of the ungodly.**
   1. *He can use calamity or whatever brings fear.*
      (a) The Philistines (1 Samuel 5).
      (b) The sailors on Jonah's ship (Jonah 1).

   2. *He may use things today to bring one to his or her knees, for example:* (a) financial crisis, (b) marriage breakdown, (c) family problems, (d) sickness, (e) unemployment.

C. **God uses suffering to increase faith in the Christian.**
   1. *What at first appears to be that which would destroy faith is in fact that which can (alone) increase it.*
      (a) It is breaking the betrayal barrier.
         (1) All Christians sooner or later feel betrayed by God.
         (2) Nine out of ten (in my opinion) back away and do not move on with God; they just barely cope.

    (b) Some – one out of ten (in my opinion) – press on and break that betrayal barrier.
        (1) They are the ones who find God real.
        (2) This is the stuff that the people of Hebrews 11 were made of!

2. *There are generally two ways by which God increases faith:*
    (a) Positive. When he just pours out his Spirit on us.
        (1) This is the way we all prefer – and pray for.
        (2) This comes through reading the Bible, praying, worship, going to church and hearing the Word preached.
    (b) Negative. When God has to discipline us to get our attention.
        (1) This is painful suffering.
        (2) But the benefit is most positive (Hebrews 12:10-11).

3. *For reasons I do not fully understand, suffering is God's chief way of getting our attention.*
    (a) Perhaps it is always Plan B!
        (1) Perhaps he comes through his Word.
        (2) Perhaps he tries to get our attention and we don't listen.
    (b) But it seems to me that suffering is mainly the way he brings real and lasting change in us.
        (1) We should pray that it won't be like this (Matthew 6:13).
        (2) But if it comes it is a call to great grace and glory (1 Peter 5:10).

4. *Suffering and God's sovereign vessels go together.*
    (a) Sovereign vessel: one chosen for a special task.
        (1) It may be very high profile (Acts 9:15-16).
        (2) It may be very low profile (Mark 5:18-19).
    (b) Those who know the Lord and who endure a lot of suffering have reason to rejoice (James 1:12).
        (1) They have opportunity for greater reward in heaven.
        (2) They may be under preparation for a work here below.
    (c) Those who were used most had a great amount of suffering:
        (1) Abraham (Hebrews 11:8ff.,17ff.).
        (2) Moses (Hebrews 11:24ff.).
        3) Joseph (Genesis 39-40).
        (4) Paul (1 Corinthians 4:10; 2 Corinthians 4:7ff.).

## 4  THE GREATEST SUFFERER THAT EVER WAS: JESUS

### A. This is the best answer of all to the problem of evil.

1. *God himself became man* (John 1:1, 14).
2. *The God-man endured everything that all of us endure, only worse* (Hebrews 4:15).
   - (a) He knew temptation (Matthew 4).
   - (b) He knew trial (Matthew 26-27).

3. *Jesus endured suffering for three reasons:*
   - (a) That he could sympathise (Hebrews 2:18).
   - (b) That he would be perfected (Hebrews 2:10; 5:8-9).
   - (c) That he could atone for sin (Matthew 5:17; Hebrews 2:17).

4. *There may be a fourth reason: to show the world that no-one understands suffering or the problem of suffering like God himself.*

### B. No-one knew unfairness, humiliation or injustice like Jesus. For example:

1. Family relationships (John 7:1-5).
2. Living conditions (Matthew 8:20).
3. Being misunderstood (John 2:18-19).
4. Being laughed at (Matthew 9:24).
5. Loneliness (Matthew 26:45).
6. Humiliation (Matthew 27:28ff.).
7. Unfair 'trial' (Matthew 27).
8. Emotional torment (Matthew 27:40).
9. Physical pain (Matthew 27:32-35).
10. Spiritual pain (Matthew 27:46).

## 5  THE CHRISTIAN IS CALLED TO DIGNIFY EVERY TRIAL

### A. Dignify: to honour, to show respect for.

1. *Why should we honour a trial?*
   - (a) Because God has trusted us with it (James 1:2).
   - (b) Because every trial has a purpose (James 1:3-4).

2. *Every trial, then, is a gift of God; to dignify it is to honour* him.

### B. Principles of trial:

1. *Trials are from God.*
2. *They have a definite purpose.*
3. *They have their time limit.*
   - (a) The trial will end.
   - (b) We may *think* it will last for ever; it will not.

4. *How we react to a trial will determine whether we 'move up higher'
   in God's grace.*
   (a) If we show contempt for it, it will do us no good.
       (1) We will have to wait for the next trial before we are likely
           to grow in grace.
       (2) God gives us a second chance to dignify it.
   (b) If we dignify it, we move up higher with God and can be trusted
       with more grace.

5. *How to dignify the trial:*
   (a) Don't complain when it comes.
   (b) Don't question God.
   (c) Accept it graciously.
   (d) Ask God to show you its purpose.
   (e) Don't abort it prematurely; let it last as long as God wills.

## CONCLUSION
Suffering will always be a mystery until we get to heaven. But we can find
some meaning in suffering to the degree we affirm God's wisdom in
everything – even if we don't understand what is happening.

# 49

# INTRODUCING ESCHATOLOGY

## INTRODUCTION

### A. Eschatology is the doctrine of 'last things'.

1. It comes from two Greek words: *eschatos* meaning 'last', or 'furthest' (it is used 58 times, including John 6:40, 11:24, 12:48) and *logos* meaning 'word'.

2. Literally it means 'word of the last', which refers to the future – prophecy, the Second Coming, the final state of the saved and lost, and also what happens at death.

### B. Why is this study important?

1. *The study of eschatology gives us a historical perspective.*
   - (a) When we consider the future we must in some way reflect on the past.
   - (b) What happens tomorrow will be a part of history after tomorrow comes.

2. *It reminds us that God has a plan.*
   - (a) God has given us promises concerning the future.
   - (b) He knows the future because he has planned what is to come.

3. *It shows there is purpose in history.*
   - (a) We are not 'thrown' into our existence by a God who does not know his own mind or the mind of others.
   - (b) What is going on in the world is under God's own sovereign control.

4. *It helps us to see that the future has been carefully thought out by an all-wise God.*
   - (a) What will happen in the end is not accidental.
   - (b) God knows the date of the Second Coming (Mark 13:32).

5. *It lets us know that we are on the winning side.*
   - (a) The devil is predestined to lose (Revelation 20:10).
   - (b) The Lord Jesus is predestined to win (Revelation 1:17-18).

6. *The Bible gives us a glimpse into 'what happens next' and we should be acquainted with what is clearly knowable.*
   (a) Not all details regarding eschatology is clear and beyond doubt.
   (b) But as Mark Twain put it, 'It is not the parts of the Bible that I don't understand that worry me, it's the parts that I understand all too well.'

7. *It brings the doctrine of salvation into sharp focus.*
   (a) Why be saved? Why must one come to faith in Christ?
   (b) Answer: because there is an eternal destiny at stake. Where will we spend eternity? What happens when we die?

8. *It reminds us that the same Jesus who died on a cross and who rose from the dead is literally coming again!*

9. *It brings us face to face with the Final Judgment.*
   (a) One day God will clear his name.
   (b) One day God will judge the saved and the lost.

10. *It makes us face the doctrine of eternal punishment.*

11. *It reminds believers of their future home: heaven.*

C. **The purpose of this study: to give a brief introduction to eschatology generally and the related doctrines particularly.**
   1. *Warning: we must beware of being 'obsessed' with any phase of eschatology.*
      (a) This would be unhealthy and lead to lack of balance.
      (b) In any case, nobody knows all of the answers for sure!

## 1  DEATH AND THE INTERMEDIATE STATE: WHAT HAPPENS WHEN WE DIE?

A. **One of two things will happen next:**
   1. *The Second Coming* (Hebrews 9:28).
   2. *Death* (Hebrews 9:27).
      (a) We all hope to be alive at the time of the Second Coming of Jesus.
      (b) That is the *only* way we will escape death (1 Thessalonians 4:17).

B. **Intermediate state: where the dead are between death and the Second Coming.**
   1. Intermediate means 'between the times'.
   2. The question is: what exactly happens when we die?

## C. **The theological issues are these:**

1. *'Soul sleep' versus conscious existence after death.*
   (a) Soul sleep theory: unconsciousness follows death; thus the body and soul are 'asleep' until the final resurrection of the dead.
      (1) According to this theory, those who are dead are aware of nothing whatever.
      (2) At the final judgment, all will awake at the same time whether they have been dead for five years or five thousand years. They knew nothing at all in the meantime. Therefore when they are awakened it will seem to them as though they died just a second before.
      (3) Those who hold to this view usually reject the idea of immortality of the soul, that all men/women have immortality by creation; they say it comes at conversion.

   (b) The New Testament does not teach the above but rather the conscious existence of the person after death.
      (1) Jesus said to the thief on the cross, 'Today you will be with me in paradise' (Luke 23:43).
      (2) Paul: 'I desire to depart and be with Christ, which is better by far' (Philippians 1:23).
      (3) Lazarus went immediately to Abraham's side when he died (Luke 16:22).
      (4) The rich man went to Hades where he was in conscious torment (Luke 16:23).
      (5) According to Paul, the only possible state for the Christian when 'away from the body' was to be 'at home with the Lord' (2 Corinthians 5:6).

2. *What is going on in heaven now?*
   (a) What we call heaven is also called Abraham's side and Paradise (Luke 16:22; 23:43).
   (b) Revelation 6:9-11 and Revelation 7:9-17 are brief glimpses into the intermediate state.

3. *What is the nature of our existence in heaven?*
   (a) Are we given spiritual bodies (2 Corinthians 5:1)?
   (b) Are we disembodied spirits (Hebrews 12:23)?

4. *Far more speculative questions are these:*
   (a) Do people in heaven know what we are doing? Are they watching us?
   (b) What are they actually doing in heaven?

(c)  What do they look like? Will they always look the way they did when they died? Will babies remain babies?

(d)  What is the difference between heaven as it now is and heaven – the New Jerusalem (Revelation 21 and 22) – as it will be after the Second Coming?

5.  *What is certain about the redeemed in heaven:*
    (a)  They are worshipping (Revelation 7:10).
    (b)  The are waiting for more to come (Revelation 6:9-11).
    (c)  They are at rest – free from further testing, trial or temptation and tears (Revelation 7:17).

6.  *Note: the subject of purgatory comes under this heading; but there is no New Testament teaching on this subject.*

## 2  THE TIME OF THE SECOND COMING

*Note:* 'No-one knows about that day or hour, not even the angels in heaven, nor the Son, but only the Father (Mark 13:32).

### A.  What is the Second Coming?
1.  The personal return of Jesus (Acts 1:10-11).
2.  The Final Resurrection of the Dead (1 Corinthians 15:51-55).
3.  The Final Judgment (Revelation 20:11-15).

### B.  What happens at the Second Coming?
1.  The 'last trumpet' sounds (1 Corinthians 15:52; 1 Thessalonians 4:16).
2.  Every eye will see Jesus (Revelation 1:7).
3.  The souls, or spirits, of the redeemed will be reunited with their bodies (1 Thessalonians 4:13-17).
4.  They will be glorified (Romans 8:30; 1 John 3:2).
5.  All will stand before God (Hebrews 9:27; Revelation 20:11).

### C.  What happens after the Second Coming?
1.  The lost are sent to everlasting punishment (Matthew 25:41; Revelation 20:15).
2.  The saved are sent to the New Jerusalem (Revelation 21 and 22).

### D.  What happens just before the Second Coming? Note: it is at this stage we find a lot of division among Christians. We want to avoid being clever or sensational and aim simply to understand the *issues*:

1.  *The millennium.* When does it take place? Or does it take place?
    (a)  Millennium: 1,000 years (Revelation 20:1-10).
    (b)  There are three main views (each held by the best of Christians):

(1) *Pre-millennialism*: that Jesus will return *before* the millennium and set up his kingdom on earth, reigning literally from Jerusalem.

    (a) Some believe the Rapture (the saved being 'caught up') will precede seven years of tribulation, which is culminated in the final Second Coming just before the millennium.

    (b) Some believe Christ will come 3½ years after the Rapture – in mid-tribulation.

    (c) Some believe that Christ's coming is at the end of the age, that the Rapture and final Second Coming are one and the same.

(2) *Post-millennialism*: that Christ will come after the millennium; that the 1,000 years (which may be more symbolic than literal) of peace and prosperity will usher in the Second Coming.

    (a) The old idea, that prior to the end the world will get 'better and better', died with World War I.

    (b) Another view, sometimes called Revolutionary Post Millennialism, is the belief that a Great Awakening, sometimes called Latter Day Glory, will immediately precede the end.

(3) *A-millennialism*: that the 1,000 years are not to be interpreted literally. In short: there is no such thing as a millennium except the reign of Christ in the life of a believer.

    (a) Some take Revelation 20:6 to refer to conversion, as described by Jesus in John 5:24.

    (b) Some hold to a Latter Day Glory before the end, believing this to coincide with a restoration of Israel.

2. *Israel.* Does the nation of Israel figure in prophecy? Is what is happening in the Middle East relevant for prophecy in the Bible? There are, generally speaking, two views:

    (a) Israel in Romans 11 refers to the people we know as the Jews.

        (1) Israel's blindness will be lifted much in the same way as salvation was received by Gentiles. This is seen as the time of the Gentiles being ended (Luke 21:24; Romans 11:25).

        (2) What is happening in Jerusalem is relevant.

        (3) Note: some would say there will be a restoration of salvation to Israel but it need not necessarily refer to what is happening in the land of Israel.

(b) Israel in Romans 11 is simply God's elect. In a word: Israel is the church, the Bride of Christ.

3. *Unfulfilled prophecy.* Sometimes called 'signs of the times'; some believe the following must take place before the Second Coming:
   (a) Unveiling of Antichrist (2 Thessalonians 2:3).
   (b) Cosmological phenomena (e.g. earthquakes, signs in heaven) (Matthew 24; Mark 13).
   (c) Gospel preached to all nations (Matthew 24:14).
   (d) Latter Day Glory (Joel 2).
   (e) Political and geographical changes.

## CONCLUSION

God the Father alone knows the time of the Second Coming of Jesus. In the meantime believers wait expectantly for the time when every eye will behold him and every knee bow before him. We have not sought to solve all of the eschatological problems that can come up. This is only a bare outline, an introduction and acquainting with the issues.

# 50

# HOW TO BE PATIENT!

## INTRODUCTION

A. **This lesson follows on naturally from the previous study on eschatology.**
   1. *What if Jesus tarries?*
      (a) Most Christians in the first century thought Jesus would come in their day.
      (b) Many Christians throughout church history have secretly hoped to see the Second Coming in their own day.

   2. *Even the Christian martyrs in the intermediate state asked the question, 'How long?'* (Revelation 6:9-10).
      (a) This suggests that even those who die and enter the Lord's very presence don't get all their questions answered immediately.
      (b) Those who are now with the Lord will have to wait until the Second Coming for God's final vindication.

B. **Patience: the calm endurance of hardship or delay.**
   1. *It is one of the most sublime virtues (Galatians 5:22). That it is a fruit of the Spirit shows that the Holy Spirit himself is patient!*
      (a) The Greek word is *hupomonee* and it is used 32 times in the New Testament (there are other Greek words which mean much the same thing). It means 'to remain instead of fleeing'; therefore the words 'endurance' or 'perseverance' are sometimes used in the New International Version.

   2. *The Lord Jesus takes notice of patience and commends it* (Revelation 2:2, 19; 3:10).
      (a) So too the apostle Paul (1 Thessalonians 1:3; 2 Thessalonians 1:4).
      (b) Patience results in the achievement of a certain kind of maturity (James 1:2-4).

   3. *The desire or need for patience is nothing new!* (Psalms 13:1-2; 27:14).
      One of the most difficult aspects of the Christian life is sheer waiting.

## C.  Why is this subject important?

1. *It connects with eschatology.*
   (a)  Obviously the Lord has delayed his coming for nearly 2,000 years!
   (b)  But aren't you glad he has?

2. *It pertains to unanswered prayer.*
   (a)  Have you put requests to God that seem reasonable to you but remain unanswered?
   (b)  Could it be that the Lord is teaching you patience?

3. *It relates to God's own promises.*
   (a)  Perhaps God has made a promise to you?
   (b)  If he did, it will be kept!

4. *It pertains to temptation or trial.*
   (a)  Perhaps you are aware of a very difficult temptation; you thought by now it would be behind you.
   (b)  You need a double dose of patience!

5. *It has to do with our worship and growth while we wait.*
   (a)  Donald Grey Barnhouse said: 'While we wait we can worship'.
   (b)  The waiting period may turn out to be the very thing we treasure the most, no matter how painful it was at the time.

## 1  GOD HAS HIS OWN TIME FRAME (Isaiah 55:8-9).

### A.  God is organised, orderly and on schedule (1 Corinthians 4:5).

1. The genealogy of Jesus shows order and planning (Matthew 1:17).
2. The time of the Second Coming of Jesus is a fixed date in history (Mark 13:32).

### B.  Our task is not to get him to fit into our way of thinking but for us to adjust to his ways.

1. He was here before we arrived; he will be around after we are gone!
2. We are fools if we dare snap our fingers at him and expect him to jump.

### C.  Everything he does has a purpose and follows a plan (Psalm 115:3; Ecclesiastes 3:1-11; Isaiah 46:10).

1. The time of the Children of Israel's time in Egypt was set in advance (Genesis 15:13).
2. The time of the Babylonian captivity was set in advance (2 Chronicles 36:21).
3. The time of Jesus' coming into the world was set in advance (Galatians 4:4).

D. **Applying this to our lives, we may safely conclude:**
   1. He has a plan for each of our lives.
   2. He has a plan regarding answering our prayers.
   3. He will fulfil what he has promised – but according to his own timing.
   4. Every trial has its built-in time scale (James 1:3-5).
   5. The God who knows how much we can bear will intervene at the right time (1 Corinthians 10:13).

## 2 GOD IS IN NO HURRY

A. **All who have got to know him even only slightly have already found this out! (Isaiah 45:15).**
   1. Jesus Christ is seen in the New Testament as the Lamb that was slain from the foundation of the world (1 Peter 1:19-20; Revelation 13:8).
   2. But God waited until 2,000 years ago to unveil this secret!

B. **God has perfect patience!**
   1. *He is called the 'God of patience'* (Romans 15:5, AV).
   2. *All which he asks of us is true of him already, and that without any limit.*
      (a) Revelation 1:9 refers to the patience of Jesus Christ (AV).
      (b) Thus our Lord Jesus Christ is exhibiting perfect patience at God's right hand.
         (1) As he intercedes (Hebrews 7:25).
         (2) As he waits for final vindication (1 Corinthians 15:25).

C. **Therefore, there is perfect peace in God's presence.**
   1. *Those who fix their eyes on him participate in that peace* (Isaiah 26:3).
   2. *They know the joy of the Lord* (Nehemiah 8:10; Psalm 16:11).
      (a) It makes for calmness in praying (Philippians 4:6).
      (b) It can make the difference in our lifestyle (1 Corinthians 15:58).
   3. *God never panics, and this spirit of calm comes to those who:*
      (a) Get to know him in ever-increasing measure.
      (b) Live in his presence and manifest his ways.

## 3 THE MOST IMPORTANT 'ESCHATOLOGICAL GRACE' IS BEING READY

A. **More important than getting our eschatology right is being right in ourselves.**
   1. This means being ready when Jesus comes (Matthew 24:44).
   2. What a pity to get the theology right but miss the main thing – being ready when he comes.

B. **There are two levels of being ready for the Second Coming.**
1. *That we are saved – and not lost.*
    (a) Being saved means that our only hope of going to heaven is that Jesus paid our debt on the cross.
    (b) Those who trust his blood will be among the saved – and will never go to hell.

2. *That we are obedient Christians – and not found out of fellowship with God.*
    (a) 1 John 1:7 clearly teaches that two things follow 'walking in the light':
        (1) Fellowship with God.
        (2) The blood of Christ cleanses from all sin.
    (b) This is a word primarily to the Christian; it follows that, if we are not walking in the light:
        (1) We are not enjoying fellowship with the Father.
        (2) There is unconfessed sin in our lives.
    (c) Not to be found walking in the light at the time of our death or the Second Coming:
        (1) Does not mean that we lose our salvation.
        (2) But it does mean that we will lose a reward.

C. **We should live our lives each day as though that were the day we would suddenly be called to give an account of our obedience to Christ (Matthew 24:45-47).**
1. *The worst thing we as Christians can do is to presume, 'My master is staying away a long time,' and begin to live carelessly* (Matthew 24:48ff.).

2. *We must never let any 'eschatological perspective' colour our readiness, e.g.:*
    (a) 'This or that must be fulfilled before Jesus can come back.'
    (b) The truth is, he will come in an hour we would not expect!

3. *There can be no more wonderful feeling than being fully ready at the moment Jesus appears* (Revelation 22:20)!
    (a) If this comes via death it will mean a 'rich welcome' (2 Peter 1:11).
    (b) If we are alive and ready at his coming it will mean a reward (Revelation 22:12).

## 4 OTHER REASONS FOR BEING READY

A. **The references to the Lord's 'coming' may not be limited entirely to eschatology.**
1. The Lord promises to come in judgment (Revelation 2:5).
2. The Lord promises to come in revival (Luke 24:49).
3. The Lord promises to turn up in unexpected ways (Hebrews 13:2).
4. The Lord promises to end the severe trial (James 1:3-5,12).
5. The Lord promises to heal (Luke 5:17).
6. The Lord promises to answer prayer (Luke 1:13).
7. The Lord promises to renew his power (Hebrews 10:37).

B. **Our state of readiness, or being prepared, can make a tremendous difference in the way things turn out when the Lord turns up. For example:**
1. Whether we are ready for revival (Matthew 25:6).
2. Whether we will recognise an angel (Hebrews 13:2).
3. Whether the trial accomplished its purpose (James 1).
4. Whether we are healed!
5. Whether we are ready for answered prayer (Luke 19:41-45).

C. **A state of readiness, then, equips us to receive the maximum benefit from his coming when he comes!**
1. It can prevent the pain of judgment (1 Corinthians 4:21).
2. It can prevent the embarrassment and exposure of our carelessness and worldliness if revival comes.
3. We will be open to the unexpected ways God works.
4. We will get the full benefit of the trial.
5. The healing, which some may have missed, will be ours.
6. We can avoid needless chastening at the times of unanswered prayer (Luke 1:20).
7. In short: we will not miss God's best for us.

## 5 WHEN GOD SEEMS TO DELAY HIS COMING WE CAN PLEASE HIM ALL THE MORE

A. **Consider two relevant parables (Matthew 25:14-30; Luke 19:12-27).**

1. *Both of these parables illustrate a point: God may not turn up for a while.*
    (a) Sometimes he seems to disappear for a long time.
    (b) He hides his face – or simply leaves us to test us – 'to know everything' that is in our hearts (2 Chronicles 32:31).

2. *Both parables illustrate a more awesome point: when God does turn up we will be happy or ashamed.*
   (a) Some found that God was pleased with their obedience and investment of time and energy.
   (b) Some, who claimed to know God so well, were solemnly and sadly condemned.

B. **We in a sense please God most when we believe without his manifest presence.**
   1. *When we are enjoying a lot of blessing, and are consequently in great obedience, we may feel good in ourselves.*
      (a) But that is not necessarily when we are pleasing God the most.
      (b) It takes little faith to trust God for something when we already have what we want.

   2. *What pleases God is sheer faith – without evidence* (Hebrews 11:1, 6).
      (a) When we 'hope in God' without anything but trust in him alone – we please him most (Psalm 42:11).
      (b) When we are at our lowest point, feeling nothing (positive), it is then we are pleasing God the most!

## 6 HOW THEN, IN THE LIGHT OF THE ABOVE, CAN WE LEARN PATIENCE?

A. **By knowing that patience pleases God.**
   1. The assumption here of course is that one *wants* to please God!
   2. Surely then patience is to be practical; no higher motive than pleasing God alone can be achieved (John 5:44).

B. **By a rugged expectancy in the light of the hope of blessing (2 Kings 2:1-18).**
   1. Elisha, who hoped to inherit Elijah's mantle, was the opposite of the man who hid his talent in the ground.
   2. Patience therefore need not be a passive thing; it is persevering and actively seeking after God.

C. **By remembering how sorry we will be when we succumb to impatience.**
   1. It may be like the man who presumed nothing was going to happen soon and began to live carelessly (Matthew 24:48ff.).
   2. Or it may be a small thing such as speaking impatiently to someone – which may turn out not to be so small after all (James 3:5).

D. **By remembering that patience counts for a lot (2 Corinthians 1:5-6).**
   1. God notices our patience.
   2. He will not forget it! (Hebrews 6:10).

E. **By recalling that God will not put on us more than we can bear (1 Corinthians 10:13).**
   1. We may think, at the time, that the trial, or temptation, is beyond our strength.
   2. But God does always make a way of escape.

F. **By realising that God is always at work (John 5:17).**
   1. He appears to be silent when he is hiding his face.
   2. But there is never a time when God is not working.

G. **By keeping in mind how glad you will be, and what satisfaction you will have, when the trial ends and God turns up brilliantly! (James 1:2-5).**
   1. All disciplining, like any trial, has its time scale.
   2. The end will reveal whether or not you really make the grade!

**CONCLUSION**

Patience, the calm endurance of hardship or delay, is an important lesson to learn as we await the Second Coming of Christ. God is the God of patience; he wants us to be more like himself. We need to make the most of the time he has given us and to be found ready when Christ returns.

'God is never too early, never too late; always just on time.'

# 51

## THE JUDGEMENT SEAT OF CHRIST

### INTRODUCTION

A. **One of the central events of eschatology is the Judgement.**
1. It follows death (Hebrews 9:27).
2. It follows the Second Coming of Jesus (Hebrews 9:28).
3. It precedes our final and everlasting destiny (Revelation 20:11-15).

B. **All human history is moving toward this great and final event.**
1. *It is prophesied in the Old Testament* (Amos 5:18; Joel 3:14).
2. *It is an assumption in the New Testament.*
   (a) By Jesus (Matthew 7:22; John 12:48).
   (b) By Paul (Romans 2:16; 1 Corinthians 1:8).
   (c) By Peter (2 Peter 2:9, 3:12).

3. *All will be present, 'great and small'* (Revelation 20:12).
   (a) Those living at the time of the Second Coming (1 Thessalonians 4:14-17).
   (b) Those who were dead (Revelation 20:11-13).

C. **This Final Judgement will deal with two classes of people.**
1. *The saved and the lost* (Matthew 13:47-50; 25:46).
   (a) The saved go to heaven (Matthew 25:34).
   (b) The lost go to hell (Matthew 25:41).

2. *The saved, of which there are two sorts.*
   (a) Those who will have a reward (1 Corinthians 3:14).
   (b) Those who will be saved by fire (1 Corinthians 3:15).

3. *The lost, of which there are two sorts.*
   (a) Those who have heard the gospel (Luke 12:47).
   (b) Those who may not have heard the gospel (Luke 12:48).

D. **The Bema Seat (Romans 14:10; 2 Corinthians 5:10).**
1. *It is translated 'Judgement Seat'.*
2. *In Corinth it was a large, richly-decorated rostrum, where rewards and punishments were given out.*
   (a) Garlands were given to winners in games.
   (b) Punishments were given to those less worthy.

3. *Paul said, 'We must all appear before the judgement seat of Christ, that each one may receive what is due to him for the things done while in the body, whether good or bad'* (2 Corinthians 5:10).
   (a) All Christians will stand before the Lord at the Judgement Seat of Christ.
   (b) But not all Christians will receive the Reward.
       (1) All Christians will go to heaven.
       (2) No Christian will go to hell.
       (3) But not all Christians will receive a Reward.
       (4) Some Christians will be saved by fire.

### E. Why deal with this subject?
1. *It has been sadly neglected.*
2. *Nothing is more important than our future destiny!*
3. *The devil doesn't want us to know about this.*
4. *The awareness of the future Judgement can change our lives now.*
5. *We should live each day as though the Final Judgement were to appear at any moment.*
6. *Many Christians are unaware of the distinction between going to heaven and receiving a Reward as well.*
   (a) Some think the Reward is heaven itself.
   (b) Wrong. You can go to heaven and still be rejected for the prize (1 Corinthians 9:27).

## 1  THE SECOND COMING OF JESUS AND THE FINAL JUDGEMENT ARE CLOSELY CONNECTED

### A. Jesus promised he would come a second time.
1. In the parables (Luke 19:11-27).
2. To the Twelve (John 14:1-3; cf. Matthew 24; Mark 13).

### B. Other New Testament writings witnessed to this:
(1) Two angels (Acts 1:10-11); (2) Paul (1 Corinthians 15:51-55; 1 Thessalonians 4:13-18; 2 Timothy 4:1; Titus 2:13); (3) James 5:7; (4) 1 Peter 1:13; 2 Peter 3:10; (5) Jude 14; (6) 1 John 2:28.

### C. Many eschatological passages show the important connection between the Second Coming and the Judgement.
1. 2 Timothy 4:1: 'In the presence of God and of Christ Jesus, who will judge the living and the dead, and in view of his appearing and his kingdom, I give you this charge.'

2. Hebrews 9:27-28: 'Just as man is destined to die once, and after that to face judgement, so Christ was sacrificed once to take away the sins

of many people; and he will appear a second time, not to bear sin, but to bring salvation to those who are waiting for him.'

3. Jude 14-15: 'Enoch, the seventh from Adam, prophesied about these men: "See, the Lord is coming with thousands upon thousands of his holy ones to judge everyone, and to convict all the ungodly of all the ungodly acts they have done in the ungodly way, and of all the harsh words ungodly sinners have spoken against him." '

4. Revelation 1:7: 'Look, he is coming with the clouds, and every eye will see him, even those who pierced him; and all the peoples of the earth will mourn because of him. So shall it be! Amen.'

5. Acts 17:31: 'For he has set a day when he will judge the world with justice by the man he has appointed. He has given proof of this to all men by raising him from the dead.'

D. **It is difficult to know which comes first: the General Judgement or the Christians' Judgement.**
1. The General Judgement is the separation of the saved from the lost (Matthew 25:46).
2. The Christians' Judgement is when all Christians are judged by their works (2 Corinthians 5:10).
3. If an eschatological order was implied in 1 Peter 4:17, then the Judgement of the saved will come first.
   (a) All will witness who is saved; all will see who will receive a reward, and who is saved without a reward (1 Corinthians 3:14-15).
   (b) Those who are lost will be judged by their works and sentenced (Revelation 20:11-15).

## 2 THE PURPOSE OF THE JUDGEMENT SEAT OF CHRIST

A. **To clear the name of Jesus.**
1. *When he came the first time he ended up on a cross.*
   (a) There was no open vindication.
   (b) He was vindicated by the Holy Spirit (1 Timothy 3:16).
      (1) He was internally vindicated.
      (2) The Holy Spirit witnesses to the family – us, for we know who Jesus is.

2. *When Jesus comes the second time he will be vindicated openly before all* (Revelation 1:7).
   (a) Herod and Pilate will witness this.
   (b) Those who crucified him will witness this.

    (c) Those who rejected him will witness this.
       (1) Those who saw him in the flesh.
       (2) Those who heard the gospel, whether from a pulpit or by someone on the streets.

3. *All will see Jesus and will be convicted:*
    (a) That he is Lord, that is, God.
    (b) That he is the very Saviour.
    (c) That he is the very Messiah.
    (d) That his death on the cross was God's way to save.
    (e) That he is fully man.
    (f) That he is fully God.

## B. To vindicate the gospel and righteousness.

1. *It will be a vindication of the Bible.*
    (a) All of the words of the Old and New Testaments will be vindicated.
    (b) The very words of Jesus will judge us as well as the books of the Bible (John 12:48; Revelation 20:11-12).

2. *It will vindicate those who confessed Christ as Lord and Saviour.*
    (a) All who trusted his blood shed on the cross will be saved.
    (b) Those who trusted in their works will be damned.

3. *It will be a vindication of holy living.*
    (a) Those who have sought to live godly lives will have their names cleared.
    (b) All that we tried to be and to do, for the glory of God, will be brought out (James 5:4).

4. *It will be a judgement on those who have been evil or unfair.*
    (a) Those who have got away with murder or whatever is wrong, will be exposed openly.
    (b) They will face those they have maligned and will receive the consequence of their deeds (2 Thessalonians 1:6).

## C. To clear the record of Christians.

1. *Some Christians have suffered greatly.*
    (a) They will be honoured, if they dignified their suffering below.
    (b) They will be given great recognition then.

2. *Some Christians have been hurt by fellow Christians.*
    (a) They suffered here below, took it quietly.
    (b) God will clear them then.

3. *Some Christians have done the hurting of others.*
   (a) They seem to get away with it now.
   (b) God will expose them then.

4. *Some Christians have not been fully obedient here below.*
   (a) They have taken warnings lightly.
   (b) They will be sorry then.

5. *Some Christians have been obedient to the full but nobody knew it here below.*
   (a) God will recognise them then.
   (b) They will have high profile then.

6. *Some Christians have had high profile here below but will be saved by fire then.*
   (a) We will learn the truth about famous Christians.
   (b) Some of them are worthy, some are not.

D. **To clear God's own name.**
   1. *The world has long argued that God has a lot to answer for.*
      (a) How could God be just and allow suffering?
      (b) Why does he let good things happen to bad people and allow the innocent to suffer?

   2. *The Bible makes no attempt to clear God's name.*
      (a) It merely affirms his justice and faithfulness.
      (b) But there is no evidence, other than God's Word.

   3. *One day God will clear his name.*
      (a) It will be an awesome moment.
      (b) I promise this:
         (1) Those who clear his name now will be glad they did.
         (2) Those who have accused him will weep and wail and gnash their teeth (Isaiah 40:5).

## 3 WHAT WILL HAPPEN AT THE JUDGEMENT?

A. **Jesus will sit.**
   1. *In ancient time sitting was a position of power and authority.*
      (a) Pontius Pilate sat when he gave his final pronouncement (John 19:13).
      (b) Jesus sat when he revealed that he was the fulfilment of Isaiah 61 (Luke 4:20-21).

   2. *When Jesus comes as judge he will sit* (Revelation 20:11).

## B. We shall stand.
1. The dead, small and great, will stand (Revelation 20:12).
2. All of us will stand before God's judgement seat (Romans 14:10).

## C. The books will be opened (Revelation 20:12).
1. This may be the sixty-six books of the Bible.
2. It may be like the scroll of remembrance of Malachi 3:16.

## D. All secrets will be revealed (Matthew 10:26; Luke 12:2-3; 8:17).
1. All unconfessed sin will be exposed.
2. Those not saved will face afresh the way they have lived their lives.

## E. Those whose names are not written in the Book of Life will be sent to their Final Doom.
1. They may wish to argue their case for a while (Matthew 7:21ff.).
2. But those not covered by the blood of Christ will have no means of appeal.

## F. At some stage all Christians will be judged.
1. Some will receive a reward.
2. Some will suffer loss of a reward.

# 4 WHAT HAPPENS AFTER THE JUDGEMENT?

## A. Those who are saved go to heaven (John 3:16).
1. *Heaven is God's dwelling place now.*
2. *Heaven is the name we commonly give to the bliss that is promised to the believer one day.*
    (a) One of the first things God will do is to wipe away the tears (Revelation 21:4).
    (b) The new heaven will feature the new Jerusalem (Revelation 21 and 22).
    (c) We will be forever with the Lord.

## B. Those who are not saved will go to hell (John 3:16).
1. *Hell is the English word that is commonly used to translate the Greek word* gehenna.
    (a) Sometimes *hades* is translated hell, but this word means the grave, or death.
    (b) *Tartarus* (2 Peter 2:4) is often translated hell, but it is simply the place of fallen spirits.
    (c) *Gehenna* is borrowed from the place to the south of Jerusalem where all the city's rubbish was burned.

   (1) It is the most common word used.

   (2) It consistently is characterised in the New Testament as a place of torment (Matthew 9:43ff.).

 2. *Other descriptions of hell refer to darkness, or a place of weeping or gnashing of teeth* (Matthew 8:12).

   (a) This is not annihilation or there could be no weeping or gnashing of teeth.

   (b) It is everlasting (Matthew 25:41).

## C. How can we be happy in heaven if:

 1. *Our loved ones are eternally lost?*

 2. *We are saved by fire without a reward?*

 3. *Answer:*

   (a) God will wipe away all tears (Revelation 21:4).

   (b) Besides, we will be glorified and we will think like God thinks and not according to fleshly, sentimental ways.

## CONCLUSION

Christians will yet be judged by Christ for their works. This judgement is not concerned with whether or not they will go to heaven – that question was for ever settled when they believed in him as Saviour. But at the *bema* their Christian lives will be examined; the illustration Paul uses is 'tested by fire' (1 Corinthians 3:12-15). In the following chapter I will examine the implications of this important subject.

# 52

## REWARDS IN HEAVEN

**INTRODUCTION**

A. **Some Christians are put off by the idea of a reward.**
  1. It may stem from a cultural prejudice.
  2. It may be the result of faulty theology.
  3. It is often a case of self-righteousness!

B. **Why deal with a subject like this?**
  1. *The Bible teaches it.*
     (a) The New Testament writer who had the most to say about justification by faith alone – Paul – also had the most to say about rewards.
     (b) Parallel with the theology of the apostle Paul are the teachings of Jesus on this subject.

  2. *This is the way God made us.*
     (a) We were created with the view to being motivated.
     (b) All obedience in Holy Scripture is set in the context of what it will mean for us if we do obey – and if we don't.

  3. *It clarifies many scriptures that are thought to contradict 'once saved, always saved'.*
     (a) What might appear to go against the doctrine of eternal security is really about losing one's inheritance (reward), not about losing one's salvation.
     (b) One can be disinherited without ceasing to be a member of the family.

  4. *It will make a difference to our lives right now.*
     (a) If a person is truly convinced that he *will* stand before God (in front of everybody) and be found out, it will make a difference in his or her life now.
     (b) One of the reasons Paul teaches this is that it will make a difference in the way we live.
     (c) Note: one test of the truth or falsehood of any teaching is whether that teaching inspires you to be more godly.

(1)  If it inspires you to be more godly it is almost certainly valid New Testament teaching.

(2)  If it does not inspire godliness, leave that teaching alone!

5.  *The more spiritual you are, the more you will aspire after reward.*
    (a)  Would you question the spirituality of Paul?
    (b)  Reward was very, very important to him (1 Corinthians 9:27).
    (c)  Note: it is only a matter of time and this matter will be of vital importance to all!

6.  *The greater our reward, the greater glory to Christ on that day.*
    (a)  That is partly the meaning of the hymn 'Crown him with many crowns'.
    (b)  If we have no crown, we will thus have none to cast before him – what an awful feeling for the Christian on that day.

C.  **There are four terms relevant to this study:**
    1.  *Reward:* The Greek word is *misthos*, and it is used 29 times in the New Testament (for example, in Matthew 5:12 and 1 Corinthians 3:14).
    2.  *Prize:* The Greek word is *brabeion*, and it is used twice in the New Testament, in 1 Corinthians 9:24 and Philippians 3:14.
    3.  *Crown:* The Greek word is *stephanos*, and it is used 18 times in the New Testament (for example, in 1 Corinthians 9:25 and 2 Timothy 4:8).
    4.  *Inheritance:* The Greek word is *kleranomia*, and it is used 14 times in the New Testament (for example, in Acts 7:5 and Colossians 3:24). The verb *kleronomeo* (to inherit) comes to much the same thing. The term 'inheritance' may at times refer just to salvation (e.g. Hebrews 1:14) but it usually refers to reward; for example it is actually called that in Colossians 3:24.

## 1   NOT ALL WHO GO TO HEAVEN WILL RECEIVE A REWARD

A.  **All who are justified, whose sins are washed away by the blood of Christ, will spend eternity in heaven.**
    1.  *This comes by personal faith in the Lord Jesus Christ.*
    2.  *Only those who believe go to heaven; all others perish* (John 3:16).
        (a)  Salvation is by grace and apart from works (Ephesians 2:8-9).
        (b)  There is nothing we can take credit for if we are among the saved:
            (1)  Our being chosen.
            (2)  Christ dying for us.
            (3)  Our having been granted faith.
            (4)  Our being kept.

B. **We are saved because we rest on the foundation, which is Jesus Christ (1 Corinthians 3:11).**
  1. *The foundation is one thing, the superstructure another.*
     (a) We are not saved by the quality of our superstructure.
     (b) We are saved by the foundation.

  2. *This foundation is perfect.*
     (a) The architectural blueprint is drawn up by an all-wise God who doesn't make mistakes.
     (b) It is perfected by the person of Jesus Christ and what he did:
        (1) By a sinless life (Hebrews 4:15).
        (2) By an obedient death (Philippians 2:6-8).
     (c) It is permanent and sure.
        (1) It cannot be shaken.
        (2) It will last forever.

C. **Important clarifications summed up:**
  1. *There is a difference between salvation and reward.*
     (a) Salvation rests on the foundation – Jesus Christ.
     (b) Reward pertains to the superstructure.

  2. *If we are on the foundation, we are saved.*
     (a) It is possible to be saved and lose the reward.
     (b) One can be on the sure foundation but have a faulty superstructure.

  3. *Our reward at the Judgement Seat of Christ will be based on the quality of our superstructure.*
     (a) If we are on the foundation, we are saved; nothing can change that.
     (b) But the superstructure is something else.

## 2 OUR REWARD IS BASED UPON THE QUALITY OF THE SUPERSTRUCTURE WE BUILD

A. **Anybody can receive a reward at the Judgement Seat of Christ.**
  1. *You can have high profile here, but no reward there.*
     (a) Some Christians have high profile here below.
     (b) High profile below means: high visibility; being busy; well known and highly regarded; position in the church, etc.
     (c) It does not follow that God sees high profile Christians in the same way as people see them!

  2. *Some Christians have little or no profile here below, but will have a great reward at the Judgement Seat of Christ.*
     (a) Low profile means: unnoticed; little or no recognition; largely unappreciated.

   (b)  But God sees differently from people. 'Man looks at the outward appearance, but the LORD looks at the heart' (1 Samuel 16:7).

## B. Salvation is based on grace; reward is based on works.

1. *Grace (unmerited favour) is what God does.*
   This does not mean we didn't have to:
   (a) Believe. We must!
   (b) Repent. We must!
   (c) Confess Christ. We must!

2. *Works are what we do.*
   (a) This does not mean we don't need God's help.
   (b) All our works are in fact by God's help.
       (1) We will not be able to boast in ourselves at the Judgement Seat of Christ.
       (2) 'So you also, when you have done everything you were told to do, should say, "We are unworthy servants; we have only done our duty"' (Luke 17:10).

3. *All believers are responsible:* 'You are God's field' (1 Corinthians 3:9).
   (a) Without obedience there will be no fruit.
   (b) The metaphor, therefore, can be either our superstructure on the foundation, or the fruit that comes from abiding in Christ (John 15:1-6).

## C. The quality of the superstructure is determined by whether or not it lasts: 'If what he has built survives, he will receive his reward' (1 Corinthians 3:14).

1. *Paul's superstructure includes the metaphors 'gold, silver, costly stones, wood, hay or straw'* (1 Corinthians 3:12). They indicate:
   (a) What is viable (something is viable according to its survival probability).
       (1) Will the superstructure survive fire?
       (2) Stones survive fire; hay, wood, straw will be burned up.
   (b) What has virtue (moral excellence).
   (c) What has visibility (a superstructure is a thing to be seen).
   (d) What has value (costly stones versus hay, wood, etc.).

## 3 HOW DO WE KNOW IF OUR OWN SUPERSTRUCTURE IS COMPRISED OF GOLD, SILVER, COSTLY STONES?

### A. Our own application of teaching and what we have learned.

1. It is not enough to sit under teaching, even the best of teaching.
2. It must be applied to our lives – even to the most intimate details.

B. **Our approach with regard to temptation.**
1. What do you do when you are tempted?
2. The best way to avoid falling into sin is to avoid temptation.

C. **Attitude toward trials.**
1. When being tested, what is your reaction?
2. Do you murmur and complain, or do you dignify the trial?

D. **Our ability in controlling the tongue.**
1. Our words will be recalled at the Judgement Seat of Christ (Matthew 12:36-37).
2. A superstructure that will survive fire is erected on the basis of our ability to control the tongue.

E. **Note: the fiery trial below is a preview of the fiery trial above.**
1. *The trial below tests the quality of our work, or works.*
2. *Our work is the sum total of our spiritual progress.*
   (a) We use the expression 'a good piece of work'.
   (b) Any work we do is the sum total of all that preceded it; the fiery trial below tests that (1 Peter 4:12, AV).
   (1) The fiery trial here below prepares us for the ultimate test on the Day of days.
   (2) That awesome Day will be the ultimate test – which we will all experience.

3. *Why call it a 'fiery trial', as Peter does?*
   (a) Fire by its light reveals what we are spiritually.
   (b) Fire by its heat reveals the quality of the superstructure up to that moment.

4. *What are the differences and similarities between the fiery trial below and that above?*
   (a) Wherein they are alike:
   (1) Both are unexpected; without warning.
   (2) Both expose where we are in our spiritual progress.
   (3) Both come from God.
   (b) Wherein they differ:
   (1) A trial below may be hidden from others; God's fire on his Day will be out in the open.
   (2) Whereas the trial below shows where we are in our spiritual progress, there may be another chance to get it right; the Ultimate Test is final – no further chance will come.
   (3) The trial below is brought on by earthly pressures (people;

illness; finances); the fire on that Day will be without the need
of earthly pressures to show where we are.
  (4)  The trial below may come from a satanic attack; the Ultimate
Trial will be God's intervention entirely: the sending of his
Son in fire and glory.

## 4  WHAT EXACTLY IS THE FIRE THAT WILL BE REVEALED?

### A. What it is not:
1. *Purgatory. The work is burned up, not the person.*
  (a)  Purgatory, not a biblical teaching, in any case refers to the
intermediate state according to Roman Catholic teaching.
  (b)  1 Corinthians 3:15 refers to the Second Coming.

2. *Propitious (that is, it does not atone for sin).*
  (a)  Only the blood of Christ is propitious.
  (b)  'Saved by fire' does not mean redeemed by fire.

### B. The fire is that which will accompany Jesus Christ at his Second Coming (2 Thessalonians 1:6-7).
1. *It will burn up the superstructure of straw; which means no reward.*
2. *Even those in Christ without a reward will be saved; they will pass through the fire.*
3. *Whether Paul is speaking metaphysically (supernatural fire), metaphorically or materially, no child of God is hurt by it.*
  (a)  Leon Morris writes: 'The imagery is that of a man who has to dash through the flames to escape to safety.'
  (b)  Like the three Hebrew children: they were unhurt by the heat of the flames.

### C. The fire will expose two things:
1. The quality of the superstructure.
2. The foundation. Perhaps the foundation nobody thought was there! But God saw it all along. 'The Lord knows those that are his.'

## CONCLUSION
Martin Luther said: 'When I get to heaven I expect to have three surprises: (1) there will be those I didn't expect to see there; (2) there will be those absent I expected to see; (3) surprise of surprises, that I myself am there!'
    My paraphrase of his words is: 'At the Judgement Seat of Christ I expect to have three surprises: (1) those who will have a reward whom I thought would not get it; (2) those who do not receive a reward but whom I thought would; (3) that I myself will hear from the lips of Jesus himself, 'Well done!'
    For that is the reward – to receive God's 'Well done!'

# 53

# WHAT HAPPENS TO THE LOST?

## INTRODUCTION

### A. Why is this study important?
1. *If there is a hell, the importance of this subject speaks for itself.*
   - (a) I, for one, do not want to go there.
   - (b) I don't want anybody else to go there.

2. *Sooner or later, we all ask the question, 'What about those who never heard the gospel?'* In this chapter I do not deal with the fate of those who have not heard the gospel. However, I have discussed it in the chapter, 'Our Responsibility to the Lost'.

3. *In recent years a number of respectable evangelical leaders have embraced the teaching of annihilation; are they right?*
   - (a) For nearly a century it was largely the cults (e.g., Jehovah's Witnesses) who rejected the traditional view of the church regarding eternal punishment and opted for annihilation.
   - (b) Is it possible that the cults got it right on this matter after all?

4. *Jesus mentioned hell more than all the writers of the Bible combined – it is surely right to know what he meant by this.*

5. *The church has sent conflicting signals to the world on this matter; surely we want to be sure where we stand lest we perpetuate an uncertain message.*

### B. The lost: those who remain unsaved after death.
1. *The term 'lost' is Jesus' term for those not yet converted.*
   - (a) 'For the Son of Man came to seek and to save what was lost' (Luke 19:10).
   - (b) 'I was sent only to the lost sheep of Israel' (Matthew 15:24).

2. *It is sometimes used interchangeably with 'perishing':* 'And even if our gospel is veiled, it is veiled to those who are perishing' (2 Corinthians 4:3).

3. *Jesus made the claim that the lost he came to save would not remain lost.*

(a) 'And this is the will of him who sent me, that I shall lose none of all that he has given me, but raise them up at the last day' (John 6:39).

(b) 'While I was with them, I protected them and kept them safe by that name you gave me. None has been lost except the one doomed to destruction so that Scripture would be fulfilled' (John 17:12).

(c) 'This happened so that the words he had spoken would be fulfilled: "I have not lost one of those you gave me" ' (John 18:9).

4. *There are at least two words that mean the opposite to 'lost' or 'perishing':* (a) found (Luke 15:32); (b) saved (John 5:34).

C. **There are therefore only two categories of people:**
  1. Saved. Those who have believed on Christ.
  2. Lost. Those who have not believed on Christ.

## 1 HEAVEN AND HELL: THE ONLY DESTINIES OF PEOPLE AFTER DEATH

A. **Heaven, the place of those who are saved.**
  1. *Heaven is the dwelling place of God* (1 Kings 8:43).
      (a) It is where Jesus is now (Acts 1:11).
      (b) It is where the saved dead are now (Matthew 22:32, Luke 16:22).

  2. *In ancient times people thought in terms of three 'heavens':*
      (a) The 'first heaven', the sky where birds fly; where clouds form.
      (b) The 'second heaven', the place of the moon and stars.
      (c) The 'third heaven', where Paul was taken up in his spirit by the Holy Spirit (2 Corinthians 12:2).

  3. *One day there will be a new heaven and a new earth* (2 Peter 3:13; Revelation 21:1).
      (a) This will be preceded by two great events:
          (1) The Second Coming of Jesus (2 Peter 3:10-12).
          (2) The Judgement (Hebrews 9:27-28).
      (b) When therefore we speak of 'heaven' we must remember that there are two phases:
          (1) Where God dwells now – with the saints and angels.
          (2) Where we will be after the Judgement.

  4. *In the meantime we refer to an 'intermediate state':*
      (a) Where people go when they die (Revelation 6:9-11; 7:9-17).
      (b) It is referred to also as: (1) Abraham's side (Luke 16:22); (2) Paradise (Luke 23:43).

## B. Hell, the place of those who are lost.

1. *There are three Greek words that are sometimes translated 'hell'.*
   (a) *Tartarus*, used only once (2 Peter 2:4).
      (1) There is doubt whether 'hell' is the best translation.
      (2) It may be the place where Satan and his fallen angels now dwell; a non-material realm in which they live and move with definite limitations.
   (b) *Hades* is used 11 times (Matthew 11:23; 16:18; Luke 10:15; 16:23; Acts 2:27,31; 1 Corinthians 15:55; Revelation 1:18; 6:8; 20:13, 14).
      (1) It basically means the grave, or death.
      (2) However its use in Luke 16:23 shows that it may be a place and that its inhabitants are very much alive and conscious.
   (c) *Gehenna* is used 12 times, although overlapping in places in Matthew and Mark (Matthew 5:22,29,30; 10:28; 18:9; 23:15,33; Mark 9:43,45,47; Luke 12:5; James 3:6).

2. *There are other descriptions of a place which is not always described as hell but which is implied:*
   (a) Darkness (Matthew 8:12; 22:13; Jude 13).
   (b) Fiery furnace (Matthew 13:42,50; Revelation 21:8).
   (c) A place (Matthew 24:51).
   (d) Eternal fire (Matthew 25:41; Jude 7).
   (e) Everlasting destruction (2 Thessalonians 1:9).
   (f) Weeping and gnashing of teeth (Matthew 8:12; 13:42,50; 22:13; 24:51; Luke 13:28).
   (g) Torment (Revelation 14:11).
   (h) God's wrath (Romans 5:9; 1 Thessalonians 1:10).

3. *It is not easy to determine to what extent the above descriptions refer to the intermediate state and the final place of the lost.*
   (a) The descriptions could refer to either or both since they do not vary in what they show:
      (1) Consciousness: 'there will be weeping and gnashing of teeth'.
      (2) Torment.
      (3) Permanence. No change of destiny (Matthew 25:46; Luke 16:26).
   (b) In Luke 16:23, though *Hades* is probably the intermediate state, it is none the less descriptive as all of the others above.
      (1) As the saved go to be with Christ, so the lost go to a place of torment (Luke 16:19-31).
      (2) They too await the Final Judgement (John 5:29).

4. *The lake of fire is the final place of the lost which parallels the new heaven and new earth.*
   (a)  It is the final destiny of the devil (Revelation 20:10).
      (1) It was made for the devil in the first place (Matthew 25:41).
      (2) Its permanence in terms of conscious everlasting torment could not be clearer: 'And the devil, who deceived them, was thrown into the lake of burning sulphur, where the beast and the false prophet had been thrown. They will be tormented day and night for ever and ever' (Revelation 20:10).
   (b)  It is the destiny of those who had been in *Hades*: 'Then death and Hades were thrown into the lake of fire. The lake of fire is the second death. If anyone's name was not found written in the book of life, he was thrown into the lake of fire' (Revelation 20:14-15).
      (1) Revelation 14:10-11, referring to people, refers to the same kind of punishment as described of the devil: 'He, too, will drink of the wine of God's fury, which has been poured full strength into the cup of his wrath. He will be tormented with burning sulphur in the presence of the holy angels and of the Lamb. And the smoke of their torment rises for ever and ever. There is no rest day or night for those who worship the beast and his image, or for anyone who receives the mark of his name.'
      (2) What was made for the devil will be the place of the lost as well (Matthew 25:41).

5. *In short: the lost go to a place of punishment.*
   (a)  There are two destinies: one for the saved, one for the lost.
   (b)  There is no 'in between'.
      (1) The teaching of purgatory is a medieval teaching.
      (2) It has no biblical foundation.
   (c)  Three descriptions summarise the place of the lost, by whatever name you give it (hell, darkness, fire, etc.):
      (1) It is conscious.
      (2) It is for torment.
      (3) It is everlasting.
   (d)  Note: Matthew 25:46 implies that the punishment lasts as long as eternal life. 'Then they will go away to eternal punishment, but the righteous to eternal life.'

## 2   CAN HELL BE ANNIHILATION?

A. **Annihilation: to be given non-existence as though one had never existed in the first place.**

1. It means utter destruction – nothing being left at all.
2. It is not a question of consciousness: there is no body, mind or soul if the person has been annihilated.

B. **There are five possible positions (that I know of) regarding the issue of eternal punishment:**
   1. *Agnosticism:* it is impossible to ascertain whether there is any such reality as hell because it is impossible to determine what happens after death.
   2. *Annihilationism:* we become nothing as though we never were.
   3. *Universalism:* all will be saved and none will be lost.
   4. *Conditionalism:* that immortality (endless existence) is not an endowment by creation but by faith. It is often referred to as conditional immortality.
      (a) Only God is immortal but he gives immortality to believers – and believers only.
      (b) Immortality and eternal life are thus used interchangeably.
      (c) Conditions must be met before the person can receive everlasting personal existence.
          (1) God must give it.
          (2) Man must receive it.
      (d) The fate of those who do not receive Christ by faith:
          (1) Obliteration of consciousness, annulment of existence.
          (2) In a word: they are annihilated.

   5. *Conscious endless existence beyond the grave, either in heaven or hell.*
      (a) This is the classic Christian belief, including both Protestants and Roman Catholics.
      (b) Man is endowed with natural immortality by virtue of creation.
      (c) The image of God in man included immortality.
      (d) Man, whether saved or lost, will therefore have conscious existence beyond the grave.

C. **The case for annihilation:**
   1. *The thought of conscious eternal torment is repulsive.*

   2. *A God of love could not treat people in a manner that allows any to suffer eternally.*

   3. *The term* gehenna *originally refers to a place of burning rubbish in a valley south of Jerusalem.*
      (a) Fire burns things up.
      (b) Therefore references to fire assume annihilation.

4. *The Greek term* appolumai *means 'to destroy', which is what fire does.*
   (a) Therefore to punish means to be annihilated.
   (b) Those who do not believe the gospel, perish.

5. *Only God has immortality (1 Timothy 6:16), therefore man must be given it (2 Timothy 1:10).*
   (a) Man does not have immortality by creation.
   (b) The gospel brings immortality to light.
   (c) One receives this by faith.

6. *Hell does indeed mean 'eternal punishment'.*
   (a) Not 'eternal punishing'; that which continues.
   (b) Rather, the punishment is final so that it does not change eternally.

7. *Those who have immortality will have endless existence in heaven; those that don't have it cease to be.*
   (a) Annihilation, then, is what happens to the person.
   (b) His body will rot and come to nothing; the soul he had ceases to be when he dies.
   (c) Note: Some annihilationists believe in the final resurrection of the body to stand judgement; but when the lost are cast into the lake of fire they cease to exist.

## D. The case against annihilation:

1. *Jesus surely intended that his descriptions of hell would be repulsive to us. I fear that the motivation behind annihilationism is largely an attempt to make God 'look good', something the Bible itself doesn't always try to do!*

2. *The earliest New Testament message, 'Flee from the wrath to come', would hardly awaken many people if they thought it meant annihilation.*

3. *Annihilation is a theological rationale for what the God-hater certainly hopes is true if there is a God.*

4. *The love of God is always set against his wrath (John 3:16); as for how God could allow the hell which the New Testament describes, two issues come to mind:*
   (a) 'Will not the Judge of all the earth do right?' (Genesis 18:25).
   (b) '"For my thoughts are not your thoughts, neither are your ways my ways," declares the LORD. "As the heavens are higher than the earth, so are my ways higher than your ways and my thoughts than your thoughts"' (Isaiah 55:8-9).

5. *Had Jesus meant annihilation by what he called 'hell' the early church would have picked up on this from the beginning, lest the wrong idea get off the ground in the church of God.*

6. *Though* gehenna *was taken from the rubbish dump outside of Jerusalem, Mark 9:41-45 was given expressly to show that the eternal fire of hell was different from* natural *fire: 'Where "their worm does not die, and the fire is not quenched"* ' (Mark 9:48).

7. *In Greek,* appolumai *does mean 'to destroy' – but not to annihilate.*
   (a) It is what we would call today a wrecked car that is a 'write-off' – it is useless.
   (b) It is the word used of the 'wasted' perfume (Matthew 26:8).

8. *There was a word in currency in Jesus' day that unquestionably means 'to annihilate'.*
   (a) *Ekmedenisis* means 'annihilation'; *ekmedenizw* means 'to annihilate'.
   (b) Had any New Testament writer wanted to show that hell means annihilation that is the word they would have used; they didn't. It is an Alexandrian word, its roots go beyond Homer.

9. *Paul's statement that God alone has immortality was not trying to prove that man doesn't have it by creation.*
   (a) He was showing what God alone has in himself; he has it because he is God.
   (b) When God chose to make man he also chose to make him in his own image (Genesis 1:26).
   (c) John 1:9 further shows that immortality was given to every man.
      (1) Immortality and light are used alongside each other in 1 Timothy 6:16 and 2 Timothy 1:10.
      (2) This shows what else it can mean in John 1:9.
      (3) The gospel alone shows how this immortality is adored and revered when we believe.

10. *Dr David Gooding has shown that Matthew 25:46 is technically to be translated 'eternal punishing'; not just 'eternal punishment'.*

11. *Jesus said that it would have been better had Judas Iscariot never been born (Matthew 26:24), a statement that would make no sense if Judas would shortly cease to exist.*

12. *That Holy Spirit fell on Jonathan Edwards preaching 'Sinners in*

the Hands of an Angry God' – a sermon on conscious eternal punishment – with so much power that can only be explained by God's own approval.

13. There is no way one can read annihilation into the devil's punishment; Matthew 25:41 shows that people will go to the same place.

14. If hell burns people up, how could they weep and gnash their teeth?

15. Annihilationists seldom if ever preach it – certainly not to the lost! Why? It won't 'preach'.

## CONCLUSION

What happens to the lost is a difficult subject to deal with. It can be tempting to soften the truth or to opt for the annihilationist view. However, the Bible leaves us in no doubt that those who are not 'in Christ' when they die will be for ever without Christ in the place of eternal punishment.

# SUBJECT INDEX

Warfare, Spiritual 262-269
Westminster Confession of Faith 341
Will of God 49, 310, 320, 338
Wisdom 189, 301, 377, 380
Witnessing 12, 336
Women, Role of, in Ministry 241-249, 286
Word, The, 11, 18, 19, 21, 26, 27, 30,
32, 35, 164, 191, 211, 214, 216, 249,
276, 288, 299, 327, 378 see: Bible,

Work 139
Works 144, 152, 159, 160, 165, 199, 278,
323, 327, 332, 358, 360, 362, 377,
396, 400, 402, 404
Worship 12, 45, 210-216, 241, 247, 286,
296, 316, 342, 378, 388
Wrath of God 154, 299, 301, 323, 353,
354, 409, 412

# Index of Persons

Abelard 115
Agricola, John 75
Ambrose 151, 201, 205
Anselm 16, 39, 40, 115
Aquinas, Thomas 16, 39, 239
Arius 32
Arminius 365
Athanasius 9, 32, 151
Augustine 9, 23, 137, 150-152, 201,
203, 239, 251, 365, 375
Barnard, Rolfe 114
Barth, Karl 6
Bewes, Richard 346
Brown, Robert 207
Bultman, Rudolf 23
Caesar 152
Calvin, John 9, 11, 19, 33, 51, 57, 115,
128, 129, 153, 154, 186, 188, 196,
203, 207, 208, 218, 220, 222, 232
Carey, William 227
Chrysostom 151
Clement of Rome 30, 201, 202, 205, 239
Constantine 203, 205-206
Coulson, Charles 376
Cranmer 232
Cyprian 201, 203- 205
Dobson, James 348
Eaton, Michael 86, 88
Edwards, Jonathan 57, 67, 186, 257, 413
Fuerbach, Ludwig 38
Gooding, David 332, 413
Graham, Billy 53
Grudem, Wayne 146, 245
Harnack, Adolf 151
Henry VIII 47
Hermas 31, 201, 203
Ignatius 30, 201, 204, 220, 368
Irenaeus 31, 39, 201-205, 368
Jackson Michael 193
Jerome 239

Justin Martyr 31, 39, 201, 203, 204
Kierkegaard, Soren 374
Leo, Bishop of Rome 202
Lloyd-Jones, Martyn 6, 7, 185
Luther, Martin 9, 19, 26, 28, 55, 75, 115, 151-
154, 208, 218, 220, 232, 239, 302, 313,
324, 342, 352, 406
Marcion 151
Montanus 186
Moody, D.L. 224
Morgan, Dr G. Campbell 6, 26, 305
Morris, Leon 406
Murray, John 146
Nero 202
Newton, John 293
Origen 114, 201, 203
Osiander, Andreas 75
Owen, John 207
Packer, J.I. 55, 56
Pawson, David 245
Pelagius 137, 138
Perkins, William 261
Piper, John 245
Polycarp 201, 368
Radbertus 220
Spurgeon, C. H. 26, 55, 196, 231
Smyth, John 208
Tatian 201
Temple, William 313
Tertullian 29, 31, 186, 201, 203, 204, 239
Ton, Joseph 254
Torrance, T.F. 152, 369
Tozer, A.W. 211, 215, 240
Twain, Mark 382
Tyndale, William 232
Wesley, John 186, 225, 313, 365
Whitefield, George 57, 186
Winfrey, Oprah 193
Valentinian III 202
Zwingli, Ulrich 208, 218, 220, 232

# Index of Bible Characters

# Scripture Index

R T Kendall is the pastor of Westminster Chapel, London where he is engaged in a much-appreciated Bible teaching ministry. He is a regular speaker at conventions, including Spring Harvest and Keswick.

He has also written over a dozen books and in addition to this book Christian Focus Publications have previously published four of his titles.

*Meekness and Majesty* is an exposition of Philippians 2:5-11 where Paul deals with the humility of Jesus in his earthly life and the glory of his present heavenly position. R.T. gives a lucid and heartwarming explanation of this well-known passage of Scripture. Derick Bingham says of *Meekness and Majesty*: 'This book exalts the Lord Jesus in everything it says. Reading it will aid you to do the same.'
*ISBN 1 871676 87 8    224 pages*

*When God Says Well Done* is an examination of the various details found in 1 Corinthians concerning the future judgement of believers by Christ when he returns. R.T. is convinced that Paul teaches that the lives of believers will be thoroughly reviewed by their Master who will reward those who served him well. However, there will be loss of reward for those believers who do not serve their Saviour as they could have. In this book, R.T. urges believers to live so as to please God and be commended by Jesus on the Day of Judgment.
*ISBN 1 85792 017 1    224 pages*

*Are You Stone Deaf to the Spirit or Rediscovering God* is R.T's way of explaining the persons described in Hebrews 5:11-6:12. Chapter 6:4-8 has worried many Christians since it seems to teach that believers can lose their salvation. Dr Kendall gained helpful insights into the teachings of the Book of Hebrews during the eleven years he preached through the book as part of the regular weekly ministry in Westminster Chapel. He believes the passage is describing true believers who have backslidden to a very marked extent, reaching the stage where they have become deaf to God's voice. However, he also finds much in the passage to encourage Christians to renew their commitment to Jesus, particularly God's oath of commitment to all his people.
*ISBN 1 85792 072 4 256 pages*

*Higher Ground* is a devotional treatment of the Psalms of Degrees (121-134) that were sung by Jewish pilgrims during their visits to Jerusalem to celebrate the annual feasts. R.T. takes one thought from each psalm and applies it helpfully to Christian living today.
*ISBN 1 85792 158 5 176 pages*

Christian Focus Publications publishes biblically-accurate books for adults and children. The books in the adult range are published in three imprints.

*Christian Heritage* contains classic writings from the past.

*Christian Focus* contains popular works including biographies, commentaries, doctrine, and Christian living.

*Mentor* focuses on books written at a level suitable for Bible College and seminary students, pastors, and others; the imprint includes commentaries, doctrinal studies, examination of current issues, and church history.

For a free catalogue of all our titles, please write to
Christian Focus Publications,
Geanies House, Fearn,
Ross-shire, IV20 1TW, Great Britain

For details of our titles visit us on our web site
http://www.christianfocus.com